SOUTHEAST ASIA

IN POLITICAL SCIENCE

EAST-WEST CENTER

SERIES ON *Contemporary Issues in Asia and the Pacific*

MUTHIAH ALAGAPPA, SERIES EDITOR

EDITED BY
ERIK MARTINEZ KUHONTA
DAN SLATER
TUONG VU

Southeast Asia in Political Science

Theory, Region, and Qualitative Analysis

Stanford University Press · *Stanford, California 2008*

Stanford University Press
Stanford, California

Printed in the United States of America on acid-free, archival-quality paper

Library of Congress Cataloging-in-Publication Data

Southeast Asia in political science : theory, region, and qualitative analysis /
edited by Erik Martinez Kuhonta, Dan Slater, Tuong Vu.
    p. cm.
  Includes bibliographical references and index.
  ISBN 978-0-8047-5810-9 (cloth : alk. paper) —
  ISBN 978-0-8047-6152-9 (pbk. : alk. paper)
    1. Southeast Asia—Politics and government.   2. Political science—
Southeast Asia.   I. Kuhonta, Erik Martinez.   II. Slater, Dan.
III. Vu, Tuong.

JQ750.A58S68   2008
320.0959—dc22   2007038749

Typeset by Newgen in 9.75/13.5 Janson

A Series from
Stanford University Press and the East-West Center

CONTEMPORARY ISSUES IN ASIA AND THE PACIFIC

Muthiah Alagappa, Series Editor

A collaborative effort by Stanford University Press and the East-West Center, this series focuses on issues of contemporary significance in the Asia Pacific region, most notably political, social, cultural, and economic change. The series seeks books that focus on topics of regional importance, on problems that cross disciplinary boundaries, and that have the capacity to reach academic and other interested audiences.

The East-West Center is an education and research organization established by the U.S. Congress in 1960 to strengthen relations and understanding among the peoples and nations of Asia, the Pacific, and the United States. The Center contributes to a peaceful, prosperous, and just Asia Pacific community by serving as a vigorous hub for cooperative research, education, and dialogue on critical issues of common concern to the Asia Pacific region and the United States. Funding for the Center comes from the U.S. government, with additional support provided by private agencies, individuals, foundations, corporations, and the governments of the region.

The publication of *Southeast Asia in Political Science: Theory, Region, and Qualitative Analysis* marks a transition for the Contemporary Issues in Asia and the Pacific (CIAP) series from the editorship of Muthiah Alagappa to a new editorial board, with John Sidel and Geoffrey White as series co-editors, and Sheila Smith, Kellee Tsai, and Peter Xenos as fellow members. This volume is the final publication in a distinguished list of books to appear under Muthiah's editorship. With his leadership from 1999 to 2006 the series took on a new visibility and importance, producing a robust list of distinguished work. The success of the series is due in no small measure to Muthiah's ability to actively encourage younger scholars such as the contributors to this new edited volume and bring their work to a broad readership. In 2006 Muthiah stepped down as editor of the CIAP series to pursue his own research and writing as a Distinguished Senior Fellow of the East-West Center. Mindful of Muthiah's intellectual vision and high standard for scholarly work, the CIAP editorial board looks forward to promoting fresh new efforts to understand the dynamic, ever-changing landscape of the Asia-Pacific in the years ahead. As we do, we want to acknowledge our gratitude for Muthiah Alagappa's hard work as series editor, and the enduring legacies he created for the series.

To the late Dan Lev and his entire
generation of Southeast Asianists

Contents

Acknowledgments

This project emerged out of debates about theory and methodology at a panel of the American Political Science Association Annual Meeting in Philadelphia in August 2003. After that panel we began to think of ways to continue this discussion. A workshop sponsored by the Southeast Asia Forum of the Walter H. Shorenstein Asia-Pacific Research Center at Stanford University in June 2004 was a crucial step in building these ideas. The result of that workshop is this book. The production of this book has been a truly enjoyable enterprise and collaborative effort among the editors and between the editors and the contributors.

We would first of all like to thank Don Emmerson for his unwavering support of this project. Don not only funded the workshop on which this book was based, but he also consistently provided sound advice and encouragement throughout the whole process. Without his mentorship this book would not have been possible.

At the workshop, numerous discussants provided intense, constructive criticism. These included Muthiah Alagappa, Annette Clear, Jim Fearon, Natasha Hamilton-Hart, Heng Pek Koon, Paul Hutchcroft, David Kang, Ben Kerkvliet, Bill Liddle, Andrew MacIntyre, Gabriella Montinola, and Danny Unger.

We are also grateful to Carolyn Emmerson, Neeley Main, Netithorn Praditsarn, Worawut Smuthkalin, and Victoria Tomkinson for helping with the logistics of the workshop.

Two anonymous reviewers provided thorough critiques of the whole manuscript. We thank them for making a sincere effort to improve our work.

At the Asia Research Institute of the National University of Singapore, Tony Reid took an interest in this project and helped sponsor a roundtable. We thank him for his support. Helpful discussants at that roundtable included Natasha Hamilton-Hart, Jomo K. S., Suzaina Kadir, and Michael Montesano.

At the East-West Center and Stanford University Press, thanks are due to Muthiah Alagappa, Elisa Johnston, Muriel Bell, Kirsten Oster, and Joa Suorez.

Finally, we wish to acknowledge our closest confidants—Kazue Takamura, Tracey Lockaby, and Lan Tran—for their constant support and encouragement.

Erik Martinez Kuhonta
Dan Slater
Tuong Vu

Contributors

Regina Abrami is an assistant professor at the Harvard Business School. She received her Ph.D. from the University of California–Berkeley in 2002. Her work focuses on the political economy of government-business and state-labor relations in emerging markets, focusing especially on Vietnam, Cambodia, and China. She is currently completing a book manuscript on the political origins of private-sector development in Vietnam and China.

Jamie S. Davidson is an assistant professor of political science at the National University of Singapore. He is co-editor of *The Revival of Tradition in Indonesian Politics: The Deployment of Adat from Colonialism to Indigenism* (Routledge, 2007) and is the author of *From Rebellion to Riots: Collective Violence on Indonesian Borneo* (University of Wisconsin Press, 2008).

Richard F. Doner is an associate professor of political science at Emory University. His research focus is on the political economy and institutional features of economic growth in Southeast Asia. In addition to numerous articles, he is the author of *Driving a Bargain: Japanese Firms and Automotive Industrialization in Southeast Asia* (University of California Press, 1991); co-author, with David McKendrick and Stephan Haggard, of *From Silicon Valley to Singapore: Location and Competitive Advantages in the Disk Drive Industry* (Stanford University Press, 2000); and co-editor of *Economic Governance and the Challenge of Flexibility in East Asia* (Rowman and Littlefield, 2001).

Donald K. Emmerson is Senior Fellow and Director of the Southeast Asia Forum in the Shorenstein Asia-Pacific Research Center at Stanford University. Recent publications include "One Nation Under God? History, Faith, and

Identity in Indonesia" in *Religion and Religiosity in the Philippines and Indonesia* (2006); "What Is Indonesia?" in *Indonesia: The Great Transition* (2005); "Security, Community, and Democracy in Southeast Asia: Analyzing ASEAN," *Japanese Journal of Political Science* (August 2005); and "What Do the Blind-Sided See? Reapproaching Regionalism in Southeast Asia," *Pacific Review* (March 2005). He received a Ph.D. in political science from Yale University.

Greg Felker is an assistant professor of Asian and international politics at Willamette University in Salem, Oregon. He has worked and published on the comparative and international political economy of development in Southeast Asia, focusing in particular on foreign direct investment and technology policy. He has been a researcher in Malaysia and Thailand, served as a consultant to several international organizations, and taught at universities in Hong Kong and Thailand.

Kikue Hamayotsu is an assistant professor of political science at Northern Illinois University. She was formerly a post-doctoral fellow and lecturer in modern Southeast Asian studies at the Weatherhead East Asian Institute, Columbia University. She completed a master's degree in Southeast Asian politics at the School of Oriental and African Studies (SOAS), University of London, and a Ph.D. degree at the Department of Political and Social Change, Australian National University, Canberra, in 2006. She has conducted research on state-Islam relations in both Malaysia and Indonesia and is currently completing a book manuscript tentatively titled *Demobilizing Islam: Institutionalized Religion and the Politics of Cooptation.* Her publications include "Islam and Nation Building in Southeast Asia: Malaysia and Indonesia in Comparative Perspective," *Pacific Affairs.*

Allen Hicken is an assistant professor of political science and faculty associate at the Center for Southeast Asian Studies and Center for Political Studies, University of Michigan. He studies political institutions and policy making in developing countries, with a focus on Southeast Asia. He has carried out research in Thailand, the Philippines, Singapore, and Cambodia. He is the author of a forthcoming book on parties and elections in Thailand and the Philippines titled *Building Party Systems in Developing Democracies* (Cambridge University Press).

Ben Kerkvliet is a professor in the Department of Political and Social Change, Research School of Pacific and Asian Studies, the Australian National University. His research emphasizes agrarian politics in Southeast Asia, particularly the Philippines and Vietnam. His recent book is *The Power of Everyday Politics: How Vietnamese Peasants Transformed National Policy* (Cornell University Press, 2005).

Erik Martinez Kuhonta is an assistant professor in the Department of Political Science at McGill University. He received his Ph.D. in politics from Princeton University in 2003 and has held fellowships at the Asia-Pacific Research Center at Stanford University and at the Asia Research Institute of the National University of Singapore. His research has appeared in *American Asian Review*, *Harvard Asia Quarterly*, *Pacific Review*, and *Asian Survey*.

Dan Slater is an assistant professor in the Department of Political Science at the University of Chicago. He received his Ph.D. from Emory University in 2005. His primary research project explores how divergent historical patterns of contentious politics have shaped contemporary variation in state, party, and regime institutions across seven Southeast Asian countries. His published work can be found in disciplinary journals such as the *American Journal of Political Science, Comparative Politics, International Organization,* and *Social Analysis,* as well as area-focused journals such as *Indonesia, Kyoto Review of Southeast Asia,* and *Taiwan Journal of Democracy.*

Ardeth Maung Thawnghmung is an assistant professor of political science at the University of Massachusetts, Lowell. Her book, *Behind the Teak Curtain: Authoritarianism, Agricultural Policies and Political Legitimacy in Rural Burma/ Myanmar* (Kegan Paul, 2004), examines farmers' perception of and interaction with local and central authorities in Burma. Her main teaching and research interests are Southeast Asian politics, political economy, and ethnic conflict.

Tuong Vu is an assistant professor in the Department of Political Science, University of Oregon, Eugene. During 2007–2008 he was a Visiting Research Fellow at the Asia Research Institute, National University of Singapore. He has taught at the Naval Postgraduate School and was a Mendenhall Fellow at Smith College. His research focuses on Indonesia and Vietnam, and he has published in *Studies in Comparative International Development, Theory and Society, Communist and Post-Communist Studies,* and *South East Asia Research.*

Meredith L. Weiss is an assistant professor of political science at University at Albany, SUNY. She was formerly a research fellow at the East-West Center in Washington. She received her Ph.D. in political science from Yale University. A specialist in Southeast Asian politics, she is the author of *Protest and Possibilities: Civil Society and Coalitions for Political Change in Malaysia* (Stanford University Press, 2005) and co-editor (with Saliha Hassan) of *Social Movements in Malaysia: From Moral Communities to NGOs* (RoutledgeCurzon, 2003). Her articles have appeared in *Perspectives on Politics, Democratization, New Political Science, Journal of East Asian Studies, Commonwealth and Comparative Politics, Asian Survey, Contemporary Southeast Asia,* and elsewhere, in addition to chapters in numerous anthologies. Her primary foci are civil society and social movements, nationalism and ethnicity, gender, Islamist activism, and electoral politics in maritime Southeast Asia.

SOUTHEAST ASIA

IN POLITICAL SCIENCE

Chapter One

Introduction

The Contributions of Southeast Asian Political Studies

ERIK MARTINEZ KUHONTA, DAN SLATER,
AND TUONG VU

After a post–Vietnam War hiatus of nearly a quarter-century, Southeast Asia has recaptured the attention of the world. In 1997 the sudden devaluation of Thailand's national currency (the *baht*) triggered a financial crisis that swept throughout Asia and threatened for a time to engulf the world's richest economies. This "Asian Contagion" had its most devastating economic effects in Indonesia—the world's fourth-most-populous country—where financial implosion helped induce the dramatic collapse of the authoritarian Suharto regime in 1998 amid swelling public demands for democratic reform. The terrorist attacks on the United States in September 2001 brought heightened attention to Southeast Asia for quite different reasons, as the region's large Islamic populations and loosely governed territories led pundits to dub it "the second front in the global war on terror." When the SARS epidemic and bird flu outbreaks struck Southeast Asia starting in 2003, they raised the specter of global pandemics from which no country would be immune. And when Indonesia and Thailand bore the brunt of the most cataclysmic natural disaster in modern history—the Indian Ocean tsunami of December 2004—Southeast Asians' unspeakable suffering not only inspired an unprecedented outpouring of emergency assistance; it also inspired unprecedented calls for international coordination in preventing and limiting the destruction caused by environmental and public-health crises, which respect no boundaries in an increasingly interdependent world.

To be sure, the eleven countries of Southeast Asia—Brunei, Burma, Cambodia, East Timor, Indonesia, Laos, Malaysia, the Philippines, Singapore, Thailand, and Vietnam—may still seem geographically peripheral to Western eyes. No other region is so distant from both North America and Europe, where global institutions are primarily housed and global images are primarily shaped. Yet these dramatic (and mostly tragic) recent events should show beyond a shadow of a doubt that Southeast Asia's diverse political systems are far from peripheral to the most momentous global trends. It is a region that the rest of the world can ill afford to ignore or misunderstand.

Thankfully, scholars of Southeast Asian politics have been accumulating valuable knowledge on this complex and crucial region for decades. Southeast Asia may have been *relatively* neglected in the study of comparative politics (especially regarding Europe and Latin America), but it has by no means been neglected *absolutely*.[1] This volume's first mission is to compile and display some of the extensive knowledge that scholars of Southeast Asian politics have produced on pressing global topics such as political Islam, state building, economic globalization, democracy and dictatorship, ethnic conflict, rural development, and civil society. Although students of Southeast Asian politics have produced an impressive range of scholarly works, Southeast Asianists still lack a systematic inventory and synthesis of the wealth of political knowledge that has been accumulated. This book's first goal is to fill this considerable void.

Our second purpose is somewhat broader and bolder. Beyond examining what we have learned about Southeast Asian politics, we also ask this: What can Southeast Asia tell us about the wider political world? This question ineluctably draws us into considerations of how theory, method, and region interact. As political scientists, we wish to consider whether the qualitative analysis of Southeast Asian politics has gone beyond generating particular, fragmented bits of empirical knowledge and whether it has produced more general theoretical insights for our discipline as a whole. We will argue that Southeast Asianists have indeed accumulated *theoretical* as well as *empirical* knowledge but that these general, portable insights are often easily missed when scholars refrain from framing their arguments in theoretically self-conscious terms, or from discussing the potential comparative implications of their arguments.

In sum, this book calls for concerted efforts to improve and invigorate the scholarly synergy between region and discipline. We see this endeavor as long overdue. In the last two decades, fresh theoretical perspectives and qualitative methodological approaches have emerged in political science, and there is much room for Southeast Asianists both to contribute to and gain from these new developments. Rather than approaching these theoretical and method-ological concerns through abstract ruminations on the philosophy of science, the contributors to this volume offer analytic reviews of state-of-the-art South-east Asian scholarship on key political topics. These reviews are structured in a manner that directly engages relevant concepts and theories in political sci-ence. Yet they should capture the interest of scholars working in other disci-plines (and other regions) as well. Indeed, we will consistently emphasize the point that some of the most insightful contributions to our understanding of Southeast Asian politics have come from *non*–political scientists.

This introductory chapter tackles four tasks. First, we assess the relation-ship between area studies and comparative politics to show that they are prop-erly conceived as complementary and mutually enriching. Second, we review recent developments in qualitative methods to bolster our call for area special-ists to take advantage of these innovations to engage the discipline—and to do so with self-confidence. In the third section, we elaborate upon how Southeast Asian political studies have contributed to knowledge accumulation through three distinct paths. We conclude the chapter by introducing the chapters to come.

Area Studies in Comparative Politics: The Merits of Dual Engagement

Studying the politics of the developing world has long meant studying the politics of a specific world region. Most prominent scholars of comparative politics have been more than just accomplished theorists: They have also been well-versed Latin Americanists, Africanists, Asianists, etc. Area studies have thus been at the heart of the subfield of comparative politics within the disci-pline of political science since World War II.[2]

But ironically, area studies and the discipline have frequently been viewed as contradictory rather than complementary fields of inquiry. Since the 1950s, political science, and comparative politics in particular, have been the site of many intense debates between those more interested in universal theory and those more focused on area studies—or, in the words of Isaiah Berlin, be-tween the fox (those who prefer to concentrate their intellectual efforts on the details of a particular region) and the hedgehog (those who advocate universal theory and abstraction) (Berlin 1953).[3] At times, relations between foxes and hedgehogs have soured to the point that mutual engagement has given way to mutual disdain. One prominent comparativist was even led to lament that although it remained clear "how much political science had to contribute to the study of the developing world," such contributions were threatened by the prospect that political science would "expire in its own disciplinary wars."[4]

Our goal here is to reframe rather than rehash existing debates. We submit that current methodological arguments within comparative politics tend to rest on two mistaken assumptions. First, we reject the view that comparativists necessarily confront a trade-off between regional and theoretical concerns. On the contrary, the chapters to follow show repeatedly that detailed research of a small number of countries can be an ideal route to developing more convincing theoretical claims.

Second, we disagree with area studies pessimists who think that qualitative researchers in political science are fighting a losing battle in a hostile discipline. The evidence suggests otherwise. As Gerardo Munck and Richard Snyder (2005) have systematically shown, qualitative studies of one or two countries not only remain *present* in the most prestigious comparative journals; they also remain *predominant*.[5] Nearly two-thirds of the articles published in *World Politics, Comparative Politics*, and *Comparative Political Studies* between 1989 and 2004 were mainly qualitative rather than quantitative, and more than 60 percent of these articles covered no more than two countries.

These data suggest that less has changed in the study of comparative politics than is commonly surmised. Although the field continues to evolve by absorbing new topics and techniques, most of the work in comparative politics is still based on two core elements: general theories and cases steeped in particular histories (Kohli et al. 1996). The existence of an "eclectic" and "messy" center of the field was observed by Peter Evans more than a decade ago, and his observation remains true today. This accords with our view that region and theory are mutually reinforcing in the production of knowledge. We agree with Evans that most comparativists become inspired to study a particular *theoretical* question because of their existing *regional* interests and passions (see Kohli et al. 1996). Although theory generation is crucial to the comparativist enterprise, this is most likely to occur after comparativists have spent significant time familiarizing themselves with one country or a small handful of countries.

The importance of area studies to comparative politics can be further demonstrated by the central role of area studies in knowledge accumulation and theory building. This has occurred through an iterated dialogue between theory and cases, and a judicious balance between deductive reasoning and inductive analysis. A few key examples should make this immediately evident. Putnam (1993) is based entirely upon Italian empirics but has generated world-wide interest in the concept of social capital (as witnessed in Varshney's [2002] careful application of Putnam's concepts to India); Stepan (1987) is based largely on Brazil, but it has long been at the forefront of studies on military politics more broadly; Bates (1981) built its argument on several African countries, while spurring a broader debate on urban bias as a political basis for economic stagnation. These are all considered landmark works in the comparative politics canon, and their theoretical contributions are rooted in a deep knowledge of one region or country. They do not disdain the particular in favor of the general. Rather, they build their general explanations with the raw material of observations from their particular regions and countries of expertise.

How much have Southeast Asianists contributed to these valuable conversations between theory and region? On this score, the data collected by Munck and Snyder (2005) suggest that Southeast Asia is not currently "punching its weight" in comparative politics. Only 4.3 percent of recently published articles in the peak comparative journals have focused on the region, far less than the Middle East (8.9 percent), sub-Saharan Africa (9.8 percent), or East Asia (17.7 percent)—to say nothing of Western Europe and Latin America, which combine to make up 63 percent of the articles in Munck and Snyder's data set.

To a large extent, this imbalance reflects the simple fact that more comparativists study these other regions than study Southeast Asia. Yet the chapters to follow will exhibit an abundance of research containing interesting theoretical implications in substantive areas of great political importance. Perhaps such work has been underrepresented in leading comparative journals because the theoretical payoff of such studies is often more implicit than explicit. It may also be the case that Southeast Asianists have perceived leading journals as unwelcoming to qualitative analyses that cover only one or a small handful of countries.

Yet comparative politics remains an eclectic enterprise in which qualitative studies of specific world regions continue to play a prominent role. We are confident that it will remain so for the indefinite future if area experts engage in theoretical and methodological debates rather than shunning them. The opportunities for Southeast Asianists to make a bigger disciplinary splash in political science would appear to be considerable. The big payoff from such mutual engagement will come when Southeast Asianists not only show how their countries of interest *reflect* current theoretical understandings but also help political scientists *rethink* these understandings in creative and rigorous ways.

The next section aims to aid such creative and rigorous mutual engagement with a practical discussion of best practices in qualitative research design. We do not seek to deny or denigrate the value of formal game-theoretic and quasi-experimental quantitative research. We wish instead to highlight and clarify the distinctive contributions of qualitative, area studies research to theoretical knowledge in comparative politics.

Qualitative Analysis in Political Science: Asserting Value Through Rigor

In the parlance of political scientists, "qualitative methods" is a rather unfortunate grab-bag category. It encapsulates the wide range of research approaches that involve neither statistical tests of probabilistic relationships between posited causes and outcomes ("quantitative methods") nor numeric formalizations of political phenomena ("formal theory"). Qualitative comparative analyses typically limit their scope to one or a few countries and use narratives to offer comprehensive accounts or explanations of certain historical events or political phenomena. How can the qualitative analysis of politics within a small number of countries inform a discipline that tends to pursue the explication of the universal rather than the illumination of the particular?

Qualitative researchers have justified their contributions to political science in numerous ways.[6] Until recently, the most common defense involved acknowledging that qualitative methods are only second best, but are still justified because of extraneous factors such as a lack of available data. This kind of defensive justification was often heard among earlier generations of researchers lacking confidence and a vocabulary to make the case for qualitative methods on their own terms.

In the past decade, qualitative researchers have moved beyond these unnecessarily apologetic responses. They have articulated impressive philosophical and methodological explanations for why qualitative analysis is indispensable in the accumulation of theoretical knowledge. Three lines of argument warrant special emphasis. First, qualitative researchers deny the common notion that hypothesis testing should be considered the central task in knowledge accumulation. Rather, the choice of research methods depends on the state of existing knowledge. As Timothy McKeown (1999: 187) remarks, "the research task is not how to move from a position of ignorance to one of certainty regarding the truth of a single proposition. Rather, it is how to learn something new about a world that one already knows to some degree." Testing is only one phase in this long process that is not always rational, consistent, or straightforward, but involves much hermeneutics. Judgment, classification, description, and thought experiments play important roles, even if they are creative intellectual processes that are difficult to formalize. It is not that case studies or contextualized comparisons are always second-best choices; rather, they are often *appropriate* responses to the existing conditions of knowledge about the subject to be studied.

Qualitative research is especially indispensable in the construction and elaboration of new theories and hypotheses. By aiding "a dialogue between ideas and data," qualitative analysis forces researchers to constantly reconceptualize the cases and reconsider the causes and outcomes: in short, the phenomena themselves (Ragin 2000: 43–44). It is not inferentially fatal if this kind of dialogue stretches or alters theories to make them consistent with new evidence (King et al. 1995: 104). It is every bit as important to elaborate and refine hypotheses as to confirm or disconfirm them in their existing form (Mahoney 2003: 146–150). Neither is it condemnable that this dialogue often serves heuristic rather than explanatory purposes. On the contrary, it matters that qualitative researchers can tackle and assess (rather than assume) the homogeneity of cases, causes, and causal impacts (Ragin 1997: 24–27).

A second noteworthy recent advance in qualitative methods has come with Henry Brady and David Collier's (2004: 252–255) useful conceptual distinction between "dataset observations" (commonly understood as *n* in statistics) and "causal process observations." This latter type of observation entails systematic attention to causal processes and mechanisms over time. This is one of the most useful analytic tools in qualitative analysis. The value of carefully accumulating observations across time as well as space has long been recognized in discussions lauding the explanatory importance of "process-tracing" in qualitative analysis (George and Bennett 2005). But Brady and Collier have made this value more explicit with their rather straightforward argument that increasing observations is not merely a matter of attaining quasi-experimental control (namely, gaining sufficient "degrees of freedom"). The best historical analyses of political phenomena in a small set of countries are not "small-*n*" studies at all, but rest on a different sort of *n* (causal process observations) than what is used in most quantitative analyses (dataset observations). In sum, determining the actual number of empirical observations in a comparative political study is not as straightforward as is commonly presumed.[7]

Third, it is important to note that not all qualitative researchers see the goal of social inquiry as one of drawing general causal inferences. For many, the more fundamental task for the researcher is to interpret and understand specific political events and phenomena (Ragin 1997: 35). In fact, causal inferences, rather than being ends in themselves, may only be a means to other ends. As Charles Ragin (2000: 15) argues, "empirical generalizations and social science theory are important, but their importance derives primarily from their service to the goal of interpretive understanding."

Unlike more positivist qualitative analysts, interpretivists believe that the ultimate goal of social science is not to search for causal regularities but to understand social phenomena.[8] It bears emphasizing that although interpretivist work is often based on fieldwork in a single village, this does not necessarily mean that it is "small-*n*" in the conventional sense. The number of individuals observed and the duration of observation decide how many "*n*" there are. If fieldwork takes place over an extended period and if the researcher is culturally well equipped, the number of observations made can be huge. To be sure, generalizations within national contexts by interpretivist studies, if made, do have to assume similar causal mechanisms and similar impacts of national particularities on individual behavior. But works that examine cross-national correlations have to make even more heroic assumptions about homogeneous causal mechanisms *across* all the countries in their samples.

In the interpretive method, as in qualitative methods more generally, hypothesis testing is embedded in the course of research rather than being a separate, formal step. The task of constructing an empirically valid and logically consistent narrative involves numerous steps by which each observation or account has to be matched with others to ensure validity and consistency. The tests are informal, but they do not necessarily lack rigor. Rigor in this method depends less on formal, public, and replicable procedures than on cultural sensitivity.

This is not to say that interpretivists totally disregard causality; they value causes as an inseparable part of their understanding of social phenomena or human behavior. Yet they commence with the insight that any causal explanation must ultimately incorporate the understandings of the people involved. Because this is inevitably a highly descriptive task, many scholars mistakenly dismiss interpretivist works as purely descriptive. Interpretivists obviously devote substantial effort to constructing a "thick description" of their subjects, but their works can be quite theoretically ambitious and informative—most notably in the research of James Scott, as we discuss at greater length below.

In sum, qualitative methodologists have made important advances over the past few years in developing a distinct logic and terminology of qualitative methods. This development is particularly helpful to Southeast Asianists embarking on projects that aim to inform the discipline of political science. We now turn our attention to some specific paths through which the qualitative analysis of a single region can foster the accumulation of theoretical knowledge in comparative politics.

Three Paths to Knowledge Accumulation in Qualitative Political Research

Each chapter writer in this book has been asked to examine the degree to which there has been *knowledge accumulation* in Southeast Asianists' study of a specific substantive topic. By knowledge accumulation, we refer to the "generation of new knowledge [that] is *dependent on* previously obtained knowledge" (Mahoney 2003: 133). We are particularly interested in locating works by Southeast Asianists that engage in active and creative dialogue with preexisting *theoretical* knowledge in political science.

Although we do imply some amount of progress in using the word "accumulation," we fully recognize that knowledge accumulation is rarely linear and almost never definitive. We see knowledge accumulation as an iterative process in which conventional theories and even received facts are challenged and amended by new empirical findings and theoretical and methodological advances. Equally important, world events have a powerful bearing on theoretical analysis, productively forcing researchers to rethink their claims. The crucial point is that knowledge accumulation entails an effort to better understand political phenomena through intensive conversation within *and across* research communities.

As a way of introducing the concept of knowledge accumulation, it may be useful to look briefly at the career trajectory of one of the most prominent scholars of Southeast Asian politics: Benedict Anderson. Anderson's research has made profound contributions to knowledge accumulation on the study of nationalism, beginning back in the 1960s through fieldwork in Java. Although Anderson has purposely ignored the fads and trends in political science, his research has persistently addressed questions of theoretical import, and has thereby maintained its broader relevance in the study of comparative politics.

Anderson's first book, *Java in a Time of Revolution* (1972), was an intensive study of a pivotal moment in Indonesian history. Anderson chronicled Indonesia's struggle for national sovereignty as a clash between the revolutionary agendas of the radical youth (*pemuda*) and the diplomatic temper of the pragmatic intelligentsia. The tension between these two visions of national sovereignty had the fading power of the Japanese occupiers and the reemergence of the Dutch and British forces as its historical backdrop. Through interviews with many key players of the period and through archival research, Anderson wove a nuanced analysis of the complexities and tensions of Indonesia's search for independence. He concluded that the pragmatic elite's pursuit of conservative policies to pacify the Western colonial powers had ensured that national sovereignty would ultimately be achieved at the expense of social reform and substantive, lasting democracy.

After being banned from Indonesia for publishing a report questioning the Suharto regime's claims that communists had been responsible for the 1965 coup d'état, Anderson trained his sights on nationalism in Thailand. His penetrating critique of the conservative character of Thai nationalism came through in his review essay, "Studies of the Thai State: The State of Thai Studies" (1978). Here Anderson argued that Thai nationalism as propagated by the monarchy was inherently reactionary, in much the same way that he had found Indonesian nationalism as propagated by its conservative elites forestalling hopes for deeper social reform. His comparative skills were brilliantly displayed with his memorable remark that none of Thailand's nationalist heroes had ever spent a day in prison. This beautifully captured the difference between Thailand's official nationalism and the more popular versions of nationalism that dominated in its Southeast Asian neighbors, where icons such as Jose Rizal, Ho Chi Minh, Aung San, and Sukarno had gained legitimacy by clashing with colonial authorities rather than accommodating them.

Imagined Communities (1991 [1983]) was the culmination—but not the end—of Anderson's writings on nationalism.[9] In *Imagined Communities*, Anderson roamed widely across world history, literature, and sociology in shaping a global analysis of the origins and growth of nationalism. Anderson argued in essence that nationalism emerged in the Western Hemisphere (first in Latin America and then in Europe) out of the confluence of several world-historical forces: the decline of Latin as a universal language; its replacement by vernacular languages enabling distinct identities; the role of administrative units in constraining the travels of civilian officials (especially in Latin America), thereby cementing their sense of place and identity; and, perhaps most powerfully, the growth of print capitalism in enabling people to imagine themselves as sharing a collective community. The erudition and breadth of Anderson's analysis, the depth of his theoretical insights, and the eloquence with which he argued his case ensured that *Imagined Communities* would become a classic in the study of nationalism.

Anderson's career trajectory is far from typical, but his writings on nationalism reflect some shared strengths of Southeast Asian political studies. First, he has shown a sustained personal commitment to the region, as evidenced by a forty-year interest in Indonesia, Thailand, and more recently the Philippines. While *Imagined Communities* has a more global reach, it is replete with Southeast Asian examples. Second, in pursuing nationalism as a central area of inquiry, Anderson has chosen a topic of real-world and worldwide significance. Third, his methodology throughout his career has combined fieldwork research, cross-country political analysis, and comparative literature—a multitude of qualitative methods that trespass disciplinary boundaries with elegant abandon.[10] Fourth, almost all of Anderson's work, whether on nationalism, democracy, or political culture, has deep historical moorings. Among Anderson's many analytical lenses, historical inquiry has remained central to his efforts to explain and interpret Southeast Asian political currents.

Finally—and perhaps most significantly—Anderson advances powerful theoretical insights that resonate beyond the region. *Java in a Time of Revolution* may not have explicitly sought to establish a major theoretical claim, but it implicitly addressed broad theoretical questions—most critically asking what the consequences are for political development when a pragmatic, accommodationist strategy prevails over violent struggle in the pursuit of national sovereignty. *Imagined Communities* initiated an ongoing conversation in the academy over the nature of constructed identities—not just in Southeast Asia but literally *everywhere*.

The following chapters will show that while Benedict Anderson might be the most renowned scholar of Southeast Asian politics, he is far from the only

Southeast Asianist to combine the virtues of deep regional knowledge with sustained attention to the most consequential theoretical topics. For now, the key point is that Anderson exemplifies a broader lesson: *Region and theory are best treated as forces in combination rather than opposition.* Knowledge accumulation in comparative politics is driven primarily by scholars who develop the regional expertise of Berlin's "fox" without losing their interest in the broad theoretical questions that preoccupy Berlin's "hedgehog."

To show more explicitly how Southeast Asian political studies have accumulated knowledge through the interplay among area studies, qualitative methodology, and comparative theory, we now turn to the different pathways through which qualitative methods can lead to knowledge accumulation. These three pathways are causal arguments, conceptual improvements, and interpretivist analysis. These represent the central approaches through which Southeast Asianists have contributed to theoretical findings in political science.

Path to Knowledge Accumulation I: Causal Arguments

Few political scientists would gainsay the value of area studies research in producing detailed descriptions and locally specific knowledge. There is less consensus on whether and how single-country studies can improve our understanding of *causal patterns* in comparative politics. We now aim to clarify how this can indeed be accomplished, using two concrete examples from the literature on military politics in Southeast Asia: Mary Callahan's (2003) analysis of military-led state building in Burma and historian Alfred McCoy's (1999) study of military socialization and coup making in the Philippines.

Drawing on the discussion above, our starting point is to distinguish between "dataset" and "causal process" observations. Single-country studies such as McCoy's and Callahan's typically have few of the former but an abundance of the latter. When they pay systematic attention to patterns of political and institutional change over time, analyses of single countries in no way suffer from a paucity of empirical observations (the "small-n problem").

"Small-n" is not the only misnomer commonly attached to such analyses. A second misconception arises from the tendency to call them "case-oriented" rather than "variable-oriented" in approach. When historical one-country analyses are squarely focused on a theoretical puzzle of general import, it is as misleading to call them "case-oriented" as "small-*n*." Such works do not try to explain cases—indeed, the notion that Callahan aims to "explain Burma" or that McCoy endeavors to "explain the Philippines" is palpably absurd. Their works echo Lijphart's (1975: 160) maxim that "a case study is a study of a certain problem, proposition, or theory" and hence oriented toward general variables *within* a specific case.

The theoretical puzzles that Callahan and McCoy tackle are among the most vital and vexing in the comparative literature on militaries and democratization. First, what makes a military more cohesive or more divided? And second, what factors increase or decrease soldiers' openness to a reformist agenda? Answering these questions helps us understand whether a military will collectively use force against citizens protesting authoritarian rule (as in Burma) or conduct coups against an elected government (as in the post-Marcos Philippines)—perhaps the two most important factors in determining whether democracy can be introduced and consolidated. These books each contribute a verse to ongoing conversations among democratization theorists, fostering the inclusion of Southeast Asian cases into one of the most robust, cumulative research agendas in political science (see Mahoney 2003).

Of course, knowledge accumulation requires that new works *inform* scholarly debates, not just *join* them. Causal arguments should be convincing as well as relevant. Crafting a compelling causal argument in comparative politics typically involves one of two strategies: either comparing and contrasting outcomes *across countries* or accounting for patterns of change and continuity within a single country *over time*. McCoy and Callahan both emphasize the latter approach. History thus serves a critical *explanatory* purpose in both books. Although many comparativists would lament these authors' focus on only one country, single-country designs can actually be ideal for ruling out alternative explanations. Ironically, this basic point was emphasized more than forty years ago by Heinz Eulau (1962: 397), one of the pioneers of quantitative and rational-choice approaches in political science: "[I]f 'control' is the *sine qua non* of all scientific procedure, it would certainly seem to be easier to obtain in a single culture . . . than across cultures."

Callahan's explanation for the remarkable durability of military rule in Burma adopts an especially long historical view. Following Robert Taylor's (1987) work on the development of the Burmese state, Callahan traces the origins of political militarization to the British colonial period (1826–1941). This helps her debunk the essentialist argument of influential scholars such as Lucian Pye (1962) that military domination in Burma derives from the country's authoritarian "national character": a causal claim that cannot explain the continuity between British and Burmese practices of rule.

Callahan usefully frames this historical continuity in theoretical and comparative perspective. She portrays Burma as an extreme example of what Charles Tilly (1992) has termed the "coercion-intensive" pattern of state formation in the European context: "The lessons of comparative history suggest that negotiation and bargaining between state builders and social constituencies are crucial to the development of responsive, representative governing institutions" (Callahan 2003: 8–9).

It is this bargaining dynamic that Callahan shows to have been utterly lacking throughout modern Burmese history. Ever since the Anglo-Burmese wars of the nineteenth century, Burma has been consistently misgoverned by a militarized Leviathan that denies the possibility of accommodation with internal rivals of all sorts. Callahan (2003: 21–22) usefully contrasts the "coercion-intensive political relationship between state and society" that British authorities crafted in colonial Burma with their approach next door, where "state-society relations in India were becoming more inclusive and more open to accommodation with Indian elites after World War I." Callahan argues that exceptionally violent and divisive colonial practices in Burma left postcolonial elites with little besides coercive institutions to hold a deeply fragmented country together.

The numerous armed insurgencies that rocked Burma after independence in 1947 thus renewed an old historical cycle of rebellion inviting repression, and repression sparking further rebellion. These insurgencies perpetuated and exacerbated political militarization, deepening the chasm between the Burmese military (*tatmadaw*) and any social forces with which it might have sought some sort of political accommodation. Burma's coercion-intensive path may have originated in colonial warfare, but it was *post-colonial* warfare that prevented these pathological colonial legacies from being overcome.

Through Burmese-language archival research and interviews with retired generals, Callahan conducts "causal process observations" to show how military leaders gradually developed both internal solidarity and intense mistrust of their civilian counterparts during the violent upheavals of the 1947–1962 period. The military has never split, Callahan suggests, because it collectively mistrusts civilian politicians as failed protectors of national unity. Shared experience as "war fighters" has given *tatmadaw* leaders a basis for solidarity behind this resolutely anti-reformist stance. Because military fragmentation is commonly viewed as a primary cause of authoritarian breakdown, Callahan's historical explanation for military cohesion in Burma contains theoretical implications that resonate beyond the Burmese case.

McCoy similarly displays the causal power of history in his analysis of military politics in the Philippines. In theoretical terms, McCoy's puzzle is one that was introduced by political sociologist Samuel Finer more than forty years ago yet insufficiently attended to ever since: "Instead of asking why the military engage in politics," Finer argued, "we ought surely to ask why they ever do otherwise" (cited in McCoy 1999: 355, n. 4). McCoy's passionate interest in this topic was by no means strictly theoretical. Having watched his beloved Philippines wracked by incessant coup attempts against the democratically elected government of Corazon Aquino during the late 1980s, McCoy (1999: 5) felt pressed by events to ask, "What is it, then, that makes an army willing to subordinate itself to civil authority?"

Because the Philippine military has exhibited substantial historical variation in this regard, McCoy was able to assess varied outcomes without taking the methodological risk of "losing control" with cross-case comparisons. After eschewing coup plotting throughout the pre-martial-law era (1946–1972), the Philippine military followed its coup against Marcos in 1986 with nine subsequent coup attempts against Aquino. Why were Philippine officers so coup-averse before Marcos and so coup-prone after him?

Political scientists have paid surprisingly little attention to the puzzle of why militaries accept or reject civilian supremacy.[11] McCoy makes this enormous theoretical question more empirically tractable by exploring the socialization processes undergone by two separate classes of the Philippine Military Academy (PMA). Like Callahan, he tries to apprehend individual soldiers' attitudes by closely examining the statements and behavior of individual soldiers themselves. The first part of *Closer Than Brothers* scours the archives and employs interviews with retired officers to trace how the PMA class of 1940 was effectively inculcated with the PMA's doctrines of obedience to superiors and subservience to civilian commands. This class helped steer the military completely clear of coup politics. McCoy then aims to explain the subsequent breakdown of military socialization, as witnessed by the leading role played by the class of 1971 in the putsches of the mid-late 1980s.

Because the content of PMA socialization did not change significantly over time, McCoy seeks his answers in broader historical shifts in Philippine politics. Much like Callahan, he sees soldiers' shared operational experiences playing the most important causal role. For PMA '40, the democratic lessons of their

"Kaydet Days" were generally *reinforced* by their armed national struggle against Japanese imperial occupiers during World War II.[12] For PMA '71, academy rhetoric about democratic principles was starkly *contradicted* by their enlistment in Marcos's brutal campaigns against leftist opponents and Muslim insurgents.

Most intriguingly, McCoy draws on an eclectic combination of psychological theory, Latin American political studies, and his own face-to-face interviews with coup leaders to develop the argument that officers' political attitudes were profoundly shaped by their personal experience as torturers: "Under the Marcos dictatorship, Class '71 became a fist of repression" and "gradually broke free from the constraints of military discipline" (1999: 347). When these officers turned their wrath against Marcos in 1986, the dictator was thus reaping his own whirlwind. Yet the whirlwind knew no loyalty to regime type: Philippine democracy struggled for years with coup attempts led by soldiers with direct experience in Marcos's torture chambers.

Both Callahan and McCoy thus elaborate causal hypotheses that are the result of countless careful observations. By grounding these observations in a single country where they possess the language skills to conduct primary research, they not only increase their explanatory depth; they also employ a research design that provides impressive control for alternative explanations. Their puzzles are both particular *and* general; their arguments are stated in terms of general causal factors that could certainly be converted to other regional contexts. These works should invite scholars of democratization in other regions to keep examining the military "at close range," and continue the effort to unravel the complex causal effects of colonial legacies, academy socialization, counterinsurgency operations, and experience with torture on military politics.

PATH TO KNOWLEDGE ACCUMULATION 2:
CONCEPTUAL AND TYPOLOGICAL ANALYSIS

[T]he progress of quantification should lag—in whatever discipline—behind its qualitative and conceptual progress.

— GIOVANNI SARTORI (1970: 1038)

A second path to knowledge accumulation comes through conceptual and typological analysis. This type of analysis precedes an explanatory, causal framework in that its main goal is to accurately describe the empirical setting at a somewhat higher level of abstraction. Before one can address the "why" question, it is crucial for the "what" question to have been solidly answered. Whereas conceptual analysis may therefore be considered "proto-theoretical," it is fundamental to advancing knowledge in comparative politics. Without an agreed-upon set of concepts for describing political structures and behavior, theoretical development will be built upon quicksand. Much of the advances in comparative politics, one should note, have come through analytic concepts developed by area studies specialists. Corporatism, bureaucratic-authoritarianism, and consociationalism emerged as concepts to describe a specific political setting, but have then been employed effectively across other regions. It bears emphasizing that these concepts, while descriptive in origin, are also rooted in a strong theoretical position.

The process of conceptual formation involves three goals. The first is primarily analytic: providing some more general level of abstraction with theoretical insights. The second is empirical: ensuring that the concept accurately describes a realistic setting. The third is normative: Concepts are often laden with certain values about politics. The process of conceptual analysis involves then a constant dialogue among theory, empirics, and the pragmatic concerns of the researcher (Collier and Mahoney 1993: 844–855). The analyst must ensure that the concept clearly represents an empirical situation while also providing an adequate level of generalization for broader analytical purposes.

In Southeast Asian politics, concept formation has been widely employed in many areas of research, but it has been particularly notable in the study of the state. The emblematic work in concept formation is Fred Riggs's (1966) idea of the bureaucratic polity. This concept was not intended primarily to describe the state, although the bureaucracy was incorporated as a key property within the concept. Rather, the bureaucratic polity was meant to give life to a vast theoretical edifice that would describe Thailand's "political system," provide an analytical framework for comparing Thailand to other developing countries, and establish a theoretical claim about political development and modernization more generally. At the same time, the concept of the bureaucratic polity contained within it a normative view about political change. Change could occur only in gradual stages, as mandated by the process of political development, rather than in the sharper, revolutionary disjunctures favored by Marxist scholars.

At the empirical core of the bureaucratic polity was the view that power was encapsulated within the military and civil bureaucracy. All other institutions within the state, such as the parliament, political parties, the judiciary, and those outside the state, such as civil society, were significantly weaker. As a consequence, political decisions as well as policy implementation became the sole prerogative of the bureaucrats. For Riggs, this meant that Thailand could not develop into a modern nation-state, for it would lack the ability to perform at its highest potential. Although the bureaucracy provided Thailand with some modern moorings, thereby distinguishing it from traditional societies, the lack of differentiation across other institutions reduced its potential for political development. In Riggs's theoretical terms, Thailand remained a "prismatic" transitional society, imbued with some amount of differentiation, but with low performance levels. Theoretically, to reach a level of successful political development, Riggs argued that a modernizing country must have high levels of differentiation and performance—thereby becoming "diffracted."

Riggs's concept of the bureaucratic polity traveled across Southeast Asia and launched a lively debate in the study of the Indonesian state. Karl Jackson borrowed its core insight about bureaucratic strength and nonbureaucratic weakness to analyze Suharto's New Order (Jackson and Pye 1978). John Girling (1981) also took the concept across the region and sought to examine its relevance for several key countries. Clearly, Riggs's concept resonated among Southeast Asianists, thus providing a solid framework for building knowledge and advancing debate.

At the same time, however, the bureaucratic polity lost some analytical depth in its traveling exploits. Most analysts of Indonesia and Thailand did not grapple with the more abstract theoretical dimensions of the bureaucratic polity, choosing instead to focus on the more mid-level generalizations about bureaucratic power. Perhaps in doing so, researchers indicated implicitly what they found useful in the concept. Yet ignoring Riggs's complex theory of political development, which was tightly woven with the concept of the bureaucratic polity, has the potential to lead to some degree of "concept misformation."

Beyond the bureaucratic polity, Southeast Asianists have also tackled other analytical concepts related to the state. The idea of the patrimonial state has figured prominently in research on Thailand, Indonesia, and the Philippines. Scholars such as Norman Jacobs (1971), Harold Crouch (1986), Thomas Callaghy (1984), and Paul Hutchcroft (1998) have used the patrimonial state to effectively describe politics in particular countries, while also theorizing about its effects on development more generally. Although there has not until now been any major effort to analyze patrimonialism at a comprehensive and comparative level within Southeast Asia, Hutchcroft's *Booty Capitalism* (1998) provides one important avenue to address patrimonialism in a more analytic, typological framework.

Building on Max Weber's writings on patrimonialism, Hutchcroft divides patrimonial polities into two types: the patrimonial administrative state and the patrimonial oligarchic state. The first type comprises Thailand's bureaucratic polity and Indonesia's New Order; the second type includes the Philippines. The key distinction between these two types is the relative strength of the bureaucratic elite or political aristocracy vis-à-vis social forces. In the patrimonial administrative state, the state elite dominates. In the patrimonial oligarchic state, the oligarchy stands above the bureaucracy. The power differential between state elites and social forces is crucial, for it helps to explain variation in political change and economic and political development more generally. Thailand has been able to pursue some amount of rational-legal capitalist development from above largely because some of its bureaucratic institutions have been relatively coherent and insulated. In the patrimonial oligarchic state, political change is inhibited by the lack of bureaucratic coherence, the dominance of oligarchic interests, and the ability of the oligarchs to prevent other social forces from emerging as potential rivals for political power.

Hutchcroft's typology of patrimonial states is useful because it enables mid-level comparisons across countries in Southeast Asia and potentially across other regions. By breaking down the concept of patrimonialism into an administrative version and an oligarchic version, Hutchcroft has made it easier to contrast polities in the region that appear to share similar properties. By linking patrimonialism to the power dynamics between state and society, it becomes clearer how patrimonialism can have a causal and varying effect on developmental outcomes. In contrast to Jackson's wholesale employment of the bureaucratic polity in Indonesia, Hutchcroft's more nuanced analysis of patrimonialism allows the concept to travel without stretching its key properties. In effect, Hutchcroft has established subtypes of the patrimonial state using radial categories. Although patrimonial states share a common, primary category (patrimonialism), they diverge on the basis of state-society relations at the secondary level (patrimonial administrative versus patrimonial oligarchic) (see Collier and Mahoney 1993; Collier and Levitsky 1997).

The process of knowledge accumulation here becomes especially evident when one places Hutchcroft's work in the context of other prominent typologies in comparative development. Peter Evans's (1995) own effort to advance a Weberian framework led to a typology of "developmental," "intermediate," and "predatory" states. Hutchcroft's elaboration of the patrimonial model disaggregates Evans's predatory state by showing that such a state can vary in terms of the power relations between state elites and social forces. Whether political elites or oligarchs possess greater power in a patrimonial or predatory state can have a significant effect on the prospects for political change. A recent state typology devised by Atul Kohli (2004) also builds on Evans's framework but imbues it with a decisively more political hue. For Kohli, the developmental state is better visualized as a "cohesive-capitalist" state and an intermediate state as a "fragmented-multiclass" state. Kohli, like Hutchcroft, distinguishes his work from Evans's by constructing two levels of analysis in his state typology: state structures *and* state-class alliances.

Concept formation thus plays a key role in Southeast Asian political studies as scholars seek to navigate an analytical terrain that adequately balances some amount of abstraction with empirical reality. In this position, Southeast Asianists generally find themselves within the medium-level categories of Sartori's ladder of abstraction. Sartori (1970: 1044) defines this level in terms of "intra-area comparisons among relatively homogeneous contexts." This is the level at which Southeast Asianists can exert their area studies expertise while thinking more abstractly and comparatively. The dangers of extending a concept beyond its "connotation" (its collection of properties) are lessened at this medium level, even though they may still be employed in ways that partly dilute their original intension—as we have seen in the case of the bureaucratic polity's application in Indonesia. Nonetheless, with a self-conscious and rigorous interplay among abstraction, case descriptions, and comparative analysis, Southeast Asianists can effectively employ conceptual analysis and typological frameworks to advance knowledge accumulation.

PATH TO KNOWLEDGE ACCUMULATION 3: INTERPRETIVISM

How is knowledge accumulated in the interpretivist tradition? Because interpretivist works do not search for causal laws, knowledge is not accumulated by repeated hypothesis testing. Rather, general insight on patterns of individual behavior (e.g., in local markets or in traditional families) is accumulated in similar but not identical social settings or social relationships. Accumulated insight leads to, first, a more precise and richer understanding of such behavior within a specific context and, second, the variations of such behavior across different contexts (Geertz 1973b).[13] The first path can be called intensive accumulation and the second path extensive accumulation.

Intensive accumulation is privileged in the interpretive methods. Interpretivists acknowledge variations, but they do not seek primarily to explain them. Rather, they use variations of the phenomenon (or the main patterns of behavior) under study to illuminate the complexity and generality of such a phenomenon. Whereas positivists tend to look for and use variations first in order to identify causal regularities, interpretivists try to understand the phenomenon as a whole or search for the main patterns of behavior before they incorporate variations into the total picture.

As Geertz (1973b: 25) observes, the task facing most interpretivist works is to plunge more deeply into the same thing that their predecessors have tackled in search of a deeper understanding. This task means that intensive but not extensive accumulation is the expected result of any particular interpretivist work. If this work is successful in powerfully capturing certain human experiences of broad generality, it may generate subsequent scholarly efforts to search for those experiences in different contexts across time and space. Extensive accumulation would take place, but the process is unpredictable in the sense that accumulation depends on the success of the first study. Of course, the universality of those experiences may be seriously questioned once subsequent works examine other contexts. This is not the reason to deny knowledge accumulation, however. Replicated tests need not yield consistent results; disconfirming existing hypotheses is progress as much as confirming them is (Mahoney 2003: 135).

The literature on peasant rebellion and resistance in Southeast Asia provides a good example of both intensive and extensive knowledge accumulation in the interpretive methods. At the center of early scholarly interest in the topic were the causes of peasants' rebellious behavior. Building on the frameworks of economic anthropologist Karl Polanyi and Marxist historian E. P. Thompson, James Scott (1976) analyzed the role of the "subsistence ethic" in regulating village life and shaping peasant behavior. The violation of this ethic due to colonialism and capitalism was argued to be the cause of peasant indignation that fueled rebellions in Indochina and Burma in the 1930s. Scott's analysis questions the validity of Marxist theories of exploitation and false consciousness. He is able to demonstrate that exploitation as a subjective perception may be far more relevant than as an objective fact, but he is unable to rule out false consciousness.

The enthusiastic response to this work indicates that it succeeded in providing a deep if controversial interpretation of peasant life. Scott's interpretation was subsequently argued to be incorrect for the very cases that Scott uses to support his thesis (see Luong 1985). Popkin (1979) questions Scott's fundamental assumptions about peasant behavior, and Adas (1979) offers a comparative study of peasant rebellions driven mostly by elite concerns, thus refuting Scott's thesis that peasant calculations mattered. On the other hand, Kerkvliet (1977), Weller and Guggenheim (1982), and Elliott (2003) conclude that Scott's interpretation, with some qualifications, is plausible for other contexts. Extensive accumulation has taken place.

Scott's later work (1985) plunges more deeply into the peasant experience of exploitation to analyze class struggle in its everyday forms. This work demonstrates that such everyday experiences may be far more salient to peasants than the rare rebellions that capture the attention of most scholars (including Scott 1976). Besides a thorough description and analysis of everyday forms of resistance, Scott is able to fully engage the Gramscian theory of hegemony and false consciousness. In particular, he (1985: 304–305) rejects this theory for failing to appreciate the ability of subordinate classes to penetrate hegemonic ideology, for overlooking the role of coercion and peasants' "hidden transcripts," and for underestimating the revolutionary power of subordinate actors whose resistance may have limited goals and whose consciousness may be far from radical. Scott (1985) provides a far richer interpretation than Scott (1976) of peasants' experience of exploitation; although it may not be a coincidence that both works are authored by the same scholar, this makes it more obvious that intensive accumulation has taken place.

Scott (1985) generated even more extensive knowledge accumulation than Scott (1976). Two edited volumes examine the issue in various contexts from Southeast Asia to South Asia, Africa, Latin America, and Eastern Europe (Scott and Kerkvliet 1986; Colburn 1989). Some works question the importance that Scott attributes to peasants' everyday forms of resistance (Adas 1986; White 1986). The role of the larger communities in which peasants live and state policies that impose certain constraints on peasant life must also be acknowledged (Brown 1989; Zweig 1989; Herbst 1989). Kerkvliet (1990) accepts part of Scott's thesis but calls for more attention to status-driven conflicts in the village world. Scott himself (1990) further generalizes the human experience of exploitation as lived by peasants under capitalism to what is lived by slaves and other oppressed groups in various social and historical contexts. Some rational choice theorists have accepted and made use of Scott's work as well (Lichbach 1995). Last but not least, Scott's framework has been taken to the unexpected context of peasants under socialism. Viola (1996), Kelliher (1992), and Kerkvliet (2005) document peasant resistance under Stalin, Mao, Ho, and their associates. The attention to the "small arms fire in the class war" allows Kelliher and Kerkvliet to offer unconventional explanations for the economic reforms in China and Vietnam in the 1980s: It was ostensibly powerless peasants, not the domineering socialist state, who caused reforms in both cases. Even though peasants' actions were carried out by uncoordinated individuals, they had a collectively felt effect on the state and forced it to abandon collectivization.

The case of peasant rebellion and resistance in Southeast Asia suggests that knowledge accumulation in the interpretivist tradition may take place through intensive and extensive paths. The intensive path is privileged, but extensive accumulation is possible, if unpredictable. The knowledge accumulated is neither "unconnected descriptive" pieces of information nor necessarily limited to certain geographic regions or historical periods. This knowledge does not offer causal laws, but it engages forcefully with Marxist or neo-Marxist theories. It has proven useful for rationalist theorists of collective action as well as for students of economic reforms in socialist countries.

Southeast Asia in Political Science: The Chapters to Follow

As seen in the previous section, our primary goal in this book is to make an explicit and forceful case for area studies and qualitative methodology in political science. Although Southeast Asia is our empirical referent, the same basic logic applies to the study of other world regions. Comparative politics has been at its best—and will continue to be at its best—when it is a pluralist enterprise, both in terms of the methods its practitioners employ and the world regions its scholars examine.

We should hasten to add that the reader need not have a stake in disciplinary debates to appreciate the chapters that follow. This is a book for anyone interested in Southeast Asian politics, not just political scientists. Knowledge has not been accumulated for knowledge's sake, but to provide "substantive enlightenment" on political events and processes in this rapidly changing region. Readers will find much to interest them if they want to better understand why Southeast Asia has experienced such rapid economic growth and such painful economic crises, produced both dramatic democratic transitions and bloody authoritarian backlashes, generated powerful state apparatuses alongside debilitated governmental structures, and incubated both highly militant and deeply tolerant strains of political Islam. Given that all these regional phenomena are of considerable global concern, the chapters that follow contain important lessons for students of other world regions as well as for policy makers in countries and international agencies with the capacity to project power and influence on a global scale.

Southeast Asia's relative geographical marginalization may be insuperable, but its relative theoretical marginalization in the social sciences should not be. Southeast Asia is home to nearly half a billion people. Its largest country, Indonesia, has a population more than twice the size of Mexico's, more than 50 percent larger than Russia's, and larger than the total populations of France, Italy, Spain, and the United Kingdom *combined*. The Philippines has more people than Germany, Europe's demographic behemoth. Southeast Asia's third-largest country, Vietnam, contains a larger population than each of the three most populous countries of the Middle East: Egypt, Turkey, and Iran.

Population is not everything, but it is certainly something. It suggests the massive normative scale on which Southeast Asian politics takes place. For instance, when Burma's military crushed pro-democracy protestors in the late 1980s and early 1990s, it disenfranchised more people than Eastern Europe's nearly simultaneous "velvet revolutions" liberated in Poland, Romania, Hungary, East Germany, and the Czech Republic. Yet Burma's tragedy appeared in the West to be a relatively marginal event, like a single rainy day amid a gloriously sunny spring. By attempting to bring Southeast Asia a little bit farther from the margins, and a little bit closer to the center of Western political consciousness, this volume hopes to give readers a better capacity to rejoice in the region's triumphs and to lament its tragedies as the momentous events that they are.

The following chapters address a political phenomenon that affects the lives of hundreds of millions of people in Southeast Asia and throughout the developing world. The first three thematic chapters address issues of governance. In the first thematic chapter, Erik Kuhonta reviews the study of states in Southeast Asia over the last forty years. States have always been an important theme in Southeast Asian scholarship. Using qualitative methods, scholars have sought to elaborate various state types, assess the role of states in economic development, and uncover state formation processes. In all these areas, Kuhonta demonstrates that Southeast Asianists have grappled with and contributed to our knowledge of issues at the core of comparative politics: from Weberian ideal-type concepts of states to neo-Marxist arguments on state autonomy to the role of war in state formation and state making.

Varying regime outcomes in Southeast Asia are a major reason that the region can make a big contribution to the study of democratic transitions and authoritarian durability in political science, argues Dan Slater in the following chapter. These variations can help scholars generate new hypotheses or elaborate on existing ones. Substantively, Southeast Asian scholarship has provided especially valuable theoretical insights into the role of structural forces such as the state, social classes, militaries, and political parties in aiding or forestalling democratic transitions. As theoretical scholarship shifts away from its previous emphasis on democratization as a product of elite bargains and contingent events, and begins to take authoritarianism more seriously in its own right, it moves into areas that have long been Southeast Asianists' strengths. Slater thus cautions that "democratization theorists can only ignore Southeast Asia to the detriment of the discipline."

Compared to state and regime studies, contributions from Southeast Asian studies on parties and elections have been more modest, in part because elections in the region have often been discounted as undemocratic. In his chapter on these subjects, Allen Hicken argues that Southeast Asian scholarship has been at its strongest when it is comparative and driven by theory. Hicken especially notes studies that have increased our general knowledge about the role of elections in authoritarian and semi-democratic regimes. Such elections do not necessarily signal a transition to democracy but instead serve to legitimize rule, gauge public support, and strengthen social control. He points out that for certain issue areas, Southeast Asian cases may offer insights that cannot be had elsewhere. These areas include parties and elections in divided societies, the causes and consequences of different party systems, and the role of leftist parties in sparking the emergence of programmatic parties more generally.

Tuong Vu's chapter on contentious mass politics is the first of five chapters that address social structures and forces. Southeast Asian conflicts in the last four decades have prompted scholars across the methodological divides of comparative politics to tackle such profound questions as why men and women rebel and how the weak resist the strong. Vu examines four genres of analysis, namely peasant behavior, political organization, comparative-historical, and quantitative modeling. Contrasting the methods employed in each genre, he argues that conventional labels in methodological debates such as "small-n" do not capture actual research practices. At the same time, testing is not the exclusive domain of positivist approaches in this literature. All four genres have accumulated knowledge and have undergone cycles of growth and exhaustion. A key insight is that knowledge accumulation consumes knowledge resources that need to be replenished.

As students of predominantly agrarian societies, Southeast Asianists have been especially tuned into peasant politics and have been at the cutting edge on this topic in political science. Reviewing this literature with the purpose of demonstrating the strengths of "in-depth research" methods, Ben Kerkvliet argues that these methods have significantly enriched our knowledge about village politics. In-depth research, as he defines it, involves extended and intense immersion in local communities, the combined use of ethnography and primary documents, and the researcher's empathy with the perspectives of ordinary people. Kerkvliet shows that the study of rural rebellions and patron-client relations in Southeast Asia has profoundly challenged the notions that villagers are passive in their attitudes, deferential to authority in their behavior, and incapable of defending their own values and ideas.

Moving to a largely urban context, Meredith Weiss focuses on the emerging Southeast Asian scholarship on civil society. Although this scholarship is still evolving, Weiss argues that it has already forced "a shift away from the simplistic, Eurocentric conceptions of civil society that have been generally taken by political scientists as benchmarks." In particular, Southeast Asian cases suggest that civil society exists in societies that are not liberal democracies, that it need not be associated with the transition from authoritarianism to democracy, that it may include ascriptive as opposed to voluntary identities, and that it may not be confined to national borders. Weiss suggests that Southeast Asianists can make further advances by devoting more efforts to achieving conceptual clarity and by conducting comparative studies both within the region and with other regions.

The remaining two chapters addressing social structures and forces examine religion and ethnicity, two prominent themes in the study of Southeast

Asian politics. In her chapter on religion and politics, Kikue Hamayotsu shows that Southeast Asian scholarship has made great strides since the early days of doctrine-based and culturally essentialist approaches to the study of religion. Works that investigate the relationship between religion and the state have enriched our knowledge about how states may shape religious institutions and how religion in some cases has helped forge a national identity and bolster state rule. Other contributions of this literature involve the causes of religious movements and the role of religion in political transformation. Researchers grappling with these issues have employed both constructivist and instrumentalist approaches to assess the impact of not just religious but also class and ethnic identities that drive many religious movements. Like Weiss, Hamayotsu calls for more comparative efforts both within Southeast Asia and with other regions to engage theoretical issues more successfully.

Given Southeast Asia's ethnic diversity, it is no wonder that regional scholarship on this topic has been rich and influential across many disciplines. Jamie Davidson's chapter traces the evolution of this scholarship from primordial, situational, and constructivist paradigms to more recent statist and neoclassist approaches. Whereas primordialism emphasized the immutability of ethnic identities, situationalism highlighted their fluidity. In contrast, constructivism focuses on the historical production of these identities in colonial and post-colonial contexts. In more recent approaches that seek to transcend old paradigms, scholars attempt to explain the consequences of states' ethnic policies in comparative perspective, as well as the seemingly declining salience of ethnic identities in the consumerist culture now pervading urban Southeast Asia. Yet Davidson points out that economic crisis and the rise of violent extremism in the region have shown that it may be premature to write off the old paradigms and that ethnicity remains as salient as ever.

Post-colonial Southeast Asia is not only a region of religious and ethnic conflicts but also of impressive economic success. Chapters 10 to 12 are devoted to the scholarship on economic development and global integration in the region. In their chapter, Regina Abrami and Richard Doner claim that with its great variations in both industrial development outcomes and potential causal factors, Southeast Asia offers a "wealth of opportunity" to students of political economy. The authors suggest three areas where the regional scholarship has made significant contributions. First, works on the role of states and state institutions in economic development have generated valuable insights by applying such concepts as veto players and the developmental state.

Second, studies on entrepreneurship in general and ethnic entrepreneurship in particular have been pathbreaking and have enriched new institutional economics by explaining why fast economic growth was possible without secure property rights. Third, Southeast Asianists are at the forefront of the field in their research on the origins of institutions.

Although the scholarship on industrial development is recent, Southeast Asian studies on rural political economy have had a long tradition—yet political scientists have been relatively absent from such scholarly discussions. In her chapter, Ardeth Maung Thawnghmung attempts to explain this phenomenon and reviews the literature on the subject to demonstrate how Southeast Asia can be valuable to political scientists. She argues that the region can help scholars assess dominant theories on urban bias, the relationship between the size of land tracts and agricultural productivity, and the linkage between regime type and rural development. Furthermore, Thawnghmung echoes the point made by Slater and Abrami and Doner that the rich variations among Southeast Asian cases offer a natural laboratory for comparativists interested in rural political-economic issues ranging from land reform to the Green revolution, and from market liberalization to rural industrialization. Last but not least, Southeast Asian scholarship can supply useful lessons for improving qualitative methods drawn from researchers' creative strategies to collect and analyze data under politically restrictive conditions.

Greg Felker's chapter concludes the chapters on development and integration by situating Southeast Asia in the international economy to assess the theoretical and empirical relationship between global structures and national agents. As Felker argues, Southeast Asian scholarship has not only enriched our understanding of the global integration process in Southeast Asia but has also questioned several implications or assumptions in the general literature on globalization. In particular, Southeast Asian cases suggest that the power of global forces to homogenize national economies in accordance with neoliberal norms is limited. Although Southeast Asian states are not generally known as strong states and have always had to take the external environment as given, state elites have proven capable of exploiting global forces to sustain domestic power relationships—a process Felker calls "illiberal adaptation." These findings challenge the structural emphasis dominant in many studies of globalization, while also showing that national agency can be expressed in more subtle and adaptive ways than pure resistance.

The last two chapters revisit the regional-disciplinary divide in light of the eleven thematic essays. Donald Emmerson asserts that the key question is not whether but *how* area studies will continue to be integrated into the study of comparative politics. He critiques proponents of the view that regional specializations are a barrier to the accumulation of theoretical knowledge, but he also chides area experts for overstating the threat of such voices. Emmerson ultimately argues that the analytic separateness of region and theory should not produce status inequalities within political science, and calls for the "creative zone of area-discipline overlap" to be nurtured. Finally, the co-editors' concluding remarks overview some of the key analytic insights from the thematic chapters and renew the volume's call for further research in comparative politics that is both locally engaged and globally relevant—not only to influence debates within academe but in international policy-making circles as well.

Chapter Two

Studying States in Southeast Asia

ERIK MARTINEZ KUHONTA

Introduction

In the 1980s, the discipline of political science witnessed a resurgence of studies on the state that was driven by theoretical dissatisfaction with the prevalence of sociologically based models. Statist scholars critiqued the modernization and neo-Marxist schools for grand theorizing and sociological reductionism, stressing instead the value of middle-level theory and the significance of "the autonomy of the political" (Kohli 1986: 17–18). Statist scholars claimed that grand social theories were elusive in establishing any convincing generalizable propositions, while arguing that political actors and structures were better conceptualized as having an independent effect that was not derivative of socioeconomic forces. The state as the very embodiment of politics and as a dominant structure that can constrain and shape outcomes thus became the pivot for analyzing economic and political development. Alfred Stepan (1978) and Theda Skocpol (1979) authored two of the most prominent early studies exploring this analytical terrain.[1] A co-edited volume titled *Bringing the State Back In* (1985) subsequently articulated the intellectual vision of state-oriented scholars.

As the study of the state returned to the mainstream of political science, Migdal, Kohli, and Shue (1994) sought to right the statist ship that they believed had veered too far off course. Although they agreed with the push to emphasize the significance of the state in politics, they argued that statist scholars were often reifying and prioritizing the state without acknowledging the messier, empirical realities of developing societies. Indeed, conceptualizing the state as an overpowering Leviathan obscured the myriad patterns in which state and society interact, overlap, and lead to unexpected, contingent outcomes. Along similar lines, Peter Evans (1995) pursued the idea that state and society could be mutually empowering. Evans argued that economic development could emerge not so much from state power alone but from synergy between state and society. As a result of this debate, the literature on the state has settled on a state-society framework that gives analytical emphasis to the state at the same time as it embeds it within its broader social and institutional context.

The literature on states in Southeast Asia shares this "second-generation" view that the state is not omnipotent and that social forces constrain, penetrate, and are fused with the state. However, this analytical position unfolded in Southeast Asian political studies more out of real-world political change than out of a self-conscious debate about theoretical frameworks. Although a number of studies of the state in Southeast Asia have sought to engage with the broader disciplinary trends, it is clear that a strong impetus for employing a state-society framework stems from the empirical realities of the region.

Economic and political liberalization in parts of Southeast Asia in the 1980s influenced the analytical thrust of research on the state. The bureaucratic polity model that had set the agenda for Thai political studies could no longer be accepted in full, now that business groups and social movements had become active in contesting politics. In Indonesia, some degree of liberalization in the waning years of the Suharto regime also formed the basis for analyses focusing on state-society relations. In the sphere of economic development, Southeast Asian analysts rejected parts of the Northeast Asian developmental state model, arguing that state-society relations had been much more porous in the region. While some scholars still emphasized the importance of the state as a driving force for development, few were willing to go so far as to crown the region as a replica of the more autonomous and heavily coercive states of the Northeast.

The focus on real-world events does not mean that Southeast Asianists have not also sought to make contributions that grow directly out of theory. The emerging body of research on the historical roots and patterns of state formation meshes well with the move among comparativists to explain how structures of governance formed and how they may relate to large-scale transformations, such as war. Some of the early work based on modernization theory, notably that of Fred Riggs (1966), was clearly linked to the trends in the discipline, although it also reflected a thoughtful effort to grapple with the particular dynamics of Thai politics. Overall, however, the twists and turns of the literature on Southeast Asian states have been influenced more by observations of politics on the ground rather than by strong predilections for particular theoretical frameworks.

Like much of the field of comparative political development, studies of states in Southeast Asia have been built on the logic of qualitative methods. The emphasis on qualitative methodology—typological and conceptual analysis, interviews, archival research, comparative history—has provided deep and nuanced analysis of the state. Through such qualitative methods, scholars have been able to effectively combine theoretical questions with area studies knowledge.

Three analytical questions have shaped the literature on states in Southeast Asia: (1) How effective are states at dominating and transforming society? (2) How do states affect economic development? (3) What are the historical bases of state structures? The accumulation of knowledge in the first two areas of study is more closely related to researchers' observations on the ground than to explicit efforts to grapple with theoretical frameworks. The third area of inquiry possesses somewhat more of a focus on theoretical ideas within the discipline.

The central argument I will drive through in this chapter is that scholarship on states in Southeast Asia has made significant advances in knowledge accumulation. This has come through two forms: by debating the value of concepts within the region and by engaging with analytical ideas from the political science discipline. It may at first glance be difficult to trace the process of knowledge accumulation, given the fact that many studies often do not engage explicitly in comparative analysis or theoretical generalization. Yet a close reading of this literature does indicate that there is an analytical conversation within the region and between the region and the discipline. But to see this conversation, it is necessary to "sum up its parts." That is the goal of this review: to draw out the elements of a conversation on states in Southeast Asia and, more generally, in comparative politics.

In this review, I have decided to focus on studies that are primarily analytical and that have had a relatively strong impact on scholarship on a particular country, on the region, or on comparative theory. In doing so, I have chosen to be selective rather than comprehensive. I should also clarify that I will confine this review to capitalist states and thereby leave out the socialist states of mainland Indochina.[2]

The rest of this chapter is divided into four parts. In the first section, I categorize states in the region through a Weberian framework and examine states' ability to govern and to maintain their dominance over society. The second section focuses on the literature on state structures and economic development. The third section examines scholarship on state formation. The conclusion of this chapter will highlight the substantive knowledge that has emerged from this conversation as well as underline future avenues of research.

Categorizing State Types: Power and Social Transformation

A central question that runs through the literature on states in Southeast Asia concerns state dominance: To what extent do states in Southeast Asia exert their authority over social forces? Tied to the issue of state power is the question of how power is structured: Do states in Southeast Asia possess rational-legal foundations that enable them to govern effectively? To answer these related questions, I frame this section using Max Weber's typology, ranging from rational-legal bureaucratic states to patrimonial states. The Philippines ranks as the standout patrimonial state in the region. Thailand (1932 to approximately 1988) and Indonesia (during the New Order) have generally been categorized as bureaucratic polities, in which clientelism and some bureaucratic procedures are both present. They therefore lie roughly in the middle of a Weberian typology. Singapore and Malaysia have been labeled administrative states, placing them closer to Weber's rational-legal ideal type.

THE ADMINISTRATIVE STATE

Using this Weberian framework, it is useful to begin our review of Southeast Asian states from the top of the ladder: the rational-legal state or a close approximation thereof. Within Southeast Asia, the state type that most closely resembles the rational-legal state is the "administrative state." The concept of the administrative state has been employed to describe the political structure in Malaysia and Singapore. Such a state is built upon the pillars of bureaucratic competence and elite autonomy. The analytical thrust of the administrative state resonates strongly with Samuel Huntington's (1968) vision of institutionalization and order as the priority for development.

Although there are numerous works on the Malaysian bureaucracy (Tilman 1964; Ness 1967; Puthucheary 1978; Johan 1984), Milton Esman's (1972) study of the administrative state stands out because of its forceful analytical position. Esman's (1972: 62) definition of the administrative state emphasizes its political dominance and autonomy from society: "The administrative state as an ideal type is one in which the state is the dominant institution in society, guiding and controlling more than it responds to societal pressures, and administrative (bureaucratic) institutions, personnel, values, and styles are more important than political and participative organs in determining the behavior of the state and thus the course of public affairs." In his study, Esman lauds the Malaysian bureaucracy for its rationality, efficiency, and high standards. Throughout, he expresses a strong belief in the importance of elite decision making and its need for autonomy from social forces. Although Esman's work may be comparable to Riggs's (1966) concept of the bureaucratic polity in terms of its emphasis on bureaucratic power and autonomy, his work is not an attempt to create a theoretical model. It is instead more descriptive and practical in its emphasis, even though it does delineate an ideal typical administrative state.

Three years after Esman's work was published, Chan Heng Chee (1975, 1976) argued that Singapore functioned as an administrative state. She defined the administrative state as having the following properties: increased power of the administrative and bureaucratic sector, reduced importance of the elected politician, and governance geared toward constraining political participation. The administrative state sees mobilization and participation as a hindrance to development and therefore seeks to ensure political order through rational and technocratic functions. This state type evidently resembles Esman's depiction of Malaysia, yet no reference was made to it.[3] And like Esman's work, its emphasis on restraining mobilization and participation echoed Huntington's own diagnosis of the problems of the developing world.

The view that Malaysia and Singapore should be conceptualized as administrative states, with the resulting emphasis on autonomy and rational-legal structures, has not gone unchallenged. Analysts working in a political economy tradition have strongly dissented from Esman's glowing depiction of the state. Countering Esman's view of Malaysia as a highly competent, rational, and autonomous state, numerous scholars have portrayed a state that is fundamentally rent seeking in its behavior and whose efforts to build a capitalist class have been based not on performance but on ascription, personalism, and particularism. In *A Question of Class*, Jomo (1986) portrays the Malaysian state as an instrument of capitalist forces or, as he terms it, "statist capitalists." In *Malaysia's Political Economy*, Gomez and Jomo (1997) emphasize the tight links between the state and business, and the way in which "money politics" has overwhelmed the polity. In these challenges to the vision of Malaysia as an administrative state, what emerges is a state that is choked by rent seeking and cronyism, rather than one driven by concerns with the public good.

In a sophisticated critique, Natasha Hamilton-Hart (2000a) counters the prevailing view of an autonomous Singaporean state.[4] Power in Singapore, she claims, flows from a tightly knit coalition of politicians, bureaucrats, and business officials. This elite coalition is held together through institutionalized bureaucratic structures and shared norms that are built upon rational-legal ideals. It is these rational-legal ideals—meritocracy, pragmatism, performance-based indicators of achievement—that prevent tight links between state and society from degenerating into clientelism and rent seeking. In this revisionist perspective, the Singaporean state does possess rational-legal foundations, but these do not emanate from autonomy, but from shared state-society norms and institutionalized procedures.

The dissenting views on the Malaysian and Singaporean state reflect real-world changes in the political landscape as well as different analytical frameworks. In Malaysia, politicians and businessmen became significantly more powerful in the 1980s. As the New Economic Policy—a redistributive program for the Malays—began to bear fruit, it brought in its wake increasing entanglement between politicians and businessmen that undermined the autonomy of the bureaucrats. This situation is captured by the political economy work of Gomez and Jomo. On the other hand, Hamilton-Hart's critique of an autonomous Singaporean state stems more from engagement with comparative politics scholarship. As the comparative literature on the state began to underscore the multiple links between state and society, Southeast Asianists have become less willing to take for granted the concept of autonomy.

THE BUREAUCRATIC POLITY

The concept of autonomy has also held a prominent place in the next ideal state type, the bureaucratic polity—a model that lies somewhere between

Weber's two poles. The bureaucratic polity model has been employed to conceptualize Thai and Indonesian politics, and its lifespan as a description of both political systems has been extensive. It is important to stress that the bureaucratic polity in its original formulation was not meant to categorize a type of state. Rooted in the lexicon of modernization and structural-functionalism, the bureaucratic polity was meant to characterize a "political system" in its entirety. Nonetheless, its emphasis on bureaucratic dominance and autonomy, on the state as an arena of naked power and self-interest, and on the weakness of extra-bureaucratic institutions clearly indicates that much of its theoretical basis was built around the structures of the state.[5]

In its vast theoretical edifice, the bureaucratic polity has in many ways shaped the analytical lenses through which scholars have visualized Thai politics. The bureaucratic polity is both a theoretical model and an empirical description of the Thai political landscape. As a theoretical model, the bureaucratic polity is ensconced in the structural-functionalist modernization paradigm that stresses the evolution of political systems. The bureaucratic polity is conceived as a transitional polity—halfway between a traditional and a modern society. Although the bureaucracy is differentiated, the rest of the state and society remain largely undifferentiated; therefore, the bureaucratic polity cannot be considered modern. Only when other institutions become more differentiated will the political system produce more effective policy and greater political accountability. Bureaucratic functions and actions will then be effectively guided, monitored, and constrained. When this occurs, the bureaucratic polity will no longer be transitional but will have matured into a modern political system.

At a more empirical level, the bureaucratic polity reflects Riggs's preoccupation with the stranglehold on power of the Thai bureaucracy (both civil and military). When the bureaucracy remains so dominant over other institutions, its administrative role becomes compromised by squabbles for political power, while policy becomes less efficient because the bureaucratic units are neither coordinated nor linked effectively to other state institutions. What was especially problematic for Riggs—and what therefore hindered Thailand's modernization drive—was not so much the lack of democracy or distribution of power in Thailand, but rather the fact that no institutionalized force existed that could serve as a countervailing source of power against the reigning bureaucrats. The bureaucracy's monopoly on power ultimately clouded any distinctions among the interests of the state, the functions of administration, and the seat of sovereignty.

Riggs's model has cast a long shadow over the study of Thai politics (Girling 1981; Ramsay 1986; Chai-Anan 1989; Pisan and Guyot n.d.). It has been adopted by many Thai scholars, particularly in its emphasis on bureaucratic dominance, but it has also elicited fierce rebuttals. The sharpest response has come from Kevin Hewison (1989: 7–13). Hewison fully rejects the utility of the model, especially its theoretical claims.[6] He assails the bureaucratic polity for presenting a distorted picture of Thai politics because of its static, neo-evolutionary, and functional dimensions. Most problematic is the bureaucratic polity's inability to account for conflict and change due to its assumptions of political development as a teleological process.

Whereas Hewison trained his artillery principally on the theoretical underpinnings of the bureaucratic polity, Anek Laothamatas (1992) questioned whether the idea of bureaucratic dominance accurately reflected the current state of Thai politics. Anek argued that by the 1980s the model of the bureaucratic polity had lost its usefulness because organized business had broken the monopoly of state power in economic policy making. Anek did not claim that the military had receded in importance, but rather that business had risen to the same level of influence as the military. What emerged in the Thai polity therefore was a positive-sum game: Both the bureaucracy and business wielded power and influence. This led Anek to assert that the Thai polity was more akin to a "liberal corporatist" polity, thereby underlining a two-way stream of influence between government and business.

The debate over the empirical validity of the bureaucratic polity has been furthered through studies of rural and local politics. Recent work on decentralization by Daniel Arghiros (2001) and Michael Nelson (1998) buttresses the earlier view that bureaucrats remain dominant players in rural politics. Arghiros claims that decentralization may have created more space for local politicians but that these politicians have nonetheless been constrained by the efforts of the provincial bureaucracy to hold on to its authority. In his in-depth study of provincial politics in Chachoengsao, Nelson concludes that the bureaucratic polity remains very much alive in the provinces. Through intensive fieldwork research, he documents that the provinces are still unable to establish any significant form of countervailing power to that of the bureaucrats.

In a highly original essay, Pasuk Phongpaichit (1999) also strengthens the case for the persistence of the Thai bureaucracy, albeit in an altered and more pernicious form. Pasuk argues that in the pursuit of its own vision of development, the bureaucracy has now extended its reach to incorporate business elites and local village leaders. Building on the earlier observation of Yoshifumi

Tamada (1991), Pasuk claims that *amnat* (power in the form of the state) and *itthipon* (influence in the form of social elites) have now become inextricably linked together against the interests of the poor. In the past, the divide between *amnat* and *itthipon* allowed the peasants to play the two sides against each other, and therefore to carve out some autonomous political space. But as state and society have become intertwined, villagers have found themselves in a more precarious position—squeezed by the powers of both the center and the periphery.

Thus, the debate on the bureaucratic polity is valuable not because of its evolutionary model, but more because it has highlighted—analytically and empirically—the historical dominance of the bureaucracy in Thai politics. The bureaucracy remains a powerful actor in Thai politics, although it must now compete with or co-opt other social forces and institutions. Even though democratization and decentralization have ushered in political change, the persistence of bureaucratic power indicates that not everything has changed. The increasing overlap and friction between bureaucrats and social forces has pushed analysts to conceptualize Thai politics through the lens of state-society dynamics.

Beyond Thailand, the concept of the bureaucratic polity has traveled to Indonesia and sparked a lively debate among its close observers. As Suharto increasingly tightened his control over the nation-state in the wake of the 1965 coup, analysts of Indonesia reached for a model that could capture its empirical realities accurately. Although not all Indonesianists used the terminology of the bureaucratic polity and some strongly disagreed with the extent of state dominance, most accepted that Suharto had on the whole forged a state that was extremely coercive, autonomous, and patrimonial.[7]

Although Indonesianists appear to have largely agreed that the New Order state resembled the model of the bureaucratic polity, analytical tensions within this framework have led to various debates, some of which mirror those among Thai specialists. The first tension regards the issue of institutionalization versus patrimonialism. To what extent was Suharto's authority based more upon patrimonialism rather than rational-legal order? The second debate that resembles the one in Thai politics revolves around the issue of bureaucratic power. How deep was bureaucratic-military power, and to what extent was the concept of Indonesia as a bureaucratic polity helpful in understanding the empirical realities on the ground?

In contrast to the Sukarno regime, Suharto's New Order had more extensive patrimonial foundations (Crouch 1986). At the same time, however, the New Order manifested important features that contradicted patrimonialism. In the economic sphere, Suharto sought to maintain high growth levels so as to assert the performance legitimacy of his regime. And for this he needed able technocrats operating within a relatively rational-legal, coherent bureaucracy. In the realm of macroeconomic policy, therefore, personal whim had to be constrained. Although technocrats may not have been dominant, they were able to play an increasingly important role in the mid-1970s. Furthermore, power and governance were structured around institutions qua institutions— the presidency, the army, and the civil bureaucracy—or, as William Liddle put it, a "New Order Pyramid." Several scholars saw this institutional structure as solid evidence of a state that would outlive its dictator (Liddle 1985).[8]

The weight of scholarship leans toward conceiving of the Suharto period as somewhat more institutionalized than patrimonial, but this does not mean that the institutionalized structure of the bureaucratic polity made it invincible. Only a few years after the image of the bureaucratic polity had been mapped onto Indonesia, some began expressing skepticism about its all-encompassing power. Indeed, some of the proponents of the bureaucratic polity later sought to soften the "hard" image that they themselves had articulated.[9]

Building on Riggs's own analysis of Thailand, Indonesianists pointed out that the autonomy of the bureaucratic polity was perhaps its greatest obstacle (Jackson 1978; Emmerson 1978). For Karl Jackson, the Achilles' heel of Indonesia's bureaucratic polity was its inability to mobilize the population for long-term goals. Whereas violence against communists and periodic voting may not have been hard to initiate, policies that required mass mobilization were seriously hampered. Without institutional forces outside the bureaucracy, as Riggs has stressed, the state remained deeply isolated and constrained. Underscoring the same point, Donald Emmerson (1978: 84, 136) placed this paradox of despotic and infrastructural power within the bureaucratic polity: "If bureaucratic strength is the capacity to dispense with feedback [therefore remaining autonomous], it may prove a weakness in disguise. . . . The irony is that coercion deprives the bureaucracy of something that its rationalization and activation make essential: sensitivity to the needs and circumstances of the public it is now technically more capable of serving."

Later on, Emmerson (1983) proposed an amended view of the Indonesian state as one of "bureaucratic pluralism." Whereas the bureaucracy under Suharto had been extensively militarized, the ministries and agencies in charge of economic policy were given some autonomous space. The idea that certain economic ministries had some distance from the executive also supported Crouch's view that the New Order demonstrated tendencies toward bureaucratic regularity and discipline in economic policy.

Building on the idea of bureaucratic pluralism, Liddle (1987) provided a nuanced view of state-society relations by looking at agricultural policy making in the sugar and rice sectors. He concluded that power was not completely centralized and that various social and political forces exerted some influence on policy—although this influence was more often indirect.[10] Andrew MacIntyre's (1990) study of business-government relations went even further than Liddle in shifting the analytical terrain away from the idea of the state as goliath. Focusing on three industrial sectors—textiles, pharmaceuticals, and insurance—MacIntyre showed that business interest groups were increasingly able to affect policy formulation in their respective areas. Although acknowledging that these changes did not indicate that democracy was emerging, MacIntyre nonetheless sought to argue that there was significantly more pluralism—especially in terms of business-government relations—within the Indonesian polity.

As with the literature on the bureaucratic polity in Thailand, Indonesianists moved away from the vision of an all-powerful Indonesian state. This reflects the fact that in the mid-1980s the Indonesian state may have slowly been losing some of its will to completely dominate society, particularly in the area of economic policy. The shift in the conceptualization of the bureaucratic polity also reflects analytical efforts by Indonesianists to disaggregate the sinews of the state and to grapple more closely with the very meaning of autonomy.

THE PATRIMONIAL STATE

Moving to the third ideal state type in Southeast Asia, we encounter the patrimonial state. This label has been used almost without exception to describe the Philippine state (Hutchcroft 1991, 1998; McCoy 1993a). Such a state is suffused by the perniciousness of personal favor and prerogative. Paul Hutchcroft (1991: 415) describes the Philippine state thus: "[T]he state apparatus is choked continually by an anarchy of particularistic demands from, and particularistic actions on behalf of, those oligarchs and cronies who are currently most favored by its top officials. . . ." As a consequence of the predatory behavior of oligarchs, the underdeveloped bureaucratic structure, and external aid from the United States, the Philippines has failed to move beyond its developmental morass—trapped in what Hutchcroft appropriately terms a system of "booty capitalism."

A patrimonial state clearly has some overlap with the bureaucratic polity because both state types are imbued with patrimonialism. But the key difference is that in the patrimonial state, power does not originate from within the agencies of the state, but from social elites with an independent economic base and regional or local electoral office. In contrast to the strength of the military bureaucrats in Indonesia and Thailand, in the Philippines the bureaucrats are largely beholden to the oligarchs.[11]

This difference in the structure of power has fundamental implications for political and social change. As the literature on the bureaucratic polity in Indonesia and Thailand has shown, in the 1980s there was some push toward the diffusion of power. In the Philippines, however, the incoherence of the bureaucracy and the lack of sustained economic growth have inhibited change from above or below (Hutchcroft 1998: 53–55). This situation has led scholars of the Philippines to view the polity in terms of patterns of political continuity despite a critical regime change in 1986.[12]

POLITICAL CHANGE

An important comparative question that arises from this analysis of the range of state types in Southeast Asia is the issue of political change. It is worth emphasizing that compared to the administrative state and the patrimonial state, the bureaucratic polity model appears to be the most vulnerable to political change. In Thailand, by the mid-1970s the model of the bureaucratic polity was already shaky. As business elites, political parties, labor unions, and students challenged the authority of the bureaucracy, they succeeded in establishing a democratic regime in 1973. Although the bureaucratic elite returned in 1976, the power structure in urban Thailand was already undergoing significant change that would lead to a more solid democratic transition in the late 1980s.

In Indonesia, political change was much slower in coming—but also more drastic when it did finally arrive. As I have argued, scholarship in the mid-1980s pointed to the greater degree of pluralism beneath the veneer of the bureaucratic polity, while still keeping to the core image of a dominant, institutionalized state. But the precipitous collapse of the Suharto regime in 1998 led to surprising analyses that would not have been predicted given the way that the New Order state had been conceptualized. Suddenly, the key question in the minds of Indonesianists was whether the Indonesian state was on the verge of collapse (Emmerson 2000; Rohde 2001; Wanandi 2002; Malley 2003).

If, as several analysts had argued earlier, the bureaucratic polity would survive its supreme leader, why did power suddenly devolve into a frenzy of institutional and social disorder? Was patrimonialism perhaps much more deeply enmeshed in state-society relations? To make sense of this tension, Crouch (1998) argues that the state's institutional and coercive capacity regarding societal forces remained strong but that the patrimonial features embedded in the nerves of the state ultimately brought down a regime that could no longer keep on feeding the patronage machine. With the financial crisis as a backdrop, the New Order state suddenly resembled a fragile shell.

In concluding this section, one might venture the following proposition regarding political change: The extreme ends of the Weberian typology—the administrative state and the patrimonial state—appear more resistant to change compared to the middle-range state type, the bureaucratic polity. Even if one contests the depiction of Malaysia and Singapore as administrative states, their structural coherence does buttress their institutional and regime resiliency. On the opposite end of the spectrum, the incoherence of the bureaucracy in the patrimonial state severely inhibits the potential for political change. Although social mobilization erupts intermittently in the Philippines, the state is unable to serve as a platform for political reform. It is in the middle of the spectrum, where clientelism and technocratic capacity rub elbows, that one finds more room for political change. Although one must be careful not to ignore the differences in the kind of change that has occurred in Thailand and Indonesia, it is notable that there is a greater balance between state power and societal interests in these polities now.

States and Economic Development

Compared to the classic studies on the developmental state in Northeast Asia (Johnson 1982; Amsden 1989; Wade 1990), Southeast Asianists have generally dissented from the view of the state as an autonomous, coercive force that can set the developmental agenda through strategic and coercive industrial policy. A central point that many analysts have advanced is that intervention in the economy has not come from a top-down vision of the public good, but from the intersection of social interests (business and ethnic groups) with politicians' interests. As a result, Southeast Asianists have emphasized the significance of state-society linkages in shaping economic development. This is true for those who tend to take a more neo-Marxist view that development is shaped by a rising capitalist class and for those who focus directly on state intervention and industrial policy.

Scholars who pursue a more neo-Marxist approach to development argue that the state stimulates economic growth not so much by "governing the market" as by fostering a capitalist class (Higgott and Robison 1985). Within this approach, Richard Robison (1986) argues that the rise of a business class in Indonesia was a direct result of state policy under the New Order. In the process, the "politico-bureaucrats" who shaped policy became so deeply entangled with the emerging capitalists (especially Chinese capital) that it became difficult to distinguish the boundary between public and private. In this analysis, the state is the central force setting the pace for capital accumulation and for the growth of capitalist forces. Yet there is also a strong emphasis on seeing the state constrained by an ineluctable class dynamic: "While we must stress that state power in capitalist society is not immediately irreducible to class power . . . the fact that the state exists in the context of a particular system of class relationships does limit and shape the form and exercise of state power" (Robison 1986: 118). There is a clear tension here between wanting to maintain an analytic separation between the state and the economy and wanting to emphasize the irrepressible power of capitalism.

Hewison's study of capital in Thailand (1989) is cut from the same analytical cloth as that of Robison and similarly demonstrates some tension between the concept of state autonomy and the idea of the state as an instrument of the ruling class. Hewison argues that the state has played a significant role in the formation of a capitalist class in Thailand. Through active intervention, the state pushed capital beyond its earlier base in trade and small-scale production toward large-scale industries and banking. By the late 1980s, capital was ascendant and, more significantly, had penetrated the state to the point at which "the interests of the state, state managers, and the nation invariably become the interests of capital-in-general" (Hewison 1989: 212). On balance, Hewison leans toward conceptualizing the state as an instrument of the capitalist ruling class. The surge of capital in the 1980s makes such an argument compelling at an empirical level, yet at an analytical level, the state is reduced to being simply a function of social forces.[13]

In a tour-de-force study of class formation in Malaysia, Jomo (1986) addresses the role of the state in development yet focuses less upon the state as an actor in its own right than upon the use of the state by "statist capitalists." Through the implementation of the New Economic Policy (NEP) and its goal of economic restructuring, the statist capitalists—politicians, bureaucrats, and businessmen—have been able to use the state to advance their goals of capital accumulation. In Jomo's analysis, the state serves not as an autonomous force for public good but as an instrument of capitalist accumulation. Gomez and Jomo's work (1997) on rent seeking and patronage in the 1980s provides a further indictment of the state's interventionist policies, although unlike the preceding study, it does not reflect a neo-Marxist bent.

Turning now to work that directly addresses the developmental state, two studies are particularly significant: *Business and Government in Industrializing Asia*, edited by Andrew MacIntyre (1994a), and *Southeast Asia's Misunderstood Miracle*, written by Jomo and colleagues (1997). Both are comparative in nature and engage deeply with the literature on the Northeast Asian Tigers, yet their theoretical emphases are perceptibly different. The first volume sees the Southeast Asian states as being significantly less competent and interventionist compared to their Northeast Asian neighbors, and the second volume tilts toward a more positive view of Southeast Asian states as well as clearly favoring interventionism as state policy.

In the introduction to his volume, MacIntyre (1994c) argues that state intervention for developmental purposes has been rather moderate compared to Taiwan and Korea, and if attempted it has been poorly implemented and characterized by rent-seeking behavior.[14] Above all, the export-oriented industrialization phase that sustained high growth rates in the region was marked not by increasing intervention, but by less. One can draw two divergent conclusions from this: (1) that the strong state thesis generated by Northeast Asia may not be that significant an explanatory variable because Southeast Asia has also developed without such strong states, or (2) that Southeast Asian development is ultimately ephemeral. MacIntyre (1994c: 17) tilts toward the latter position, noting that "the principal reason for this is the belief that the limited capacities and insulation of Southeast Asian state institutions outside the macroeconomic policy citadel of the liberal technocrats is likely to be a serious constraint on economic performance."

Jomo's volume is a direct response to the World Bank's *East Asian Miracle* report (1993). Jomo challenges the World Bank's view that Southeast Asian newly industrializing countries (NICs), compared to Korea and Taiwan, would be the better model for the developing world specifically because of their minimal state intervention and heavier reliance on economic liberalization. Whereas the level of state intervention in Thailand, Malaysia, and Indonesia is considered moderate, Jomo argues that industrial policy has in fact played a pivotal role in the region's economic boom. Of the three countries, Thailand comes closer to the Northeast Asian developmental state because of its ability to maintain relatively effective macroeconomic policies, advance capital accumulation, and engage in skills upgrading as well as labor repression.[15]

In Indonesia and especially in Malaysia, state interventionism has been significant, but its focus on industrialization and capital accumulation has been distorted by ethnic considerations. In Malaysia, the strengthening of a Malay rentier capitalist class has been the central goal of the state's industrial policy. Yet Jomo (2001: especially 472–473 and 480–482) also notes that had it not been for state intervention, Malaysia would not have succeeded in establishing itself as the leader of palm oil exports or as a major site for electronics assembly.

Although Jomo and MacIntyre concur that a significant part of state interventionism in Southeast Asia has been built upon rent-seeking pursuits, Jomo (1997) concludes that states in the region have been crucial for economic development. They may not possess the same prowess as Northeast Asian states, but their difference is more one of degree than of kind. As Jomo (1997: 156) writes, "Despite all the flaws and abuses involved, there is now little doubt that the structural transformation and industrialization of these economies have gone well beyond what would have been achieved by exclusive reliance on market forces and the private sector initiatives."

Even while accepting that Southeast Asian states have played a significant role in development, numerous scholars lean toward the view that Southeast Asian states are less effective and less autonomous than their Northeast Asian brethren, precisely because of denser links between state and society. In his study on business associations in Thailand, Anek (1992) claims that these associations have had greater influence on economic policy compared to their counterparts in Northeast Asia. This is in large part because the Thai state does not possess the same coercive and institutional capacity as that of Korea or Taiwan. Anek's study thus highlights the significance of societal forces, rather than of the state, in explaining policy outcomes. On similar lines, Hamilton-Hart (2002) argues convincingly that it is not the autonomy of the bureaucracy that explains Singapore's developmental performance, but the rational-legal norms shared by elites in state and society. The pervasive interaction between state bureaucrats and business elites in the formulation of policy in Singapore indicates that a purely statist perspective is inadequate.

Perhaps among all scholars working on political economy in Southeast Asia, Richard Doner (1991b, 1992) has been the most persistent voice in advocating a state-society framework that places institutions as the central, analytical force. In his study of the automobile industry, Doner (1991a) examines state-society linkages and patterns of bargaining with automobile transnational corporations in four Southeast Asian countries as well as South Korea. Doner argues that the relative success of the local auto industry cannot be explained by state strength. Collective action dilemmas have been solved by institutional structures, such as business groups and public/private consultative bodies. Only when one looks at the interaction of state and society and at the coalitional arrangements that drive policy does one get a more accurate picture of policy implementation.

In distilling some generalization from the literature on states and development, it appears that the state in Southeast Asia is far from being autonomous and being in possession of similar bureaucratic capacities as the Northeast Asian NICs. Class and ethnicity deeply penetrate the state in Thailand, Indonesia, Malaysia, and the Philippines such that industrial policy often becomes a function of a particular social group. Whereas for some this indicates that the state is weak and unable to fulfill a developmental role, others point out that the state still maintains important developmental functions that—although they may not reach the coherent and coercive nature of a Korea or a Taiwan—nonetheless represent significant capacity in its own right.

Placed in a comparative perspective, economic development in Southeast Asia is best understood through a state-society dynamic precisely because the relative balance of power among class, ethnicity, and the state appears to be much more in flux compared to the quintessential developmental state model. One should stress that this state-society dynamic has become accentuated due to the liberalizing trends in the region in the 1980s. Perhaps this does make Southeast Asia a more suitable region for comparative analysis of Third World development because developing regions are characterized more often by the permeability of state and society.[16]

State Formation

Scholarship on state formation in Southeast Asia has a long pedigree that can be dated to studies of colonialism. A central theme that runs through several of these early works is the tension that colonial administrators faced in trying to accommodate local values and authority structures with modernizing, universalistic rules. John Furnivall's (1991 [1939]) *The Fashioning of Leviathan* provides an illuminating account of British administrators' efforts to establish control and authority over Burma, including the notable difficulties that administrators faced in trying to reconcile local law with more imperial directives. In the first half of *The Crescent and the Rising Sun*, Harry Benda (1958) similarly analyzed the problems of colonial administration in Indonesia. Benda focused especially on the tensions between the liberalizing political and legal reforms of the Ethical Era with the rising dominance of the more conservative Dutch Adat Law School.[17]

These works on colonial state formation, however, did not necessarily advance an explicit, analytical argument. Recent work on state formation in Southeast Asia tends to be more theoretically focused to the extent that it addresses a central analytical question in comparative politics. A significant part of this work directly addresses Charles Tilly's idea of war making and state making (Tilly 1975, 1985, 1992). This recent scholarship thus joins an emerging trend in comparative political development that focuses on the origins of state structures (Waldner 1999; Centeno 2002; Kohli 2004; Lange and Rueschemeyer 2005). Largely because we now have a better understanding of the characteristics of state structures as well as their impact on social order and economic development, it now becomes imperative to ask how these structures emerged in the first place.

It is perhaps possible to trace part of the current scholarship on state formation in Southeast Asia to Benedict Anderson's critique of the New Order state. In his essay, Anderson (1983) provided a stark contrast between the interests of the nation and those of the state. Empirically and normatively, he castigated the New Order as a violent and repressive Leviathan. Analytically, Anderson sought to establish a comparative-historical framework with which to study the formation of nations and states. Although not all work in this genre harks back to Anderson's essay, the themes of state violence on the one hand, and comparative-historical development on the other, characterize several of these works.

A key theme that has emerged is the relationship between war and the state. Studies of the state in Burma have been important in this regard. Robert Taylor's work on the formation of the Burmese state is primarily a historical narrative, but its introductory chapter explicitly calls for more comparative analysis of state formation: "[A]nalyzing the contemporary Southeast Asian state solely in terms of its colonial predecessors has cut off comparative study from the literature on the development and perpetuation of the state in Europe. But comparable experiences in the formation and perpetuation of the state in mainland Southeast Asia are apparent" (Taylor 1987: 6). Taylor then goes on to argue that Tilly's six general conditions of state formation and survival in Europe can be reasonably applied to political development in Burma. This exercise has much comparative potential, but unfortunately Taylor does not elaborate on these similarities.

Mary Callahan's (2004) study of the formation of the Burmese military state is also primarily a historical narrative, yet its analytical moorings are deeper. Callahan seeks to explain why the Burmese military state has been so durable since 1962. Central to her thesis is the idea that the military officials are primarily "war fighters"—not politicians in military outfits. These war fighters have been shaped by a perpetual history of war making dating from the colonial period to the post-colonial regime. As a consequence of this history of violent conflict, military authorities have established a repressive-coercive apparatus through which citizens can be perceived only as enemies of the state.

The theoretical insights of Callahan's book go well beyond its contribution to Burmese studies. Callahan frames her study analytically by first delineating why state building in Europe had significantly different long-term consequences compared to state building in the developing world. Because war making in Europe was externally directed, there was also more sharing of power between the monarchy and social constituencies. By contrast, the modern state in the developing world emerged out of *internally* imposed war. This began with the colonial state's repression of indigenous rebellions and protests, but was subsequently taken over in the post-colonial period by nationalist regimes' efforts to quash ethnic and communist centrifugal forces. Although most Southeast Asian countries were mired in civil strife and counterinsurgency in the early post-colonial period, Burma's military, like that of Indonesia, refused to accommodate civilian interests, in contrast to the Philippines and Malaysia. Burma then stayed on a purely military course because external pressures generated by the Cold War forced the state to maintain an aggressive posture. In *Making Enemies*, we thus have a rich case study of the Burmese military state, a clear analytical focus on violence, and a comparative framework that can provide much insight into processes of war making and state formation.

Richard Stubbs's (1989b) study of the Malayan Emergency (1948–1960) shares with Callahan's work a focus on war making and the consequences for state formation.[18] Stubbs shows clearly how a powerful coercive state apparatus emerged out of the Emergency—the Malaysian state's war against communism. The gravity of the communist threat compelled the state to coordinate and tighten the sinews of power. As a result, the federal system became highly centralized, and the internal security apparatus was significantly institutionalized. The bureaucracy was enlarged to mobilize resources, and the government initiated a more effective tax structure that would fund the expanding Leviathan. During the early years of the Emergency, the police and the armed forces increased substantially in size, thereby strengthening their position in the state. The Internal Security Act still in place today is perhaps the most notorious legacy of this period. At the same time, the warlike method of strategic coordination employed during the Emergency became the model for the implementation of rural development programs in the 1960s.

In Malaysia, war making strengthened the state, but in the Philippines, Patricio Abinales (1997) argues that the state apparatus did not benefit from war making. Initially, the war against communist insurgency did lead to the enlargement of the military and to the centralization of state power under the Marcos regime, but the tenacity of the communist movement eventually began to erode the capacities and morale of the military. As the military failed to quash the communists, the patrimonial and sultanistic features of the state resurfaced, evident in the lack of military discipline and in intense factional rivalry among the officer corps. In the Philippines, the unified force of the communist opposition coupled with a legacy of factionalism and patrimonialism ultimately limited the potential for state building in a period of anti-insurgent struggle.

John Sidel's (1999) study of bossism in the Philippines also addresses state formation through detailed case studies and within-case comparative analysis. Sidel's main analytical goal is to emphasize how the process of state formation has led to bossism in the Philippines. Sidel shows that the creation of subnational elective offices throughout the archipelago during the U.S. colonial period has led to the subordination of the central state to the periphery. The fact that this subnational structure developed prior to advanced forms of capital accumulation has enabled local elites to consolidate their power through capital, coercion, and crime. This is a state that is predatory at its very core.

Although there are some significant analytical problems in the way Sidel conceptualizes state strength and weakness, his study provides a useful comparative-historical framework for analyzing local despotism.[19] Historical timing is a key factor that leads some countries toward the strengthening of local power while others evolve in the direction of central control. Had U.S. colonialism not instituted a vast electoral system at the provincial, district, and municipal levels, local fiefdoms might not have had the means to extract resources from the state with such impunity. Had the structure of the economy been less "primitive" during the institutionalization of local government, elites might have been somewhat more constrained. Sidel's work thus opens up important avenues for exploring the rise of local power elites in relation to processes of capitalist development and state formation.

Work by Callahan, Stubbs, Abinales, and Sidel is distinct from the bulk of the literature on states because of the greater emphasis placed on historical processes. Although at an early stage, this research strand has already made clear progress in terms of engaging theoretical questions in the discipline. Callahan and Stubbs have persuasively argued that internal war making in the developing world has been distinct from that in Europe. Although war has strengthened the state, it has also been internally directed and has therefore limited opportunities for cooperation between state and society. However, war making does not always lead to a stronger state, especially when its lineage is deeply patrimonial. Historical patterns in Southeast Asia and in the developing world more generally suggest that different structural conditions from those delineated by the European literature on state making have been critical.

Conclusion

Scholarship on states in Southeast Asia has made important advances in knowledge accumulation. At one level, there has been knowledge accumulation *within* Southeast Asian political studies. Concepts such as the bureaucratic polity and the administrative state have been challenged based primarily upon real-world changes but also upon analytical shifts in the discipline. At another level, knowledge accumulation has occurred through deep engagement with broader theories in comparative politics. The literature on states and economic development has moved beyond the developmental state model of Northeast Asia to highlight the importance of state-society relations in aiding and constraining economic growth in Southeast Asia. Recent work on state formation has also addressed comparative theoretical ideas but has rejuggled them based on the region's own historical trajectories.

I wish to highlight now some key substantive findings that we have gained from our survey of the literature. First, in terms of the balance of power between state and society, it is clear that bureaucratic forces in Malaysia, Thailand, and Indonesia are no longer completely autonomous and omnipotent. It might still be debatable how influential the bureaucracy may be in Thailand, but it is no longer possible to deny the increasing importance of social forces throughout the region. Class and ethnicity are critical forces that shape and penetrate the structures and policies of these states and affect the economic development of these countries.

A more even balance between state and society is precisely what ties the Southeast Asian literature to that in comparative politics. Although the Southeast Asian literature has come to emphasize state-society relations in greater part because of the change in power dynamics within countries rather than because of clear theoretical predilections, this literature nonetheless shares with analysts such as Evans, Migdal, and Kohli a view of the developing world in which state and society mutually constitute each other. Although some Southeast Asianists working in a neo-Marxist tradition tend to reduce the state to class interests, most make a clear analytical differentiation between state and society as much as they show that state-society relations are often deeply intertwined. A state-society framework thus provides an optimal approach that integrates the on-the-ground, messy, empirical realities that only an area studies scholar would perceive with the more theoretical disposition of the discipline. This, then, is the healthy "messy and eclectic" center of comparative politics (Kohli et al. 1996).

Second, in terms of the state's ability to transform society and pursue developmental goals, the contemporary variation among states in the region is clear. At the more effective end, closer to the rational-legal ideal type, lie Singapore and, to a lesser extent, Malaysia. Although the Malaysian state has become more penetrated by "money politics" since the 1980s, it remains a relatively coherent institution. In the middle are Thailand and Indonesia. At the low end is the Philippine patrimonial state.

What is perhaps most striking about such a continuum is that state capacity in the contemporary period has not changed that much from the way it was diagnosed in earlier studies in the 1960s. Although it is true that when one looks at the bureaucracy in specific countries there has been notable change in terms of its dominance over social forces, a comparative analysis of states in Southeast Asia as a whole indicates that their position *relative to one another* has not changed that much. Malaysia and Singapore have historically possessed a more effective civil service, but the Philippines has remained institutionally inept since state building under U.S. colonialism. Indonesia and Thailand have gone through structural changes in the past years that have weakened the bureaucratic hold on power, yet *when examined on a comparative canvas* they have not changed that much: They have neither fallen into abysmal failure nor risen to become developmental powerhouses. In other words, they continue to hold the middle position when compared to Malaysia and Singapore on one end and the Philippines on the other end.

What this situation points to, then, is the importance of historical analysis that examines the origins of current state structures and their institutional continuity. Indeed, this is precisely where the cutting edge of scholarship on the state is moving, both in comparative politics and within Southeast Asian political studies. The section on state formation has shown that several of these studies engage and rethink Tilly's work on states in Europe.[20] Recent work on the Philippines has also emphasized the historical-institutional legacy of U.S. colonialism as a central determinant of political development (Sidel 1999; Abinales 2000; Hutchcroft 2000a). Further analyses of state building in particular countries and in comparative perspective will help elucidate contemporary problems of state capacity or incapacity.

A number of recent studies of state formation and political development have also addressed long-term, macro questions of historical sequencing, equity, and institutional origins. What are the consequences for political development when electoralism precedes a capable bureaucracy (Anderson 1996; Sidel 1999)? How does the development of states and parties affect patterns of equitable development (Kuhonta 2003)? What are the political origins of the developmental states (Doner, Ritchie, and Slater 2005)? Although Southeast Asianists have not yet fully immersed themselves in the conceptual analytics of qualitative methodology, such as the idea of "critical junctures," it may be interesting to see how useful such concepts might be in tackling pivotal historical events in the region.[21]

One should point out that the bulk of the literature on states in Southeast Asia has generally been historically oriented. Even studies of the modernization school, which theoretically tend to be ahistorical, have had historical roots. After all, Riggs's *Thailand* opened with a comparative-historical analysis of the Burmese and Thai monarchies' responses to imperialism. Yet what distinguishes the new crop of historical work in Southeast Asian political studies is its engagement with history as a theoretical framework rather than as a backdrop to contemporary politics. Historical events do not simply matter as context, but rather as patterns. These patterns have theoretical import for understanding why certain states are effective while others are not.

Another significant point to emphasize in this emerging body of literature on state formation is its comparative potential. By asking how patterns of state formation have varied across the region as well as between developing regions, comparative theory can be significantly advanced. Work by Miguel Centeno (2002) on war and state formation in Latin America, or by Jeffrey Herbst (2000) on geography and state formation in Africa, is beginning to establish distinct arguments for developing regions. What is Southeast Asia's response to these theoretical claims? Case studies are crucial in tackling these questions in a detailed manner, but ultimately it is comparative analysis that will bring forth with greater forcefulness a theoretical statement that can captivate comparative politics.

This brings me to one critical weakness of the literature. Many of the studies we have surveyed have focused on only one country. The concepts of the bureaucratic polity and the administrative state have traveled to at least one other country in the region, but explicit comparative analysis has been rare.[22] The literature on the bureaucratic polity in Thailand has been almost completely insular, as has that of Indonesia.[23] The study of the administrative state in Singapore has virtually ignored its earlier origins in Malaysian scholarship.

In recent years, Southeast Asianists have been moving toward more comparative analysis. Notable here are the studies of Doner and Hamilton-Hart. My push for more comparative work should also not obscure the fact that there are important comparative studies at the subnational level, such as those of Sidel and Abinales, and that a number of case studies have anchored their work in comparative analytical frameworks. Hutchcroft's sophisticated analysis of patrimonial state types and of variations in forms of capitalism, and Sidel's imaginative use of bossism across developing countries, are excellent examples of area studies work with comparative scope and analytical thrust.

Still, there is strong reason to push for more explicit comparative research. Systematic comparison may provide both theoretical and country-specific insights that might not be as evident in case study research. Comparative analysis also enables a Southeast Asianist to think as a regionalist rather than principally as a country specialist. In turn, this provides justification for arguing that Southeast Asia is not just an artificial, geographical construct but a region linked by common analytical questions.

The most compelling reason, however, goes back to theory, and here the lack of comparison in terms of the bureaucratic polity or the administrative state exemplifies this problem. Had greater effort been made to think of this concept more comparatively, perhaps Southeast Asian studies would have articulated broader theoretical insights about bureaucratic power in the developing world. Comparative analysis by itself does not generate theory, but it is a powerful engine to move toward theory building and to effectively pinpoint key explanatory factors.

Despite this relative lack of comparative analysis, the literature on states in Southeast Asia remains robust and vibrant. Much progress has been made in terms of building descriptive knowledge and appropriate conceptual containers for the study of Southeast Asian states. Our understanding of state structures and state formation is clearly more sophisticated now than it was forty years ago. What I encourage Southeast Asianists to do now is to grapple further with comparative analytics that will bring them in direct engagement with the classics of the discipline. I suggest then that Southeast Asianists deepen their conversation with the founders of the comparative-historical canon: Barrington Moore, Reinhard Bendix, Stein Rokkan, and Charles Tilly.[24] There is much that can be gained from juxtaposing comparative-historical work in Southeast Asia with work in other regions, including Europe. This process of engagement will enable Southeast Asianists to visualize their region in more theoretical terms while at the same time making further analytical contributions to the study of states in the developing world.

Chapter Three

Democracy and Dictatorship Do Not Float Freely

Structural Sources of Political Regimes in Southeast Asia

DAN SLATER

If recent democratization is, indeed, a global process, then the terrain of these studies should better reflect that fact. Moreover, only by expanding the geographical horizons can we know whether our conceit as social scientists—that is, our presumption of generalizability—is well founded.

—VALERIE BUNCE (2003: 168)

Democratization and Divergence:
Regions and Regimes in Political Science

Southeast Asia specialists have paid significant attention to democratization, but leading theorists of democratization have exhibited precious little interest in Southeast Asia.[1] This chapter will argue that Southeast Asia provides extraordinarily fertile territory for assessing and improving existing theories in political science about why some authoritarian regimes collapse (while so many others survive) and why some new democracies flourish (while most flounder). I hope to convince the reader that democratization theorists can only continue to ignore Southeast Asia to the detriment of the discipline.

The most compelling methodological rationale for taking greater account of Southeast Asia is the region's astonishing variation in regime outcomes: what

Kevin Hewison rightly calls its "remarkable range of political forms" (1999: 224). Whereas Samuel Huntington's (1991) famed "Third Wave" of democratization has indeed resembled that mighty metaphor in some regions (e.g., Latin America, Southern Europe, and Eastern Europe), it has represented nothing more than a faint ripple in others (e.g., Central Asia, North Africa, and the Middle East). This makes it nearly impossible to know whether domestic, regional, or global factors are primarily responsible for producing such region-wide patterns of democratic transition or authoritarian durability. In a region exhibiting significant variation in regime outcomes, such as Southeast Asia, it is easier (though not entirely unproblematic) to control for confounding regional and global factors, and focus on the divergent domestic factors driving intra-regional divergence in democratization.

By any metric of regime variation, Southeast Asia represents a motley crew. Two countries in the region can be considered electoral democracies (Indonesia and the Philippines), while a third (Thailand) has recently seen its democratic procedures interrupted, almost certainly temporarily, by a military coup aimed at removing the polarizing figure of Thaksin Shinawatra as prime minister.[2] Four other Southeast Asian countries are unambiguously and unabashedly authoritarian (Vietnam, Burma, Laos, and Brunei), and another three present varying mixes of competitive and authoritarian features, while falling short of the minimum procedural definition of electoral democracy (Malaysia, Cambodia, and Singapore).[3] Democratization in Southeast Asia has been more than a mere ripple, but less than a full-fledged wave.

Consolidation is trickier to gauge than contestation, in part because political scientists disagree about what consolidation actually means. But by any reasonable definition, Southeast Asia's regimes are very diverse along this dimension as well. On the authoritarian side of the contestation continuum, ruling parties in Vietnam, Malaysia, Singapore, and Laos are confronted by weak or nonexistent oppositions. Regime change in these cases (as in Brunei's oil-soaked sultanate) is not unthinkable, but neither is it on anyone's radar screen. By contrast, Burma's freakishly durable military regime faces a highly determined opposition that refuses to disappear. Similarly, Cambodia's electoral authoritarian regime can hardly be said to countenance its democratic opponents, but neither has it managed to crush them entirely.

This substantial variation in regime outcomes provides enormous opportunities for improving regime theories, via comparative studies of contemporary divergence within Southeast Asia itself. By contrast, students of the world's "wave" and "ripple" regions find themselves pressed either to devise cross-regional comparisons or to examine earlier historical epochs, when regime outcomes in their region of interest still differed.[4] The latter approach entails an unfortunate silence on the most recent events in global democratization. The former approach—conducting research across rather than within regions—comes with the danger that, in a wide-ranging search for cases that vary in *outcomes*, researchers will compare cases that vary too greatly in potential *causes* as well. As Valerie Bunce sensibly puts it in her defense of intraregional research designs, "The most illuminating comparisons are those that restrain the universe of causes while expanding the range of results" (2003: 169). Controlling for all potential independent variables is tough enough in one world region; doing so in a cross-regional research design is even more nightmarish.

Yet some regions are more nightmarish for comparative research than others. Herein lies the biggest obstacle to comparing regime outcomes in Southeast Asia. The region may exhibit greater variation in outcomes than regions such as Latin America and the Middle East, but it also contains greater variation in factors that might plausibly cause that variation (e.g., economic development, colonial legacies, and ethnic and religious distributions). Donald Emmerson has called Southeast Asia the most "recalcitrant" region for students of democratization, in large measure because its "contiguous states are so diverse, despite their proximity, as to make it difficult to generalize across them" (1995: 225). The opportunities presented by Southeast Asia's diversity in regime outcomes are thereby matched by the obstacles posed by Southeast Asia's diversity in potential causal factors.

Southeast Asian regime theorists have tended to display more anxiety about the region's comparative obstacles than anxiousness to take advantage of the region's comparative opportunities. Multi-country studies remain the exception, not the norm. Yet there is a wealth of single-country studies of Southeast Asian regimes (and at least a handful of comparative works) that have provided valuable empirical insights and surprising theoretical challenges to what we think we know about democratization. By "broadening . . . the geography of the conversation" to include Southeast Asia, we might build democratization theory in fruitful and surprising new directions (Bunce 2003: 168).

Knowledge Accumulation in the Study
of Southeast Asian Democratization

How should we assess the theoretical contributions of Southeast Asian regime studies to political science? A good starting point is James Mahoney's emphasis on "knowledge accumulation" as a proper benchmark for the progress of any research tradition. In the broadest possible terms, knowledge accumulation occurs whenever researchers "generate useful knowledge about phenomena of interest" (Mahoney 2000a: 1).[5] But how do we determine whether the knowledge produced by a particular research tradition is "useful," and how can we decide whether that knowledge is "of interest" or not?

Research on Southeast Asian democratization has indeed produced useful findings that should be of interest to more than just Southeast Asianists. As Robert Taylor argues, the finest scholarship on Southeast Asia finds ways "to study its politics on its own terms, but without ignoring the universal features to be found there" (1996: 11). The best work on Southeast Asian regimes speaks directly to pressing theoretical debates on democratization in political science (and is therefore broadly "of interest"). It also expresses its findings in terms that can be translated from context into variables (which makes them broadly "useful" to the study of democratization). On issues ranging from the role of ethnic divisions in hindering democratic transition to the importance of ruling parties in sustaining authoritarian rule, Southeast Asian regime studies provide new thinking, convincing evidence, and compelling arguments with profound implications for democratization theory.

To be sure, Southeast Asianists often neglect to situate their arguments in wider theoretical literatures, treating their cases as *sui generis* by default, if not necessarily by design. Moreover, when Southeast Asian regime studies do directly address existing theoretical explanations, it is rarely if ever with a mind to test these hypotheses in the sense of confirming or falsifying them in any definitive way. Rather, these analyses tend to help accumulate knowledge through *"hypothesis elaboration,"* in which scholars either (1) "introduce new independent variables that work in conjunction with previously identified ones," (2) "extend independent variables . . . to a new set of outcomes," or (3) "[identify] the scope conditions that govern a hypothesis." This type of analysis "serves as a springboard for the creation of a new hypothesis that yields additional information about causal patterns" (Mahoney 2003: 135, emphasis in original).

This emphasis is noteworthy, insofar as methodological discussions in political science tend to focus on the role of scholarship in either *generating* new hypotheses or *testing* existing ones, with more status typically accruing to the latter task. Hypothesis elaboration is something different, yet equally important. It aims not to have the first word or the final word in a scholarly conversation, but to intervene in that conversation in a way that invites further interventions. Although political scientists often see such an enterprise as properly relegated to a "pre-testing" phase of the research cycle, hypothesis elaboration can be quite useful at any stage. Even after causal hypotheses have been subjected to rigorous quantitative testing (and even when the correlations they uncover are entirely convincing), important questions invariably remain as to the causal mechanisms through which apparent causes produce outcomes of interest. Using deep knowledge of particular cases to assess causal processes serves the valuable purpose of *regenerating* hypotheses for further consideration and assessment—and, in some instances, for a return to the theoretical drawing board.

Southeast Asianists' emphasis on elaborating (or "regenerating") hypotheses rather than testing them is not a weakness, I argue; it is a proper response to the democratization literature's excessive reliance on European and Latin American cases. Before we can test hypotheses in any convincing or remotely definitive way, we must first construct a more complete universe of hypotheses that reflects a more representative sample of cases. It is simply premature to conclude that Southeast Asia's "refusal to conform" to theoretical expectations exemplifies the "anomalousness" of the region's democratization experience (Emmerson 1995: 226, 223). Bringing Southeast Asia's diverse regime experiences into the theory-building process might well show that the region fits broader causal patterns that *have not yet been identified*, due to the selection bias that has afflicted regime theory in political science to date.

In considering the prospects for research on Southeast Asia to make a bigger theoretical splash, I argue that the region contains the greatest possible lessons in domains where it exhibits the greatest variation. For instance, Southeast Asia can probably tell us little about the historical origins of democracy—a primary focus of studies of Europe and Latin America[6]—because democratic procedures initially arose more or less simultaneously throughout the region, through global diffusion, as part and parcel of the decolonization process after World War II. For much the same reason, Southeast Asia provides limited guidance in analyzing the theoretically salient topic of democratic breakdown.

Having been introduced from the outside during the "second wave" in the 1940s and 1950s, electoral democracy collapsed *throughout* Southeast Asia during the "second reverse wave" between the mid-1950s and early 1970s.[7]

Where Southeast Asia potentially has the most to teach us is in the core theoretical concerns of the "third wave," when the region's contemporary regime variation actually emerged. First, how do we explain the fact that some countries have undergone *democratic transitions*, while many have not? Second, on the opposite side of the same coin, how can we explain the sources of *authoritarian durability* in those regimes that have avoided democratization? And third, among those countries where transitions have taken place, why have some had significant success with *democratic consolidation*, while most new democracies face such serious problems of political performance that regime survival is far from assured?

Southeast Asianists have produced a wide array of works addressing these phenomena of theoretical interest. Yet the shared strength of these diverse studies, I argue, lies in their careful attention to the *structural forces* that influence regime change, stability, and consolidation. Regional specialists have long recognized that regimes are not simply disembodied rules or practices of governance, or the straightforward product of contingency and elite choice. Like ideas, democracy and dictatorship do not float freely. In trying to understand how regimes work, it is essential to examine—and Southeast Asianists have been exceptionally effective at examining—the supporting institutions that actually shape their performance, cohesion, and prospects for survival: (1) states, (2) political parties, and (3) militaries. At the same time, regional specialists have climbed outside the state to examine two other key structural forces shaping Southeast Asia's political regimes: (4) social movements and (5) social classes.

In short, democratization involves not just *individual decisions*, but *organizational collisions*. Recognizing this, Southeast Asianists have never fallen victim to a major "mistaken assumption" of the leading "transitions paradigm" in democratization theory: namely, that "the underlying conditions in transitional countries . . . will not be major factors in either the onset or the outcome of the transition process" (Carothers 2002: 8). Even the strongest proponent of a voluntarist approach to democratization in Southeast Asia, William Case, acknowledges that one can adequately apprehend elites' behavior only after properly "specifying their institutional or social grounding" (Case 2002: 28). As leading regime theorists seek to "thicken" their analyses with more attention to the political structures that influence processes of regime transition and consolidation, Southeast Asian studies provide a wealth of examples of how this might be achieved.

It is these structures-as-factors and regimes-as-outcomes that guide the discussion from here. To avoid overlap with Meredith Weiss's chapter on civil society and Kikue Hamayotsu's chapter on religious politics, I set aside the role of social movement organizations and focus on the other four structural forces mentioned above: (1) social classes, (2) states, (3) militaries, and (4) political parties. In assessing the potential contributions of these studies to regime theory, I focus my attention on democratic transitions and authoritarian durability, rather than democratic consolidation. I do so in part because Allen Hicken covers topics related to democratic consolidation in his contribution on parties and elections, and partly because political scientists are already much more cognizant of the structural sources of democratic consolidation than democratic transition. That the consolidation of democracy depends on capable states and effective political parties is well understood; that prospects for democratic transition also depend on the character of state and party institutions is much less widely recognized.[8]

Structural Foundations of Democratic Transitions and Authoritarian Durability

No aspect of political regimes has attracted more theoretical interest than the puzzle of democratic transitions. Two streams of analysis have dominated the discussion for the past three-plus decades: (1) the Barrington Moore (1966) research tradition, which sees class structure as the primary factor driving democratization, and (2) the Dankwart Rustow (1970) research tradition, which sees regime change as a product of highly contingent elite bargains during moments of political crisis. Whereas social-structural analysis dominated examinations of democratization's "first wave" in Europe, elite bargains have attracted the most interest since the "third wave" spread to Latin America in the mid-1980s.[9]

Regime studies have consistently been less diverse than the regime outcomes demanding explanation, however. Scholars' fascination with uncovering the diverse dynamics of democratization has never been matched by interest in unraveling why authoritarianism so often endures. Only recently, with

Barbara Geddes's pathbreaking research on authoritarian institutions (1999a, 1999b), has any sort of research agenda on *authoritarian durability* emerged. This approach has two enormous merits. The first is methodological: It captures much-needed variation in outcomes. The second big benefit is theoretical: By calling attention to authoritarian *institutions*, it steers a middle path between the apolitical determinism of the "social prerequisites" literature as well as the asocial and ahistorical contingency of the "transitology" literature.[10] By looking at political institutions, we can show that social structure is not political destiny and that democratization and authoritarian durability are much more than the result of random accidents.

Given Southeast Asia's long-standing variation in regime outcomes, experts on the region have never ignored the structural foundations of authoritarian durability in their efforts to illuminate the dynamics of democratization. This can be seen not only in sophisticated treatments of Southeast Asian states, parties, and militaries, but also in a number of sensitive studies regarding the effect of class structures on democracy and dictatorship.

SOCIAL CLASSES

Although choice-theoretic approaches to democratization have gained predominance in political science in recent decades, social-structural perspectives have by no means run their course. The main point of consensus in this literature is that economic development fosters democratization by strengthening classes with an interest in avoiding authoritarian rule, while weakening the position of the group generally seen as the major class antagonist of democratization: labor-repressive landed elites.[11] However, disagreements abound over whether it is the bourgeoisie, the middle class, or the working class that tends to serve as the "carrying class" for democracy.[12] More recently, a debate has arisen as to whether development and democracy are correlated because development presses dictators to *introduce* democracy (via "endogenous democratization") or because national wealth helps *sustain* democracies over time (via "exogenous democratization").[13] The big theoretical debates thus surround not *whether* but *how* economic development and related class shifts improve prospects for democracy.

Like these leading theorists, leading Southeast Asianists have consistently highlighted the role of social classes in their studies of political regimes. For instance, successive edited volumes during the 1990s by Kevin Hewison,

Richard Robison, and Garry Rodan; Anek Laothamatas; and James Morley similarly attempted to assess the impact of Southeast Asia's swelling middle class and bourgeoisie on democratization in the region (Hewison, Robison, and Rodan 1993; Anek 1997; and Morley 1999).

The contributors to these volumes were confronted by the same basic puzzle: Considering that Southeast Asia's capitalist economies had experienced faster growth rates and more dramatic class transformation than most regions in the developing world, why was democratization still so rare? More to the point, why were the two countries with the fastest growth rates and the largest urban middle classes in the region—Malaysia and Singapore—proving more resistant to democratization than Thailand and the Philippines? And why did the Philippines—the Southeast Asian country with the most intransigent class of landed elites—have less experience with outright authoritarianism than any other country in the region? From a class-analytic perspective, Southeast Asia appeared to be uniquely and intriguingly plagued by both unlikely democracies and unlikely dictatorships.

Indonesia's transition to electoral democracy in the late 1990s seemed only to compound the puzzle of Southeast Asia's glaring mismatch between development and democratization. Harold Crouch and James Morley continued to assert the value of a class-analytic approach, insisting that economic development produced powerful pressures for political change. Yet even by their own coding of socioeconomic development—which considers Indonesia, Thailand, and the Philippines insufficiently developed to sustain democracy—only four of Southeast Asia's eleven countries support this hypothesis. And all four are poor dictatorships (Burma, Cambodia, Laos, and Vietnam), not rich democracies. "Endogenous" theory is thus called into question by the resilience of rich dictatorships, whereas "exogenous" theory seems stymied by the persistence of poor democracies.

Southeast Asia's striking nonconformity to theoretical expectations pressed these volumes' editors and contributors to consider additional causal factors. Using Southeast Asian cases alone to reject the class perspective on democratic transitions outright would have been an untenable move, considering this literature's long-standing value in illuminating democratization in other world regions. Rather than rejecting the importance of class, these authors sought to qualify it by introducing an array of auxiliary hypotheses. The good news for theory building was that these studies generally stated these new hypotheses in terms of causal variables that could be applied to other cases, rather than attributing Southeast Asia's apparent exceptionalism to under-specified contextual factors. As argued earlier, this type of "hypothesis elaboration" represents a vital (if underappreciated) step in processes of knowledge accumulation in comparative politics.

To be sure, these analyses are no paragons of parsimony. They adopt more of an additive, "let a hundred variables bloom" approach to explanation, rather than attempting the daunting task of mediating among the multitude of potential explanatory factors that they introduce. For instance, Anek's introductory essay posits at least six variables of importance in breaking the causal chain from development to democracy: (1) statist economic development; (2) political culture, especially collectivist and subservient mass attitudes; (3) communal divisions; (4) performance legitimacy deriving from rapid growth; (5) electoral legitimacy, in those regimes that countenance at least a modicum of political contestation; and (6) the weakness of social capital (Anek 1997: 11–17). Meanwhile, Crouch and Morley bring even more potential "suppressor variables" to the table: (7) country size, (8) external threat, (9) elite cohesion, and, most interestingly for our discussion, (10) political institutions—specifically the state, party, and military organizations that provide authoritarian regimes with their necessary institutional spine (Crouch and Morley 1999: 317).

Many political scientists might dismiss these works as failures to provide parsimonious causal models. Yet at this stage of theory development, I would argue that this type of work is absolutely essential. Southeast Asia's diverse regime experiences are yet to be meaningfully incorporated into democratization theory. The effort to do so must begin by recognizing the wide range of factors that might plausibly influence regime outcomes in these theoretically neglected cases. Causal messiness cannot simply be wished away in a headlong rush to parsimony; it must be gradually and carefully reduced with informed, controlled comparisons of cases that theorists have heretofore largely ignored.

A valuable effort to trim this thicket of independent variables comes from Jacques Bertrand's (1998) discussion of growth's ambiguous effect on democratization in Southeast Asia. His explanation for variation between democratic Thailand and authoritarian Indonesia and Malaysia is parsimonious in the extreme. Relative ethnic harmony explains why capitalist economic growth undermined authoritarian rule in Thailand while greater communal friction precluded such political transformations in Indonesia and Malaysia.

By arguing that Thailand in fact supports the "endogenous democratization" hypothesis, Bertrand usefully highlights a nation's economic *growth* rather than its total economic *wealth* as a possible stimulant for authoritarian collapse. If Bertrand had expanded his purview to the Philippines, a case of much slower growth, he might have concluded that it is not growth per se but the expansion of the educated, urban middle class that provides a necessary social precondition for democratization—even as Singapore and Malaysia continue to make it abundantly clear that such a class transformation is no sufficient condition. Including the democratic Philippines would also have lent powerful additional support to Bertrand's hypothesis that muted ethnic and religious tensions represent a necessary condition for democratic transition to take place.

In making his intriguing argument that communal frictions suppress the impact of economic growth on democratization, however, Bertrand was not only hindered by suboptimal case selection. He was also the victim of bad timing: Indonesia experienced a dramatic democratic transition in the month after his article was published. Because Indonesia is by most measures the most ethnically diverse country in the region, these events called Bertrand's straightforward correlation between communal diversity and authoritarian durability into question. On the other hand, Malaysia experienced a nasty deepening of authoritarian rule only months later, and analysts commonly cited the country's deep communal divides as a barrier to opposition unity and democratic change.

Southeast Asia's democratization experience thus suggests that social-structural variables such as class and ethnicity should neither be expected to explain outcomes on their own nor dismissed out of hand as causally insignificant. This mirrors the consensus of sorts that seems to be emerging in wider democratization theory. Indeed, it is worth recalling that even Dankwart Rustow (1970), the godfather of the voluntarist approach to democratization, argued that national unity and a balance of social power among competing factions were necessary social-structural precursors for democracy to result from elite negotiations. More recently, pathbreaking work by Eva Bellin (2002) has muscularly reasserted a central role for social classes in shaping third wave democratization. Yet even in Bellin's work, the impact of business and labor on democratization depends not on development per se, but on the state's role in guiding it. Theorists are thus well advised to go beyond purely class-based explanatory models and to consider the causal significance of political institutions in democratic transitions: a theme that has long captured considerable attention among Southeast Asianists, but not among democratization theorists.[14]

The natural place to start our institutional analysis of democratization is with *the state*—the institutional apparatus that authoritarian regimes control and that their opponents hope to seize. Authoritarian regimes are sharply differentiated by the extent to which leaders personalize rule, typically undermining the effectiveness of the state apparatus in the process. In its most extreme form—"sultanism"—personalization tends to produce sharp and violent conflict between regime loyalists, whose future depends on the survival of their patron, and regime opponents, who know that the ruling clique is too desperate to hold on to power to negotiate a peaceful exit (Bratton and van de Walle 1997).

Mark Thompson has applied this model to the Philippines, where Ferdinand Marcos's personalized rule bore a family resemblance to classic Latin American and African cases of sultanism.[15] Thompson shows how the collapse of the Marcos regime was not simply the result of severe economic crisis and the contingencies of elite calculations, but was deeply influenced as well by the weakness of the Philippine state. Indeed, the economic crisis of the mid-1980s that helped destroy the Marcos regime cannot be properly understood absent an appreciation of Philippine state incapacity. "Marcos had to increase foreign borrowing because government institutions were too corrupt to be effective revenue collectors," Thompson argues. "A stagnant tax base could not finance the mounting demands on public resources by his inner circle, whose greed seemed to know no bounds" (1995: 66). If the Marcos regime had enjoyed access to a more effective state, this analysis suggests, it might have avoided financial crisis and subsequent democratic transition altogether.

In Thompson's framework, personalization of regime power weakens the state, which undermines a regime's durability by restricting its access to revenue for patronage purposes. But as Richard Tanter and William Liddle have shown, the personalization of power that took place in Indonesia under Suharto had a less pernicious effect on the state than Marcos's sultanism exhibited in the Philippines. For Tanter, Indonesia's access to oil revenues and foreign aid produced double-edged rather than purely debilitating effects. On the one hand, these revenues had given rise to "the hypertrophy of the state vis-à-vis other social organizations." Yet Suharto's Leviathan also appeared to stand upon clay feet, as Tanter concluded that "this power is highly vulnerable, since the stoppage of external rents can severely damage the government finances" (1990: 71, 70). From this perspective, Suharto's fall in May 1998 was not simply the contingent product of an unforeseeable economic crisis, but a regime outcome shaped significantly by historical patterns of state formation in Suharto's New Order.

Whereas Tanter usefully highlights the role of external revenues in shoring up sultanistic patronage networks, Liddle more fundamentally questions the notion that regime personalization and state weakness are opposite sides of the same coin.[16] Suharto personally dominated Indonesia as surely as Marcos dominated the Philippines, yet Suharto ruled through what Liddle terms a "presidential-military-bureaucratic complex," not simply an ad hoc array of personal alliances. Even after Suharto began cultivating a narrower personal clique in the late 1980s, it remained the case that "the bureaucracy pervades society. . . . Its health centers, agricultural extension services and marketing agencies, religious affairs offices, and requirement of personal identity cards make it for better and worse a daily reality which most Indonesians cannot escape" (Liddle 1985: 71). It thus appears that the lack of stateness under Marcos cannot be ascribed to regime personalization alone, but must be traced to deeper patterns of state building in Philippine history.

The causal significance of Philippine state weakness in the fall of Marcos is drawn even more sharply in works that directly compare that country's democratic transition with the (later) transition in Indonesia. When Philippine specialist Vincent Boudreau compares the country's "people power" movement in 1986 with Indonesia's *"reformasi"* movement in 1998, he uncovers a series of important contrasts where most analysts have seen similarities. Rather than representing sudden and unpredictable shifts in the sociopolitical terrain, mass anti-regime mobilization in both cases followed patterns that were "entirely in keeping with the larger themes of opposition" *throughout* the Suharto and Marcos eras (Boudreau 1999: 10).

Boudreau expertly shows how these contrasting patterns of opposition were analytically inseparable from the contrasting "authoritarian architecture of the two regimes" (1999: 10)—especially differences in state power. Whereas the Indonesian regime had successfully crushed its mass opponents at the onset of the New Order, its Philippine counterpart lacked the capacity to do so. This left Marcos with fewer options than Suharto enjoyed. Boudreau argues that "expanding guerrilla and protest organizations, in combination, forced Marcos into accelerated and amplified cycles of political liberalization and crackdown that propelled the regime toward its mass-mobilization-caused demise" (1999: 6).

Suharto's state consistently held a greater power advantage over its potential challengers, who were more often lawyers than guerrillas. Suharto thus faced no pressure to gamble with relatively free national elections, as Marcos fatefully did in February 1986. Boudreau shows that this divergence was not simply a contingent result of elite miscalculation in the Philippines and elite shrewdness in Indonesia. Rather, it reflected deep structural differences in the two countries' authoritarian regimes. Similarly, there was far more than contingency at work in the Philippine opposition's success at seizing political power, whereas Indonesia's more scattered opposition managed only to "convince those in power to exercise their authority to move Suharto aside" (1999: 13). In sum, "the institutions of state rule and the legacies of that state's domination over Indonesian society essentially foreclosed the 'people power' option to the Indonesian protestors" (1999: 15).

Yet Boudreau's statist model cannot explain how Indonesian protestors managed to overcome legacies of repression and help stimulate authoritarian collapse at all. At first blush, this seems to recommend closer attention to the manifold contingencies of Suharto's fall: for example, Indonesia's severe economic crisis, the president's declining health, and the nonrevolutionary character of Suharto's strongest elite opponents. Alternatively, scholars might try to undertake an even deeper and more systematic analysis of the structural factors that shaped Suharto's fall.

Eva-Lotta Hedman adopts this latter approach in her recent comparison of mass mobilization and democratization in Southeast Asia. She goes beyond Boudreau's analysis in two important and impressive ways. First, she expands the comparison, adding Thailand and Malaysia to Boudreau's Indonesian and Philippine cases. By bringing in Malaysia, Hedman gains analytically valuable variation on the dependent variable of democratization. Second, she is more diligent about expressing the contextual factors that differentiate these four cases in terms of clear variables. The result is a staunchly structuralist causal account that provides intriguing comparative implications. Whereas most studies of civil society "privilege voluntarism, agency, and contingency," Hedman's approach aims to "underscore the importance of examining the underlying conditions and mobilizational processes anticipating such 'euphoric moments' within a structured comparative analytical framework" (2001: 922).

Hedman locates the source of cross-case divergence in four variables, which closely parallel the factors emphasized by Boudreau. First, she highlights "salient variation in the nature of regimes," especially the degree to which they are institutionally prone to internal division and vulnerable to electoral challenge. Second, Hedman argues for the significance of "the constellation of classes," most notably the extent of upper-class co-optation accomplished by the ruling regime. Third, Hedman calls attention to "the legacies of the Left," as countries experiencing a history of robust socialist movements possessed stronger opposition resources for confronting authoritarian rule from below. And fourth, Hedman highlights "the institutions of religion," particularly the degree to which these institutions enjoyed some measure of autonomy from state control.

Like Boudreau, Hedman argues that to understand the nature of opposition to authoritarian rule, one must first understand the nature of the state in patterning its emergence and evolution. By stating her complex argument in terms of variables, she presents it in a fashion that speaks directly to broad theoretical concerns and debates in democratization theory, and in a way that can be applied to cases outside Southeast Asia. Particularly resonant is her argument that the state's relationship with organized religion shapes prospects for anti-regime mass mobilization—a causal pattern that comes into sharper relief when comparing the relative autonomy of Islamic institutions in Indonesia with their more co-opted and controlled counterparts in Malaysia. This serves as a hypothesis that can be widely tested, as well as a useful corrective to Boudreau's dismissal of Indonesian civil society as weakly organized across the board. In sum, authors such as Thompson, Boudreau, and Hedman provide powerful empirical evidence that the state plays a central role in processes of democratic transition—a structural pattern that is largely and surprisingly neglected in the "transitions paradigm."

Theoretical attention to the role of "stateness" in consolidating democracy is yet to be matched by attention to the importance of the state in consolidating dictatorship as well.[17] But if Southeast Asia specialists appear to be surpassing democratization theorists in their attention to the state, theorists are setting the pace in examining other regime institutions that Hedman hints at in her discussion of "salient variations in the nature of regimes" but does not address systematically: militaries and political parties.

MILITARIES AND POLITICAL PARTIES

In an agenda-setting effort to give the bargaining-centered "transitions paradigm" a stronger structural foundation, Barbara Geddes has introduced and tested new hypotheses regarding the role of authoritarian regimes' political institutions in shaping prospects for regime change. Coding all nondemocratic regimes as (1) military, (2) single-party, (3) personal, or some hybrid thereof, Geddes (1999a, 1999b) attempts to show that single-party regimes are more resistant to democratic transitions than personalized regimes, which are more resilient, in turn, than military regimes.[18]

Her logic is crisply game-theoretic, and her evidence is correlative. Military regimes are especially brittle because of intrinsic divisions between political and professional soldiers, whereas ruling parties more effectively avoid internal splits because politics *is* the profession of party elites. With no barracks to retreat to, party leaders hang together and hang onto power for dear life. Personal regimes generate similarly hard-core support from loyalists who fear political extinction in any democratic transition.

Geddes finds impressive empirical support for her conclusions in a sweeping quantitative test confirming the greater durability of single-party regimes than their personalized and militarized counterparts. Yet if statistical analysis can indeed help convince us *that* single-party regimes last longest, such techniques cannot show us *why* they last longest. In assessing the validity of Geddes's arguments in Southeast Asia, we must be attentive not only to the presence or absence of a causal correlation between specific regime institutions and regime durability, but also to the accuracy of the causal mechanisms underlying her hypotheses.

On the first question, Southeast Asian evidence clearly supports Geddes's argument regarding the relative robustness of single-party rule in a correlative sense. From relatively wealthy Malaysia and Singapore to low-income Laos and Vietnam, ruling-party apparatuses have helped authoritarian regimes avoid democratic transitions by managing elite relationships and quashing mass dissent (Slater 2003). Meanwhile, the three Southeast Asian countries that have undergone democratic transitions had never developed party institutions that superseded either the organized power of the military apparatus or the political authority of the individual leader.[19] When transitions occurred in Thailand, the Philippines, and Indonesia, the military was a stronger broker than those regimes' respective ruling parties. However, the Burmese military regime's bucking of this trend is a puzzle for Geddes's model, as we will discuss shortly.

For now, it is worth considering how some of Geddes's other hypotheses fit Southeast Asia's diverse set of regime outcomes. Two of her arguments in particular warrant further scrutiny: that (1) personalized regimes are more resistant to democratization than military regimes, and that (2) the most durable authoritarian regimes of all are so-called "triple hybrid" regimes, or those with an institutional profile combining party, military, and personalistic elements in roughly equal measure. Taken together, these arguments suggest that military regimes can enhance their durability by building strong party institutions and by cultivating a clique of hard-core loyalists surrounding the individual ruler.

We have already discussed Mark Thompson's argument that the personalization of power in the Philippines fostered democratization rather than forestalling it, by undermining the state apparatus that Marcos needed for both patronage and repressive purposes. Alfred McCoy (1999) similarly traces the debilitating effects of personalization on the Philippine *military*. McCoy details Marcos's venality in military appointments and convincingly shows how this politicization and personalization destroyed the ethos of apolitical professionalism that had broadly characterized the officer corps during the Philippines' first few decades of independence.

Such tensions between professional and political soldiers are crucial for our story because they are precisely the mechanism through which Geddes argues that military regimes derive their extreme brittleness. It is good news for Geddes that McCoy supports this interpretation of military regime breakdown, broadly linking the intra-military friction that produced the fateful 1986 coup d'état to the cleavage between political and professional officers. But it is more problematic for Geddes's overall framework that personalization clearly *worsened* military factionalism, especially by producing widespread loathing of Marcos's top crony general, Fabian Ver. This made democratic transition more likely rather than less. Geddes thus gets partial support from the Philippine case. Her posited causal mechanism of breakdown in military regimes fits the historical material nicely, but her suggestion that personalization should help military rule endure sits uncomfortably with Philippine evidence.

Long-lived military-led regimes in Burma and Indonesia provide greater challenges to Geddes's causal framework. The stunning durability of the Burmese military regime is particularly vexing. How has the Burmese military managed to avoid the sort of splits between political and professional soldiers that Geddes sees as dooming military rule? Mary Callahan provides powerful evidence that militaries are not necessarily riven by the political-professional divisions that Geddes portrays as intrinsic to military institutions. Whereas ruling parties tend to cohere because professional considerations are insepara- ble from political concerns, Callahan adroitly shows that the Burmese military has cohered because the political is never allowed to distract attention from the professional. In short, Burma's ruling generals "are war fighters who are not adept at politics. But they are war fighters, first and foremost" (Callahan 2004: 2). Pathologically fearful of any political opponents who might divide the fragile nation-state, the Burmese military has engaged in a disastrously violent confrontation with democratic activists rather than coming to the sort of compromise that Geddes sees as the natural terminus of military rule.

The point is not that the solitary Burmese example definitively falsifies Geddes's arguments about military regimes. Rather, the point is that the di- visiveness or cohesion of military and party institutions is a research question demanding intense empirical scrutiny, not a matter to be determined deduc- tively. By climbing inside the belly of the Burmese military beast, Callahan exemplifies how statistical "outliers" can serve to keep fascinating research questions on the agenda in comparative politics. Most intriguingly, Callahan argues that the Burmese military's cohesion—and hence the military regime's remarkable survival—derives from Burma's abnormally simultaneous strug- gle against both domestic insurgents and foreign incursions during its decolo- nization process.

Such historical considerations weigh heavily in the finest studies of the In- donesian military as well. Like Callahan's, Harold Crouch's analysis calls into question Geddes's fundamental assertion that military regimes "carry within themselves the seeds of their own disintegration" (Geddes 1999a: 5). If divi- sions between political and professional soldiers in Burma were dampened by shared and simultaneous operational experience against domestic and for- eign enemies, Indonesian soldiers developed significant professional solidarity through shared traumas during the national revolution of the 1940s, the sepa- ratist rebellions of the 1950s, and the communist upsurge of the 1960s. With its ideology of *dwifungsi*, or dual function, the Indonesian military defined politics as inherent to its professional mission. Seizing power in the mid-1960s did not suddenly turn the military into a political animal, for "it had never previously regarded itself as an apolitical organization" (Crouch 1978: 344).

The Suharto regime thus rested on a highly unified and politically ambitious military apparatus at its onset. The military's cohesion and shared will to power more closely resembled Geddes's portrayal of ruling parties than ruling militaries.

Like Burma's, Indonesia's military-led government lasted for decades—but unlike Burma's, it ultimately collapsed in the face of popular upheaval and elite fragmentation. Geddes's model would attribute the Suharto regime's impressive durability to its "triple hybrid" institutional character, for it rested on a combination of military, party, and personal power rather than military power alone. But this raises two big questions. First, why did Indonesia's "triple hybrid" regime prove *less* durable than Burma's pure military regime? And second, can we really explain the Suharto regime's considerable resilience in terms of its relative reliance on civilian party elites and the president's personal clique?

Close attention to the dynamics of Indonesian democratization suggests otherwise. Suharto's personalization of the military had the same sort of debilitating effects on military cohesion as Marcos's personalization of the military in the Philippines. Jun Honna's (2003) analysis of Indonesian military politics during the 1990s shows how seriously *esprit de corps* had eroded since the era when Crouch conducted his research—a historical slide paralleling the one detailed in McCoy's longitudinal study of two classes of the Philippine Military Academy.

As in the Philippines, a dictator obsessed with personal power made loyalty rather than seniority or merit the primary basis for appointments and promotions, as best witnessed in Suharto's blatant cultivation of his son-in-law, Prabowo Subianto. The division between military "hardliners" and "softliners" that hastened Suharto's collapse was not a matter of differences in ideology or democratic proclivity, Honna shows, but of differences in how particular factions fared in Suharto's reshuffles. The prevailing military faction was no more democratically inclined than its opponents but rather more desperate "to preserve the integrity of the institution and not leave it vulnerable to the type of political machinations that wreaked such havoc under Soeharto" (Honna 2003: 200).

When combined with the Burmese example, the Indonesian experience with democratic transition suggests further grounds for questioning the hypothesis that personalization bolsters military rule. Even more problematically for Geddes's framework, the Burma-Indonesia comparison suggests that the *military* might have been the primary institutional source of authoritarian cohesion in both cases, rather than any party apparatus or personal clique of the leadership. Perhaps both regimes proved so durable because they were constructed upon the shoulders of military elites who had been unified by shared operational experiences. And perhaps military-backed rule collapsed in Indonesia before Burma because Suharto tried harder than Burma's Ne Win to lessen his dependence on the military through personalizing political power.

Not only did Suharto build a more personalized regime than Ne Win; he also devoted far more resources to party building, as captured in Geddes's coding of the Suharto regime as a "triple hybrid" regime. Geddes argues that these multiple institutional foundations should serve as a source of strength, especially relative regime dependence on a supposedly loyal and cohesive ruling party, as opposed to a presumably more fractious and apolitical military.

John Sidel (1998) calls this argument into question with his detailed examination of the collapse of the Suharto regime. Sidel clearly agrees with Geddes that the regime had taken on "triple hybrid" qualities. Whereas the military was obviously the major institutional support for the regime upon its establishment in the mid-1960s, Suharto ultimately elaborated a national political party (Golkar) to mobilize civilian support, and nurtured a coterie of personal loyalists to assume top positions in all of Indonesia's leading political and business organizations. But Sidel argues that Suharto's construction of multiple institutional sources of support proved to be his undoing rather than his salvation:

> [T]he most important tensions within the regime, it may be argued, stemmed from the peculiar mix of institutional bases and personal networks through which Suharto entrenched himself in power and exerted authority over the more than thirty years of his rule. In this regard, one key structural tension within the regime developed between the pattern of *circulation* within the Armed Forces and the process of personal *accumulation* by the President, between the *military* circuitries of his regime and the more *civilian* networks for his electoral and ideological legitimation and his (and his family's) economic enrichment. (Sidel 1998: 162, emphasis in original)

For our purposes here, the most interesting aspect of this argument relates to the tensions that arose between the New Order's military and civilian wings—in institutional terms, between the military and Golkar. Suharto accelerated his party-building efforts in the late 1980s in a concerted effort to gain a civilian counterweight to military power, but this move did not necessarily have beneficial consequences for his regime. Instead, the "elevation of civilians to new heights of influence in the regime inspired disaffected elements in the military to promote oppositional activities against the President" (Sidel 1998: 174).

As the regime began to look less like a military regime, and developed more of a "triple hybrid" institutional bricolage, it seemingly produced worsening elite conflict rather than heavier institutional ballast. In fact, it is worth conjecturing that Indonesia might never have undergone a democratic transition at all if Suharto had allowed his regime to sustain the purely military character of its early years. As the Burmese example shows, military regimes can exhibit astounding resilience, even in the absence—or perhaps *because* of the absence—of countervailing powers in a ruling party or loyalist clique.

To be sure, the Indonesian case does not falsify Geddes's arguments regarding either the general durability of "triple hybrid" regimes or the fortifying effect of ruling parties, any more than the Burmese case falsifies her argument that pure military regimes tend to be exceptionally brittle. Suharto's regime collapsed, but it enjoyed a long run in power before doing so. Nevertheless, Sidel's analysis suggests that far more attention needs to be paid to the causal mechanisms through which authoritarian regimes endure or implode. Statistical tests of correlative hypotheses are valuable, but they should not be seen as the end of the road. They should be treated as one important stage in the process of knowledge accumulation, which can be fruitfully followed by critical examination of such hypotheses' empirical implications at close range.

POLITICAL PARTIES AND THE STATE

We might best advance this "hypothesis elaboration" process by turning our attention back to the political institution that was discussed at length earlier in this chapter, but that is glaringly absent from Geddes's institutional model: *the state*. As we have seen, the relative strength of the Indonesian state when compared to the Philippine state provides an important clue in understanding Suharto's greater ability than Marcos's to withstand pressures for democratization. This suggests that strong parties might effectively forestall democratization when they are combined with strong states, but foster authoritarian collapse when they are forced to coexist with strong militaries.

Further evidence in support of the notion that robust *party-state combinations* provide the strongest institutional bulwark against democratization is presented in studies of two of Southeast Asia's highly consolidated single-party regimes: Singapore and Vietnam. Quite tellingly, Chan Heng Chee's (1976) classic study of Singapore's ruling party finds it impossible to ignore the role of the state, while Stein Tønnesson's (2000) highly original study of the Vietnamese state consistently addresses the role played by the ruling party.

Chan examined the grassroots organization of Singapore's People's Action Party (PAP) in the mid-1970s, seeking sources of institutional robustness that would explain its stranglehold on power. What she found, to her evident surprise, was that the PAP's grassroots presence had atrophied since the heady days of decolonization in the late 1950s and early 1960s: "The party no longer stresses the importance of socializing the new recruit into party life nor organizing activities to mobilize its members. It is striking that practically no political education exists at branch level; and party-building by the PAP, in terms of recruiting members and inducting them into party thinking and party life so that they may perpetuate the party commitment, is not a priority" (1976: 131–132). The conventional wisdom that the PAP served as a quasi-Leninist political machine appeared to be greatly exaggerated.

The key to Singapore's exceptional political stability, Chan concluded, was not the PAP's internal organization and practices, but its firm command over a highly effective state apparatus: "With the assistance of the bureaucracy, the PAP has built an image of effectiveness." Credit for Singapore's rapid growth and quasi-welfare state accrued directly to the PAP, as "the long years of partnership between the PAP and the civil servants have undoubtedly accelerated the fusion of the party and Government identity." Simply put, Singaporeans had come to view "the party as synonymous with the State" (1976: 224).

Tønnesson provides a vivid metaphor for such party-state fusion in Vietnam, where economic reforms have seemingly forestalled the need for political reforms. Rather than seeing states and markets as oppositional forces, Tønnesson views "the state as a system of bones, muscles, lungs, nerves, and veins, and the party as the head, employing market forces to take care of feeding and digestion" (2000: 250).

To keep vital revenues flowing to the party-state's coffers after the catastrophic collapse in Soviet aid, Vietnamese Communist Party (VCP) leaders had little choice but to welcome foreign direct investment. "Despite certain declarations to the contrary," Tønnesson argues, "the Vietnamese communist leaders endeavored to keep the new 'business management layer' *inside* the state" (2000: 247, emphasis in original).[20] Joint ventures between foreign corporations and state-owned enterprises have seized the commanding heights of the Vietnamese economy, often with the help of sectoral monopolies granted by—who else?—party leaders. This keeps the VCP's revenue lifeblood flowing, strengthening regime institutions amid the challenges for regime maintenance presented by rapid socioeconomic change in a society lacking easily manipulated communal divisions. Although social-structural conditions seemingly make Vietnam a prime candidate for democratization, institutional factors appear to be pushing in the opposite direction.

Perhaps the most intriguing evidence in support of the causal linkage from party-state power to authoritarian durability comes from Kate Frieson's (1996) study of Cambodia's aborted democratic transition in 1993. This book chapter is extraordinarily valuable in methodological terms because it examines the only instance when a Southeast Asian single-party regime was defeated at the ballot box—thus providing much-needed variation in regime outcomes, via a fascinating snapshot of a ruling party actually losing its uncontested grip. In elections bankrolled and monitored by the United Nations, the long-ruling Cambodian People's Party (CPP) was outpolled by the royalist Funcinpec and forced, for a four-year period, to share power with its rivals.

Why did the CPP lose in the 1993 vote, when no other ruling party in Southeast Asia's post-colonial era has done the same? At one level, this surprising result was due to the pure contingency of events. The UN had intervened in Cambodia's civil war and was committed to securing a fair electoral result, devoting $2 billion to the task of reconstructing Cambodia's war-torn economy and polity. Should this rare defeat of a single-party regime thus be seen as the result of contingent rather than structural factors?

When one reads Frieson's analysis against the backdrop of the studies we have just examined, one sees that external intervention was not simply a contingent, unpredictable factor in the regime-change equation. Rather, the intervention of the UN authority, known as UNTAC, helped to loosen both the coercive and the financial stronghold of the *Cambodian state*—dominated by CPP apparatchiks—over Cambodian voters. With its $2 billion in aid funds, largely distributed through nongovernmental organizations rather than the Cambodian bureaucracy, UNTAC was perceived by voters upon its arrival in March 1992 as "the richest patron in centuries" (Frieson 1996: 232). It was only a mild exaggeration to say that by the time of the vote, "UNTAC was the state" (233).[21] To be sure, the CPP still attempted to link party and state power to its electoral benefit, as it "rallied its administrative structures and civil servants, including teachers, soldiers, and police, to work for the CPP. Those who refused were told they would lose their jobs" (234). But with state power temporarily fragmented, rather than monopolized by the CPP, Cambodian voters enjoyed a moment of relative immunity from the ruling party's electoral intimidations and inducements.

This victory for Cambodian democracy did not long outlast the UN-mandated disruption of party-state power, however. The 1993 elections forced CPP elites to share power in the legislature, but the state apparatus remained overwhelmingly controlled by pro-CPP elements. The withdrawal of UN forces left CPP leader Hun Sen with a free hand to overturn his power-sharing arrangement with Funcinpec—which he did, unilaterally and violently, in 1997. Cambodia's return to authoritarianism cannot therefore be understood simply as the contingent result of one man's desire for absolute power. Hun Sen was as power hungry in 1993 as in 1997. It was only when he had regained his previous structural advantage, with unencumbered access to combined party-state power, that he enjoyed the institutional capacity to destroy democratic procedures for his own political benefit.

In sum, Southeast Asian regime studies have tended to be strongest where democratization theory has tended to be weakest. They have consistently contributed thought-provoking analyses of the structural underpinnings of democracy and dictatorship. As democratization theorists ponder "the end of transitology," and increasingly examine the social and institutional forces that shape regime outcomes, they would be well advised to take a closer look at studies of democratic transition and authoritarian durability in Southeast Asia.[22]

Accumulating Knowledge by Marrying Big Questions with Deep Answers

One of the most distinguished figures in modern American political science, Adam Przeworski, was recently asked to comment upon the successes and failures of knowledge accumulation in comparative politics over the past three decades. His commentary on what he sees as the field's biggest failings is rather remarkable, considering the studies of Southeast Asian democratization and authoritarianism just discussed in this chapter:

We still do not know why and when people with guns obey people without them: the determinants of civilian control over the military. We still don't understand political parties very well. This is truly an important topic, which we have neglected. . . . Though we have learned a lot in general about authoritarianism, I also think we know disastrously little about the structure of dictatorships. (Quoted in Munck and Snyder 2004: 30)

If political scientists indeed know "disastrously little" about these vital subjects, it might be in part because of a disciplinary predilection to doubt whether area studies can produce knowledge of theoretical value. Przeworski implies as much when he comments on where he currently sees the biggest theoretical contributions being generated: "I think some of the best research in comparative politics is done these days by economists. They don't know enough about politics, particularly about institutions, but they address central questions and get provocative answers" (quoted in Munck and Snyder 2004: 30). We seem to have reached a peculiar juncture in the development of our discipline if one of our finest comparativists suggests that "some of the best research in comparative politics" is being conducted by scholars who "don't know enough about politics."

Knowledge accumulation in the study of democratization is most likely to occur if we can marry the deep knowledge of politics and institutions displayed by the authors discussed in this chapter with those askers of big and provocative questions who are praised by Przeworski. Big questions demand deep answers, but deep answers will attract substantial attention from theorists only if they address the biggest political questions imaginable. This will require unprecedented levels of mutual engagement between deductive theorists and area specialists. If our understanding of democratization and authoritarianism is to grow, theorists and area experts alike need to consider spending some quality time in unfamiliar sections of their university libraries.

Chapter Four

Developing Democracies in Southeast Asia
Theorizing the Role of Parties and Elections

ALLEN HICKEN

Introduction

Political parties and elections lie at the center of modern democratic politics. Elections function as the chief means of holding leaders accountable for their actions in democratic societies. Political parties, defined most simply as a group of candidates who run for election under the same label, provide a means of aggregating interests as well as organizing and coordinating voters, candidates, political donors, legislators, executives, and interest groups around a common set of objectives. It is little wonder, then, that parties and elections are the subject of so much attention from political scientists.

When I was first asked to write this chapter, I immediately sat down with a pen and paper and tried to list all Southeast Asia–focused works that have had a major impact on the study of political parties and elections in political science generally. The list was depressingly short. With a few important exceptions, very little work on Southeast Asian parties and elections turns up on reference or reading lists outside of regionally focused materials. This lack of impact stands in sharp contrast to areas in which scholars of Southeast Asia have played a more prominent role in advancing our knowledge—for example, in the study of nationalism, state building, state-society relations, and the political economy of development. Clearly, the explanation for this state of affairs does not lie in a dearth of bright minds writing about Southeast Asian politics. Nor is it due to a lack of attention to parties and elections by Southeast Asia–focused scholars. In preparation for this paper I began constructing a bibliography of works that had as their primary focus parties or elections in Southeast Asia. I stopped compiling when the list reached fifteen pages with no end in sight.

Among these works are some outstanding pieces of scholarship. However, with some notable exceptions, most of the works on this list are (rich) descriptions of single countries, single elections, or single parties.[1] In addition, scholars have generally paid scant attention to what Southeast Asia can contribute to broader debates in the parties and elections literature. As a result, while the universe of facts at our disposal is much richer because of these studies, the relative lack of theorizing and comparative analysis has hindered the accumulation of knowledge about how elections and parties operate in developing democracies.

To a degree, this state of affairs is understandable. In the past, with most of Southeast Asia less than democratic and few electoral outcomes in serious doubt, parties and elections were not the major story.[2] In part, this view was a misrepresentation of the facts and discounted too steeply the role that elections and parties played, even in semi-democracies. Still, it is somewhat understandable that Southeast Asia scholars have not been major contributors to the analytical debates in the field of parties and elections.

Regardless of one's view of the past, however, the peripheral status of parties and elections is no longer appropriate. During the past two decades, democratic elections have come to Thailand, the Philippines, and Cambodia. In Malaysia, there has been increased uncertainty about the future of party politics since the retirement of Prime Minister Mahathir in 2003. The *coup de grace*, of course, is the democratic transition under way in Indonesia. Indonesia's prosperity and, more fundamentally, its very survival as a nation depend in part on the success of its democratic experiment. The transitions in Indonesia and elsewhere in the region have Southeast Asia scholars grappling with some of the core questions in the field of comparative parties and elections. Can democracy work in Indonesia, Thailand, the Philippines, and Cambodia? If so, what types of electoral and party arrangements are most supportive of that goal, and which are inimical to it? What are the expected consequences of different electoral/party systems for economic governance, corruption, and ethnic/religious harmony? How accurate and appropriate are existing models of party/electoral politics for Southeast Asian cases?[3]

These and other questions relating to parties and elections in Southeast Asia are being asked and answered by a growing number of scholars, both new and established. With the increased focus on parties and elections comes the prospect that studies of parties and elections in the region will emerge as not only important parts of Southeast Asian scholarship, but as vital contributions to our understanding of parties and elections generally. In short, it helps to have a critical mass of scholars working on similar sets of questions, though perhaps in different countries and employing different research methods. As this occurs, there is no reason that Southeast Asia scholars cannot contribute to theory development, advancement, and refinement in the same way their Latin American counterparts have been doing for the past fifteen to twenty years.

In the pages that follow I review a sample of the literature on parties and elections in Southeast Asia.[4] As I mentioned above, this literature is quite extensive. I will therefore not attempt in the space allotted to present a comprehensive review. Rather, my goal is to be as representative as possible. Drawing on the literature, I argue that Southeast Asia–focused research is at its strongest, and has had the broadest impact, when it meets two conditions: (1) it is theory driven, and (2) it is at least implicitly comparative. In a sense, both of these conditions are essentially comparative in nature. With the first, we compare our observations to a set of ideas—theories—about how the world works. (These need not be grand, all-encompassing theories, nor does the primary goal of a study need to be theory creation/development.) For example, we can compare observations about vote buying in Thailand to existing ideas about the role of reciprocity and patron-client relations in Thai society and/or to theories about how different electoral arrangements affect candidates' incentives to buy votes (Hicken 2007a, 2007b). We might compare the electoral performance of female candidates for public office against existing ideas about the role of women in certain countries and/or against theories about how features of the electoral system can discourage or encourage the nomination of women candidates (Reynolds 1999). Regardless of the topic, the reference to theory, whether developed by the author or imported from elsewhere, puts observations in context, clarifies the contribution (Does the study [dis]confirm existing ideas? Does it suggest a new way of looking at the world?), and ultimately enables the study to contribute to the accumulation of knowledge in our country, field, or discipline.

The same can be said for the second condition—use of the comparative method. Of course, research can be comparative in a number of ways—for example, across countries, across time within a given country, across units (parties, regions, etc.) within a given country. Regardless, some sort of comparative referent (explicit or implicit) is extremely valuable. For example, consider Benedict Anderson's wonderfully perverse take on murder, movies, and elections in Thailand (Anderson 1990b). Students consistently rank this as a favorite in my Southeast Asia and comparative elections courses. Why?[5] The article does not contain any new data—the facts and events described by Anderson were widely reported in the press and fairly well known, at least to Thai scholars. But it takes someone to analyze the facts, identify patterns, and put events in context before the result can usefully advance our knowledge. Anderson's ability to do this is what resonates with students. He invites the reader to compare the state of the Thai polity in the 1980s to earlier periods. He argues that the political killings he describes are not just a reflection of the increased violence surrounding Thai elections; they also reflect the growing value of elected office. For the first time, elected office is worth competing, fighting, and even killing for. This marks a significant departure from the heyday of the bureaucratic polity in Thailand, when elected officials and political parties were virtually without power or influence (Riggs 1966).

In the next section I briefly review some of those works that, like Anderson's, bring a comparative, theoretical approach to the study of parties and elections in Southeast Asia. In so doing I highlight areas where studies of Southeast Asian cases have also had an influence on the broader discipline and where there has been a serious accumulation of knowledge. I then discuss three major areas of research in the field of party and electoral studies—areas where theoretically informed work drawing on Southeast Asian cases can, I believe, make an important and immediate impact (and, in some cases, is already doing so). The final section concludes.

Consistent with the focus of this volume, it is worth highlighting the indispensable role that qualitative approaches play in the study of elections and parties. Scholars rely on the careful use of qualitative methods to generate and test novel hypotheses, as well as to confirm/refute existing arguments in the field.[6] Although in recent years quantitative methods have become more commonplace in the study of parties and elections, in most cases they complement rather than replace qualitative approaches.[7] Likewise, qualitative methods will continue to be the foundation of much of the work on Southeast Asian parties and elections, even as the availability of more numeric data allows for greater use of psephology and other quantitative approaches.

Parties and Elections in Southeast Asia

No one should mistake my argument for more theoretically informed comparative work as a denigration of the many largely descriptive pieces of scholarship that exist in the literature.[8] These studies often accomplish the necessary but relatively thankless task of clearing the brush away so we can better see the lay of the land. This is particularly useful in a region such as Southeast Asia, where language or logistical/bureaucratic barriers can make it difficult for non–country specialists to get access to information on parties and elections. Things such as a summary of national election results from around the region (Nohlen et al. 2001), a historical review of a region's electoral systems (Hassall and Saunders 1997; Hicken and Kasuya 2003; Hicken 2004), a description of the region's party systems (Sachsenroder and Frings 1998), and a catalogue of Filipino political parties (Banlaoi and Carlos 1996) are valuable resources for scholars of parties and elections. In the sections that follow I will make note of some of these brush-clearing contributions while focusing most of my attention on more theoretically motivated, comparative work. I first review works on elections and electoral systems and then turn my attention to parties and party systems, while recognizing that these two literatures often overlap.

ELECTIONS AND ELECTORAL SYSTEMS

The Southeast Asia elections literature contains a large number of the type of brush-clearing studies described above. These can be anything from publications focused on cataloging the electoral rules and results for a single country (e.g., Peralta 1977; Rachagan 1980, 1993; Carlos 1998; Carlos and Banlaoi 1996) to analysis of the conduct, results, and implications of a single election within a given country. These studies appear frequently in journals such as *Contemporary Southeast Asia, Asian Survey,* and *Electoral Studies* (Liddle 1978; Weiss 2000; Funston 2000; Croissant and Dosch 2001); appear in local in-country publications (de Leon 1986; Kalaw-Tirol and Colonel 1992; Nelson 2000); or are produced by organizations such as IFES, NDI (National Democratic Institute), and IRI (International Republican Institute) (e.g., NDI 2001 and IRI 2003). By necessity, these studies are heavily descriptive and often serve as the indispensable raw material for further in-depth, theoretically informed studies.

As useful as these brush-clearing studies are, by themselves they do not do much to advance the accumulation of knowledge about parties and elections. For this to occur, descriptive data must be grounded within a theoretical and comparative context. The best work on elections in Southeast Asia does just this—using rich empirical data as a springboard to talk about a broader set of theoretical concerns.[9] For example, Herbert Feith's *The Indonesian Elections of 1955*, together with his subsequent book, used the election of 1955 and its fallout as a lens through which to analyze the decline of democracy in Indonesia. This sparked a debate about the viability of democracy in Indonesia that still resonates (Feith 1957, 1962, 1982; Benda 1982).

Dwight King's recent book is another such example (2003). It is primarily an analysis of the 1999 Indonesian elections, but the study's strongest contribution comes from its comparison of voting patterns across the 1999 and 1955 elections. Drawing on existing ideas about the way social and geographic cleavages might affect voting in Indonesia, King tests whether voting loyalties have changed in the nearly forty-five years since Indonesia's last democratic election. Among his findings is the discovery that the 1999 elections largely reproduced the religious, class, and regional voting patterns observed in 1955.

Imagine, for a moment, if King's study had simply focused on voting patterns in 1999. Though still interesting, the lack of a comparative referent would have diluted its power and contribution. It is the marriage of in-depth country knowledge, solid qualitative and quantitative methods, and a theoretically motivated comparative research design that makes for an extremely interesting study of democratic and electoral reform in Indonesia.

As mentioned in the introduction, where there exists a critical mass of scholars working on similar sets of questions—critiquing and building on one another's work—knowledge accumulation is more likely to happen. This has begun to occur around the issue of voter behavior in Indonesia. For example, King's argument in favor of enduring patterns of religious or class-based voting has been challenged on both methodological and empirical grounds by Liddle and Mujani (2004). They find that sociological variables are weak predictors of voter behavior compared to a voter's attachment to local or national political leaders. An interesting and fruitful debate between the two sides is emerging that should advance our understanding of voter behavior in diverse polities such as Indonesia.

Another welcome development in the literature is the greater attention being given to the dynamics of elections at the local level. Kimura's study of electoral politics in the city of Lipa, Philippines, is an excellent example, as are Nelson's and Arghiros's work on local politics and elections in Thailand (Kimura 1997; Nelson 1998; Arghiros 1995). The need for studies of local electoral politics will only increase as greater decentralization in many Southeast Asian states magnifies the divergence between national and local politics. Although the synergistic use and critique of work on local elections outside of one's particular country are still largely lacking in this literature, the potential is certainly there. When one reads these studies, certain common themes emerge—foremost among them the distinct dynamics of politics in local (usually rural) settings versus those at the national level (or in urban areas).

Another research area that has attracted the attention of a growing number of elections scholars in recent years is the role of money and the influence of business interests. Anek and Pasuk and Baker chronicle the growing influence of Bangkok-based business interests on elections in Thailand, and Ockey, Robertson, and the authors in McVey's edited volume do the same for provincial business interests (Anek 1992; Pasuk and Baker 1995; Ockey 1991; Robertson 1996; McVey 2000b). Anusorn, de Castro, and Sidel describe the vital role that money plays in fueling the modern campaign machines in Thailand and the Philippines (Anusorn 1995; de Castro 1992; Sidel 1999). In Malaysia, Gomez and Jomo have analyzed the vital role that business interests play in financing UMNO's electoral efforts (along with the resulting quid pro quo) (Gomez and Jomo 1997).

Of these, McVey's edited volume comes closest to a kind of synergy, with each chapter author analyzing the role of provincial business interests in Thai political life from a slightly different perspective, combined with McVey's competent synthesis of the state of our knowledge. What is largely missing from the volume is any sort of comparative or theoretical framework. Is the role that provincial money plays in elections something unique to Thailand? Probably not. I am struck, for example, by the similarities between the literature on the provincial elite in Thailand and the work on political clans in the Philippines.[10] Considering the Thai experience through a more comparative and/or theoretical lens might better enable researchers to draw new connections and tackle important questions that are of interest not only to Thai specialists, but to parties and elections scholars as well. For example, is there a connection between the role that money and moneyed interests play in campaigns and the level of economic or political development? What effect do electoral and campaign finance rules have on the role of money? Do funding and campaign strategies vary with the relative strength of political parties, the state, or private business interests?

PARTIES AND PARTY SYSTEMS

Like the literature on elections in Southeast Asia, the literature on political parties has mostly focused on the development and condition of political parties within a given polity. Yet there has been some useful cross-fertilization across countries and even across regions. In the 1950s and 1960s, for example, a body of literature emerged that aimed to understand the makeup and development of political parties in newly independent states.[11] Southeast Asia scholars were important contributors to this literature. Indonesia experts explored the connection between political parties and *aliran*—underlying religious, social, and cultural cleavages (e.g., Lev 1967; Liddle 1970).[12] Landé focused on the role of existing patron-client patterns in the types of parties that were emerging in the Philippines (Landé 1965). Although these studies were focused on Southeast Asia, the ideas and frameworks they advanced were usefully applied in other comparative contexts.

More recently, scholars working on the Philippines have led the way via a number of interesting and diverse studies attempting to explain why the Philippine party system looks and operates as it does (Kimura 1992; Rocamora 1998; Montinola 1999; Choi 2001; Kasuya 2001; Hicken 2002; Hutchcroft and Rocamora 2003). These build on the pioneering work of Landé (1965) and Liang (1970) on the development of the Philippine party system. By addressing common questions and generally relying on a theoretically informed comparative research design, significant progress has been made toward understanding the nature of the Philippine party system and, to some extent, party systems in developing democracies more generally.

Two questions relating to the Philippine party system have received the most attention from scholars.[13] First, how do we account for the weak and under-institutionalized nature of the party system? Second, how do we account for the demise of the stable two-party system after Marcos? Regarding the first, the conventional wisdom is that party cohesion in the Philippines is minimal—parties are factionalized or atomized, party switching is rampant, and party labels are weak. Parties are generally temporary electoral alliances between candidates who tend to have narrow/local constituencies. Through the work of several scholars, a consensus has begun to emerge about why this is the case. Namely, the origins of the weak party system can be traced to a combination of three factors: (1) a weak state vis-à-vis societal actors (oligarchs) (Wurfel 1988; Tancangco 1992); (2) early local and national elections under the U.S. colonial administration (Landé 1965; Stauffer 1975; Wurfel 1988; Magadia 1999; Hutchcroft and Rocamora 2003); and (3) features of the electoral system (Wurfel 1988; Hicken 2002).[14]

The death of the stable two-party system after Marcos is a second issue that has received a good deal of scholarly attention. Two sets of arguments exist, and the debate between advocates of each has spurred the advance of knowledge on this interesting question. The first group of scholars argues that changes in the structure of local politics in the Philippines account for the end of the two-party system. In the premartial law era, bifactionalism at the local level was the norm (Landé 1965, 1971; Wolters 1983). This began to break down in the 1960s, and by the end of the martial law period, multifactionalism was the norm in many localities (Laquian 1966; Nowak and Snyder 1974; Kimura 1992, 1997). Whereas prior to martial law there was no local organizational base for third parties to rely on, this was not the case after martial law. A second group of scholars argues that the shift from local bifactionalism to multifactionalism cannot fully account for the growth in the number of parties after Marcos (Kasuya 2001; Hicken 2002). Instead, the blame or credit must go to changes to rules and institutions in 1986. These include changes to rules regulating party representation on election monitoring bodies (Carlos 1997; Velasco 1999; Teehankee 2002), the shift to synchronized local and national elections (Velasco 1999), and the advent of presidential term limits (Choi 2001; Hicken 2002).

The literature on political parties in Thailand and Indonesia is less developed than it is for the Philippines, no doubt in part due to the shorter electoral histories of those two nations.[15] For Thailand, the two best-known works in English are Kramol's interesting, but now somewhat dated, application of political party theories to the Thai case and Murashima and colleagues' edited volume titled *The Making of Modern Thai Political Parties* (Kramol 1982; Murashima et al. 1991).[16] In Indonesia, many scholars have focused on the division between secular and religious parties in both past and more recent elections.[17] The democratic transition under way in Indonesia has also sparked a new interest in the characteristics and implications of the country's emerging party system (Suryadinata 2002; Tan 2002; Ananta et al. 2004). Sherlock's recent study is notable for its careful consideration of the way in which recent changes to Indonesia's electoral rules should affect party strategies and party development (Sherlock 2004). In another study, Tan (2001) draws on existing theories to argue that party institutionalization has occurred in Indonesia, but in an incomplete and potentially dangerous way. Party ties to societal/communal groups are strong, but on other important dimensions of institutionalization Indonesian parties remain weak. Tan argues that this presents challenges for democratic consolidation and stability. Through her use of the Indonesian case, Tan has raised questions for the broader field about how we measure and think about party institutionalization.

Studies such as those by Tan, King, and others discussed above reflect a new and positive trend in the study of parties and elections in Southeast Asia. These scholars not only target the country- and region-specific literature, but also explicitly engage and critique the theories, models, and debates within political science more generally. This empowers them to move the debates within the field forward and thus contribute to our understanding of parties and elections. Although this shift toward theoretical engagement is for the most part a relatively recent development, there is at least one area in the field of party/elections studies where Southeast Asian scholars have, for many years, been leading contributors: the literature on the relationships among parties, elections, and democracy.

Although perhaps less well known than people such as Fareed Zakaria (1997) or Larry Diamond (1998), Southeast Asian researchers have been important contributors to debates about parties and elections in less-than-ideal democracies (a.k.a. semi-democracies, demi-democracies, pseudo-democracies, illiberal democracies, halfway democracies, Asian-style democracies, Cacique democracy, etc.). Southeast Asian cases have been key pieces of evidence used to drive home the point that the presence of regular elections and political parties does not necessarily signal a transition toward democracy (Zakaria 1989; Chai-Anan 1995, 1998; Liddle 1992; Anderson 1988; Neher and Marlay 1995; Emmerson 1999; Case 2002).

In most Southeast Asian countries, there have been extended periods when there was little doubt about the outcome of elections and no hope of holding leaders accountable by voting them out of office. Why then would regimes in these countries bother to hold elections in the first place? What purpose could elections in such polities serve? Edited volumes by Taylor and Anek (1996) tackle these questions head-on, as do portions of edited volumes on political legitimacy and political opposition in Southeast Asia by Alagappa

(1995) and Rodan (1996). We can distill three sets of arguments from this literature. First, elections serve legitimating functions for both domestic and international audiences, and victory at the polls can also help provide leaders with a mandate to rule. Second, elections serve as a source of information. Even if there is no serious threat of removal from office, a small dip in support for the incumbents, a rise in support for the opposition, or a fall in turnout can convey important information to leaders about public sentiment. Indeed, the leadership of Malaysia and Singapore has proved very adept at responding to very small changes in voting patterns with timely reform (of both the carrot and the stick variety). Finally, elections can also be a means of social control (Tremewan 1994). They can be used instrumentally by regimes in an attempt to pacify the public, demonstrate the strength of the incumbents, or legitimate certain forms and avenues of participation while delegitimating others. Elections can also convey information about new opponents and possible sources of opposition. The regime can then respond by co-opting or marginalizing those opponents.

A subset of this literature focuses on single-party dominance in regular elections in Malaysia, Singapore, and Indonesia (e.g., Tremewan 1994; Case 1996a; Jesudason 1999; Mauzy 2002; Slater 2003; Mutalib 2003). This literature is concerned with both explaining the emergence of single-party dominance in these states and accounting for these parties' resilience over time.[18] Indeed, Malaysia and Singapore are crucial cases for scholars interested in transitions from single-party rule. These are the dogs that haven't barked. During the past decade, dominant parties around the globe have given way to more competitive party systems. The LDP in Japan, the KMT in Taiwan, the PRI in Mexico, and, closer to home, Suharto's Golkar in Indonesia are just some examples. Yet UMNO and the PAP have remained entrenched in Malaysia and Singapore. What is it about these parties, or the underlying political and social systems, that makes them more enduring and resilient?

Some argue that what makes Malaysia and Singapore different is the ability of the dominant parties in these states to remain relatively unified—avoiding the crippling internal splits that often presage a transition. Jesudason (1996), for one, posits that as long as UMNO remains unified, single-party dominance will continue. Case, on the other hand, argues that although transition is unlikely to come via a split within UMNO, other factors exist that may pave the way for the defeat of UMNO at some future date, even though enduring ethnic and religious divisions continue to limit opposition efforts.[19]

Specifically, Case (2004) argues that dominant party regimes eventually lose the ability to control patronage—especially during times of economic crisis, when there is economic uncertainty. Conversely, it is during times of crisis that public tolerance for patronage/corruption is at its lowest. In the wake of heightened public discontent, governments resort to baser forms of authoritarianism, limiting civil liberties and further restricting elections. By doing so, however, the regime undermines its electoral legitimacy and risks triggering a backlash that could lead to its defeat. Case argues that there were signs that such a dynamic was beginning to emerge in Malaysia's 1999 election, but the persistence of ethnic and religious differences undermined collective action on the part of opposition social forces.[20]

Case's study is notable for its careful engagement with the existing literature on democratization. He uses evidence from the Malaysian case to provide a useful corrective to some of the prevailing theories in political science. More such theoretically grounded research on the critical cases of Malaysia and Singapore promises to shed greater light on the process by which dominant party systems end or endure.

New Directions for Research

As the previous discussion makes clear, Southeast Asia scholars have made some important contributions to the literature on parties and elections, particularly regarding parties and elections in semi-democracies. Still, when compared to the contribution of Southeast Asia scholars to other literatures, there is room for improvement. Likewise, the field of party and election studies would greatly benefit from quality contributions from Southeast Asia–focused scholars. More cases with which to test theories and hypotheses is always a welcome development, but the Southeast Asian cases bring more than simply a potential for increasing "*n*" to the table. First, the cases of Southeast Asia are a welcome addition to a literature that has been dominated by Western European and, in recent years, Latin American cases. Second, for certain questions the insights to be gleaned from Southeast Asian cases cannot be had elsewhere. Below I discuss three areas where theoretically informed work drawing on Southeast Asian cases could have an important and immediate impact on our understanding of parties and elections: (1) parties and elections in divided societies, (2) institutional engineering and the (unintended) consequences of reform, and (3) the causes and consequences of different types of party systems.[21] Where appropriate, I review existing Southeast Asia contributions to these three areas.

PARTIES AND ELECTIONS IN DIVIDED SOCIETIES

One of the most crucial questions in democratic theory is whether democracy can work in deeply divided societies. Can democratic participation help reduce ethnic or religious tensions, or does it just add fuel to communal fires? Perhaps not surprisingly, the answer is that it depends. Under some conditions, democratic elections can mitigate social conflict, but under others they actually can exacerbate existing tensions. The debate in the literature on democracy in divided societies is over what types of electoral and party systems are most conducive to conflict mitigation.[22]

Briefly, there are two contending schools of thought.[23] The first, championed by Lijphart and dubbed the consociational or power-sharing approach, argues that democracy works best when societal cleavages are acknowledged and an effort made to ensure that each group gets a share of power (Lijphart 1977). To do this, one seeks to make ethnic/religious groups the building blocks of political parties and then ensure that each group is represented in a "grand coalition" government (Reilly 2003a). As a practical matter, this requires the adoption of proportional representation and the creation of ethnically based political parties. A second approach argues that constructing a political system on a foundation of contentious societal cleavages is inherently unstable. Instead, the centripetalist approach advocates moving the focus of politics away from societal cleavages by creating institutions that encourage moderation and cross-cleavage accommodation and cooperation (see Horowitz 1985, 1991; Sisk 1996; Reilly 2001). Two pillars of this approach are an electoral system that allows for preference voting and vote pooling,[24] and a party system with broad-based parties or party coalitions that transcend cleavage boundaries.

My purpose here is not to critique these approaches or to advocate one over the other. Rather, it is to point out that Southeast Asia can supply something that this literature desperately needs—a fresh batch of relatively understudied cases. The region contains two ethnically, religiously, and geographically divided societies, Malaysia and Indonesia—each of which have, at the moment, functioning political systems. Lying at the other extreme is ethnically diverse Burma—for most of history a political and economic basket case. Important ethnic and religious divisions exist in most other Southeast Asian states as well. The various attempts by countries within the region to manage these divisions, including the use of both consociational and centripetal strategies, have not received much scholarly attention.

A partial exception is Malaysia. Two of the most prominent scholars in this field, Lijphart and Horowitz, have both used the Malaysian case to support their (contradictory) arguments (Lijphart 1977; Horowitz 1985). However, even in this case the frequent manipulation of the electoral and party systems by Malaysia in an effort to moderate ethnic tensions leaves room for further analysis.[25] The interesting cases of Burma and Indonesia have been almost completely neglected.[26] Particularly intriguing is Indonesia's current attempt to marry an element of the consociational model, proportional representation, with a new system for electing the president of the sort often advocated by supporters of the centripetal approach. Careful analyses of this and other Southeast Asian cases could significantly advance the debate about democracy in divided societies.

Southeast Asia is also an ideal laboratory for studying the process by which nascent societal cleavages become (or do not become) politicized or particized (Lipset and Rokkan 1967). It is interesting to note, for example, that while religious and ethnic cleavages have given rise to political parties in Malaysia and Indonesia, the same has not occurred in the Philippines or Thailand. Islamic groups in Mindanao are highly politicized, and this is increasingly the case in Southern Thailand, yet this has not translated into any significant effort to form political parties. A thorough analysis of this research question would need to consider a variety of possible variables, but these would include the role that the electoral system plays in providing incentives and opportunities for the creation of new parties and the interaction of electoral rules with societal cleavages.[27]

INSTITUTIONAL ENGINEERING AND THE (UNINTENDED) CONSEQUENCES OF REFORM

During the past twenty years, Cambodia, East Timor, Indonesia, the Philippines, and Thailand have all either adopted new constitutions or greatly overhauled existing charters. These and other reforms resulted in dramatic changes to the rules pertaining to parties and elections in these countries. Institutional engineering is often an attractive option for would-be political reformers for two reasons. First, electoral rules have predictable and discernible effects on outcomes. They help determine which actors will have a seat at the table, and contribute to the incentives and capabilities of those actors. Second, although institutional reform is by no means easy (institutions, after all, create groups with a vested interest in the continuation of those institutions), electoral rules are arguably more malleable than cultural norms, social structures, or levels of development in the short to medium term. The promise and peril of such institutional engineering is an area of great interest to students of electoral and party systems.

Southeast Asian cases can help shed light on several questions related to institutional reform. First, how do such reforms come about? (Must they always be crisis driven?) Second, how effective are institutional reforms at achieving the goals set out by reformers? Third, is institutional engineering actually a useful means to bring about changes in the party system?

Consider the cases of Thailand and Indonesia. In both countries, much of the blame for past democratic shortcomings and failures was laid at the feet of the party system. As a result, reformers in each country sought to engineer new party systems that would be more conducive to political stability and good governance.[28] Among other things, they wanted to encourage the development of national political parties—parties that draw broad support from across the country rather than from one particular region or ethnic/religious group. As Reilly states, for Indonesia "the development of such a national party system was seen as an essential step both in counteracting secessionism and in building a viable democracy" (2003b: 3). A second, related goal was reducing the number of political parties in an effort to improve government stability and reduce gridlock in the policy-making process. Finally, in the case of Thailand there was also desire to improve party cohesion.[29]

In an attempt to engineer these party systems, an impressive variety of reforms were introduced. These include, for example, adopting vote thresholds (both countries),[30] switching to single-seat districts (Thailand), adopting stringent branch and membership requirements for political parties (both), adding a national party list tier to the electoral system (Thailand), restricting the ability of politicians to switch parties (Thailand), and requiring a winning president to garner not only majority support, but support across most regions as well (Indonesia). Reform on this scale is relatively rare and represents a golden opportunity for researchers. In essence, we have the chance to field-test theories about the effects of institutions and institutional reform.[31]

Is institutional engineering producing the expected outcomes? If not, what does that say about the validity or generalizability of existing theories?

The scale of the reform effort in Thailand and Indonesia also affords us the chance to better understand how different types of reforms interact with each other. When developing and testing theory, one often relies on comparative statics. What happens if we change one particular variable while holding all else constant? This is useful and necessary, allowing one to isolate the independent effect of that particular variable. However, in the real world, *ceteris* is never *paribus*. Institutional reform doesn't proceed in isolation of other variables. Economic and political conditions, social structures, and other reforms can interact with a particular reform to reinforce or undermine stated goals. In short, reforms may produce unintended consequences.

We can illustrate this point with some examples from the region. In Indonesia the rules designed to encourage national parties and discourage separatism may in fact inflame separatist sentiments, especially when applied to provincial and district elections. The de facto ban on provincial or regional parties may effectively block legal, moderate alternatives to groups such as the Free Aceh Movement or the Free Papua Organization (Sherlock 2004: 7). The 1997 Thai constitution introduced a number of reforms designed to change elections from candidate-centered affairs to battles between competing party platforms (e.g., the addition of a party list tier and the elimination of block voting). However, other constitutional reforms, adopted in pursuit of other goals, push in precisely the opposite direction—toward more candidate-centered campaigning (e.g., the method of electing the Senate and smaller electoral districts) (Hicken 2007b). In the Philippines, decentralization and a single-term limit for the president were adopted with an eye to undoing the extreme concentration of power under Marcos. However, these reforms also changed the nature of the party system and the organization of election campaigning. Finally, also from the Philippines, the reservation of a small number of seats for parties and groups representing marginalized interests has produced some unintended side effects. Although the party list provision has probably resulted in more diverse interests being elected to Congress, it has also partially ghettoized those interests. Mainstream political parties and politicians seem largely content to leave programmatic campaigning and the representation of marginalized interests to party list groups.

Clearly, institutional reform, especially on the scale attempted in Thailand, the Philippines, and Indonesia, is both a promising and potentially perilous undertaking. The unintended consequences of institutional reform that result from the type of interactions discussed above are an understudied topic in the field and one to which Southeast Asia–focused scholars can immediately contribute.

THE CAUSES AND CONSEQUENCES OF DIFFERENT TYPES OF PARTY SYSTEMS

A party system is an enduring pattern of electoral competition between parties for public office. The marked differences in party systems across countries (and within a country over time) are of great interest to many scholars. Party systems can differ along any number of dimensions, including the number of parties that compete regularly at the national and lower levels, the stability of the governing and opposition party coalitions, the durability of party loyalties within electorates, and the frequency of new party formation. These differences are interesting because they have real consequences, affecting the quality and nature of democratic representation and accountability, economic governance, and the stability of governments and political systems.[32] There is evidence, for example, that the number of parties in governing coalitions—which is related to the number of parties in the party system—affects the ability of governments to respond to economic shocks (Franzese 2002; MacIntyre 2003). Likewise, voter turnout across countries is positively correlated with various aspects of party systems (Blais and Dobrzynska 1998). And some scholars have linked the success of regional parties to secessionist pressures (Filippov, Ordeshook, and Shvetsova 2004).

Because party systems are so vital to the political life of a country, researchers have studied various features of party systems seeking to understand both the causes and consequences of these features. I will briefly review three of these features and argue that Southeast Asia scholars have something to contribute to our knowledge about each. Perhaps the most familiar feature is the number of parties. For measurement, political scientists tend to use Laakso and Taagepera's (1979) "effective number of parties" index, or N, which gives greater weight to parties that get higher proportions of the vote.[33] We know a good deal about the factors that correlate with the effective number of parties in a given electoral district. Specifically, evidence strongly supports the idea that the electoral system and social structure interact to influence the effective number of parties at the district level (Duverger 1954; Taagepera and

Shugart 1989; Ordeshook and Shvetsova 1994; Lijphart 1994; Amorim-Neto and Cox 1997; Cox 1997). A district can have few parties because it uses a restrictive electoral system or because it has few social cleavages. Likewise, a multi-party system can arise as the result of many cleavages or a permissive electoral system.

Southeast Asian cases are certainly useful for evaluating these theories, especially because the region is home to some relatively unusual electoral systems.[34] For example, evidence from the Thai case suggests that electoral rules can produce predictable outcomes, even where the electoral system is complex, democracy is new, and political information is relatively scarce (Hicken 2002). The Thai case also highlights the need to consider more carefully the assumptions that underlie existing theories.

Existing theories of electoral systems make predictions at the level of the electoral district but have little to say about how many parties we should expect to see nationally. The possibilities for the number of national parties run the gamut from a few large nationwide parties, to a large number of regionally based parties, to extreme party system fragmentation. There is, in fact, often a huge difference between the effective number of parties nationally and the effective number of parties locally. (For example, the average effective number of parties at the district level in Thailand is around three, versus more than seven nationally.[35]) This issue should be of more than just academic interest to Southeast Asia scholars, given that fragmented party systems have been blamed for the breakdown of Indonesian democracy in the 1950s and for a variety of governance problems in Thailand.

There has been little research on how the numerous district party systems in a given country come together to form a national party system, but this is beginning to change.[36] Among the variables that seem to affect the size of the national party system is the degree of economic and political centralization. Given the decentralization campaigns under way in several countries, Southeast Asia is an excellent laboratory in which to study the variables that shape the size in which of the national party system. Evidence from the Thai and Philippines cases has already shaped debate, suggesting that the concentration of economic and political power cannot alone account for the size of the national party system. Instead, concentration interacts with other features of the political environment to shape the national party system (Hicken 2002).

Second, a growing group of scholars is interested in the distinction between programmatic and clientelistic party systems. There are various definitions of political clientelism, but most include the direct exchange of goods and services by politicians in return for (expected) political support (Medina and Stokes 2002). In clientelistic party systems, these exchanges typify party-voter linkages. By contrast, programmatic party systems contain parties that compensate supporters indirectly through the promise of specific policy packages (Kitschelt et al. 1999). A portion of this literature focuses on explaining the origins and evolution of programmatic or clientelistic parties/party systems. Others focus on the effects of these party system characteristics on policy outcomes and on the policy-making process (Kitschelt et al. 1999; Cox and McCubbins 2001; Medina and Stokes 2002; Golden 2002).

There has been a good deal written about clientelism in Southeast Asia, but unfortunately very little of it has thus far engaged this literature. The potential synergies from marrying the Southeast Asia–focused literature with the broader theoretical and comparative literature are significant. One challenge for this literature is isolating and disentangling the relative weight of possible independent variables. Various scholars ascribe the origins of clientelistic or programmatic parties to the level of socioeconomic development (Brusco et al. 2002), the degree of bureaucratic professionalization (Shefter 1994), electoral rules (Carey and Shugart 1995; Golden 2002; Hicken 2007a), or the nature of executive-legislative design (Blondel 1968; Sartori 1976; Coppedge 1998; Knutsen 1998).

For each of these variables, Southeast Asia contains an interesting set of cases. Thailand's rapid economic development over the last twenty-five years went hand in hand with regular elections. Did rising incomes, urbanization, and greater education lead to changes in the mix of clientelistic versus programmatic appeals? Are differences discernible in the demand for and supply of clientelism between richer and poorer areas within Thailand? Comparing the Philippines, Thailand, and Singapore, with their varying levels of bureaucratic professionalization, could also yield useful insights. Changes to Thailand's electoral rules offer a chance to study the effect of formal rules on the incentives for clientelism. Cross-country comparisons of the effects of different electoral environments (for example, between majoritarian Philippines and proportional Indonesia) are another avenue to explore. Finally, Southeast Asia contains variation in executive-legislative relations that is lacking in places such as Latin America. (Studies of party systems in Latin America are, by default, studies of presidential party systems.) We can, for example, get some useful analytical leverage by comparing Thailand and the Philippines.

Each has similar levels of economic development and similar electoral rules, but one is a parliamentary system, and the other is presidential. How, if at all, is this difference reflected in their party systems? In short, there are still plenty of unanswered questions, and quality research drawing on the region has the potential to shape the debates and set new research agendas.

A third oft-studied feature of party systems is the degree of ideological polarization (Blondel 1968; Sartori 1976; Coppedge 1998; Knutsen 1998). This concept usually refers to the ideological distance between parties, with scholars interested in how the degree of ideological polarization affects democratic stability, public policy, etc. In the many countries where ideological differences are the basis for competition between parties, this focus is completely appropriate. However, there are other countries where ideology seems to play little if any role in electoral politics—for example, Thailand and the Philippines. The lack of ideological or programmatic differentiation in these Southeast Asian cases sets them apart from most of their European and Latin American counterparts and raises interesting questions. First, what factors determine the extent to which parties differentiate themselves on the basis of ideological appeals? Second, what are the consequences of a lack of ideological diversity in the party system? How does this affect policy making, voter turnout, interest representation, capacity for reform, democratic stability, and other aspects of politics?

Southeast Asia scholars are well placed to begin providing answers to these important questions. Consider specifically the second of these questions. What are the consequences of a lack of ideological diversity in the party system? Phrased differently, what are the consequences of the absence of a partisan left in most of noncommunist Southeast Asia? This is an intriguing question for Southeast Asianists, certainly, but also for party and election scholars more generally. The development of party systems in much of the rest of the world takes place in an ideologically diverse atmosphere with parties arrayed along a left-right dimension.[37] Yet a partisan left did *not* emerge in most noncommunist countries of Southeast Asia. (The exceptions are pre-1965 Indonesia, which I will discuss below, and perhaps more recently the Philippines.) By comparing party and party system development in Southeast Asia with development in other areas of the world, it is possible to begin to isolate the effects of a partisan left on the party system.

By way of preliminary speculation only, let me suggest three hypotheses that might be worth exploring in connection with this question. First, the presence of a partisan left is a catalyst for the development of programmatic political parties (from across the ideological spectrum). The *raison d'être* of parties on the left generally includes the promotion of certain sets of policies— for example, land reform, poverty alleviation, and wage protection. The presence of a partisan left, campaigning on these types of programmatic appeals, might induce competing parties to respond with alternative programs. Where there is no electoral threat from the left, other political parties may lack strong incentives to move toward more programmatic campaigning—relying instead on more traditional strategies (e.g., mobilizing patron-client networks).

Closely related to the first hypothesis is a second: The presence of a partisan left is associated with greater attention by governments (left or right) to issues of rural development, social safety nets, and labor protection. In other words, the presence of a partisan left should not only shape the attraction of programmatic appeals generally; it should also shape the mix of specific policies that get placed on the political agenda by whichever party is elected. Where leftist parties succeed in politicizing an issue, it will be difficult for competing parties to ignore it.

The third hypothesis is related to the organizational structure of parties—a key component in Mainwaring and Scully's definition of party system institutionalization. Wherever a partisan left is present, parties are more likely to develop a stable, grassroots organizational apparatus (e.g., local party branches). This hypothesis assumes that leftist parties typically place greater emphasis on local, grassroots organizing and party building from the ground up than do other parties—an assumption that would first need to be verified empirically. If the assumption holds, we might find that just as parties respond to programmatic appeals by leftist parties with programs of their own, so too do they respond to electoral threats by adopting some of the left's organizational strategies.[38]

Cross-regional comparisons are one way to begin to investigate these hypotheses, but within the region there are also interesting variations to explore. For example, Indonesia is the one Southeast Asian state with a long history of an active, partisan left, in the form of the PKI. Until its destruction in 1965, the PKI was an electoral/political force to be reckoned with. How did this affect party system development in the pre-1965 period? How has the legacy of the PKI shaped the party system since 1965? What are the consequences of the lack of an explicitly partisan left for Indonesia's newly reestablished democratic party system? The point is not whether these hypotheses turn out to be right or wrong, only that they, and numerous others like them, are worth exploring in the context of Southeast Asia.[39]

To summarize, party systems in Southeast Asian states differ in interesting ways from one another and from party systems in other regions. Exploring the origins and consequences of these differences should yield important empirical and theoretical insights.

Conclusion

I have said very little in this chapter about the use of various research methods for the study of parties and elections in Southeast Asia. The choice of which method to use—qualitative, quantitative, or formal—should be driven by the nature of the research question and the types of data that are available. Most of the existing research on Southeast Asian parties and elections relies on qualitative methods, and this is likely to remain the case. Indeed, careful qualitative work in one or a few countries is an integral part of the study of parties and elections. However, the use of quantitative methods is also becoming more common as more and better data suitable for large-n analyses become available. The key to Southeast Asia scholars contributing to the core debates in the field is not the use of any particular method, but rather the combination of an engaging research question, sound research design, and careful analysis.

To date, the contribution of Southeast Asia scholars to the field's collective knowledge about parties and elections has been relatively modest. Altering this state of affairs will take a conscious effort by more researchers to engage and add to the broader literature on parties and elections. I have argued that Southeast Asia–focused research is at its strongest and has had the broadest impact when it is theory driven and (at least implicitly) comparative. Placing more of our work within a theoretical and comparative context will enable us to better connect with scholars outside of the region and contribute to our collective knowledge about parties and elections.

Chapter Five

Contentious Mass Politics in Southeast Asia
Knowledge Accumulation and Cycles
of Growth and Exhaustion

TUONG VU

Introduction

Why do men and women rebel? How do the weak resist the strong? Why did
certain revolutionary movements develop the way they did? Why did a few
succeed but most fail? These are some nagging questions that have preoccupied political scientists for the last forty years. Throughout the twentieth century, Southeast Asia was rife with conflict, from peasant rebellions to urban
revolts to communist revolutions.[1] These conflicts, especially the civil war in
Vietnam, have inspired the scholarly quest for explanation and understanding
by both generalists and regional specialists. In this quest, Southeast Asianists
have pursued distinctive approaches and have made major contributions to the
study of contentious mass politics.[2] These contributions are concentrated in
the areas of peasant behavior and political movements.

This essay will begin with a historical overview of the four main genres
of analysis in the study of contentious mass politics in Southeast Asia since
the mid-1960s.[3] These genres include political organization, peasant studies,
comparative-historical, and quantitative modeling.[4] The overview suggests
that (1) there has been a close relationship between scholarship and politics
in the real world and that (2) certain genres of analysis have been much more
popular than others in Southeast Asian studies. The second section of the

essay contrasts the goals and methods employed by different genres: from research questions to data collection, from ontological to epistemological assumptions, and from the use of cases to that of comparison. The analysis will stick to actual research practices as explained by researchers themselves in their works. Actual practices cannot be assumed to fit neatly into conventional labels in methodological debates such as "small *n*/large *n*," "qualitative/quantitative," and "positivist/interpretivist." In fact, based on concrete examples of works on contentious mass politics, I will argue that (1) the label "small *n*" is misleading and should be dropped from use and that (2) validity testing is not the monopolized domain of positivist approaches.

The final section will discuss how knowledge has been accumulated through four different modes. Whereas some works enrich our knowledge about certain themes, others specialize in the variations of such themes in different national contexts. Whereas some genres accumulate knowledge by hypothesis testing, others do so by generalizing or universalizing human experiences across times and societies. No genre monopolizes the truth, and knowledge accumulation in all genres tends to indicate complex realities rather than produce conclusive findings. Last but not least, the four genres in the study of contentious mass politics in Southeast Asia have all undergone cycles of growth and exhaustion. Periods of growth are followed by times of exhaustion, when a genre becomes overburdened with too rigid or complex meta-theoretical frameworks, or when it runs out of fresh cases to test its hypotheses. Accumulating knowledge is thus not "free" in the sense that it consumes resources (meta-theories, cases, and empirical data) that may be depleted and often need to be refilled or renewed.

A Historical Overview

Since the turbulent 1960s, which sharply raised scholarly interest in political conflicts,[5] four broad genres of analysis have developed in political science. The peasant study genre (*Peasant*) is concerned solely with peasants as the main forces in many revolutions. The second genre, political organization research (*Organization*), supplies in-depth case studies of revolutionary organizations and is especially interested in explaining why these movements develop and possibly defeat government authorities. At a macro level, the comparative-historical genre (*Comparative*) views revolutions as important social events to be systematically compared and explained. This genre of analysis traces the historical unfolding of these events and seeks to identify common causal patterns across a few national cases. Finally, the quantitative modeling genre (*Quantitative*) develops econometric models and statistical tests to search for correlates between conflict attributes and systemic variables (e.g., macro socioeconomic indicators).

These genres had certainly had long pedigrees in political science before the 1960s, but they have taken on distinct shapes only since then. Among the pioneering works were Johnson (1962) for Organization, Moore (1966) for Comparative, Wolf (1969) for Peasant, and Feierabend and associates (1972 [1966]) and Gurr (1970) for Quantitative. Seven Southeast Asian countries were included in Feierabend and associates' data set of eighty-four cases. Wolf had a chapter on the Vietnamese "peasant war." Even though subsequent authors would challenge their arguments, the five studies were influential with respect to the study of mass conflicts for the following decade.

During the 1960s and the early 1970s, Quantitative was probably the fastest-growing genre, with several statistical studies on the relationship between inequality and insurgency in South Vietnam and the Philippines (Mitchell 1968, 1969; Paige 1970; Sansom 1970; Russo 1972). Paige (1975) used statistical analyses to evaluate the revolutionary potential of different kinds of peasants within the peasantry, both at the global level and within the three selected cases (Peru, Angola, and Vietnam). Based on opinion surveys and regression analyses, Jackson (1980) sought to explain the origins of an Islamic rebellion in Indonesia.

For the Organization genre, Race (1972, 1974), Zasloff (1973), and Berman (1974) dealt with communist insurgencies in South Vietnam and Laos. These studies analyzed the complex dynamics among the revolutionaries, the government, and the people caught in between. Standing out for its comparative scope and historical topic was Adas (1979), which examined five cases of millenarian movements under colonial rule in the Dutch Indies, German East Africa, British India, Burma, and New Zealand.[6]

Appeared in the mid-1970s were four ambitious works in the Peasant genre that explained why peasants joined rebellions. Migdal (1974) built a theoretical framework inductively on the basis of fifty-one ethnographic monographs about rural politics in various countries, including (for Southeast Asia) Burma, Malaysia, the Philippines, Thailand, and Vietnam. Scott (1976) developed the moral economy theory of peasant behavior, to be illustrated by the cases of peasant rebellions in colonial Burma and Indochina in the 1930s.[7] Kerkvliet (1977) traced the peasant movements in the Philippines that arose in the 1930s and culminated in a failed communist rebellion in the mid-1950s. Finally, Popkin (1979) presented a deductive theory of peasants' "rational" behavior with illustrations from Vietnam.[8]

Important changes took place in Southeast Asia in the mid-1970s and onward. The end of revolutionary tumult in Indochina was followed by violent interstate wars between a reunified Vietnam and its former communist allies China and Cambodia. As the Cambodian revolution turned into a mass genocide, "social revolutions" no longer appeared as romantic to younger scholars as they once had to the previous generation. Elsewhere in Southeast Asia, the 1970s and 1980s witnessed a remarkable surge in urban unrest, including the riots in Indonesia (1974), the student uprisings in Thailand (1973–1976), the "people power" movement (1986) that ousted Marcos in the Philippines, and the student protests in Burma (1988) that failed to topple military rule. At the same time, peasant protests flared up in northern Thailand in the mid-1970s and in the Philippines in the early 1980s. By the end of the 1980s, however, armed communist insurgencies in Burma, Thailand, and the Philippines had withered away. The 1990s continued the trend of the 1980s, with urban movements mobilizing for elections in the Philippines, protesting authoritarian regimes in Burma (1990s) and Malaysia (1998), and overthrowing military rule in Thailand (1992) and Indonesia (1998). Sporadic peasant and labor protests also emerged in Vietnam, this time against a communist authoritarian regime.

In Southeast Asian studies, the 1980s saw no major works on the new urban uprisings in the region.[9] Probably the most popular genre in the late 1980s was Peasant, in which Scott (1985, 1990) attracted considerable attention.[10] These two works analyzed peasants' "everyday forms of resistance," a phenomenon that Scott argued was far more common and probably more beneficial to peasants than revolutions. Scott and Kerkvliet (1986) and Colburn (1989) presented further evidence of "everyday forms of resistance" in Southeast Asia and other continents. Sharing a concern about peasants' everyday life with Scott were Kerkvliet (1990), which examined the politics of class and status in a Philippine village, and Kerkvliet (2005), which dealt with peasant resistance to collectivization in Vietnam.

In the early 1990s, the Organization genre continued to grow, with studies such as Marks (1994) and Rutten (1996) on the communist movements in Thailand and the Philippines, respectively. Marks (1996) examined four cases of failed Maoist armed struggles in Thailand, the Philippines, Sri Lanka, and Peru. Elliott (2003) was a massive two-volume study that traced the course of the Vietnamese revolution in a single province over fifty years.

The Quantitative genre saw a drop in interest in the 1980s and a recent revival. Analysts in this tradition were now aided by new econometric techniques, game theory, the massive Singer-Small data set of war correlates,[11] and simply faster computers. New lines of inquiry tackled comparative genocides and the economics of civil wars. Representative works in this emerging literature include Harff and Gurr (1988), Collier (2000), Collier and Hoeffler (1998, 2001), Bhavnani and Ross (2003), and Collier and Sambanis (2005). Burma, Cambodia, and Indonesia were among the Southeast Asian cases that inspired this literature.

In contrast with all the other genres, the Comparative genre that Barrington Moore pioneered never took root in Southeast Asian studies even when it developed a large following in comparative politics and historical sociology.[12] Since the 1980s, new research in this genre has moved away from the classic revolutions and taken on newer cases such as Iran, Nicaragua, and Eastern Europe. Only four works have systematically discussed Southeast Asian cases: Walton (1984), Parsa (2000), Goodwin (2001), and Thompson (2004).

In the late 1990s, a younger generation of Southeast Asianists began applying theories of democratization and social movements in their studies of urban movements and uprisings. These works continued the Organization genre, with the form of political organizations now being urban mass movements instead of rural communist ones. Major studies include Eldridge (1995) and Clarke (1998) on the politics of NGOs in Indonesia and the Philippines, Thompson (1995) and Boudreau (1996a, 2001) on the "people power" movement in the Philippines, Hadiz (1997) and West (1997) on labor movements in Indonesia and the Philippines, and Uhlin (1997) on the democratic movement in Indonesia. Hedman (2001), Boudreau (2004), and Schock (2005) are explicitly comparative studies that focused on urban mass movements and democratic transition. Aspinall (2005) studied the anti-Suharto movement in Indonesia.

What the future trend will be can be inferred from a brief survey of unpublished recent dissertations. A search of University Microfilms' dissertation database yielded a dozen recent studies; from their abstracts, most of these studies dealt with urban movements.[13] The ethnographic approach to studying mass politics was found in several unpublished dissertations that employed concepts such as everyday forms of resistance and hidden transcripts. Topically, both published and unpublished works in recent years have shown interest in compliance as well as resistance, and in nonviolent as well as violent forms of resistance. Furthermore, not just new cases but old cases such as the Huk rebellion were now reexamined from a gender perspective.[14]

Philosophies and Methods in Contrast

The historical overview above suggests that the Organization and Peasant genres have dominated the study of contentious mass politics among Southeast Asianists. The Organization genre borrows heavily from economics and sociology, whereas ethnographic research has been the most influential method within the Peasant genre. The Quantitative genre, which has foundations in economics, sociology, and psychology, flourished early on but lost popularity until recently. There is a growing trend to develop systematic comparisons across national cases (along the Comparative tradition), but this is still at an infant stage.

This section will examine how analysts of different genres view the goals of their enterprises and the causal structures of the world, what kinds of questions are asked, what units of analysis are focused on, what forms of data are collected, what style of analysis and reasoning is used, and what the strengths and weaknesses of each genre are in dealing with the subject matter. Table 5.1 summarizes the main characteristics of each genre.

Methodological debates in political science sometimes resemble ideological conflicts.[15] They give the impression that the battle lines are clear and fixed, that the fights are about non-negotiable principles, and that the overall development of social scientific research has been a rational and predictable process. The historical evolution of the scholarship about contentious mass politics in Southeast Asia since the 1960s suggests that this impression is not accurate. Methods have often been applied to solve specific problems, not as dogmas: Many studies combine statistical analyses and in-depth case-study

TABLE 5.1

Studies of Southeast Asian Contentious Mass Politics by Genre

Political history	Kahin (1952), McVey (1964a), McAlister (1969), Anderson (1972), Mortimer (1974), Huynh (1982)
Peasant studies	Wolf (1969), Migdal (1974), Scott (1976), Kerkvliet (1977), Popkin (1979), Weller and Guggenheim (1982), Scott (1985), Scott and Kerkvliet (1986), Colburn (1989), Scott (1990), Kerkvliet (1990, 2005)
Political organization	Race (1972, 1974), Zasloff (1973), Berman (1974), Adas (1979), Marks (1994, 1995), Eldridge (1995), Thompson (1995), Boudreau (1996a, 1996b), Rutten (1996), Hadiz (1997), West (1997), Uhlin (1997), Goodwin (1997), Clarke (1998), Boudreau (2001), Hedman (2001), van Klinken (2001), Missingham (2003), Elliott (2003), Boudreau (2004), Aspinall (2005), Schock (2005)
Comparative-historical	Walton (1984), Parsa (2000), Goodwin (2001), Thompson (2004)
Quantitative modeling	Feierabend et al. (1972), Mitchell (1968, 1969), Gurr (1970), Paige (1970), Sansom (1970), Russo (1972), Paige (1975), Jackson (1980), Harff and Gurr (1988), Boswell and Dixon (1990, 1993), Collier (2000), Collier and Hoeffler (1998, 2001), Bhavnani and Ross (2003), Collier and Sambanis (2005)

methods,[16] participation observation and archival research,[17] and formal modeling and interviewing.[18] Some scholars are loyal to certain methods throughout their careers. Others adopt new methods to solve new problems or as a result of changes in their thinking.[19] The discussion below will stay away from fixed *hypothetical* methodological positions and try to capture the messy practices in *actual* research as perceived by researchers themselves and as modified by different generations of researchers over time. It hopes to identify continuities as well as discontinuities, and consistencies as well as inconsistencies in many research genres.

The Peasant genre is primarily interested in understanding and explaining what motivates peasants and how they resist their oppressors. The focus is on the salience of certain themes concerning peasant behavior and not the possible variations in their behavior across different communities and at different times. As Scott writes, "for our purposes, what is important is that the peasant community embodies a set of communal and local class interests—a moral economy—that can and do form the basis of violent confrontations with elites. The strength of that moral economy, to be sure, varies very much with local social structure, but it is a variation around a constant theme" (1977b: 280). Another way of expressing the same idea is found in Scott (1977a: 237): "The probability of [peasant] revolt depends . . . on the coercive force of those who would prevent it. The capacity to experience the anger that comes from a sense of exploitation, however, is universal. . . ." Thus, the goal is to uncover peasant anger as a universal condition, not to predict the probability of a revolt. By proposing a deductive theory and applying it in three cases (precolonial, colonial, and post-colonial Vietnam), Popkin (1979) also stresses a main logic of peasant behavior despite variations across cases and times. As Skocpol rightly observes, comparison as used in this genre is global but not cross-national (Skocpol 1982: 367). Scholars of this genre are interested in explaining peasant behavior but not in explaining the variations in such behavior across national contexts.[20]

There are two opposing causal ontologies[21] within the Peasant genre. In Scott (1976, 1985) and Kerkvliet (1977), the causal ontology lies in the moral world of village communities. The alternative ontology in other Peasant works such as Migdal (1974) and Popkin (1979) is centered on the individual peasant as a rational actor. Cases play different roles from one author to another. Kerkvliet (1977, 1990) is primarily interested in the cases (the Huk rebellion and social relations in a Philippine village), although he discusses at length the implications of his empirical findings for the moral economy hypothesis. Popkin (1979) and Scott (1976, 1985, 1990), in contrast, use cases to illustrate their theories of behavior applicable to both peasants and other groups. For Migdal, and Scott to a lesser extent, cases are also used to inductively derive and test theory; cases are integrated in theoretical development rather than playing only an illustrative role.

Scott (1985, 1990) and, to a lesser extent, Kerkvliet (1977) are among the most important studies in the genre that employ an interpretivist epistemology.[22] For them, the search for "generalizations from within" makes "case selection" in the positivist sense unnecessary (Geertz 1973b: 23). More important than "cases" are their fieldwork sites: villages that can offer them access to accounts of events in their interest (e.g., participation in the Huk rebellion or post–Green revolution changes) or some control for certain factors (e.g., a rice farming village with minimal off-farm employment opportunities).

Data-collection techniques indicate both changing methods and the common concerns underlying most works in the Peasant genre. Data come from diverse sources: direct observations, archival documents, works of fiction, and other secondary sources. Popkin (1979) counts mostly on secondary sources, whereas Scott (1976) mines official colonial records for data. Reversing himself, Scott (1985, 1990) turns to direct observations as the only valid source for his analysis of peasants' everyday forms of resistance. Official records, he argues, recount only those events perceived by state agents as directly threatening the state. Everyday resistance is thus left out despite its significance *from the peasants' perspective.*

For Scott and his collaborators, the resort to ethnography involves more than a practical concern about the limits of historical records. Normatively, these scholars assume that legitimacy rests with the weak and the oppressed. They don't treat all participants in rebellions the same way and like to point out that peasants, not the "political commissars," are the true revolutionaries (Scott 1979). This concern for the "little guys" differentiates these authors from those of the History genre, who often identify themselves with national revolutionary leaders (Sukarno, Tan Malaka, or Ho Chi Minh), or those of the Organization genre, who tend to display unambiguous sympathy for anti-government movements but who do not distinguish between elite and non-elite activists,[23] or from those of the Quantitative genre, who often treat rebels as either angry or greedy people.[24] Whereas this normative concern leads to the romanticization of peasant lives (Skocpol 1982: 360), it helps works in the Peasant genre avoid the mistake that many students of revolution make in assuming that peasants would fare better under communist regimes because they participated in the revolutions that put those regimes in power.[25]

Privileging ethnography is also based on the ontological assumption that class consciousness should be inferred not from structural economic relationships (as in classical Marxism) but from the lived experience of those involved. Class conflicts are rarely expressed in the form of violent struggles in which a class overthrows its oppressors, but are lived everyday. Scholars should be deeply concerned about the impact of their own class backgrounds on their scholarship, as Scott (1977a: 232, 245) reviews the "dismal science of peasant revolution" below:

> As larger human emotions than trucking and bartering are involved in the enterprise of rebellion, one would expect that a theory based largely on models of bourgeois calculus [i.e., rational choice theory] would fail to do it justice. . . .

It is instructive to go directly to the human participants of such dramas, where they have been heard or recorded, and ask them what moved them to act. . . . To read [peasants' accounts] is to realize what most social scientists (myself included), who have never experienced the humiliations or hunger or poverty, fail to capture in their theories of peasant revolution.

In criticizing a study of peasant rebellions in the Philippines, Kerkvliet (1978: 772) echoes the same point: "Beginning with the belief that these rebels are unrealistic and possibly irrational, [the author] precludes an understanding of these people in their own terms. He gains knowledge about them, but does not come to know them." Although ethnography is privileged in this genre, it is not the only method used. Kerkvliet (1977, 2005) successfully combines official records and peasant voices to study Philippine and Vietnamese peasants. Popkin (1979) shows that deductive reasoning can explain an important part of peasant lives or at least offer a plausible alternative to explanations obtained by ethnographic methods.

Ethnography and interpretivism are controversial in political science.[26] "Weapons of the weak," "everyday forms of resistance," and "hidden transcripts" are catchy and widely applicable phrases but may be criticized for lacking analytic and explanatory power.[27] The real voices of participants and the liberal use of literary tales permit rich narratives of conflicts, but positivist scholars have dismissed this kind of evidence as impressionistic and unsystematic.[28] Scott is the first to admit that the interpretation of the lived human experience is "treacherous" because behavior may be automatic (i.e., meaningless), contradictory, deliberately misleading, and uninformed of larger events (Scott 1985: 46–47). The proposed standards of evidence and inference are that interpretations be economical, logically consistent with observations, capable of incorporating anomalies, and found plausible by the actors themselves (139). Implied in this list is the practice of conducting validation tests not as a formal process separated from other phases of research (as in statistics) but as numerous iterated informal steps embedded throughout the course of research: For each observation the researcher makes, he or she has to match it with others, identify inconsistencies in the main story, search for additional observations that can account for anomalies, revise the story, and go back to his informants to find out if the revised story is still plausible. Far from being "small-*n*" and lacking rigor, the process in ethnographic research involves huge amounts of data and numerous tests of consistency and plausibility. As Yanow (2003: 10) argues, interpretivist-qualitative research must be characterized as "large-*n*" because it entails numerous observations over extended periods combined with extensive interviews and documentary evidence.

Turning to the Organization genre, the primary research questions of earlier works are how revolutionary organizations gather mass support and compete with governments for authority. In answering these questions they also address the related question of what motivates ordinary people to join those organizations. In contrast, more recent studies on urban movements deal with a more diverse range of issues, such as the diffusion of foreign democratic ideas (Uhlin 1997) and the impact of regime type or state repression on the modes of protest and character of anti-government movements (Thompson 1995; Boudreau 2004). Although most Organization studies focus on only one case, concepts are widely applied and research questions are often framed broadly enough to enable their potential application to other cases. In fact, Adas (1979: xxv) claims that his findings about peasant-based prophetic rebellions can be useful to the study of movements based on other groups such as the urban poor.

Comparison plays varying roles within Organization studies. For most authors who study communist insurgencies, comparison is unsystematic, and generalizations beyond their cases are made only reluctantly. Exceptions are Race (1974), which proposes a general theory of revolution based on the Vietnamese case and tests it with the Thai case, and Marks (1995), which presents parallel contrasts of five Maoist insurgencies that failed for the same reasons. Boudreau (1996b) compares Northern and Southern sociopolitical conditions to highlight different strategic dilemmas facing Southern movements. Boudreau (2004: 3) systematically compares protest movements in Burma, Indonesia, and the Philippines to "illustrate" the variety of repressive strategies available to states, and the connection between state strategies and modes of resistance. Parallel/contrast comparison is also used in Adas (1979: xxii), which selects the most different cases among the phenomena of prophetic rebellions and analyzes the differences as well as similarities among them. The focus on a single national case in most Organization works does not necessarily make them "small-*n*" or unsystematic. Berman (1974) quotes extensively from more than 1,000 interviews and applies statistical analyses throughout to evaluate competing hypotheses about the motives of participants. Elliott (2003: 7) combines more than 400 interviews of nearly 12,000 pages of transcribed materials with numerous postwar memoirs and thousands of captured documents. To the extent that these authors generalize about human motives and human relationships inside the movement or between the movement and ordinary peasants, their studies should be characterized as "large-*n*."

Ontologically, some authors in this genre reject macro causes of revolution. For example, as Rutten (1996: 111) states, "We should avoid looking for 'big' causes (for instance, a wide gap between rich and poor, or a deep socioeconomic crisis) to explain a 'big' change (massive support for a revolutionary movement) but consider, instead, the accumulation of microprocesses out of which a specific large change is built." Berman similarly calls his approach "a microstructural" one while acknowledging the importance of macrostructural factors (Berman 1974: 9). However, the genre generally seems not to be too concerned with limiting itself to only one level of causality. All authors assume human agents to be rational actors "who are not slaves to their environment" and who "seek goals and make choices within the constraints of their environmental situation" (10). Yet whereas Thompson (1995) and West (1997) assign great weight to macro factors such as regime type, state structure, and history of protest, Berman (1974) and Rutten (1996) emphasize meso-level organizational processes (e.g., mobilization, integration, and socialization). For individual works, this ontological ambiguity may cause confusion as to how micro, meso, and macro levels are integrated in the causal structure of things, but for the genre as a whole the ambiguity may be seen as strength rather than weakness because it offers scholars more flexibility to frame their research questions.[29] Rather than accumulating knowledge *intensively* through iterated tests of some key hypotheses, the genre may grow *extensively* as researchers' work on different levels can still be connected in a loose ontological framework.

We have seen that Peasant and Organization styles of analysis are popular in the study of Southeast Asian contentious mass politics. In contrast, the Comparative genre is the least popular.[30] Comparative works do not focus on a particular class or the revolutionary organization as the Peasant and Organization genres do. Instead, they ask why historically "revolutions" happened (or should have happened but did not) and what determined variations in their outcomes. The goal is not to seek causal regularities or universal laws but to identify common patterns across a small number of disparate cases (Goldstone 2003: 50). Generalization beyond the case studies is generally avoided, but arguments are often framed in terms broad enough to aid generalizations

(Skocpol and Somers 1980: 19). There is no such thing as a general theory of revolution, Goodwin (2001: 8) writes in one of the most ambitious Comparative works ever, which compares Southeast Asian, Central American, and Eastern European "peripheral revolutions." His goal is to demonstrate that their outcomes were "the results of general (if not universal) causal mechanisms."

More than for any other genre, systematic comparison is the hallmark of Comparative works. In the words of Comparative pioneers Skocpol and Somers (1980: 182), "the logic involved in [Comparative works] resembles that of statistical analysis, which manipulates groups of cases to control sources of variation in order to make causal inferences when quantitative data are available about a large number of cases. [The Comparative genre] is a kind of multivariate analysis to which scholars turn in order to validate causal statements about macro-phenomena for which, inherently, there are too many variables and not enough cases." Many later scholars of this genre have since moved away from this strong positivist stand. For instance, Walton's study of "national revolts" in the Philippines, Colombia, and Kenya (1984: 25) explicitly rejects the positivist logic and quasi-experimental design as "not entirely appropriate" because his study does not focus "on three cases of similar revolutionary outcomes, but on three distinctive processes of national revolt that followed rather different courses and produced different results."

Walton signals a fundamental change in the methods used to study revolutions among many later Comparative researchers. Whereas John S. Mill's methods of agreement and difference are accepted as the foundation for early works (Skocpol and Somers 1980: 183), a recent comprehensive review of this genre does not even mention Mill (Goldstone 2003).[31] Mill's controversial methods have been replaced by "process tracing" aimed at uncovering the specific causal mechanisms that link macro structures and processes to the events as they unfolded over time (Goldstone 2003: 49). The change reflects a more methodologically confident generation of Comparative researchers who no longer have to rely on quantitative terminologies to describe themselves. Stylistically, the change helps make Comparative narratives less "mechanical" and "unaesthetic."[32] More important but less unanimously recognized is that process tracing performs the function of robust validity tests in which macro causal hypotheses are matched and evaluated against numerous points of data.[33] For instance, in studying how centralized and exclusive state rule affected the likelihood of revolution in her cases of Iran, Nicaragua, and the Philippines, Parsa presents several causal mechanisms and demonstrates how these unfolded in different national contexts over extended periods. The number of national contexts ("dataset observations") may be limited, but the extended time frame and the various institutional sites subjected to analytical investigation mean a huge number of "causal process observations."[34] Instead of accepting the condescending label "small-n," which counts only dataset observations and ignores the contribution of causal process observations, Comparative scholars now may proudly claim that their methods can produce rigorously tested results based on adequate data.

Ontologically, most Comparative works attribute the causes of "revolutions" to the conjunction of macro structures or factors such as state and regime type, state and social class structure, the international system, and demographic pressure. For instance, in his study of "anticolonial revolutions" in Southeast Asia, Goodwin (2001) argues that exclusionary and repressive colonial regimes (in Indonesia and Vietnam but not Malaysia and the Philippines) made available broad strata of population for revolutionary parties to mobilize. Western and Japanese support for populist nationalists (in Indonesia, Malaysia, and the Philippines but not Vietnam) pre-empted communists from leading anti-colonial movements. However, structural arguments no longer dominate Comparative works as they once did.[35] Walton (1984: 22) calls for "a merger of developmental and revolutionary theory as necessary allies in the explanation of modern rebellions."[36] Parsa (2000) treats structural factors almost as background variables for his analysis of collective action. Even Goodwin (2001: 133), who goes furthest among recent works in promoting a structural "state-centered perspective," implicitly acknowledges that in many cases the state may be little more than an intervening factor: "Scholars of revolutions need to pay attention to states not only because control of state power is, by definition, central to revolution . . . , but also because states powerfully determine the precise ways in which a range of other factors may (or may not) contribute to both the mobilization and impact of revolutionary movements." Thompson (2004) studies fifteen "democratic revolutions" in Asia and Eastern Europe since the 1980s, using an eclectic explanatory framework that includes regime types, political opportunities, and actors' motives.

For the Comparative genre far more than for others, case selection is of paramount importance. (In contrast, data, which mostly come from secondary sources, are relatively of less concern to researchers.) Besides practical issues, the selection of cases is made with great care for the purpose of (dis)confirming certain theories, highlighting particular patterns of interest, isolating or controlling for the effects of particular variables, and avoiding "selection bias." Several opposing methods of selection have been used, including regional versus global samples [37] and urban-based versus peasant revolutions.[38]

Because theory is sensitive to which cases are "constituted"[39] and selected, and case selection in turn is sensitive to how "revolution" is defined, it is remarkable that Comparative researchers have not agreed on a common definition of *revolution*. The only attribute of revolution commonly accepted is the presence of mass- or class-based mobilization. Scholars disagree on whether other aspects of revolution, such as the successful overthrow of the state, the use of violence, and the "basic, rapid transformations of state and class structure," must be viewed as necessary conditions for events to be defined as "revolutions."[40] This ambiguity concerning the very phenomenon or phenomena to be investigated has never been (and will probably never be) successfully resolved. It is thus left to individual scholars to pick what particular set of "revolutions" they want to study: "social revolutions" (Skocpol 1979; Parsa 2000), "national revolts" (Walton 1984), "urban-based revolutions" (Farhi 1990), "Third World social revolutions" (Foran 1992), "anticolonial revolutions" and "persistent insurgencies" (Goodwin 2001), or "democratic revolutions" (Thompson 2004). On the one hand, it can be argued that this conceptual fuzziness hinders the accumulation of theoretical (as opposed to empirical) knowledge because each study tackles a different species of the beast. How can scholars falsify the results of other studies if they don't study the same phenomenon?[41] On the other hand, the genre has been able to grow largely because the conceptual ambiguity has allowed researchers to study new events as they happened. Interest, ideas, and secondary sources would have dried up quickly had all scholars been required to study the same three classic "social revolutions" that Skocpol (1979) did.

The popularity of the Comparative genre in comparative politics during the last two decades stands in stark contrast to the Quantitative genre, which enjoyed popularity in the 1960s but largely slipped into oblivion until recently. Quantitative works focus primarily on specifying, modeling, and testing statistical correlations between certain macro-level political and socioeconomic variables (e.g., regime type, social inequality, economic development level) and the risk that a country may experience large-scale political violence or rebellion. Some early Quantitative works such as Feierabend and associates (1972 [1969]) and Gurr (1970: 13) deduce the correlations from a general theoretical framework that explains how relative deprivation induces discontent or frustration, which in turn spurs action. Whether action is politicized and actualized depends on intervening cultural, historical, and institutional variables. More often, Quantitative studies involve the tests of certain correlations of theoretical or policy interest, without any attempt at developing a general theory. Based on these correlations, the researcher can predict how much and in what direction the risk of civil war or rebellion in a country may change when particular independent variables change in their values. Or she can infer motivation from patterns of observed behavior expressed in statistical relationships. For instance, Collier (2000) and Collier and Hoeffler (2001) find that after controlling for several variables, a statistically significant correlation exists between a country's share of primary exports in GDP and the proportion of uneducated young men, on the one hand, and the risk of civil war in that country, on the other. They then infer that conflicts are more likely to be caused by economic opportunity than by grievances because the looting of those exports and the availability of easy recruits can be assumed to lower the cost of organizing a rebellion.[42]

Because statistical samples used in these studies are supposed to cover nearly the entire universe of the phenomenon under investigation, Quantitative researchers often present their findings as universal relationships: "inequality is associated with insurgency" (Mitchell 1969), or "economic and political dependency contributes to rebellion" (Boswell and Dixon 1990: 541). Sometimes these researchers are content with only probabilistic statements, such as "increased development is associated with a decreased likelihood of civil war" (Henderson and Singer 2000: 289), or "unlootable resources are more likely to produce separatist conflicts, and lootable resources are more likely to produce nonseparatist conflicts" (Ross 2003: 67).

Early Quantitative works attribute causality to systemic variables at the national level. "Social frustration" is assumed to be the uniform aggregation of psychological "deprivation" at the individual level. Social frustration in turn is a function of systemic changes in traditional societies caused by modernization. Although deprivation is the overarching theme, sophisticated Quantitative works (e.g., Feierabend et al. 1972 [1966]) examine numerous variables that may be related to the quality of life and the nature of the political system such as regime type, level of economic development, and political freedom. Since modernization and functional system theories became discredited in the early 1970s, Quantitative works have continued with the same approach, although their techniques have improved greatly. However, the absence of "an integrated theory" (Gurr 1970: 16–17) has made these works appear eclectic at best and ad hoc at worst (Lichbach 1989: 448). Marxists and dependency theorists have developed a separate line of analysis and made occasional contributions to this genre, including Paige (1975) and Boswell and Dixon (1990, 1993). Causality for these works operates at both the level of domestic class relations and that of core-periphery dependency. A line of analysis that has recently been resurrected by (political) economists suggests a causal ontology that rests with individual motives. Rebels are rational actors and motivated by greed as much as, if not more than, grievances.[43] As Collier and Hoeffler (1998: 1) argue, "civil wars occur if the incentive for rebellion is sufficiently large relative to the costs" (for groups that want to rebel).

Quantitative works make explicit hypotheses, offer creative ways of measuring concepts, perform massive tasks of coding and data entry, and devise mathematically rigorous tests of their hypotheses. These methods are sound in abstract statistical theory but are fraught with difficulties in practice. These problems include conceptual measurement (death rates per day or month as a measure of the risk of civil war); model specifications (should the relationship between democracy and rebellion be linear or curvilinear?); endogeneity (does greed for resources cause rebellion, or does continuing rebellion increase the need for resources?[44]); systematic sampling biases (are coded reports of events in the *New York Times* index reliable?); and sometimes trivial conclusions ("countries with larger populations have higher risks of war, and these wars last longer"[45]).

Although new statistical techniques, better databases, and cumulative research skills may gradually eliminate these practical problems, Quantitative works face a far more fundamental criticism that involves the assumptions in statistical methods about the homogeneity and independence of cases, causes, and causal impact (Ragin 2000: 13–27; P. A. Hall 2003). For example, among the Asian "cases" of "civil wars" in Collier and Hoeffler (2001: 22) are Afghanistan (1978–1992; 1992–ongoing), Cambodia (1970–1991), China (1967–1968), Indonesia (1975–1982), Laos (1960–1973), the Philippines (1972–1996), and Vietnam (1960–1975). Although these "cases" are assumed to be the same by Collier and Hoeffler, regional specialists may argue that this list represents events that are too diverse, even for successive wars in the same country such as Cambodia, to be lumped together in the same "population" under the label "civil war."

Some criticisms of the Quantitative genre are unwarranted, however.

A common criticism is the generation of conflicting findings, especially on the relationship between inequality and rebellion (Lichbach 1989; Goldstone 2003). Clearly this is due in part to the use of different measures of similar concepts and different data sets. However, no genre can escape this problem. Mahoney (2003: 140) shows that iterated tests of Barrington Moore's hypothesis in the Comparative genre about the importance of a strong bourgeoisie for democracy have similarly found conflicting results. Another criticism asserts that "statistical analysis presumes a world in which the only prior knowledge one has is a null hypothesis, based on ignorance of causal relationships, and uses data to identify causal relationships that depart from the null hypothesis. In contrast, [a Comparative work] rarely starts from ignorance of causal relationships" (Goldstone 2003: 44–45). Although this may be true from the perspective of abstract statistical theory, in practice all the Quantitative works reviewed here start with some theoretical puzzles, if not a deductive framework. Often the conflicting implications of two different theories are first cited before the researcher proceeds to modeling and testing, presumably to solve the contradiction.

The review of methods used by different genres of analysis suggests that most of what is often labeled "qualitative research" is not "small-n." National contexts may be limited, but data sets are huge. Interpretivist works in the Peasant genre are often based on a single village, but because they search for analytical knowledge about human behavior in structural social relationships, national contexts may or may not matter. The number of individuals observed and the duration of observation decide how many "n" there are. Similarly, national contexts ("cases" in Quantitative studies) may or may not be important for most Comparative works because their focus is on revolutionary processes that are observed in numerous institutional and social sites. Generalizations across national contexts by Peasant and Comparative works, if made, do have to assume similar causal mechanisms and similar impacts of national particularities on individual behavior or on revolutionary processes. But Quantitative works that examine cross-national correlations have to make similar but much less realistic assumptions about homogeneous causal impacts and mechanisms within a national context. "Small-n" is a misleading term that belittles qualitative research through the lenses of quantitative theory.

A second lesson from the methodological review is that testing is not the monopolized domain of positivist approaches. Contrary to conventional perceptions, interpretivist works in the Peasant genre do carry out testing as an integral part of their constructing a valid and consistent narrative. These tests are informal, but they are appropriate for the purpose of the research involved, which does not focus on variations but on the main theme: a generalizable human experience. Rigor in this case depends less on formal and replicable procedures than on cultural sensitivity; logical rather than numerical consistency is the goal.

Knowledge Accumulation and Cycles of Growth and Exhaustion

Against the backdrop of tumultuous events in Southeast Asia in the 1960s, the study of contentious mass politics since then has proceeded along four different paths. Different genres tackle different pieces of the puzzle. Whereas the Peasant genre concentrates on peasants—the everyday resisters and the foot soldiers of many revolutions—Organization examines the organizations that make revolutions happen. Comparative deals with macro processes believed to shape the origins and courses of those revolutions. Quantitative identifies and tests causal relationships among macro-level variables applicable universally. The divisions among the genres do not preclude scholars from occasionally crossing the lines. Some works are hard to categorize: Paige (1975) straddles Peasant and Quantitative; so does Parsa (2000) with respect to Comparative and Organization. Some researchers try several genres: Goodwin (1997) belongs to the Organization genre, whereas Goodwin (2001) takes the Comparative path. Ross (2005) lies in the Comparative tradition, whereas Ross (2003) is a Quantitative work. Despite what seems to be a reasonable division of labor among the genres, Peasant and Organization have been more popular in Southeast Asian studies than Comparative and Quantitative.

Has knowledge been accumulated, and, if so, what kind of knowledge? As Table 5.2 indicates, even though they may study the same events or phenomena, different genres view their objects of analysis differently, employ different methods of explanation, and suggest different modes of knowledge accumulation.

For the positivist Comparative and Quantitative genres, causal knowledge is central to their enterprises.[46] Knowledge is accumulated through the improvement of causal theories and repeated tests with new cases. Replicated tests need not yield consistent results; disconfirming existing hypotheses is progress as much as confirming them is (Mahoney 2003: 135). In the Quantitative genre, among the most tested relationships are those between rebellion or violence and a range of systemic variables, including inequality, modernity, democracy, dependency, primary commodity exports, military spending, and national income. Repeated tests of these relationships have been done with better data, different measures, more complex models, and new techniques. Overall, repeated tests have succeeded less in settling any debates than in showing that the issues are complicated and need further testing or theoretical refinement. Theoretical development in the genre has moved away from relative deprivation toward rational choice theory. New taxonomies of genocides and natural resources (in relation to civil wars) have been constructed recently, but further progress remains to be seen (Harff and Gurr 1988; Collier and Hoeffler 2001). Southeast Asian case studies have offered criticisms and contributed to the development of these taxonomies (Fein 1993; Ross 2003, 2004).

Compared to their Quantitative counterparts, Comparative works make far more complex causal arguments that are embedded in particular contexts. Later works add to early ones new cases, new explanatory factors, and invariably more complex causal arguments. Old hypotheses are refuted, reformulated, or accepted with important qualifications. Complexity, rather than conclusive findings, is again the result. This genre has not developed much in Southeast Asian studies but does have some potential for that very reason. A key insight from this literature is how regime types and state policies shape the character and outcomes of movements. Another insight about the various conditions under which revolutionary coalitions form is also relevant to Southeast Asian cases.

The interpretivist works that dominate the Peasant genre are not interested in a social phenomenon or an event per se, but in the generalizable experience of peasants: how they think and why they act in certain ways. Geertz's (1973b: 25) discussion of knowledge accumulation in the interpretivist social sciences is relevant here:

> Our knowledge of culture . . . cultures . . . a culture . . . grows: in spurts. Rather than following a rising curve of cumulative findings, cultural analysis breaks up into a disconnected yet coherent sequence of bolder and bolder sorties. Studies do build on other studies, not in the sense that they take up where the others leave off, but in the sense that, better informed and better conceptualized, they plunge more deeply into the same thing.

What is observed in the development of the Peasant genre over time confirms Geertz's characterization, even though not all works in the genre are

TABLE 5.2
Genres in Contrast

Genre	Normative concerns	Causal ontologies	Epistemology	Objects of explanation	Methods of explanation	Modes of comparison	Modes of knowledge accumulation
Political history	Sympathetic to leaders of rebellions	Unspecified	Atheoretical interpretivist	Unique historical events and the particular details of these events	Implicit	Comparison rarely done	Descriptive knowledge of specific events through cumulatively richer and more coherent narratives
Peasant studies	Sympathetic to peasants and nonelites	Micro-level	Theoretical interpretivist	Peasant behavior as a general theme and as a generalizable human experience	Explicit	Global, not cross-national	Descriptive, analytical, and causal knowledge of certain (generalizable) human experiences

Political organization	Sympathetic to anti-government protests	Micro and meso levels	Weak positivist	Movements or revolutionary organizations as social collective units; their variations in different contexts	Explicit	Infrequent, cross-national	Analytical and causal knowledge of specific social organizations
Comparative-historical	Rebels and authorities assumed not to matter	Macro-structural	Medium to strong positivist	Rare social phenomena and the variations of their characteristics in particular contexts	Explicit	Cross-national	Causal knowledge about a category of social phenomena
Quantitative modeling	Rebels viewed as angry or greedy	Macro-systemic	Strong positivist	Correlations of macro-variables	Explicit	Cross-national	Knowledge about the magnitude and direction of macro-causal relationships

interpretivist. Scott (1976) analyzes how peasants reacted to the advance of colonialism and capitalism. This work contrasts sharply with Migdal (1974) and Popkin (1979), which focus on the same theme while starting from very different assumptions about the nature of peasants. Scott (1985) and Kerkvliet (1990) dwell on far more details and observe at close range how peasants live during post-colonial capitalism. They are far more incisive than their predecessors. They are preoccupied not with the rare rebellions but with peasants' everyday life. The time frame is no longer restricted to the colonial period. Scott (1990) further generalizes the human experience of exploitation as lived by peasants under capitalism to what is lived by slaves and other oppressed groups in various social and historical contexts. Scott's (1985) framework has also been applied to the unexpected context of peasants under socialism. Kelliher (1992), Viola (1996), and Kerkvliet (2005) document peasant resistance under Stalin, Mao, Ho, and their associates. The attention to the "small arms fire in the class war" allows Kelliher and Kerkvliet to offer unconventional explanations for the economic reforms in China and Vietnam in the 1980s: It was powerless peasants, not the domineering socialist state, that led agricultural reforms in both cases. Scott's concepts of "moral economy" and "everyday forms of resistance" have also helped rational choice theorists build their own theories of rationality (Popkin 1979; Lichbach 1995). All in all, the Peasant genre showcases how contentious mass politics in Southeast Asia can enrich our knowledge of social conflicts in general. This genre brings to the study of contentious mass politics not causal analyses of events but the attention to certain aspects of contention that other genres overlook, such as uncoordinated but still significant individual acts of passive resistance and hidden discursive forms of contention.

Organization studies are interested in radical organizations viewed as social collective units operating in particular contexts. The findings in Race (1972), Berman (1974), and Rutten (1996) accumulate the analytical and causal knowledge of insurgencies on strategy, organizational processes, and the reasons for their success or failure. An issue of central concern to researchers of this genre is the role of violence in the outcome of the struggle. Although both the government and revolutionaries used violence, Race (1972: 181) argues that the latter won because violence was used not as a military tactic but as an integral part of a comprehensive strategy of revolution. In this strategy, the revolutionary organization announced social policies that appealed to the class interests of most peasants; their support or at least sympathy caused a shift in the balance of social forces in favor of the movement. Once this shift had taken place, government suppression was only counterproductive. Berman (1974: 72–75) shows that coercion was important to draw peasants into the movement but that retention required positive attractions. Coercion was indirect: The revolutionary organization controlled the environment of village life and established authority to the extent that joining became what was expected of young people. Although both sides engaged in violence, government violence violated cultural norms and alienated people rather than generating their support. Elliott (2003: 5) agrees that terror was a main feature of the South Vietnamese insurgency and was effective at critical junctures but not sufficient to produce broad popular support. Rutten (1996: 150–152) also confirms a complex picture rather than a simple causal relationship between repression and rebellion in the Philippines.[47] Repression at one point prompted church activists and victims to rally to the movement but at another time narrowed the opportunities for mobilizers to solicit support and made people less willing to follow the movement out of fear. People's responses to repression varied depending on the place, timing, targeting, and type of repression.

Quantitative and Comparative works have generally concluded that the relationship between repression and rebellion is either linear (more repressive regimes, greater risks of rebellion) or curvilinear ("semi-democracies" experience the greatest risk of rebellion).[48] By focusing on the micro and meso levels of political events, Organization works are able to grasp more subtle causal mechanisms and the nuanced dynamics of the political process than are most structural Comparative studies.

As this genre turns to urban movements, it has borrowed a wide range of concepts from the democratic transition and social movement literatures. Nevertheless, except Boudreau (1996a, 1996b, 2001, 2004), who deeply and directly engages social movement theorists, students of Southeast Asian movements have not really integrated these borrowed concepts into their works. Instead, "high-risk activism," "frames," "contentious repertoires," and similar notions have more often been used as convenient metaphors and idioms (Rutten 1996; van Klinken 2001; Missingham 2003; Leheny 2005). This limited borrowing thus does not bear out some regional specialists' concern that the encompassing framework provided by social movement theorists has become the dominant language of Southeast Asian collective action at the expense of in-depth research. In none of these works have borrowed concepts substituted for careful analyses, although they do help the authors organize empirical materials and inject a comparative perspective into the analysis. As such, the use of a common set of concepts can make Southeast Asianists' works more accessible to a larger scholarly community without sacrificing the depth of research that has been the hallmark of the genre. For those studies that are able to combine careful analysis of the cases with a critical engagement with theories, there is the added benefit of contributing to theoretical building based on Southeast Asian cases.

Although knowledge accumulation has taken place, all the genres have experienced cycles of growth and exhaustion. The genre that achieved the earliest success, the Quantitative genre, was also the first to be exhausted. The success in formulating an "integrated theory" of relative deprivation based on the combined ontologies of modernization and functional-system theories (e.g., Gurr 1970) led to the wholesale abandonment of the project once those theories were discarded. The genre has experienced a recent revival thanks to the growth of rational choice theory. Yet many statistical modelers are still working in the tradition of relative deprivation without the explicit use of this theory.[49] They have not yet accepted the deductive premises of rational choice theory.

As I argue, the Comparative genre has been able to grow thanks to its conceptual and ontological fuzziness, which allows researchers to incorporate new cases and ideas into the general (originally structural) framework. The Comparative genre seems to have run its course as well. The most recent and ambitious work by Goodwin (2001: 5) is forced to justify at the beginning why "there needs to be *another* comparative study of revolutions" (emphasis in original). Goodwin (132) also admits that "there are now virtually as many theories as there are cases of social revolutions." Theories have been developed at an unsustainable rate: The proliferation of Comparative works in the past two decades has almost exhausted the available cases. Because most Comparative works rely on secondary sources and most make exhaustive use of these sources, there are few new findings expected if old cases are reopened. The ongoing expansion of the original structural framework to incorporate new factors also makes new studies less original and less differentiated from one another. The clearest evidence of this intellectual exhaustion is found in Goldstone's (2003: 76) ironical advice in his review of the genre that students of revolutions turn their focus to the causes of stability, the very opposite of revolution!

The Peasant genre has grown thanks to its ability to generalize the human experience from peasants under colonialism, to peasants under post-colonial capitalism and socialism, then to all exploited and oppressed classes or groups. Theories of exploitation, hegemony, and class consciousness have been exhaustively analyzed, with Marx and Gramsci being chided numerous times. The concepts developed about hegemony and resistance are still useful and will, of course, be further elaborated. But unless new theoretical orientations are found, the chances of the genre making major findings, as it did in the 1980s, may be small. Here the sign of intellectual exhaustion is also suggestive: The most creative researcher in the Peasant genre has turned to studying the state, the oppressor and exploiter of peasants in his earlier studies (Scott 1998).

The Organization genre has similarly exhausted its cases of communist insurgencies, which had mostly been defeated by the 1990s. However, there are now more urban social movements and new forms of radical organizations in Southeast Asia. The popularity of peasant and communist studies led to the neglect of urban movements in the region, with the important exception of the "people power" movements in the Philippines. Studies of old urban movements or new religious fundamentalist ones may break new theoretical and empirical grounds. The genre may also benefit from a boom in social movement theories that explain from cycles of protests to repertoires of collective action to cultural framing to social networks. These theories were first developed to explain politics in the West but are now widely applied in Third World polities. These theories not only allow researchers in the genre to study new phenomena but also offer tools to exhume old cases for reexamination.

In sum, there have been many reasons for exhaustion. Intellectual impulse (supply side) and intellectual interest (demand side) on the topic may run out (the cases of revolutions and communist movements). Knowledge resources, including cases (again, revolutions and communist movements) and sources of theoretical inspiration (e.g., Marxism and neo-Marxism), may be depleted. Theoretical frameworks may become too rigid to incorporate new information (the case of relative deprivation), or they may become too complex and vague to be original. The Quantitative and Organization genres are orienting toward new sets of theories and cases, but the Comparative and Peasant genres have not yet found new intellectual resources and inspiration for growth in the near future.

The historical development of the four genres in the study of contentious mass politics in Southeast Asia suggests that knowledge accumulation uses up knowledge resources. These resources include not only methodological tools and meta-theories but also cases as sources of fresh empirical data. One often hears warnings that too much "unconnected descriptive knowledge" has been produced (Mahoney 2003: 134). These warnings may undervalue empirical knowledge, or they may simply be based on a partial examination of a genre that is still growing. By studying several genres at the same time *and* over time in a particular area of research, this essay suggests that too fast and too much theorization also hurts in the sense of generating a rapid depletion of knowledge resources. To be sure, these resources can be replenished by theoretical and methodological innovations or borrowings that increase the extractive capacity of scholarship from the empirical world. Yet it must be acknowledged that such developments are unpredictable and often external to the genres.

Chapter Six

In-Depth Research and Knowledge Accumulation About Agrarian Politics in Southeast Asia

BENEDICT J. TRIA KERKVLIET

Introduction

Has in-depth research, which emphasizes qualitative data and analysis, enhanced our understanding of politics in Southeast Asia? Put simply, is such research useful? "Yes" would seem to be the obvious answer. Showing how is not so easy and is the task of this essay.

I focus on two topics regarding agrarian politics involving peasants and agricultural workers: rebellion and patron-client relations. For each I start from a "benchmark" composed of studies done as of the 1950s through the mid-1960s and then refer to what has accumulated since through in-depth studies. I hasten to point out that the literature drawn on here is limited to publications (mainly books) in English; the discussion would probably be different were materials from other languages included. Another limitation is that the cited publications by no means exhaust all that are available. I also stress that my purpose is not to compare the quality of the studies used here, but only to show how in-depth research can augment our knowledge.

Social science research that contributes to knowledge accumulation has two main characteristics.[1] One is that it interacts with work done before. That interaction may involve using and augmenting what previous studies did, but it need not be limited to that. It may criticize, correct, or even reject earlier studies. The point is that researchers are mindful of where their work sits in relation to what others have done. The second characteristic is that the research enriches our understanding through deeper or more comprehensive explanations. That enrichment can result from using more appropriate methodologies, analyzing new information and other material, applying or developing theories, or having a combination of these.

In-depth research refers to a type of qualitative investigation and analysis. It involves lengthy and intense immersion in the society in which the events and phenomena being studied occur. Often, even for subjects that happened long ago, in-depth research is done in the countries where the phenomena being investigated occurred or are still happening. Frequently, it involves living among people relevant to the topic. Second, it uses diverse means and methods to find information and gain insights. A typical combination is extensive interviewing and observing of people relevant to the topic, searching widely for documents and other written materials, gathering and analyzing numerical data, and searching for other sources of information (such as songs, films, photographs, and poetry) that might prove useful for understanding the phenomena. Typically, researchers know the languages relevant to the subject of investigation. Third, in-depth research tries to see the phenomena being studied from the perspectives of the people involved. Their perspectives become an important, though not the sole, part of the analysis as the researcher seeks as comprehensive an understanding as possible.

Although this chapter emphasizes the value of in-depth research, I am not saying it is the only way to study agrarian politics or other political phenomena. Qualitative research that is not in-depth, as found in many comparative studies, has its place; so do other methods and approaches, including quantitative ones. Whether in-depth research is appropriate depends on a researcher's questions and puzzles. It also depends on whether such research is possible. Constraints—such as government restrictions that forbid scholars from investigating particular topics, living in certain areas, or using archival records—affect what researchers investigate and the methods they use. In other words, the applicability of in-depth research depends on what one is trying to study and various practical considerations. When it is possible, in-depth research can add significantly to knowledge accumulation. Let me turn now to examples.

Rural Rebellion

To many social scientists as well as journalists and Western government officials writing about Southeast Asia in the late 1940s to mid-1960s, the region was "in turmoil," as the title of one of the more popular accounts put it (Crozier 1965). From the Philippines to Burma, violent upheavals were prominent on the region's political landscape. Given that Southeast Asian countries then were still largely agrarian societies, their rebellions and revolutions were primarily rural as well.

Although books on the phenomena were numerous, research was sketchy.[2] The materials on which analysts relied were usually not well referenced, and writers said little about their methods. Information in the studies apparently came from government pronouncements and accounts, newspapers, and secondary sources. Some writers drew on their experience as military men fighting the rebellions. The studies examined the rebellions and revolutions from a macro, often international level. They treated each rebellion or revolution primarily, if not entirely, as a single unit. Consequently, the studies say little about dynamics within the movements. Nor do they say much about the people who were rebelling and why they did so. The people they do mention are a few prominent leaders. Occasionally, writers showed an interest in knowing about lesser leaders and the nameless rebels but provided scanty information. Nevertheless, most studies posited that terror, coercion, and propaganda by radical leaders and organizations were the main reasons that rural people become involved.

The studies rarely engaged literatures about rebellion, revolution, and rural unrest beyond Southeast Asia. They did not use the comparative studies of revolution then available, such as books by Crane Brinton (1938) and George S. Pettee (1938), to query what was happening in Southeast Asia, nor did they use their findings to interrogate other scholars' generalizations. Nor did they show much interest in studies of the Communist Party and revolution in China, an obvious place to look for possible comparisons.[3]

Writers sometimes drew on previous scholars for information while augmenting previous findings with new material, practicing what James Mahoney calls descriptive knowledge accumulation. Rarely, however, did they engage the arguments of previous works. To the extent they did it was about the mix of nationalism and communism. Some early studies highlighted the importance of nationalism in struggles involving Marxists and communists in Southeast Asia.[4] By the late 1950s and early 1960s, however, many analysts framed the rebellions and revolutions in the Philippines, Malaysia, Laos, and Vietnam as communist movements. They either ignored nationalism—and, for the most part, other motivations or objectives—or claimed that communists used nationalist sentiments to advance their different agenda. Frequently analysts wrote about "nationalists" and "Marxists" (or "Communists") as distinct from and usually at odds with each other.[5]

Since the mid-1960s, political scientists and other analysts have done in-depth research that has expanded considerably our collective understanding of rebellion and revolution in Southeast Asia and contributed to the broader literature on those subjects. This does not mean consensus on all major issues or that all questions have been answered or even asked. It does mean that in-depth research has advanced knowledge to levels substantially higher than scholarship was before. Three advancements illustrate this.

The first is that in-depth research has taken us past the national and international view of rebellion or revolution and beyond seeing each as a unitary event or process. The beginning of this development is partly traceable to John Smail's study of the Indonesian revolution. Rather than focusing on what he called "Dutch-Indonesian relations," Smail took a local-level perspective to analyze what the revolution looked like and meant to people in Bandung, a city in West Java (Smail 1964).[6] Smail was engaging George Kahin's study (1952) of the Indonesian revolution done a decade earlier. Kahin's book was unusual for its time in that it emphasized what Indonesian revolutionaries did and why, and it drew heavily on their own writings and words, including numerous interviews that Kahin had done during his lengthy research in Indonesia.[7] But the book focused on the struggle between the Dutch and Indonesians, in particular on prominent leaders and their groups. Smail's study found another dimension of the revolution. In Bandung, according to Smail, the nationalist revolution and the Dutch were in the background. In the foreground was a struggle among Indonesians themselves over power, religion, status, and economic matters, all part of what Smail argued was a social revolution.

Since the mid-1960s, other scholars have done similar research.[8] They have looked at rebellion and revolution from the perspectives of various parts of a country and different groups and types of people—youth, women, gangsters, plantation workers, religious communities, among others. Usually their research involves finding new resources—previously unused documents and newspapers, interviews, and other conventional materials but also songs, poems, and other unusual sources. The studies show that rebellions and revolutions are far more complicated and less unified than research taking primarily a national or international perspective conveys. Such studies suggest that putting a single label such as "nationalist" or "communist" on a particular rebellion or revolution may bring a degree of understanding but is highly inadequate for characterizing what was going on and why.

Several studies of Indonesia's revolution in the 1940s, for instance, show that what occurred was a "series of largely autonomous regional revolutions. . . ." Whereas an independent Indonesia was a common goal, what people expected from it varied according to "traditions and changing social dynamics in each region" (Kahin 1985: 281–282).[9] Many ordinary Indonesians, especially peasants and workers, associated independence closely with egalitarianism, an aspiration not widely shared among participants from better-off walks of life. In-depth research on the Philippine revolution against Spain, Southeast Asia's first national revolution against Western colonial rule, and agrarian revolts that followed uncovered similar egalitarian sentiments among lower-class Tagalog revolutionaries—sentiments that propertied participants opposed (Ileto 1979: 144–154, 230–231).[10]

Different aspirations among participants relate to another complexity that in-depth research has found. The objectives and purposes espoused or sought by top leaders do not necessarily convey the main concerns and aims of lower-level leaders or ordinary participants and sympathizers. Among Muslim Filipinos involved in rebellions against the Philippine government during the 1970s–1990s, prominent leaders sought a new nation that would secede from the Philippines. However, local leaders and ordinary people were frequently dubious about such goals or even rejected them. They were more concerned with protecting themselves and communities against the harassment, aggression, and violence that Philippine authorities inflicted on them (McKenna 1998: 23–24, 195–196, 280, 286).[11] During the Huk rebellion (1946 to mid-1950s), several objectives of the Philippine Communist Party, which claimed to lead the uprising, were out of sync with the objectives and purposes of most Huk members and supporters (Kerkvliet 1977: 164–174, 223–229, 264–265).[12]

A second advancement resulting from in-depth research is a better understanding of people's reasons for supporting and joining rebellions and revolutions. Exceptional studies in the 1950s started to move toward more nuanced explanations. The research was not in-depth but did include talking to people who had been or still were involved in rebellions or revolutions. From interviews with former Huk members, Alvin Scaff concluded that although coercion and terror by "Communists" were factors in why people joined, those were less important than "agrarian issues" and that most people joined for a combination of reasons (Scaff 1955: 117–122). Lucian Pye's interviews with captured or surrendered people who had been in or close to the Malaya Communist Party during a rebellion in the early 1950s found that they were attracted to the party mainly because of their "rootlessness," being separated from their traditional ways, and their "quest for advancement and personal security" (Pye 1956: 128, 343, 354). Wilfred Burchett traveled in several provinces of northern Vietnam during the mid-1950s, along the way talking to peasants, coal miners, and other ordinary participants in the "people's war" against the French army. They fought, according to his account, mainly because of their anger against repression and abuse under the French and their strong desire for a better life (Burchett 1956).[13]

Repression and other gross abuses by government authorities turn out to be among the common reasons that villagers in Southeast Asia resort to violent rebellion. This is the finding of several in-depth studies done since the mid-1960s. In Malaysia, large-scale military operations and sweeps of towns and villages alienated Chinese residents and created considerable support for the guerrilla movement there in the late 1940s–early 1950s (Stubbs 1989b: 88, 90, 92).[14] In the Philippines, lawless and exceedingly violent actions by government authorities, its armed forces, and local elites contributed significantly to the growth of the Huk rebellion in Central Luzon in the mid-1940s, the New People's Army in central Mindanao and elsewhere during the 1970s, and the Bangsamoro rebellion in southwestern Mindanao in the 1970s–1980s (Kerkvliet 1977: 256, 260–262; Collier 2002: 284–285; Hawes 1990: 289–292; McKenna, 1998: 183–184, 191, 195–196).[15] In Vietnam's Mekong delta, the behavior of Saigon government authorities—arbitrarily arresting villagers, extortion, "draconian" actions against anyone suspected of opposition, and forcing people to reside in "Agrovilles"—instead of eliminating nascent rebellion in the late 1950s and early 1960s greatly accelerated it (Elliott 2003: 194–209, 865).[16] The authorities' main approach to governing, argues another study, continued to be "reinforcement," which among other measures included forcing people out of their homes to live in government-assigned locations, compelling people to join the government's army, using torture, and suppressing any opposition, all of which helped rebellion to grow (Race 1972: 155, 159–160, 180, 183–184).[17] Military destruction and killing, particularly the U.S. government's intensive bombing, also drove many people to support the National Liberation Front in southern Vietnam and the Khmer Rouge in Cambodia (Race 1972: 230, 235–236, 266; Kiernan 1985: 349–356, 390; Kiernan 1996: 16–25).[18] It might not be stretching the findings in these and other in-depth studies too far to say that terror by revolutionaries is relatively insignificant for explaining rebellion and revolution whereas terror by governments, especially their militaries, is a major factor.[19]

Revolt is often the last resort of people who have tried nonviolent methods to overcome harsh political, economic, and social conditions. Those conditions, the in-depth studies just referred to and others have found, are among the main underlying and often long-festering causes of rebellion and revolution. Studies published forty years ago paid little attention to such matters. Even in the late 1960s and early 1970s, numerous social scientists—and, more fatally, many U.S. government and military leaders—doubted whether people's miseries and their hopes of a better life were significant factors. Particularly disputed was whether land inequality, tenancy conditions for sharecroppers, working conditions for agricultural laborers, and other agrarian issues were important for understanding rebellions and revolution, especially in Vietnam. One influential social science study in 1968, for instance, showed through regression analysis that "Vietcong" areas of southern Vietnam were strongly associated with land ownership and relatively equal land distribution; Saigon-government-controlled areas were, in contrast, associated with tenancy and land inequality. The implication was that land inequality and other grievances regarding land use were not very relevant for understanding the revolutionary movement there (Mitchell 1968: 421–438).[20] However, in-depth research found that agrarian reform, especially a more equitable distribution of land, was a major aspiration among lower classes of rural Vietnamese and a chief reason that many of them supported or joined first the Viet Minh against the French throughout the country and later the National Liberation Front against the Saigon government and U.S. military in the southern half.[21]

In-depth studies in Vietnam and other countries in Southeast Asia have also refined our understanding of how agrarian conditions contribute to rural unrest and rebellion. Widespread tenancy, land inequality, or landlessness per se is not necessarily a causal factor. More telling are the conditions of tenancy and agricultural labor, which often cannot be assessed without close examination. For example, the fact that a large proportion of villagers were tenant farmers and agricultural workers could not account well for why revolt in lower Burma and volatile agrarian conflict in Central Luzon (the Philippines) occurred during the 1930s. More telling was the rapid deterioration of traditional patron-client relations between landlords and their tenants and workers. Suddenly, tenants could no longer get concessions or loans from their landlords, they had to pay higher rents, and a large proportion of villagers had no work (Adas 1974: 188–191, 200–203; Kerkvliet 1977: chapters 1–2).[22]

A third aspect of rebellion and revolution to which in-depth studies have brought greater understanding is the role of leadership and organization. A well-received argument in the mid-1960s and early 1970s put organization at the center of the explanation for how rebellions developed. Some who arrived at this conclusion did no in-depth research. They relied heavily on deductive reasoning, which started with certain premises about "rational" behavior. They stressed that bad living conditions exist in many countries but that rebellion and revolution arise only in some. The difference was the growth of organizations that take advantage of those conditions to create rebellion, even if a majority of people do not actually support it (Wolf 1966; Leites and Wolf 1970). Others gave more importance to people's living conditions but came to a similar conclusion about the centrality of organization and leadership by analyzing documents from the rebellions and revolutionary movements and interviews with former members, particularly former leaders.[23] Other researchers who did in-depth research, including in some cases living among villagers in the midst of Vietnam's revolution, dispute this heavy emphasis on organization and leaders as a causal factor. Yes, they essentially say, organization is important, but the big question is, what does the organization do, particularly in relation to rural people? The same can be asked of governments and their militaries, which are also organizations. A successful revolutionary movement addresses villagers' problems and in return attains support, new members, and a stronger organization.[24] By the same token, important to defeating rural rebellions is for governments to alleviate villagers' hardships, including drastically reducing repression (Stubbs 1989b: chapters 6–8; Kerkvliet 1977: 233–248). In-depth studies also find that leadership that helps villagers to link their views and concerns to broader ideas and structural problems and to see their experiences in ways compatible with revolutionary aspirations is also crucial for strengthening and expanding the revolutionary organizations (Rutten 1996: 110–153; Collier 2002: 150–153, 165–180, 229–233, 282).[25]

Virtually all in-depth studies on a particular rebellion or revolution in Southeast Asia done since the mid-1960s refer to earlier work and try to enhance and improve scholarship on it. They add, in short, explanations about what happened, why, and how. They have also contributed methodologically to knowledge accumulation. Far more than earlier studies did, they tell readers where their information comes from, reflect on the strengths and limitations of their sources, and demonstrate how to learn from and about those involved in the movements through interviewing them, living among them, and scrutinizing documents and other materials for evidence about events and processes inside and outside the rebellion or revolution as each evolved.

However, most in-depth studies published before the late 1970s did not compare their findings to other scholarship on rebellions and revolutions within or beyond Southeast Asia. Consequently, few of them directly contributed to generalizations and theories.[26] Since the late 1970s, that tendency has lessened noticeably. More scholars using in-depth methods now compare their findings to studies of other rebellions and revolutions in the region.[27] And several of them, by engaging debates in the social science literature, have made notable contributions to the general study of rebellions, revolutions, social-political movements, and related phenomena (Hawes 1990; Luong 1992; Rutten 1996; McKenna 1998; Collier 2002). For instance, Thomas McKenna tackles head-on the debate about the meaning of hegemony and the concept's value for explaining ordinary people's behavior and their involvement in ethnic and nationalist movements. His study of Muslim Filipinos in and on the fringes of armed separatist movements forcefully argues that hegemony has only modest value for explaining what ordinary people do and their relationships to authorities, and his findings reinforce scholarship elsewhere that subordinate people are frequently engaged in multiple forms and layers of resistance (McKenna 1998: especially chapters 1 and 11). Laced through David Elliott's stupendous study of war in southern Vietnam, from its historical origins until its end in 1975, is an argument that two major theories—moral economy and rational peasant—help explain why people join revolutions and why they remain involved, but even the two together are inadequate (Elliott 2003: 603, 686, 689–691, 1224–1226, 1234–1235, 1393–1398, and elsewhere).

One of the first to study rebellion or revolution in Southeast Asia using in-depth methods that deliberately sought to contribute to theory is Samuel

Popkin (1979).[28] Drawing on literature regarding collective action and decision making, he develops the "rational peasant" argument for why rural people supported and joined several movements in rural Vietnam, among them the Viet Minh and Communist Party. His theory emphasizes the strategic choices and calculations that peasants make individually as they weigh the political and economic pros and cons of being involved with religious and political organizations. Popkin's book takes issue with a "moral economy" explanation advanced by other scholars studying peasants and agrarian movements in various parts of the world. That theory stresses peasants' values and the economic conditions that make peasants angry, though not necessarily rebellious.

The most forthright and vigorous advocate of this moral economy interpretation is James C. Scott (1976). Although he is a Southeast Asianist and the book is primarily about agrarian societies in that region, Scott did not do in-depth research to write it. He did collect new documentary evidence about Vietnam and Burma, but primarily he drew on other scholars' studies regarding village life, agrarian conditions, rural unrest, colonialism, capitalism, and other subjects to develop an elegant argument. Both his argument and Popkin's rejoinder have become extremely influential in social science discourses on peasant societies and rural unrest, including recent quantitative research into "greed and grievance" motives for rebellions.[29]

Scott's use of secondary sources illustrates another contribution of studies based on in-depth research. Valuable theories often rely heavily on other people's in-depth research. Reinforcing this fact are several comparative studies that use examples from Southeast Asia to generalize about rebellion and revolution (Wolf 1969; Migdal 1974; Paige 1975; Adas 1979; Walton 1984; Rice 1988; Marks 1996; Goodwin 2001). Without other scholars' in-depth research on a range of agrarian topics (not necessarily limited to rebellion and revolution), authors of those comparative studies could not have included Southeast Asian cases and might not have been able to develop their generalizations.

Other Rural Politics

In addition to rebellions and revolutions, social scientists have paid some attention to other forms of politics involving Southeast Asian peasants and agricultural workers. Studies done during the benchmark period, the 1950s to the mid-1960s, emphasized elections and political parties and usually stressed the centrality of patron-client relations, a phenomenon that political analysts of other "developing nations" were then examining and anthropologists had been analyzing in Southeast Asia.[30] Votes and other forms of political support, the studies said, were mobilized primarily through factions, alliances, and other networks of patron-client dyads; political parties were unstable associations of factions and alliances built largely of numerous patrons and their clients (Hollnsteiner 1963; Landé 1965; Nash 1965: 77–78, 90–93, 279–280; Swift 1965; Phillips 1965; see also Wilson 1962 and Riggs 1966). Because patron-client relations and the alliances and other units they composed cut across class and status, these studies often claimed or implied that relations among people in different classes and status groups were generally harmonious. Consequently, the political landscape in rural Southeast Asia seemed to have peasants who were either rebels and revolutionaries or docile clients of landlords, faction leaders, and local elites.[31]

Several in-depth studies since the mid-1960s have found that the quality of patron-client ties and similar interclass relations helps to explain changes and continuities in rural communities. Some scholars, as noted earlier, showed that the breakdown in patron-client relations between landowners and tenants contributed significantly to rural unrest. Studies also indicate that the persistence of patron-client relations contributes to continuity at the local level despite considerable changes in the national political system. During both the Sukarno and the Suharto regimes in Indonesia, village politics in North Lombok and East Java continued to revolve primarily around people associating themselves "with a locally influential person, to become part of his following" (Cederroth 1991: 265–294).[32] In the southern Luzon provincial town of Batangas, Philippines, factions made up of a myriad of patron-client ties persisted before, during, and after the Marcos regime (Kimura 1997).[33] In some Cambodian villages, patron-client relations continue to be prominent, although in somewhat modified ways, despite the tumultuous upheavals that lashed the country in the 1970s–1980s (Ledgerwood and Vijghen 2002: 109–150).

In-depth research has also uncovered considerable complexity regarding the political importance of relations between people in different class or social strata. Some have found that patron-client ties and entourages are not the only or even the main feature of relations between superiors and subordinates. Often mixed with vertical linkages between wealthy and poor villagers, landowners and tenants, large landholders and small ones, employers and employees, and local officials and ordinary residents are linkages among people in similar class and status positions and antagonism between them and others holding different ranks in the social structure (Wolters 1983; Kerkvliet 1990; Peluso 1992).[34] Patron-client ties are but one aspect of complex class relationships. On the other hand, studies have found that political organizations featuring intraclass alliances may also involve members' other identities and relationships, including patron-client networks (Stoler 1995: especially 91, 209; Hefner 1990: 193–244).[35]

Several in-depth studies dispute the rather benign depiction in patron-client/factional analyses of political parties and alliances and how elections are won. Mafia-like organizations and political bosses, for instance, dominate elections, government offices, and public resources in Cavite and Cebu, two provinces in the Philippines. And they do it through fraud, skullduggery, intimidation, and violence, not networks of patron-client relationships (Sidel 1999).[36] Paying villagers for their votes is another factor in many rural areas of Southeast Asia. Research in central Thailand, for instance, found that money, rather than patron-client relations, has become the principal method for mobilizing villagers and rural townspeople to support and vote for candidates. In particular, candidates and their local advocates buy people's votes. Meanwhile, the idiom of patron-client relations remains. Politicians frequently talk as though they are patrons yet do not act as patrons, and some voters feel obliged, even though they are not clients, to reciprocate, as they would to a patron, by actually voting for the candidate giving them the cash (Arghiros 2001: 7–9, 92–94, 98–99, 124–125, 262–263).[37]

Issues are frequently important in elections, a finding that is incompatible with a patron-client/factional interpretation. One of the earliest in-depth studies of post-independence local politics in Indonesia found that concerns regarding land, religion, and the future of the nation significantly influenced votes and party affiliations among villagers and townspeople in northern Sumatra during the 1950s–1960s (Liddle 1970: chapters 3–4).[38] Whether personal relationships also figured in those Indonesians' electoral activities is not addressed in that study. But research in the Philippines shows that even though patron-client relations and factional loyalties are important considerations for rural voters, so are other matters, including their worries and discontent regarding living conditions, corruption, and other social, economic, and political matters.[39] In a Malaysian Chinese village, personal and clientelistic followings remained important in the 1970s, but local and national issues also aroused people to become involved in electoral politics (Strauch 1980: 213–239).[40] In Malaysia's state of Kelantan, personal followings were an aspect of how the Pan Malayan Islamic Party grew in the 1950s–1960s, but the party won elections primarily by attracting support among peasants. The party expressed, however imperfectly, many peasants' antagonisms against an old elite and their abiding concerns about land and its distribution (Kessler 1978: chapters 9 and 12).[41]

Besides showing that elections and political parties in rural Southeast Asia involve much more than patron-client relations and factions, in-depth research has revealed the political significance of the mundane behavior of ordinary villagers. Michael Adas was perhaps the first Southeast Asianist writing in English to take seriously such behavior when he analyzed "avoidance protests" by villagers in colonial Burma and Java (Adas 1981). The study draws out the political significance of peasants moving from place to place and doing other things arising from their discontent while avoiding clashes with their oppressors. Scott pursued the matter much further in an in-depth village study. Analyzing verbal remarks, villagers' characterizations of one another, people's recollections of past events, as well as pilfering, sabotage, and other "everyday forms of resistance," his research shows that daily life is rife with class struggle that only occasionally bursts into the open (Scott 1985).[42] Other in-depth research has investigated similar resistance elsewhere in rural Southeast Asia (Stoler 1995: 11, 61–62, 128–130, 160–161; several scholars' chapters in Scott and Kerkvliet [eds.] 1986; Kerkvliet 1990: chapters 5–6; Peluso 1992: 18–19, 70–71, 194–199; McKenna 1998; Oorthuizen 2003; Kerkvliet 2005).[43] Some of these studies demonstrate how resistance can feed into confrontational protest and rebellion. A few show that subtle, nonconfrontational resistance is part of a broader phenomenon of "everyday politics," which can significantly affect conventional politics and even national policies.

Most researchers investigating resistance, electoral behavior, patron-client relations, and the other political phenomena discussed in this section have related their findings to previous studies. Usually they build on or take issue with earlier work pertaining to the country they are studying. And these studies are frequently linked to work done elsewhere in Southeast Asia and beyond. Consequently, their research has fairly self-consciously tried to contribute both to knowledge claims about politics in particular places as well as to broader literatures and debates and thus to generalizations and theory. Perhaps the Southeast Asian literatures in this realm of research on politics most used by scholars studying other parts of the world and most prominent in theoretical debates are those regarding patron-client relations and everyday resistance.

Conclusion

In-depth research on agrarian politics of Southeast Asia illustrates the argument made in Chapter 1 of this book about the value of qualitative methods and analysis for advancing knowledge accumulation. Collectively and in several individual studies, in-depth research has contributed to theory. Its findings have nourished efforts, particularly through comparative analysis, to generalize about the causes, processes, and outcomes of agrarian revolts. Research on patron-client relations and everyday resistance has advanced social-scientific efforts to conceptualize and theorize class and status relationships in agrarian societies.

Our understanding of agrarian unrest and rebellions in the region and elsewhere has improved substantially compared to what scholars had produced in the 1950s and mid-1960s. In-depth studies have provided textured, nuanced, and deep comprehension of those rebellions and revolts examined in that earlier scholarship as well as of others that occurred in more recent decades. Additionally, through in-depth research we have a fuller understanding of rural political life in "normal" times, when villagers are not in the throes of turmoil and unrest. Patron-client relations are part of that political landscape but are not as predominant as benchmark studies of the 1950s and mid-1960s suggested.

Also emerging from in-depth studies is a better appreciation of peasants and agricultural workers' political outlooks and orientations. Benchmark literature on rebellion and revolution has little to say about the ordinary people who rebel and why they are up in arms. The few comments it does contain give the impression that villagers have little say in the matter. Villagers seem to be swept into the movements by the terror and propaganda of ideological leaders. Benchmark literature on other politics portrays ordinary villagers as being deferential to authority and other people in more powerful status or class positions. Research done since the mid-1960s, by trying hard to understand what ordinary villagers do and think, shows that such depictions are decidedly incomplete. The views and orientations of ordinary villagers in Southeast Asia are rarely so simple and straightforward. In-depth research finds that although people can be deferential and be pushed around, they can also assert claims to subsistence, better living conditions, and dignity. Villagers can get angry with duplicitous and hypocritical leaders. They can trace their poverty to abuses by wealthy people and exploitation. In-depth research also shows that outward appearances of subscribing to dominant classes and rulers should not be taken at face value. Even when joining organizations that reinforce the status quo, subalterns are not necessarily convinced (Bowie 1997: 283–286).[44] Peasants and agricultural workers are likely to have alternative values and ideas. And they are unlikely to subscribe fully to how people in superior positions depict them. In 1965 the Indonesianist W. F. Wertheim observed that societies are often composed of contentious views about how life is and should be. Frequently at odds with views prominent in the dominant classes are different convictions and outlooks among lower classes (Wertheim 1965: 26–37). Considerable research done since the mid-1960s has confirmed, elaborated, and given us a better understanding of those contending ideas and outlooks.

Chapter Seven

Civil Society and Close Approximations Thereof

MEREDITH L. WEISS

In line with larger disciplinary trends, questions related to the form, development, function, and impact of civil society have peppered works on Southeast Asian politics, especially since the mid-1990s. Although a core concept in political science, civil society admits of a gamut of definitions, from the broad area between the family and the state to precisely elaborated and far more specific mappings. The concept, in other words, remains poorly specified; debates about it are "both fascinating and unclear" (Kaviraj and Khilnani 2001: 1). Works on civil society in Southeast Asia have made at least four key contributions to these debates. First, studies of Southeast Asia affirm that civil society may be implicated in all sorts of political change, not just democratization. Second, these cases demonstrate that organizations based on ascriptive identities may constitute a core part of civil society. Third, studies of the region find viable civil societies in a range of regimes, not just in liberal democracies. Finally, this literature suggests that civil societal activism may transcend the borders of any given nation, even if it is the state that largely constitutes civil society. The present chapter cannot hope to offer definitive answers to intractable questions such as why variations persist in civil societies across the region. However, an analytically focused stock taking and synthesis may move the discipline closer to such insights, recommending ways to further such progress while validating continued attention to Southeast Asian cases and the methods commonly used to study them.

It will be helpful to begin with at least a working definition of civil society. Larry Diamond (1996: 228) offers a comprehensive and useful one:

> Civil society is . . . the realm of organized social life that is voluntary, self-generating, (largely) self-supporting, autonomous from the state, and bound by a legal order or set of shared rules. It is distinct from "society" in general in that it involves citizens acting collectively in a public sphere. . . . Civil society is an intermediary entity, standing between the private sphere and the state. Thus it excludes individual and family life, inward-looking group activity . . . , the profit-making enterprise of individual business firms, and political efforts to take control of the state. . . . [C]ivil society not only restricts state power but legitimates state authority when that authority is based on the rule of law.

Most definitions, including this one, presume a degree of democracy—freedom of assembly, for instance—as well as rule of law and exclude "uncivil" (for instance, violent or exclusionary) activity. Whether or not all Southeast Asian polities, few of which approach liberal democracy, could thus be said even to have a civil society is dubious. Unfortunately, as Kaviraj and Khilnani bemoan (2001: 4–5), "Actual political processes in the Third World are mostly very different from political life in the West; yet strangely, the language used to describe, evaluate, and express the experiences of politics are the same everywhere." I would argue that this language has become more nuanced and better informed over time, a shift in large part reflecting the influence of works such as those described here on Southeast Asia. Definitions such as Diamond's are still commonly glossed as "standard," but in practice, comparative politics has become more tolerant of variations on its themes as our knowledge has accumulated.

Still, many younger scholars in particular have been keen to disprove assumptions of Southeast Asian exceptionalism. It is true that state-society relations in Southeast Asia tend to differ from those in the Western states in which civil society was first "discovered." In Southeast Asia's post-colonial, developmental states, the middle class has been actively fostered by state policies and remains largely dependent on that state's good graces, the boundaries of the public and private sphere are more often porous than impermeable, and the state tends to exert more ideological and programmatic control than in democracies with a sturdier tradition of individualism. Yet civil society and/or its component organizations can develop and thrive even in "Asian democratic," semi-authoritarian, and free-market communist states, and this sphere may as well be indigenous as developed through mimicry of the West. This understanding is reached in part by eliding the terms of the debate—introducing some conceptual ambiguity for the purpose of expanding or recentering our understanding of a useful term. Unfortunately, these efforts have largely been conducted in isolation from important and clearly cognate work being done on other regions.

Until recently, studies of civil society in Southeast Asia were largely single-country case studies, using qualitative, especially ethnographic, methods and engaging with other case studies primarily just at the level of the literature review, if at all. In the past few years (and sporadically before then), there have been a few attempts to develop intraregional analyses, though not all these efforts have been particularly theoretically coherent or integrative. However, even the less theoretically informed single-country case studies in this literature do (or could, if read by a broader audience) play an important theory-building function. Works on Southeast Asia add to political scientists' understanding of civil society by disaggregating it, disrupting assumptions of a teleological progression from authoritarianism to democracy under its aegis, and pointing out how limited and limiting an understanding of civil society only as it appears in Western liberal democracies may be.

The discussion that follows makes no claims to being exhaustive, but rather offers a critical overview of landmark works and trends within the field in order to spotlight seminal contributions. My aim in the next section is to give a sense of the breadth and nature of the studies with which we are currently engaged, and of how civil society is understood in works on the region. I then go on to elaborate upon four domains in which works on civil society in Southeast Asia force an important theoretical and empirical shift away from the simplistic, Eurocentric conceptions of civil society that have been generally taken by political scientists as benchmarks—kinds of political change, identities engaged, regime type, and transnationalism. Finally, I conclude by assessing the level of engagement between Southeast Asianists and others in studying civil society and suggesting where we might go from here, conceptually and methodologically.

Studies of Civil Society in Southeast Asia: Concept (Re)formation

Its diversity of regime types and cultures, coupled with widespread evidence of societal organization and activism, makes Southeast Asia an excellent region in which to interrogate the parameters and significance of civil society.

Indeed, studies of civil society in Southeast Asia have not just built up our empirical knowledge of the region but have also at least begun to shore up middle-range theories. The fact that a simplistic understanding of civil society clearly does not reflect reality in this region advocates for a more carefully elaborated concept. Of course, Southeast Asian cases are not the only ones that add thus to this realm of comparative politics; it is unfortunate that conversation across areas is so generally muted. Theorists and specialists in other areas may hardly encounter works on Southeast Asia, given the general positioning of these texts within the literature,[1] and even Southeast Asianists may have limited exposure to work done on other countries in the region. All the same, meta-analysis of work on civil society in Southeast Asia suggests a significant degree of knowledge accumulation and theoretical elaboration over time. That contribution begins at the fundamental level of concept formation: The range of institutional and cultural cognates for civil society in the region mandates that we rethink our sense of the term and lays the ground for more targeted theoretical interventions.

CONCEPTUALIZING AND NAMING THE PUBLIC SPHERE

Attention to civil society blossomed with growing awareness of its apparent democratizing potential amid a rash of "third wave" regime transitions. Referring to democratization in South Korea, Poland, Chile, Nigeria, and elsewhere, Larry Diamond insists: "[T]o comprehend democratic change around the world, one must study civil society"—although he concedes that other forces matter as well (1996: 228). The organizations to which he refers are characterized by their attention to public rather than private ends, relation to the state, embrace of pluralism and diversity, and "partialness" (as no one association seeks to represent all society) (1996: 229–230). Diamond—a leading light in comparative politics, especially in the area of democracy and regime transitions—sets a high standard, and one that presumes a link, whether causal or correlative, between civil society and democracy. Works on Southeast Asia have challenged this standard by suggesting that states in the region boast what look like civil societies, but not always in the context of substantive democracy (and hence real autonomy of societal actors from the state, civil liberties, etc.) or democratization.

All these accounts are concerned with the public sphere. Habermas clarifies: "By 'the public sphere' we mean first of all a realm of our social life in which something approaching public opinion can be formed. . . . Although state authority is so to speak the executor of the political public sphere, it is not a part of it" (1974: 49). Some works speak explicitly in terms of a public sphere or civil society; others engage more obliquely with organizations that form and present "public opinion" as opposed to just "opinion" (Habermas 1974: 50). Indeed, some of the most significant works on this topic in the region hardly engage with the civil society literature. For example, Anthony Milner (2002 [1995]) examines the historical establishment of a public sphere in Malaysia without really speaking in terms of civil society operating therein. Similarly, several scholars ponder the limits of democracy in Malaysia and include some discussion of civil societal actors, but are more concerned with the nature of the state than of its comparatively weak antagonists (e.g., Barraclough 1985; Case 2001; Tan 1990). Other studies cover just specific sectors and are designed more to educate about particular issues or groups than to lay out a theoretical argument on civil society—for instance, regarding Malaysia, Nicholas (2000) on indigenous people's mobilization, Karim and Hamid (1984) on student activism, Tan (1997) on the Chinese education movement, Stenson (1970) on labor mobilization, and Weiss and Hassan (2003) on several key movements. Still, one may discern a shift over time toward greater terminological self-confidence: using concepts developed in a very different, Western context to refer to phenomena in Southeast Asia, but specifying what is meant by those concepts rather than sidestepping or warily obfuscating them.

Aiding this trend has been the combination of in-depth, single-case, qualitative studies and (increasingly) comparative volumes, including a selection of cases from across Southeast (and sometimes also South or East) Asia. Although the latter design tends to be more theoretically self-conscious, the former may contribute at least as much to concept formation and theory testing, and implicitly makes the case for inductive, qualitative work as necessary to concept development and refinement. The coverage of countries by single-case studies of civil society has been highly uneven—and much of what has been written has been quite clearly targeted at an area specialist rather than a disciplinary audience. The civil societies of Indonesia, the Philippines, and Malaysia have been quite well studied by anthropologists and historians as well as political scientists, whereas very little has been written about civil society (such as it is) in mainland Southeast Asia, apart from Thailand.[2]

Some of the first comparative works that stimulated thinking about civil society within the region were on political opposition generally—for instance, *Political Oppositions in Industrializing Asia* (Rodan 1996). Editor Garry Rodan presents a narrow definition of civil society: Civil societies feed into political parties, but social and political forces outside both formal politics and civil society may be central to political opposition. The expansion of civil society in many states is presented as a form of accommodation by the state to emerging social forces as part of a sequence of socioeconomic change and shifts in political opportunities. The volume engages usefully with modernization theories, positing through several country case studies (Thailand, Singapore, Malaysia) that diversification of social forces and elaboration of class structures with economic development may bolster the state more than civil society. Independent political spaces may thus be co-opted or abrogated, curbing the possibilities for both civil society and for the development of a coherent, politically transformative opposition.

At around the same time as this volume came a string of others homing in on nongovernmental organizations (NGOs), an approach dominant from the mid-1980s through the mid-1990s. Most were relatively mechanistic, empirically oriented progress reports on the status and functions of NGOs and related organizations. Most magisterial among these works is *Emerging Civil Society in the Asia Pacific Community*, edited by Tadashi Yamamoto (1995). Yamamoto's overview develops general themes on the formation of nonprofit sectors in the Asia-Pacific region, the significance of the growth of a middle class in promoting the development of civil societies, and the emergence of both national and transnational advocacy and resource networks. However, the country case studies themselves are generally atheoretical surveys of NGOs, research institutions, and philanthropic organizations. Sponsored by the Japan Center for International Exchange, Yamamoto's volume exemplifies the growing and pervasive interest in civil society on the part of a host of funding agencies and transnational institutions, from the Asia Foundation to the World Bank. As purveyors of funds, these groups influence not only the development of civil societal groups and programs but also research agendas. Still, however substantial, their influence is more often amorphous and indirect than clearly traceable or univalent.

By the late 1990s, more scholars of Southeast Asia were speaking and writing in terms of "civil society," even if doubtful of the concept's applicability.

These works gradually became more theoretically aware, reinventing the civil society wheel perhaps a few too many times with drawn-out literature reviews from the Scottish Enlightenment onwards, but at least trying to place Southeast Asia in a broader context (for instance, Hudson 2003). Even so, the aim of such examinations seems often as much to prove that the states of the region "fit" as to assert how distinctive these cases are and how much of a reevaluation of concepts they mandate. For instance, David Schak and Wayne Hudson's edited volume, *Civil Society in Asia* (2003a), aims to highlight identifying characteristics of civil society (used in the dubious singular [3]) in Asia and to determine whether and how civil society in Asia differs from its counterparts in Europe. The editors take it as a strength that the book "does not impose a single model of civil society on different and very diverse Asian countries." However, this flexibility may also be read as incoherence: Rather than all working within and elaborating upon the same general theoretical framework, only some chapter writers [4] take a more theoretically informed approach, and few make any explicit reference to the other cases and ideas in the volume.

Building on these prior initiatives is the more analytically coherent *Civil Society and Political Change in Asia: Expanding and Contracting Democratic Space* (Alagappa 2004e). Organized by regime type and framed by several theoretical and comparative chapters, contributions on Southeast, East, and South Asian cases offer convincing evidence of the significance of civil society organizations as political forces. The volume investigates "the state of the nonstate public sphere in Asia and the importance of civil society organizations relative to other domestic and international actors, and the specific functions and consequences of civil society organizations in promoting or preventing political change in the direction of open, participatory, and accountable political systems" (Alagappa 2004c: 8). Aside from weighing in on debates regarding the links between civil society and political change (discussed below), this volume also suggests an analytically useful definition of civil society "as a distinct public sphere of organization, communication and reflective discourse, and governance among individuals and groups that take collective action deploying civil means to influence the state and its policies but not capture state power, and whose activities are not motivated by profit" (Alagappa 2004c: 9). Moreover, rejecting the tendency in the civil society literature to focus on democratization per se, the volume considers all sociopolitical change "in the direction of open, participatory, and accountable politics," thus sidestepping the issue of whether the states in question are, or are becoming, "democratic" (Alagappa 2004c: 10).

COMPLICATING CIVIL SOCIETY

As these works suggest, the diversity of states and societies in Southeast Asia demands a complex treatment of civil society. An adversarial or otherwise transformative civil society is not necessarily to be found in every state in the region. Still, we do find public spheres populated by voluntary, reasonably autonomous, rule-abiding associations critically engaged with the commonweal, and organizing not just to benefit their own constituents. Garry Rodan cogently summarizes that while a flourishing civil society is not inevitable in Asian states, whether or not such a sphere emerges has more to do with state-business and state–middle class relations than with cultural predispositions, and aspirations for political change may be met as effectively by selective co-optation as by civil societal agitation. However, not all social forces are amenable to co-optation, nor are all East and Southeast Asian states equally able to support "alternatives to civil society" (1997a: 156–157).

Philippe Schmitter also asserts the diversity of Asia as a region. Asian societies, he argues, have a tradition of self-organization, despite diffusion of Western conceptions of civil society, state mediation of the public sphere (not least through state-corporatist arrangements), and the blurring of private/public lines. Moreover, unlike in Europe, in Asia it has been outside large urban areas that intermediary institutions have been most likely to develop; these institutions may not be autonomous with respect to primary and ascriptive social groups (1997: 251–259). Still, evidence seems to indicate that Southeast Asians may be simultaneously "ethnic" and "democratic" political actors (Saravanamuttu 1997: 8)—suggesting that we reconsider whether, as opposed to scholars such as Robert Putnam (1993), vertical networks *can* sustain trust and cooperation and build social capital.

Schak and Hudson (2003b) largely concur with Schmitter, with stronger empirical grounding. They propose that civil society in Asia needs to be understood in dynamic terms, as its strength waxes and wanes with larger political changes. Civil society is path dependent, and it manifests idiosyncratically across states. They find also that public and private spheres may be less clearly distinguishable in Asia than in Europe, as the state has played a more central role in the former in establishing civil society, and not just "autonomous non-state voluntary organizations" are included in Asian civil society (3–4). This finding directly contradicts the assertions of autonomy of organizations central to definitions such as Diamond's—the ones most commonly taken as authoritative within the canon of comparative politics—but brings the concept of civil society more in line with Southeast Asian reality, rendering it useful. Johan Saravanamuttu stresses this same point in his survey of civil societies across the region: They are weak compared to the state because they "have had their incipient features shaped primarily by the economic milieu engendered by a dominant state structure," rather than having grown organically out of politics (1997: 2).

As Rodan explains, "groups that exist outside the state have divergent values and agendas, not all of which are marked by political tolerance or liberal democracy. . . . [T]here is no inevitability that civil society will prove to be the most effective or common political accommodation . . . to the pressures for change from domestic populations" (1997a: 157–158).[5] Exemplifying this variety is Katherine Bowie's (1997) discussion of the mass-based, state-sponsored Thai Village Scouts, a quasi-fascist group that was pivotal in the anti-communist military crackdown of 1976. Bowie's narrative finds an obvious parallel in Sheri Berman's (1997) documentation of the fascist-supporting tendencies of German mass organizations in the Weimar period. However, in Berman's example, a nascent state could capitalize on social capital and organizational networks developed in civil society, whereas in Bowie's, the state (specifically, Thai intelligence) created a movement that later retreated into civil society. As Alagappa's definition suggests, in this region as others, groups are generally perceived to be outside civil society once brought into (or taking over) the state, and the methods of civil society organizations are at least predominantly "civil"—although these distinctions may admittedly be fine ones. Overall, then, Asian civil society may not be so consistently a force for democratization or so staunchly independent of the state as the literature presumes, yet may still be an important space, among others, for political engagement and transformation. This recalibration of the concept "civil society" should not be presumed to be Asia specific, but offers a clearer lens on the concept more generally in political science.

Interactions with Political Science

The conversation between Southeast Asianists and political science has been disjointed, but not absent. Asia has been less central than Europe (Western, Central, or Eastern) or Latin America in the literature on civil society—and when engaged at all by nonarea specialists, Southeast Asia tends to be lumped with East Asia or "the developing world," or taken as a homogeneous unit. Schmitter's "Civil Society East and West" (1997) is a case in point: Although he deems the contrast between Asian and European civil societies a "potentially novel contribution" (250) and asserts that Asian cases defy generalization, he oversimplifies to the point of caricature. More generally, presumptions about "Asian values," the prevalence of Confucianist or Islamic orientations, and the persistence of nondemocratic or illiberal democratic regimes in the region have seemed to exclude Southeast Asian cases from the mainstream.

Certain debates simply have not really been engaged by Southeast Asianists, even though vital to larger discussions within the discipline. This rift may stem from the empiricist orientation of so much of this literature in the region: Some concerns seem more pressing in the abstract than on the ground. Faced, for instance, with an antagonistic state and grappling for space, activists may be less concerned with absolute autonomy when they can achieve more through strategic cooperation with the state. Issues of whether groups based on ascriptive identities should be considered part of civil society or can generate social capital, or whether violent means may at times be found in civil society, likewise tend to be taken for granted or defined out of consideration by the preemptive setting of relatively inclusive parameters (for instance, Alagappa 2004e). However, studies of civil society in Southeast Asia have contributed particularly to four core debates in political science: examinations of processes of political change, the role of religious organizations as nonstate political actors, the varieties of associational life to be found across regime types, and the nature of and potential for transnational activism. These studies highlight how we might reconceptualize civil society to make it more relevant to and reflective of non-Western experience. Their theory-building significance is less apparent when taken singly; only a more synthetic approach makes it clear how far these studies have advanced our knowledge and challenged common assumptions.

CIVIL SOCIETY AND POLITICAL CHANGE

Of particular prominence in political science today are studies of the role of actors from civil society in promoting various sorts of political change. Regime transitions in Central and Eastern Europe helped to jump-start this field of inquiry (for instance, Weigle and Butterfield 1992; Ekiert and Kubik 1998), as political scientists pondered whether mass protests represented contingent, singular episodes or something more enduring and broadly transformative. Studies of Latin America (for example, Oxhorn 1994; Alvarez 1990), Africa (Chazan 1992), and China (notably Chamberlain 1993; Wakeman 1993; and the rest of that special edition of *Modern China*) also explored civil society as an agent for change and largely deemed civil society a necessary and perhaps even sufficient prerequisite for democratization. As sociologist John Hall notes, "we value democracy in large part because we expect it to be married to civil society" (Hall 1995: 26–27). Certainly, not all Southeast Asianists have been immune to the tendency to construe civil society as an agent for democratization above all (e.g., Uhlin 1997), yet works on the region present a far wider range of reforms to which civil society may contribute.

Works on Southeast Asia bear directly on the issue of what types of changes that civil societal engagement may effect and represent significant contributions to the debate. The aforementioned volumes by Schak and Hudson and Alagappa are especially germane. The theoretical thrust of the former is toward asserting the diversity of forms and trajectories to be found among civil society organizations. The latter volume reiterates this stance and makes a strong case as well for the varieties of political change that activism may bring about: institutional and cultural, liberal democratic and not.

An array of more focused works also highlight this point, suggesting the relevance of Southeast Asian cases for untangling the role of civil society in promoting political change apart from establishment of full-scale liberal democracy. For instance, a major theme of Duncan McCargo's *Reforming Thai Politics* (2002) is the variety of meanings of "political reform" available: urging democracy, a yen for technocracy, limiting patronage and corruption, or transformation of sociopolitical relations. Along with this more nuanced understanding of reform comes a broader conception of what constitutes civil societal engagement in reform processes, for instance, as elaborated in Ockey's comparison in the volume of civil society, politics, and political reform in Thailand in the 1950s and the 1990s (Ockey 2002).

Still, the experience of activism in several Southeast Asian states suggests that civil society may be relatively impotent, even where organizations exist and have at least some space for maneuvering. For example, Kerkvliet explains that while we can identify an emergent civil society in Vietnam, it remains highly constrained. Increasingly, individuals and groups in Vietnam organize around and advocate for their issues and interests, in a civil and tolerant way, and in the context of enabling institutions, laws, and communications media. All the same, Vietnamese civil society organizations are not allowed to criticize Communist Party leaders or officials, the military, and the like, and thus cannot be unreservedly "political" lest they lose what space they have (Kerkvliet 2003: 15–16). Likewise, David Brown and David Martin Jones find that in Singapore, the dominant party regime has successfully co-opted and accommodated the middle class, thus averting the possibility of bourgeois demands for political participation and liberal values. An overriding concern with protecting one's hard-earned middle-class status, coupled with a culture of deference for authority and preference for technocratic management, has rendered the process of democratization in illiberal democratic Singapore "the expansion of political participation and consultation within the limits defined by the state" rather than the project of an adversarial civil society (Brown and Jones 1995: 84; also Jones and Brown 1994).

Jones later expands this argument, puzzling out just what the character and political role of the new middle class are in East and Southeast Asia and how studies of the region expand our theoretical understanding of the links among economic development, civil society, and political liberalization. He finds that a "modular civil society"—one premised on the differentiation of political and socioeconomic spheres—is not emerging in the region. Rather, "political change reflects a conservative, managerial strategy to amplify political control by forging a new relationship with an *arriviste* middle class" (Jones 1998: 163). Puzzled by this same phenomenon, Gillian Koh and Ooi Giok Ling propose a different solution, one suggested by the Singapore government's own differentiation between *civic* and *civil* society. They posit "two unequal halves of civil society in Singapore": one composed of reformist organizations aligned with the state and the other of independent organizations with potentially competing views (Koh and Ooi 2000: 74). This formulation encapsulates and effectively builds upon the findings of previous studies of Singapore and of civil society by interrogating what sort of power or influence civil society organizations have or seek, and what sort of political change they may engender.

Several studies of Malaysian politics propose a central role for NGOs in both electoral and informal politics, rendering the state more democratic in practice than its institutional constraints (meek judiciary, curbed press, etc.)

might suggest. For instance, Francis Loh (2003) argues that Malaysians disillusioned with political parties and electoral politics have the option of engaging instead in informal politics. What has made this option possible, he suggests, is the proliferation of NGOs since the 1980s and their increasing political importance since the late 1990s. Not only do these organizations offer venues for participation outside the channels of electoral politics, but the engagement of civil societal organizations with opposition political parties also helps "to enrich those parties as well as hasten the process of political reform" (Loh 2003; also Weiss 2006). As Saliha Hassan (2002) warns, however, to be truly effective in expanding the space for democratic participation, NGOs need to beware of both exclusionary tendencies and state co-optation.

Similarly, Gerard Clarke's impressive *The Politics of NGOs in Southeast Asia: Participation and Protest in the Philippines* (1998) explores the ways in which NGOs simultaneously strengthen and weaken civil society, how collaboration with NGOs has fortified the state in small but significant ways, and how NGOs have expanded political participation. Through in-depth analysis of the Philippines (and less-comprehensive treatment of the rest of the region), Clarke also notes that NGOs may simply poach members from more radically activist (and even more effective) civil societal organizations rather than drawing new participants into political struggles, may bolster as well as check the power of the state, and may stand in for inadequately representative political parties and the decline of class-based, left-wing movements.[6] Hence, this work also forces us to disaggregate "civil society" in order to understand and evaluate its aims and impacts, as these may vary across organizations.

Finally, a range of works on Southeast Asia have contributed to the literature on civil society and political change by considering not just the varied intended effects of engagement, but also the novel ways in which this influence may manifest itself or be understood. Most works on civil society consider the sorts of autonomous advocacy organizations that Diamond describes and assume that a rather straightforward analysis is both possible and adequate. Works on Southeast Asia highlight the need to read between the lines in understanding civil society—to seek out the hidden transcripts (Scott 1990)—especially where the media are constrained, and for citizens to develop innovative and often contained rather than transgressive strategies for protest (see McAdam, Tarrow, and Tilly 2001).

Two examples are William Callahan's *Imagining Democracy: Reading "The Events of May" in Thailand* (1998) and his comparative study, *Pollwatching,*

Elections and Civil Society in Southeast Asia (2000). In the first of these texts, Callahan underscores the significance of interpretation: How we understand the influence of civil society on political change depends substantially on who tells the story. Given that in Southeast Asia as elsewhere, the rise of social movement organizations has been accompanied by a proliferation of electronic and other media, this narrative analysis broaches an important set of questions: How do we as researchers understand the inspirations or aims of protest, what are the dimensions of conflict, and what sort of change is effected by activism? Albeit an empirically rich analysis of a particular contentious episode in Thailand, Callahan's work makes a key methodological contribution in demonstrating the use of discourse analysis as a tool for understanding political processes and the importance of careful evaluation of sources.

In the latter text, Callahan considers the significance of election monitoring as part of broader movements against political corruption and in contributing to the development of alternative political cultures. As he explains, Thailand's 1995 PollWatch "does not quite fit into the standard categories" and "both confirms and calls into question hegemonic understandings of civil society" (2000: 79). Callahan sees election monitoring organizations as critical to developing a sociopolitical infrastructure, fostering a more democratic political culture, and transforming election campaigns into mass movements (2000: chapter 6). Although the theoretical implications of the work could be more carefully elaborated—and could go far toward bridging the segregated literatures on elections and on civil society—Callahan's text sheds light on the dynamic interplay between political reform and civil society and on an understudied but critical element of the latter. These extensions become all the more obvious when the work is read in tandem with, for instance, Clear (2000) and Hedman (1998). The former traces the extent and impact of foreign funding for democratization assistance in Indonesia, and the latter uses a structured longitudinal analysis of the Philippines to explore how mobilization of citizens for free elections occurs, foregrounding especially preexisting social networks and changes in the transnational context.

All in all, then, especially when considered in quantum, works on Southeast Asian civil society clearly indicate that civil society should not be presumed a force just for democracy, that less than fully autonomous organizations cannot simply be written out of the sphere, and that we need to take a broad view in identifying and evaluating the diverse forces within civil society in a particular context.

RELIGIOUS ORGANIZATIONS AND CIVIL SOCIETY

Mainstream theories of civil society tend to privilege organizations premised on voluntaristic rather than ascriptive criteria, and are oriented along horizontal rather than vertical lines. As such, religious organizations are deemed lacking in pro-democratic potential. Emblematic of this tendency is Robert Putnam's famous study of why democracy "works" in northern but not southern Italy, in which he cites the social capital nurtured in secular, horizontal associations, but not in affiliates of the Catholic church (Putnam 1993).[7] And Ernest Gellner (1994) insists that Islamic societies cannot support a civil society at all. Such societies, he argues, are too clientelistic and supranational in orientation (more focused on the Islamic *ummah* than on the nation-state) to be conducive to development of a civil society, and the people judge their rulers "by applying the religious norms of sacred law, rather than the secular principles of a Civil Society" (Gellner 1994: 22). On much the same lines, studies of Asian political cultures tend toward reductionism, presuming that a Confucianist or Islamist legacy leaves Asian citizens happy to accept strong, authoritative regimes and limitations on the individual rights associated with liberal democracy (for instance, Bell et al. 1995; Pye 1985).

Works on civil society in Southeast Asia challenge these assumptions. First, studies of Indonesia, the Philippines, and Malaysia in particular suggest the clear democratic potential of certain sectarian associations. More broadly, the variety of political predilections and traditions of civic engagement revealed by a close examination of states in the region belies simplistic formulations of deferential, authoritarian political culture, even if Western-style liberal democracy seems less common and culturally accepted than a communitarian variant (see Chua 1995). However, what complicates comparison both within and beyond the region is the rather atheoretical bent of much of this research—as well as its neglect by so many specialists on Islamism in the Middle East, even though Islam is a primary ascriptive identity invoked in these debates and the implications of this identity are certainly open to comparative treatment.

Generally speaking, Southeast Asia's Muslim societies do not fit the pattern that Gellner describes.[8] Most notable in asserting this point is Robert Hefner's *Civil Islam: Muslims and Democratization in Indonesia* (2000). Hefner characterizes Indonesia as having an emergent discourse of an Islamic state as supporting "democracy, voluntarism, and a balance of countervailing powers in a state and society" (2000: 12–13). Much as Anthony Milner (2002 [1995]) posits that Islamists, royalists, and nationalists all converged in early-twentieth-century Malaysia on a common sense of a democratic accountability and "politics," Hefner also speaks of the emergence of a Habermasian public sphere in Muslim Indonesia. He notes the multiple political possibilities associated with Islam, but highlights one of these as especially relevant to Indonesia: "civil pluralist Islam." As he notes,

> In embracing the ideals of civil society, this democratic Islam insists that formal democracy cannot prevail unless government power is checked by strong civic associations. At the same time, . . . civil associations and democratic culture cannot thrive unless they are protected by a state that respects society by upholding its commitment to the rule of law. (2000: 13)

Evoking the lessons on civil society and regime type discussed in the next section, Hefner faults the predations of the New Order regime rather than Muslim culture for the stuntedness of civil society in modern Indonesian history (2000: 215).[9]

Writing on Malaysia, Vidhu Verma takes a somewhat different perspective on the relation of Islam to civil society. She acknowledges the work of civic associations in developing civil society and notes that both Islamic and secular symbols are manipulated in the struggle for democracy, but concludes (apparently presuming a democratizing function of civil society), "Malaysia's democratic potential depends upon its society's rich precedents regarding tolerance and civility. Thus the emergence of independent sites of protest against authoritarianism does not imply the transition to a strong civil society" (2002: 7). Like Hefner, Verma faults the nature of the state—its institutional framework, its sponsorship of countervailing organizations, and the greater priority given to religious communities than to civil liberties—more than political culture for the weakness of civil society. The dominant position of the Malaysian government, and not the prevalence of Islam, has prevented civil society from developing an "autonomous space" from which to "empower citizens" (193–196).

Furthermore, studies—especially of Malaysia, but also to a lesser extent of Indonesia—detail a specifically Islamist variant of civil society: *masyarakat madani*, or a society modeled on that of Madinah in the time of the Prophet Mohammad and marked by high moral standards, self-sufficiency, civic consciousness, and consensus-building sociopolitical debate (MINDS 1997; Verma 2002: especially 5–7). This concept remains more an academic one than a term of common parlance; it sometimes serves just as a translation for civil society rather than being seen as something distinctive (e.g., Hikam 2000; Panggabean 2000). Regardless, these works add to the literature on civil society by mining non-Western contexts for indigenous forms and conceptions of the sphere, thus directly refuting the Europeanist bias of dominant theories and enhancing our sense of the concept.

CIVIL SOCIETY AND REGIME TYPE

Given the sheer variety of regimes in Southeast Asia, considered across either states or time, both in-depth case studies and cross-regional surveys offer real contributions to the literature on civil society in different contexts. Indeed, works comparing the emergence and attributes of civil society across regime types within Southeast Asia present an important new frontier, still substantially unexplored (but see Alagappa 2004e). Definitions of civil society generally presume the sort of regime in which voluntary organizations are free to form, meet, and express critical opinions, and in which the state is not overly intrusive or coercive (e.g., Diamond 1996; Hall 1995; Schmitter 1992). By demonstrating that civil society–like spaces persist even in far less conducive environments, studies of Southeast Asia confront the question of whether the existence of a civil society presupposes a particular sort of regime and investigate how it looks under others. Along these lines, Schak and Hudson (2003b), for example, point out that the late development of modern states in Asia and the different functions (for instance, with regard to public welfare) of those states compared with European counterparts implicitly expand the debate as we see those civil societies in perspective.

Some of the best-theorized such works are the comparative chapters of multi-country volumes. For instance, Kevin Hewison and Garry Rodan (1996) point out that although conventional wisdom would associate a vibrant civil society with advanced economic development, the reverse is often true in Southeast Asia. There, emerging business and middle classes constitute a force for moderation, prompting the narrowing of space for the political left and for independent political activity more broadly. The contributors to that volume trace out these linkages—for instance, James Jesudason's discussion of Malaysia's "syncretic state" as "a particular historical-structural configuration that has allowed the power holders to combine a broad array of economic, ideological, and coercive elements in managing the society, including limiting the effectiveness of the opposition as a democratising force" (1996: 129).

Other authors conclude much the same, for example, by positing a *civic society* rather than a civil society (with the latter more an arena for political action to challenge state power) in tightly managed Singapore and elsewhere (Saravanamuttu 1997: 8; Rodan 1997a: 162; Koh and Ooi 2000). Even amid legal restrictions and a degree of ideological hegemony, however, voices may emerge from civil society to engage government agencies in debate, even if with limited or veiled effect. In fact, as Chua Beng-Huat describes, citizens may determine that their best chance for efficacy is by working within rather than against state structures—for instance, choosing to express dissent via feedback to a generally effective and appreciated state rather than by supporting opposition parties or adversarial NGOs. This possibility, most obvious in Singapore, suggests a very different state–civil society dialectic than the liberal democratic one most common in the literature (Chua 1995: 203–212; also Koh and Ooi 2000).

The limitations on civil society's reformist potential in such a state are explored further in Tan Boon Kean and Bishan Singh's *Uneasy Relations: The State and NGOs in Malaysia* (1994). The authors cite the "interventionist role of the state" (1994: 13) as the major issue facing Malaysian NGOs. The state is not merely coercive—though it curtails a range of civil liberties—but it has also effectively co-opted many groups and activists. Moreover, the pervasiveness of state power and patronage has served to fragment NGOs' efforts, and the partisan spin placed on opposition has rendered the state more resistant to policy demands originating in civil society but echoed also by opposition parties. The inability of interested parties to influence policies affecting them, Rodan suggests, is a sign of the limited capacity of civil society as a force for political liberalization (1997a: 157). Still, Sheila Nair posits that the fact that these challenges are broached at all represents a symbolic threat to existing political institutions and implies the rise of new, noninstitutional politics: "[I]t is not the policy 'successes' but rather their politics which matter" (1995: 267).

Amid burgeoning interest in the theme in the 1990s, Indonesia's New Order regime informed a number of studies on the potential for a civil society to develop and function under conditions of near-authoritarian rule. Two of the most substantial of these studies are Muhammad A. S. Hikam's *Demokrasi dan Civil Society* (1996) and Philip Eldridge's *Non-government Organizations and Democratic Participation in Indonesia* (1995). The former book analyzes Indonesia in the context of Latin American bureaucratic authoritarianism and Eastern European democratization, determining the extent to which Indonesia fits theories derived from those sets of cases. Hikam makes less conscious an effort to revise extant theory than to suggest where Indonesia falls short— for instance, in the fact that intellectuals in Indonesia have grown increasingly elitist and exclusive over time, precluding the sorts of pro-democratic coalitions previously possible there and central to changes in political culture and institutions elsewhere (Hikam 1996: 214–215). Overall, he concludes that capitalist penetration, industrialization, urbanization, modern education, and rising political consciousness among elites and in modern social organizations since the early twentieth century have fostered a civil society in Indonesia, but its path has not been clear. The period of Guided Democracy under Sukarno, for instance, rendered mass mobilization a means to legitimate rather than to contest the regime, and the political significance of the new middle class that developed under the New Order was dampened by its dependence on the state and resilient primordial ties, as well as by the strength of the state itself.

Philip Eldridge (1995; also 1990, 1996) homes in on that last phase, surveying the subcutaneous political activity of New Order NGOs, which aimed to strengthen society as compared to the state, regardless of orientation and public profile. Reinforcing Nair's point about noninstitutional politics, Eldridge argues that "[i]t is misleading to see only actions designed to confront power structures or capture the levers of governmental power as 'political'"; any enhancement of the capacity of less-advantaged groups to engage on more equal terms with state agencies and other forces falls within the same rubric (1990: 503–505). Although NGOs might not have forced much of a political opening, they did open up the debate and encourage political participation. All the same, that influence should not be exaggerated, especially if the nondemocratic setting raises expectations that NGOs can simply substitute for the lack of independent political parties, trade unions, and the like. Walker (1996) also explores the enormous range of NGOs and government-organized NGOs (GONGOs) in New Order Indonesia, detailing their historical precedents, environment, characteristics, and foci, and reaches conclusions similar to Eldridge's. NGOs as of the mid-1990s could report a "negligible" record of influencing government policies and structures, but Walker still optimistically opines that their activity was "bound to raise the consciousness of the village population in Indonesia," even if it might "take a while for this to translate into community empowerment" (19–20).

More comprehensive is *State and Civil Society in Indonesia*, edited by Arief Budiman (1990), which considers ways in which Indonesia's economy, state, and civil society had changed and the interactions among these dimensions of change through the 1980s. Budiman's introduction traces the simultaneous rise of neoliberal economics and civil societal activism, such that portions of both the elite and the masses supported democratization, whether to bolster their own position or to gain access to the system. Subsequent chapters do not all carry forward this theme, but explore specific aspects of nonstate political engagement—for instance, Zifirdaus Adnan's chapter on the ways in which Islamist activists redirected their efforts (for instance, adopting a less overtly "political" cultural approach) in light of the New Order state's intolerance of Islamic political ideology; or Philip Eldridge's, on the ways in which NGOs adopt a similarly "apolitical" public profile but then perform politically significant tasks of social organization outside state structures.

Other works are likewise empirical and targeted at area specialists but still constitute remarkable contributions to our knowledge of Indonesia and the region, and of how civil society might emerge and function in a nondemocratic regime. Two examples are Edward Aspinall's working paper, "Student Dissent in Indonesia in the 1980s" (1993),[10] which offers a nuanced, historically informed argument about why students engaged as they did in Indonesian politics, but makes only a limited effort to link this discussion with a larger theoretical debate; and Michele Ford's work on the place of NGOs within the Indonesian labor movement (for instance, Ford 2000). Taken as a whole, these studies of civil society and its organizations in relatively stable, semi-democratic to authoritarian regimes substantially supplement a literature that grew out of works on consolidated liberal democracies or states in the process of attaining that status, and should be of interest to political scientists beyond area specialists.

TRANSNATIONAL CIVIL SOCIETAL ACTIVISM

Studies of Southeast Asian cases have also contributed significantly to the burgeoning literature on transnational activism. The links between civil society and the state would seem to suggest that civil societies are confined within nation-state boundaries. Civil society both legitimates and restricts state authority—and it is not clear what transnational political entity might create the space and rules for a transnational civil society (see Rudolph 1997: 2). A growing body of work on Southeast Asia, only some of it explicitly engaged with ASEAN as a transnational organization, takes as a given the fact that transnational civil societal organizations exist, engage in political discussion and advocacy, and even foster aterritorial national identities (Parreñas 2001). Such studies force us to rethink both our use of concepts and the interplay between state and civil society.

Previously, this work mostly took the form of investigations into the activism of nonindigenous groups in Southeast Asia, most notably "overseas Chinese" (for instance, the discussion of Chinese nationalist activism in Heng [1996]). More recently, works on Southeast Asia have contributed explicitly to the nascent field of transnational advocacy networks and social movements.[11] Two of the leading participants in this endeavor are Nicola Piper and Anders Uhlin. Uhlin's *Indonesia and the "Third Wave of Democratization"* (1997) offers an exceptionally careful elucidation of the sources of, adherents to, and impacts of various imported influences on pro-democratic discourses in Indonesia.[12] This volume both predates the more recent rash of attention to the border-crossing potential of civil society activism and focuses more explicitly on discourse than most empirically grounded works on civil society, suggesting a fruitful, but difficult, approach to studying social movements.

In a different vein, Piper and Uhlin's collaborative work on East and Southeast Asian female labor migration adds a feminist analysis of the implications of neoliberal economic globalization and engages directly with the theoretical literature on transnational advocacy networks and political opportunity structures. In fact, the authors define their objective as not primarily empirical, though based upon a strong grasp of the details, but as an effort "to bring political economy and politics into migration studies" through an investigation of state interventions and transnational NGO activism (Piper and Uhlin 2002: 174). Their work adds to understandings of transnational activism in its explicit attention to gender—specifically, how the position of women in the global economy and as transnational activists is mediated by their differential access to political opportunities and resources.

Drawing together some of these strands on transnational influences, power relations, and potential for civil society activism is Piper and Uhlin's edited volume, *Transnational Activism in Asia: Problems of Power and Democracy.*

The book combines four empirically driven chapters on Indonesia, Malaysia, Singapore, and Taiwan with six theoretically oriented chapters—an unusual, but useful, balance for such a work. The editors describe their objective as "contextualizing transnational activism within broader power structures between state and civil society organizations as well as between non-state organizations, and . . . providing an analysis of how this is related to problems of democracy," with reference to East and Southeast Asia as regions understudied in the literature (Piper and Uhlin 2004: 1). Piper and Uhlin's introductory chapter is an excellent critical entrée into transnational activism theory and ways in which to frame and to understand cross-border, nonstate initiatives.

The other chapters, especially the empirical ones, form a less coherent whole: The "theory" chapters hover at an abstract level, and the empirical chapters generally fail to engage meaningfully with the theoretical literature or with comparative cases outside the region. Still, Keck's discussion of "discursive representation" (the representation of issues rather than individuals in international governance regimes) or Smith's on efforts at democratization at a global level fall squarely within a theory-building tradition; the empirical chapters address questions such as when transnational networks do and do not develop, or why activists engage in domestic versus transnational endeavors; and Piper and Uhlin's introductory chapter helps to tie these perspectives together. All in all, these works move beyond empirical descriptions to sustain and inform ongoing theoretical debates about whether we can identify an enduring, potentially efficacious transnational civil society.

Methods and Approaches

Work on civil society in Southeast Asia has generally rested squarely within a political science tradition. Central questions have concerned power: how disadvantaged actors can effect political change, means of achieving policy influence, and so forth. Yet methods and approaches tend to be interdisciplinary in key ways, as in their reliance on ethnographic methods and a tendency to take history seriously. In challenging too-simplistic definitions of civil society, works on Southeast Asia argue for a dynamic, context-specific approach (probably requiring qualitative research) and maintenance of "proper nouns" if aspects of civil society are to be understood and evaluated meaningfully.

Furthermore, much work on Southeast Asian civil society grows out of the authors' personal, activist involvement with the region, regardless of their academic roots. As Heryanto and Mandal explain of their volume,

> The central questions it raises and the answers it attempts to offer do not descend directly from the exogenous logic and imperatives of academic production from outside the societies it studies . . . [but] from years of personal practical engagements, grounded analytical reflection, serious doubts, and a series of intellectual dialogues with Western-based social sciences and humanities. (2003a: 15)

This tendency may privilege indigenous over external observers, but it also validates a wider range of voices than generally heard in political science work.

The methods used in almost all these studies have been qualitative, reflecting a commitment to various forms of "thick description" among area specialists.[13] A prime example of sophisticated qualitative methodology is Ben Kerkvliet's renowned examination of agrarian unrest in the intra-war and postwar Philippines, *The Huk Rebellion* (1977).[14] More recent is Vince Boudreau's *Grass Roots and Cadre in the Protest Movement* (2001). This cogent study of protest in the Philippines in the mid-1980s highlights the potential of meticulous ethnographic research—primarily large numbers of interviews, close observation of the events described, and "systematic storytelling" (Boudreau 2001: see 12–13 for more on his methods). Detailed exploration of the experience of three autonomous mass organizations at the time of the democratic transition allows Boudreau to shed light on one of the more intractable problems in the study of civil society and social movements: how mobilization actually occurs.[15] Boudreau uses the term "civil society" sparingly but engages explicitly with the theoretical literature, positioning his work as representative of a research agenda. In his framework, protest movements are continuous with other periods in participants' lives, and the study of them takes into account dynamics between the movement and macropolitical structures and among the movement's various constituencies, implying the connections between episodes of extraordinary contention and the more usual workings of civil society (Boudreau 2001: 165–168). Heryanto and Mandal's volume also advocates an "insider" approach to studying civil society: Only someone with intimate access to the organizations and individuals in question could conduct the sort of investigation that might reveal the actual workings of civil society.

The focus on in-depth case studies need not preclude cross-national or cross-regional comparisons, but tends to do so in practice. For instance, like Boudreau, Gerard Clarke (1998) relies upon extensive interviews, both published and unpublished sources, and "insider" access to the primary organizations that he discusses. Although he gives some attention to other states in the region and clearly aspires to theory-building comparison, his research is so much richer on the Philippines than on the other cases that the volume as a whole could hardly be considered other than a case study.

Those works on civil society in Southeast Asia that attempt to position themselves as appealing not just to narrowly defined area specialists largely target students of the concepts or theories engaged rather than specialists on other regions. This tendency toward insularity is unfortunate given the fertile possibilities of explicitly cross-regional analysis, but seems slowly to be changing. For example, Heryanto and Mandal (2003a: 14–17) explain that their comparative treatment of political opposition in Indonesia and Malaysia requires a more nuanced approach than is standard in the literature, including transcending pat definitions and taxonomies or even modifiers such as "soft authoritarianism" to focus on ever-changing qualities such as subjecthood and social relations in different regimes. This approach moves beyond most work in Southeast Asian studies by its explicit comparativism and in political science more broadly by its avoidance of a reductionist resort to abstractions and concrete terms that obscure social and cultural realities.

Conclusions: Broadening the Perspective and the Audience

Clearly, then, works on Southeast Asia suggest the necessity of disaggregating the collective noun "civil society" in discussing this sphere across states and of a realistic view of the place and implications of civil societies. Hence, Alagappa, for instance, refers not to "civil society" but to "civil society organizations" and underscores the range of implications of civil societal activity in the region. On the nature and development of Asian civil societies, his volume concludes:

* Civil society organizations exist in Asia and have grown significantly since the mid-1980s;
* Different social factors have spurred the development of civil societies in Asia;

- Asian civil societies are diverse in composition, resources, and goals, and are marked by both cooperation and internal conflict;
- The composition and dynamics of Asian civil societies have been changing and will continue to do so;
- Asian civil societies bear features of both neo-Tocquevillian/liberal democratic (associational) and neo-Gramscian/New Left (cultural and ideological) frames (see Alagappa 2004b), with the former gaining ascendancy as state institutions gain legitimacy;
- The proliferation of civil society organizations has not resulted in institutionalization of a nonstate public sphere, and civil society is seen more instrumentally for its fostering or preventing political change than as an autonomous arena for societal self-governance. (Alagappa 2004c: 10, 2004d) [16]

The Alagappa volume draws similarly nuanced conclusions regarding the connections among civil society and democracy, the state, and political society. The work proposes that civil society organizations may expand or contract democratic space depending on their dominant discourse, other environmental factors, and countervailing or coordinating forces. It acknowledges the impact of the state on the nature and development of civil society but finds that civil society has limited the power and reach of the (still-strong) state. Interactions between these two spheres may not be confrontational, but vary significantly in contemporary Asia. Finally, like Schmitter's or Schak and Hudson's work, this volume recognizes the porosity of the boundary between civil and political societies in the region, and posits a synergistic relationship between the development of these spheres (Alagappa 2004c: 11, 2004a). The volume thus effectively synthesizes our accumulated knowledge regarding civil society in Southeast Asia, and sets out to engage the disciplinary concept accordingly.

Still, the foregoing discussion returns all too often to the attenuated dialogue between studies of Southeast Asian civil societies and other themes and cases within political science. Even when scholars of these civil societies invoke theories and frame their work to be more analytical than descriptive, their primary audience remains the ranks of area specialists, especially when their methods are the ethnographic, qualitative ones favored in this subfield. The paucity of this engagement is neither fully consistent nor inevitable, though. Non–Southeast Asianists could take works on the region more seriously (so long as they were exposed to them), and these works could be made more purposefully theoretical and bridge building, hopefully without sacrificing empirical depth.

More broadly, as Mahoney and Rueschemeyer (2003) suggest of the extension of comparative-historical analysis (CHA) to ever more sites of investigation, the proliferation of studies of civil society raises tensions between historical particularity and theoretical generalization. The sort of introspection as to method and conceptualization that they find among devotees of CHA is also evident in the comprehensive—even tortured—literature reviews prefacing every recent work on civil society in Southeast Asia. These efforts have produced a literature that at least speaks in the general direction of theory, even if those links are not always so well specified beyond the literature review as political scientists might like. Several strategies could focus and intensify its theory-building predilections, including rigor in definition and use of concepts and terms, diversifying the n of studies, and more attention to case selection.

First, one of the core issues yet to be resolved is one of conceptual clarity. The trend is unproblematically to accept a broad definition of "civil society." The "unproblematically" part of that tendency could be rectified. Alagappa (2004e), for instance, works with a capacious definition, but the scope of "civil society" is clearly specified at the outset, and the chapters hold consistently to it. Second, while thick description of single cases performs critical theory-testing and theory-generating functions, the field could benefit from more small-n comparative studies (or innovative research designs that explicitly present a larger number of cases—regions, periods, etc.—within a single country). Most multi-country studies on the topic are compilations of single-case studies, with little or no connective tissue to link the chapters. A step in this direction is Heryanto and Mandal (2003b), in which most of the chapters explicitly compare aspects of political protest (the role of public intellectuals, labor activism, the contributions of arts workers, etc.) across Indonesia and Malaysia. The volume takes as its central mission to draw out connections and contrasts between the two states, even in those chapters primarily oriented around one or the other case (see Heryanto and Mandal 2003a: 11–14 for why this task is logical but rare). Seldom are these links so clearly elaborated, yet the institutional diversity, regional dynamics, and cultural affinities across Southeast Asia make the region a terrific laboratory for theory-building research on civil society and political change. CHA would be a particularly helpful technique in such endeavors (and, indeed, clearly informs at least several chapters in Heryanto and Mandal).

Finally, individual scholars could make more of an effort to think outside the region. In studying the role of Islamic organizations in processes of political change, for instance, Indonesia and Malaysia are certainly worth comparing—but so is either of these cases with Egypt, Jordan, or Algeria. For instance, David Camroux (1996) offers an excellent description of the combination of accommodation, co-optation, and confrontation through which the Malaysian state has negotiated Islamic resurgence, but makes no real effort to consider the extensibility of this framework or how political Islam in Malaysia differs from its counterparts elsewhere. Extrapolating beyond real or presumed regional peculiarities not only precludes recourse to dubious arguments of geographic/cultural exceptionalism and shifts the focus instead toward structural determinants, but also taps into different audiences and critics, opening the discussion to a redefined intellectual community. Such efforts can only serve to integrate studies of Southeast Asia better within the larger corpus of comparative politics, with positive implications for all sides.

In conclusion, studies of civil society in Southeast Asia have not just added to our knowledge of the specific noteworthy experiences of a range of states, but significantly challenge and improve our understanding of civil society as a concept. By presenting the diverse sorts of political change that civil societal activism may promote, works on civil society affirm the influence such engagement may wield but challenge a presumed teleological connection between civil society and democratization. By asserting that organizations based on ascriptive identities may be part of civil society, these studies usefully contradict some of the more prominent and authoritative works in the field. By exploring the nature of civil society under various types of regime, works on Southeast Asia show that liberal democracy and individual freedoms are not necessary preconditions for what looks otherwise like a civil society. Finally, works on Southeast Asia support the concept of transnational civil society, in the process interrogating the connection between civil society and the state. Taken together, these contributions suggest that scholars of Southeast Asia are not stretching the concept of civil society by uncovering the deficiencies of "mainstream" definitions. Rather, they are disaggregating and refining the concept, proving the theory-building value of inductive, qualitative area studies work, and making their mark on political science as a discipline.

Chapter Eight

Beyond Doctrine and Dogma
Religion and Politics in Southeast Asia

KIKUE HAMAYOTSU

Introduction

One of the most prominent scholars of the Middle East lately acknowledged that political scientists have long neglected the study of religion (Anderson 2003). Since the 1980s, however, the rising prominence of religious institutions in the public sphere has increasingly drawn the attention of scholars, including political scientists.[1] Among Southeast Asianists, studies of religion and politics seem abundant and quite familiar. Yet we are not sure to what extent these studies have generated knowledge that helps advance general theories. Should scholars of the Middle East, for example, care about Islamist movements in Indonesia? Can studies of political Islam in Indonesia or Malaysia tell them something that will excite them? This chapter assesses Southeast Asia scholars' theoretical contributions to the study of religion and politics.

The study of religion and politics can be divided into three bodies of scholarship. One analyzes colonial and post-colonial states' attempts to use religion for nation building and their efforts to domesticate religion. A second body of literature analyzes the origins of religious movements. State penetration has evoked societal responses in the form of religious movements or resistance, but states are not the sole cause of religious movements. Studies on Southeast Asia have identified four additional factors: primordialism, socioeconomic changes, religious ideas, and ethnicity. A third body of literature analyzes the effect of religious movements and religion on political transformation. Variations in the impact of religion on political transformations, particularly democratization, are debated from a culturalist and institutionalist perspective.

ISSUES AND THEORETICAL DEBATES

Scholars have engaged the aforementioned questions in a variety of ways from one of three perspectives that I refer to as primordialist, constructivist, and instrumentalist/functionalist. Primordialist approaches claim that religious mobilization is driven primarily by religion and culture, and is ultimately a struggle to defend a religious and cultural cause. This approach entails an essentialist assumption that "religious identity always exists in a crystallized fashion as a primordial, that is nationally strong and dominant, collective sentiment." Moreover, this view asserts that "primordial sentiments are assumed to emerge *inevitably* in the realm of politics, usually through a vehement eruption" (Kalyvas 1996: 8, emphasis added). In other words, the transfer of religious identity into politicized cleavage is considered automatic.

The constructivist view, on the other hand, regards religious identity as an identity *constructed* by political agents. According to this view, "the process of cleavage and identity formation is linked to mobilization and organization and, in turn, to the choices and decisions about mobilization and organization made by political actors" (Kalyvas 1996: 10).[2] Instrumentalists regard religious mobilization as an automatic response to a variety of exogenous forces such as industrialization, modernization, Westernization, and secularization. From this perspective, religion provides an ideological and organizational instrument to articulate adherents' political and socioeconomic demands.

At a general methodological and theoretical level, Southeast Asia scholars have confronted two prevailing paradigms concerning religion and politics. A classical-oriented doctrinal approach to religion regards it as an "unchanging corpus of key doctrines and practices or the classical statements that define a particular belief-system," and religious doctrines as a key determinant of political behavior (Ileto 1999: 194). This orientation has reinforced parochial boundaries, emphasizing the specificity of each religious tradition, thereby impeding vigorous inter-religious comparative analysis.[3]

A second school of thought has grappled with the long-prevailing thesis of modernization. The original modernization school regards religious forces as irrational and traditional. Its secularization assertion expects that religion survives as a potent public force only in a traditional society and disappears or is privatized when society becomes modern. Religious forces are considered secondary to rational economic, social, and political forces. The "clash of civilization" thesis advanced by Huntington is based on this premise. It relies upon—and reinforces—the static cultural assertion that there is an intimate correlation between culture (e.g., religious traditions) and political development, and democratization in particular (Huntington 1984, 1996).[4] Other modernization scholars debate the link between culture and the level of economic development (e.g., Harrison 1992; Davis 1987).

These two paradigms overlap in an analytically significant way: Both essentialize religion and culture, making cross-religious comparison less likely or, as pursued by Huntington, crude. This is painfully evident in earlier studies of Southeast Asia. For example, Geertz is the scholar most prominently associated with this culturalist view. His study of Indonesian Islam emphasizing primordial identity has been extremely influential in the analysis of political cleavages there (Geertz 1960). The immense influence of, and the impulse to uncritically accept, his conceptualization of three streams of Muslim culture—*abangan* (nominal Muslims), *santri* (orthodox Muslims), and *priyayi* (hereditary aristocrats)—have led to the assertion that political divisions are inevitably shaped by this cultural division.

Recent scholars have dealt deftly with the theoretical and methodological problems posed by these two paradigms. Through their theoretical engagement and methodological innovation, these studies exhibit substantial knowledge accumulation. Despite disciplinary boundaries and their focus upon one geographic area and religion, these studies critically engage—and even challenge—theoretical premises ensuing from the two prevailing paradigms. They acknowledge change in religion (in terms of ideas and institutions), and they seek to evaluate the impact of such change on broader political processes. Moreover, they emphasize the function of practical religion or popular religion, and explore how transcending/universalizing faiths take on locally specific meanings and functions according to political and socioeconomic conditions.

This chapter evaluates the main theoretical debates arising from the study of religion and politics. In particular, it examines scholars' efforts to resolve theoretical and methodological tensions arising from the culturalist claim associated with the classical-oriented doctrinal approach and the modernization thesis in the three bodies of scholarship delineated above. This chapter concludes with an assessment of the contributions and shortcomings of Southeast Asian scholarship within the broader study of religion and politics.

The State and Religion

In contrast to the modern secularist assertion that the state and religion should be separate, Southeast Asian states—both colonial and post-colonial—have actively interfered with religion. In particular, states here attempted to mobilize religion in order to forge national identity. States also attempted to domesticate religion because they feared that popular mobilization via religion could pose a political threat to the state.

The question of whether states should recognize a particular religion has also been contentious in Southeast Asia and has stirred considerable scholarly debate. The central issue has been not purely religious or symbolic, but also a matter of practical interest, because state sponsorship of one religion would clearly benefit one group at the expense of others. Religious leaders, for example, were fighting for political and economic benefits and social recognition in the realignment process that followed national independence. This also involved struggles to preserve local cultural institutions against the onslaught of modernization, a process that was aggressively launched by Western-educated national leaders.

RELIGION, STATE, AND NATION BUILDING

Early Southeast Asian scholarship espoused a functionalist position emphasizing the ideological function of religion in the nation-building process. Such works argued that Buddhism and Islam played a role in the nation-building process that was *functionally* equivalent to the secular nationalism in the West (Hefner 1997: 19). These studies shed light on the political significance of cultural power, suggesting that modern states cannot rely exclusively on coercive and secular administrative mechanisms to integrate a religiously and ethnically fragmented nation. Southeast Asian states, they demonstrate, deployed cultural and religious forces—both ideologically and organizationally—to achieve their national development goals and to consolidate power over social forces. However, these studies do not explain why some nations succeeded whereas others did not.

A key proponent of the functionalist approach, Keyes (1971, 1987) high-lights the role of Theravada Buddhism in the formation of national identity in Thailand. By focusing upon the Thai state's traditional use of Theravada Buddhism to integrate an otherwise ethnically and religiously fragmented populace into a modern nation-state, Keyes emphasizes the consolidating—rather than divisive—character of religion. The central thrust of Keyes's analysis is historical continuity: He traces Thai national cultural heritage back to the pre-modern period and contends that the monarchy and Buddhism have been and remain cultural institutions that are central in all corners of social, economic, and political life.[5]

However, Keyes does not argue that Thai national identity is a primordial sentiment, but rather that it is the product of political and social forces. Thai rulers recognized that the integration of the *Sangha* was crucial for achieving their political ends, so they co-opted it, by statutory means, to promote the government's national goals. This state-church formula also provided political legitimacy. Moreover, state leaders recognized that the organizational and doctrinal coherence of the *Sangha* was a prerequisite for political stability. They feared that monks not sanctioned by the *Sangha* could form an organizational agent for extra-state activism and therefore threaten national security and their political predominance.

A doctrinal approach has constrained studies on religion and politics by emphasizing the peculiarity of each religion. Scholars influenced by this approach, for example, repeatedly emphasize the anti-secular doctrine proscribing separation between church and state in Islam to account for Muslims' demands for establishing an Islamic state. However, the deficiency of the doctrinal approach is readily apparent when one considers the questions concerning the official position of religion—and conflict over it among various groups—in newly independent states in Southeast Asia. For example, Malaysia and Indonesia have had markedly different experiences in this respect (Hamayotsu 2002). Despite the fact that some 90 percent of the Indonesian population is Muslim, Islamic nationalism has never prevailed over secular ideologies. Post-colonial debates about whether Islam should form the ideological basis for the republic have been extremely contentious. When does a particular ideological position prevail, and why?

Earlier studies were greatly influenced by Geertz's primordialist conceptualization of Islam, which attributed political conflict to the cultural differences between the *abangan* (nominal Muslim) and *santri* (orthodox Muslim) communities. Samson, for example, explained the government's hostility to Islamic forces as a clash between the *abangan*-oriented armed forces and the *santri*-oriented modernist Islamic forces (Samson 1971–1972).[6]

However, recent scholarship presents an alternative perspective that emphasizes the fluidity of Islamic thinking and the flexibility of Islamic actors in altering the place of Islam in the state and national vision. Effendy's *Islam and the State in Indonesia* (2003), for example, sheds light on Islamic intellectualism and ideas to argue that the emergence of a new intellectual movement that emphasized doctrinal renewal and the reinterpretation of classic texts in the 1970s and onward helped alter the antagonistic relations between the state and modernist Islamic forces. By popularizing novel idioms such as *reactualisasi* (re-actualization) and the secularization of Islam, the movement managed to push aside the doctrinal ideal that religion and politics should be joined.

Bowen, an anthropologist, similarly emphasizes the role of religious intellectuals in the formation of state-religion relations. His ethnographic exploration of the evolution of Islamic legal institutions in Indonesia (2003) reveals that Muslim intellectuals actively engaged in public reasoning (public interpretation of religious doctrines) in light of local, cultural, social, and legal norms and in a political context (2003: 18–20).[7] It was this process of intellectual reasoning, he asserts, that influenced the role of the state in religious affairs and the growing significance of Islamic jurisprudence in Indonesia's legal system. By focusing on strategic interactions among various religious actors, his study dismisses the dogmatic position that "Islam consists of a fixed set of rules—as if a codebook called 'sharia' contained a timeless and repressive plan for abolishing rights and diversity" (2003: 19).[8]

STATE DOMESTICATION OF RELIGION

Religion can serve or oppose government power. To confine opposition, states—both colonial and post-colonial—have maneuvered in a variety of ways to deal with religious forces. Studies on Southeast Asia have amply documented these efforts. These studies have contributed to knowledge accumulation about the various forms—and various levels—of states' efforts to domesticate religious forces: Why and how do states domesticate religions in the particular ways they do? What are the consequences of particular policies? The studies find that the state's promotion of a particular ideology or religion often corresponds to greater state intervention in religious affairs and the state's penetration of society, and has a significant impact on the long-term relationships among the state, the church, and society.

As already noted, Keyes's studies (1971, 1987) of Thailand reveal that the organizational and doctrinal development of religious institutions was used to cultivate national identity.[9] The Thai state has been fully involved in—and rendered lavish patronage to—the organization and administration of the *Sangha* and the codification of its religious doctrines. This pattern of ideological and institutional formula allowed the religious institutions to evolve into a highly coherent and well-structured hierarchical body under the tight control of the state.[10]

Smith's study on Burma (D. E. Smith 1965) also acknowledges the state's functional use of religious institutions for the promotion of national development objectives. However, the Burmese case exhibits significant deviation from the Thai case. According to Smith, the Burmese state was largely unsuccessful in domesticating religious institutions under both colonial and postcolonial regimes. Unlike in Thailand, state patronage for the *Sangha* in Burma was never institutionalized, leaving the latter largely fragmented, unregulated, and undisciplined. Consequently, the *Sangha* played a leading oppositional role in anti-colonial mobilization, alongside other secular-based nationalist organizations led by Western-educated elites (Smith 1965: 92–114; von der Mehden 1963). This oppositional potential of the *Sangha* was also manifested in anti-authoritarian mobilization under the post-independence military regime (Matthews 1993).

Benda's study of Dutch policies toward Islam in Indonesia explores how colonial authorities manipulated religion, why they did so, and with what effect (Benda 1958). Dutch colonial policy was inconsistent, but generally reflected Dutch officials' suspicions about Islam. The Dutch government's early policy of administrative noninterference minimized the organizational development of religious institutions.[11] On the other hand, this policy allowed various nongovernmental Islamic organizations and activities to flourish, provided they didn't exhibit any indication of political mobilization and agitation. Traditional religious leaders—*kiyai* and *ulama*—were thus able to exercise relatively independent authority over a range of religious affairs, including education and other social welfare activities. Moreover, state manipulation of religion under Japanese rule invigorated further popular religious mobilization and organization at the societal level.

Roff (1994) and Yegar (1979) analyze the contrasting case of Malaysia. The British colonial government officially endorsed Islam and sponsored a variety of religious activities such as pilgrimages to Mecca and religious education in government-sponsored Malay schools (Roff 1994; Yegar 1979). British rule also resulted in a more formal and organized system of *Syariah* (Islamic law). The state's heavy involvement in Islamic affairs significantly shaped the way that British colonial authorities institutionalized and consolidated Islam legislatively and administratively (Yegar 1979: 265–266). This created a new hierarchical ecclesiastic order, comprising a corps of religious officialdom under the state. Consequently, state authorities came to exert enormous authority over religious activities and teaching at the societal level. This institutional formula largely constrained religious mobilization against the state.

The institutional difference set under the colonial regimes in Indonesia and Malaysia was not fundamentally altered in the period after independence. Zifirdaus, for example, suggests that the post-colonial Indonesian government under Sukarno suppressed any opposition to the national ideology, *Pancasila*, including Islam, although he allowed religious organizations to continue adhering to their own ideologies (1990: 452). Under Suharto, the government considered Islamic forces a major threat to the army's dominance in society and adopted a variety of means to suppress the political involvement of those Islamic forces (Zifirdaus 1990: 454). Overall, the political activism of religious movements—like that of all other social movements—was greatly curtailed under the Suharto regime.

Origins of Religious Movements

Scholars have vigorously debated the origins of religious movements, whether in reformist or radical form. Scholars of Southeast Asia lag behind other area specialists in an effort to make use of their empirical findings about religious movements to advance theories of social movements. But their exploration of grassroots religious mobilization has helped extend our understanding of the causal mechanisms of collective action among religious communities. One cause of these movements is state penetration. Official claims that a nation should be based on one particular religion have confronted multiple ideological and practical challenges. Official national visions primarily indended to *integrate* multi-religious populations have ironically served to *divide* them along not only religious but also ethnic, regional, class, and gender lines. Of course, the state has not been the sole instigator of religious movements. Scholars of Southeast Asia have also highlighted the role of social forces from primordialist, constructivist, and instrumentalist/functionalist perspectives.

Studies of religious movements—especially Islamic movements—have grappled with the secularist assumption in mainstream comparative politics: Religion and politics should be separate. This assumption has largely led political scientists to dismiss the important practical function played by religious movements: expressing multifaceted sociopolitical interests such as class, ethnicity, gender, and political opposition. For example, Islamic movements were often simplistically regarded as fundamentalist or radical and treated as a source of disturbance to civil liberty and pluralism (Esposito and Piscatori 1991). Once separatist movements expressed their aspirations in religious terms, they were regarded as fanatical. Consequently, religious movements were inadequately understood in the comparative politics literature.

In recent years, however, political scientists, especially scholars of the Middle East, have shed light on the complexity of religious movements. By employing and elaborating social science methods and theories used to analyze nonreligious social and political movements, these area specialists (e.g., Norton 1995, 1996; Wiktorowicz 2004) critically engaged the culturalist and secularist assumptions and discredited the textual and dogmatic approach adopted by the older generation of Western-oriented scholars.

Studies on Southeast Asia have contributed to those theoretical debates by engaging a range of questions concerning religious mobilization at the societal level. These studies have critically engaged major debates—although often only implicitly—to advance a variety of explanations for the rise of religious movements, such as ethnicity, class, and religious ideas.

ETHNIC-REGIONAL NATIONALISM AND RELIGION

Southeast Asia specialists have vigorously debated the cause of ethnic/religious separatist movements arising in the margins of national territories. Why do some ethnic/religious minorities revolt against the state whereas others do not? Reactions have varied across place and time. Some have sought greater autonomy from the state, whereas others have fought for independence. However, not all have openly organized against central governments. Some studies have found that there is considerable difference of opinion and tension *within* minority communities, significantly affecting patterns of conflict, cooperation, and compromise with national governments. Southeast Asianists have explored and elaborated these complexities.

Scholars have varied in the extent to which they stress the importance of religion in minority struggles against the state. Early Southeast Asianists advanced the primordialist view to account for the emergence and popularity of separatist movements. In "Islam and Malay Nationalism" (1982), for example, Surin argues that the Muslim separatist movement in Southern Thailand is ultimately the result of a clash between two contending cultures, Thai-Buddhists and Malay-Muslims. Although the form and intensity of the movements have varied over time, he contends, Islamic sentiment has been the foundation of ethno-regional identity and the chief motive of the Muslim community for seeking cultural autonomy.[12] The government's culturally and religiously insensitive integration policies, it is argued, helped fuel and perpetuate anti-Bangkok Muslim resistance.

Subsequent research has repudiated such primordialist assumptions. McVey (1989), for example, highlights class tension among Muslim elites and between elites and the peasants, arguing that mass participation was motivated primarily by socioeconomic interests. Kell's study on the Acehnese rebellion (1995) similarly emphasizes socioeconomic factors to explain Acehnese separatism.

McVey challenges Surin in a number of fundamental ways. Whereas Surin stresses the special nationalistic sentiment attached to cultural institutions such as traditional religious schooling within the Muslim community, McVey dismisses such sentiment. McVey argues that Muslim peasants, in fact, did not always care about religious schooling. Better-off Muslim peasants, who were the financial and social backbone of the *pondok* system, began to question the value of religious learning and the wisdom of boycotting the Thai schools as they realized the importance of advanced secular schooling and proficiency in Thai for their career advancement (McVey 1989: 46). McVey thus emphasizes the socioeconomic interests of a minority population while deemphasizing antagonistic religious and cultural aspirations.

McKenna's study on separatism in the Southern Philippines also refutes primordialist approaches that depict the separatist movement as a Muslim rebellion against Christian enemies (McKenna 1998). He does so by adopting a combination of constructivist and instrumentalist perspectives and focusing upon "everyday politics" to explain popular support for the insurgent movements. He especially highlights intra-Muslim (Moro) political and economic relations, and the immediate concerns and material needs of ordinary Muslims. His critical assessment of the rebellion, from the perspective of followers, reveals that the ideal of fighting for the *Bangsamoro*—a nation of Philippine Muslims united by common culture and history—was but one of those motivational factors, and it was not an especially potent one. Compliance was based not only on Muslims' "possession of a common enemy" but also on "a host of collateral intentions: self-defense, defense of community, social pressure, armed coercion, revenge, and personal ambition, among others" (McKenna 1998: 286).

Although these studies complicate primordialist approaches to religion, they do not completely reject the significance of religion as a focus of collective mobilization. In the case of the Southern Philippines, McKenna argues that there *was* a significant religious element in the movement. McKenna suggests that at least two components of the Islamic appeals of the *ulama* worked to mobilize ordinary Muslims. The first was the notion of Islamic unity, which referred to the establishment of a more uniform Islamic community (*ummah*) in Cotabato. The concept of *ummah* offered a solution to internal divisions rooted in class, ethnic, familial, and political differences. The second component was the ideal of juridical equality for all Muslims (McKenna 1998: 281–282). In short, McKenna's findings suggest that religious identity constructed by political agents also played a role in the mobilization of support for the separatist movement.

RELIGIOUS MOBILIZATION FROM BELOW:
ECONOMIC CHANGE, CLASS, AND GENDER

State penetration, and government-initiated national development programs in particular, have brought about rapid economic transformation in local communities, reinforcing not only inter-regional and inter-ethnic tension but also inter-class tension. Some scholars have adopted an instrumentalist view, arguing that religion expresses class interests. In this view, religious mobilization is essentially a result of economic and social change: Economic transformation causes socioeconomic cleavages, and religion provides ideological and organizational instruments by which affected communities can express their class interests. In other words, religion is regarded as epiphenomenal, masking real causes such as class conflict and bourgeois aspirations.

The interactions among class interests, religious ideology, and political mobilization are explored by Clive Kessler's pioneering study, *Islam and Politics in a Malay State* (1978). By focusing on the use of religious ideology, Kessler explains the political and electoral success of the Pan-Malayan Islamic Party (commonly referred to as PAS) in the Muslim-dominant state of Kelantan from 1959 to 1969. Kessler argues that conflict between the two political parties, PAS and its archrival UMNO, was essentially a result of class tensions. The PAS enjoyed electoral success, he argues, because of its ability to capitalize upon enduring class antagonisms between two elite groups: new commoner elites identified with PAS, including religious teachers, and aristocratic elites associated with UMNO. Toward this end, the party leaders employed Islam "as a politically persuasive idiom for the apprehension of mundane social experience" (Kessler 1978). PAS tapped into fundamental Islamic appeals, such as social justice and moral equality, to mobilize opposition against UMNO leaders, who were depicted as being obsessed with immediate material interests and therefore unfit to meet religiously defined moral standards.

By adopting historical sociology, Kessler elucidates the link between class formation in a Muslim rural community and the effectiveness of the Islamic party's ideological mobilization of the impoverished class through a religious idiom. Theoretically, the study was innovative because it emphasized the exploitation of class tensions in refuting the platitude that the Islamic party simply manipulated religious slogans and religious-inspired racial feelings among the rural Muslims to mobilize religious fanaticism. This analytical emphasis thus discredits the essentialist view that Islam is a special case because of the intimate relation between religious doctrines on the one hand and the political behavior of Muslims on the other. Kessler reminds us, time and again, that Islamic doctrines and ideas cannot determine political behavior.[13]

Drawing from this earlier scholarship, Hefner emphasizes the role of class to account for the rise of Islamic resurgence movements (1993, 1997, 2000). His studies show that since the 1970s, flourishing Islamic activism—termed "cultural Islam"[14]—in Indonesia arose primarily from rising bourgeois aspirations. In the 1980s, moderate Muslims sought to develop new Islamic initiatives, especially in the fields of education, the economy, and social welfare. Hefner emphasizes that "the most spectacular evidence of cultural Islam's advance was visible" in the booming metropolitan regions of Indonesia, especially at universities (1997: 90). In order to Islamize secular universities, students adopted relaxed, democratic forms of dress, amusement, and interaction while encouraging strict adherence to Muslim devotional acts, including the daily prayers, the fast, and payment of alms (*zakat*) to the poor (1993: 12–13).

Other scholars establish that the emergence of this type of Islamic activism cannot be detached from the rapid economic transformation that occurred under the Suharto government, and the subsequent growth of a Muslim urban middle class that became self-consciously more Islamic in its devotion and lifestyle (e.g., Barton 1994; Effendy 2003; Federspiel 1998; Ramage 1995).

Class interests are not homogeneous, however, as various essays in the volume edited by Andrew Willford and Kenneth George, *Spirited Politics* (2005), demonstrate. Some religious movements expressed a gender-specific urban, middle-class perspective.[15] Brenner's essay, for example, explores the emergence of Muslim feminist activists and organizations in late New Order Indonesia. Brenner adopts an instrumentalist position to demonstrate that the Islamic resurgence provided an important means for "those who were disaffected with the conditions of New Order Indonesia to become involved in grassroots efforts to transform their society" (2005: 94).

Brenner's essay suggests that the rise of Muslim liberal feminist groups in Indonesia and their approach to women's issues were not only products of the Islamic movement itself, or of its intersection with other transnational movements (such as those of global feminism). The trend also derived from local political conditions: the gender ideologies and policies of the Suharto regime that raised questions about women's positions in the family and broader society. Muslim feminists rose to fight the rising influence of conservative Islamist factions over these questions.

What is distinctive about some of these feminist movements is their tactical use of religious techniques. To fight the dominant patriarchal interpretations of Islamic texts and the conservative approaches of religious leaders, they engaged in *ijtihad* (independent reasoning) to interpret Islamic texts for themselves to debate religious leaders over their interpretations of particular passages in the Qur'an and Hadiths. This approach enabled these activists to demonstrate that women's rights did not conflict with the basic tenets of Islam. It also helped them distance themselves from secular feminist groups, who tend to be considered Western or alien among conservative Muslims (Brenner 2005: 108–112).

Religious reformist movements are not peculiar to the Muslim world. Thailand has also witnessed similar movements (Jackson 1989). Jackson analyzes the conspicuous trend of Buddhist reformist movements that emerged in the 1970s, focusing on the transformation in religious thought. Placing the religious ideological transformations in their institutional and sociopolitical contexts, this study contends that the growing influence of the capitalist class and middle class in Thai society greatly contributed to the rise of reformist movements.[16]

Some scholars also associate socioeconomic transformations with the formation of noninstitutional popular religious practices and movements. Such popular religions may not appear overtly political, but their potential to mobilize a network of believers has considerable political significance, as shown later by Ileto's *Pasyon and Revolution*.

Philip Taylor's study *Goddess on the Rise* (2004), for example, explores the growth of popular worship of deities—pilgrimage to the shrine of the goddess, the Lady of the Realm—in southern Vietnam in the postwar era. Taylor demonstrates that the worship is closely associated with socioeconomic transformations in a particular historical context. The decline of a centralized socialist command economy and Vietnam's increasing economic openness since the mid-1980s—coupled with limited state intervention—created a context in which the female deity has become very popular among a particular *class*: the petty entrepreneurs. Those petty entrepreneurs, especially women, have greatly benefited from the region's growing exposure to global markets, but at the same time have had their fortunes and prosperity subjected to highly unpredictable and unstable economic forces. Under such vulnerable and at times helpless circumstances, Taylor argues, people sought a sense of insurance and assistance from a cast of powerful spirits and attempted to come to terms with uncontrollable and invisible forces by propitiating these deities (Taylor 2004: chapter 3).[17]

RELIGIOUS MOVEMENTS: RELIGIOUS IDEAS

Much of the recent theoretical work on Islamic activism is devoted to identifying the cultural frames that motivate, inspire, and demand loyalty among adherents. These studies insist that "because Islamic activism operates in contexts of repression, the dynamics of framing may differ from similar processes in Western, liberal democracies" (Wiktorowicz 2004: 25). In other words, cultural difference needs to be taken into account in fully understanding the root of Islamic movements. Methodologically, deep understanding of the language, culture, and history of local communities is crucial.

Wickham, for instance, advances this cultural framing approach in explaining the success of Islamist outreach to Egypt's university-educated youth, and challenges rational actor models, another prominent approach in the mobilization literature (Wickham 2002, 2004). An underlying theoretical issue is how movement leaders forge and sustain linkages with recruits (i.e., the "micro-mechanisms of mobilization"). Wickham's assertion is that rational actor models of mobilization can help explain the involvement of those recruits in initial, low-risk forms of activism, but they alone cannot explain an eventual progression to riskier, more overtly political forms of Islamic activity. To fill this theoretical gap, she advances a moral-based mobilization theory. She contends that "to facilitate a progression toward high-risk activism, Islamists framed activism as a moral 'obligation' that demands self-sacrifice and unflinching commitment to the cause of religious transformation. Such a frame encouraged graduates to view political participation as a religious duty" (2004: 232). What is important here is that the appeal of the Islamist message is not simply attributed to the intrinsic appeal of Islam. Rather, Wickham emphasizes, the movement's appeal was rooted in a particular ideologized form of Islam, transmitted through grassroots networks and reinforced through intensive small-group solidarity aided by prior family, friendship, and neighborhood ties (2004: 247).

Such ideational approaches to the mobilization of popular religious movements are not entirely new among Southeast Asia specialists. Ileto's *Pasyon and Revolution* (1979) is the most acclaimed study in this field. By examining millenary movements in the Philippines during the Spanish and early U.S. colonial periods, Ileto suggests that ideas encoded in popular religious traditions help explain the mass appeal of those movements and the durability of the movements' resistance against the colonial authorities. Drawing upon a rich array of informal materials—such as poems, songs, autobiographies, confessions, prayers, and folk sayings—Ileto rewrites the history of popular resistance from the perspective of the masses. He demonstrates that the masses' experience of Holy Week fundamentally shaped the style of peasant brotherhoods and uprisings. In so doing, Ileto challenged conventional explanations, which stressed patron-client ties and material interests in their explanations of mass mobilization.

RELIGIOUS RADICALISM AND TERRORISM:
TRANSNATIONAL OR LOCAL?

In more recent years, scholars of Southeast Asia have made a considerable contribution to the debates concerning the causes of religious radicalism and terrorism.[18] The central debate asks if the rise of radical Islamic movements in the region since the late 1990s should be attributed to transnational forces or to local factors. Here we see a distinct theoretical divide between so-called terrorist experts and area specialists.

Scholars such as Rohan Gunaratna and Zachary Abuza belong to the former camp (Abuza 2003; Gunaratna 2002). These terrorist experts typically emphasize the global network of terrorism to claim that radical Islamic movements such as *Jemaah Islamiyah* (JI) are essentially the offspring of transnational terrorist networks, most notably Al-Qaeda. These scholars heavily rely on intelligence and secondary sources without much knowledge about local conditions—political, social, and cultural (including religion)—to come to this conclusion. They seem to recognize that local conditions have some relevance to the spread of radical groups and terrorist activities. But even when they do, they are primarily concerned with security dimensions (e.g., police forces and intelligence operatives) and largely dismiss characteristics of social mobilization or the function of religion. From their perspective, these local factors are secondary at best, and the content and context of Islam are irrelevant.

Area specialists, in contrast, emphasize local conditions to account for the rise of radical Islamic movements. Scholars and local experts such as Noorhaidi Hasan, Sidney Jones, John Sidel, and Martin van Bruinessen belong to this camp and consciously dispute the views advanced by the terrorist experts (Hasan 2002; Jones 2005; Sidel 2003; van Bruinessen 2002).[19] They adopt a historical and sociological approach to identify particular local conditions under which radical Islamic movements have made significant inroads. They pay close attention to the function of Islam as a significant ideological and organizational channel to mobilize a particular segment of society. From their perspective, a radical Islamic movement such as *Laskar Jihad* or JI can be viewed as a social force having deep historical roots in a particular local setting. Sidel (2003) highlights variation in the forms of radical mobilization and the recruitment of adherents among Muslim communities in Indonesia and the Philippines. To account for the variation, he traces the process of capital accumulation, state formation, and national integration under which Muslims were systematically disadvantaged and excluded.[20]

Religion and Political Transformation: Culture, Ideas, and Institutions

How and to what extent does religion affect democratic transition and other political changes? More specifically, do particular religious traditions foster or impede the development of democratic practices and institutions? These theoretical questions have been increasingly debated among scholars, especially those concerned with the role of political culture in aiding democratic transition and consolidation. This approach focuses on "the need to develop civic and participatory norms at the level of the individual citizen" (Tessler 2002: 338).

Essentialists such as Huntington identify religion as an indispensable attribute of political culture and assert that some religions are favorable to democratization whereas others are inimical (Huntington 1984). This view posits that "democracy is not attained simply by making institutional changes or through elite level maneuvering. Its survival depends also on the values and beliefs of ordinary citizens" (Inglehart, quoted by Tessler 2002: 338).

Debates about the correlation between political culture and democracy are particularly rife among Middle East specialists.[21] Against the backdrop of widespread authoritarianism in the region, scholars have questioned if the absence of democratic regimes can be attributed to Islamic culture and tradition (e.g., Esposito and Voll 1996). These scholars have adopted a variety of methods to challenge culturalist assertions. Tessler, a political scientist, uses public opinion data collected in four Middle Eastern countries to conclude that Islam seems to have less influence on political attitudes than is often suggested by scholars of Arab and Islamic societies (Tessler 2002).[22]

Islam specialists Esposito and Piscatori also repudiate the culturalist assumption that Islam and democracy are incompatible, on empirical and doctrinal grounds. They argue that there are pressures for liberalization and the potential for homegrown democracy movements in the Middle East. Moreover, they emphasize that Islam lends itself to a variety of interpretations and that many Muslims support democratic values (Esposito and Piscatori 1991).

Norton not only writes off the culturalist approaches; he also advances a civil society approach that emphasizes the presence of associational life as an alternative variable (Norton 1999).

Studies on Southeast Asia have contributed to the study of political transformation by focusing on the role of religious institutions and practices. Many of these studies are country specific, descriptive, and informative rather than analytical. The explanatory power of the propositions advanced by these studies is limited to specific circumstances—geographically and temporally. Yet the country-specific knowledge and propositions provided by these studies are valuable for analyzing religious organizations and activities. An adequate understanding of these informal religious activities—which is made possible only by extensive field research and detailed historical knowledge—is a prerequisite for formulating and elaborating convincing hypotheses. Despite the limited scope of these studies, the propositions that they advance resonate in other regions.

THE RISE OF CIVIL ISLAM DISCOURSE: RELIGION, CIVIL SOCIETY, AND DEMOCRATIZATION

Only recently has the theoretical literature recognized religious organizations as a force within civil society. Studies of civil society in Indonesia, for example, have paid relatively little attention to large religious associations such as *Nahdlatul Ulama* (NU) and *Muhammadiyah* (van Bruinessen 2003).[23] Against the backdrop of resurgent religious movements, however, the genesis and activities of nongovernmental religious movements, and their role in the promotion of civil society, have increasingly drawn scholarly attention.[24]

Scholarship on Indonesian Islam has made a significant contribution to the debates about the relationship between culture and democracy. Since the early 1990s, scholars have advanced the "civil Islam" thesis, which links the rise of an Islamic intellectual reformist movement with an expansion of democratic culture (e.g., Barton 1994; Ramage 1995; Federspiel 1998; Effendy 2003). Spearheaded by eminent modernist Islamic intellectuals, the reformist movement emphasizes the interpretation of classic religious texts according to historical and sociocultural contexts rather than the orthodox application of their strict rules. The reformist movement also advocates participation in cultural, educational, and socioeconomic development rather than formal participation in politics. In this way, Muslim intellectuals hope to allay the suspicion of ruling elites about the threat of political Islam, and to contribute to national development. Scholars of this religious renewal movement assert that it has fostered a pluralistic and democratic form of Islamic culture in Indonesia.

Hefner's *Civil Islam* (2000) elaborates upon how such Islamic cultural traits contribute to democratization. Building on democratic theories that emphasize civic-minded cultural resources, Hefner argues that rich civic precedent, a tradition of cultural pluralism, the prevalence of Muslim voluntary associations, and pluralistic Islamic thought that enshrines democratic values all contributed to "make democracy work" in Indonesia.[25] Moreover, the argument goes, in the last days of the authoritarian Suharto regime, Muslim democrats and their secular counterparts joined forces in a pro-democracy campaign that ultimately brought Suharto down. After all, the prime intention of civil Islam is to emphasize the pluralistic nature of Islamic thinking and practice, along with the role played by Muslim intellectuals and organizations in the process of democratization.

Hefner's work has sparked theoretical and methodological controversies (e.g., Fealy 2001; Sidel 2001). One question raised is the extent to which key Islamic individuals sympathetically portrayed as democrats could represent the nature of the Islamic culture of the whole nation. Evidently, these highly prestigious modernist Muslim thinkers had only limited appeal to a segment of the Muslim urban, middle class. How could such a small number of Muslims play a central role in the fall of the authoritarian regime? Moreover, the reformist credentials of some of the figures—such as Abdurrahman Wahid—are suspect. When there was a chance, these reformist Muslim figures and associations sought to associate themselves with the state and sought its patronage. Finally, we are also left uncertain whether civil culture alone can make democracy work without considering the nature of state institutions and their broader structural factors. Interestingly, some argue, the more established Islamic organizations—such as NU and *Muhammadiyah*—were both unable and/or unwilling to commit themselves to the pro-democracy struggle both before and after the fall of the authoritarian regime (Kadir 2002).

THE AUTHORITARIAN REGIME AND ISLAM

Another controversy arising from the general debate about religion and political transformation concerns the relationship between an authoritarian regime and Islamic forces. As suggested in the prior section, authoritarian regimes do not always adopt the same repressive means to deal with Islamic groups. The controversy here is over when and why these regimes adopt a more accommodating position and what the likely consequences of such change are.

Scholars on Indonesia have engaged this question by focusing on the changing relationship of Suharto's authoritarian regime to Islam. Since the 1970s, Indonesia—like many other Muslim nations—experienced a flourishing Islamic resurgence. Against this backdrop, the Suharto regime adopted an accommodative approach to Islam, culminating in the formation of the Association of Indonesian Muslim Intellectuals (ICMI) in 1990. This marked a clear departure from the regime's essentially hostile approach to political Islam in the past. The central controversy is whether ICMI should be seen as a mass-based organization representing the aspirations of the urban, middle-class Muslims or a corporatist mechanism for Suharto to court important segments of modernist Islam.

The former view derives from a sociological analysis advanced by Hefner, among others. His essay "Islam, State, and Civil Society" (1993) contends that the organization should be regarded primarily as a consequence of the larger socioeconomic and cultural transformation of the Muslim community, especially the rise of middle-class Muslims who grew more self-consciously Islamic and more influential in the urban private sector and the bureaucracy.[26] Against this backdrop, sociocultural transformations stimulated changes in the regime's attitude toward Islamic groups.

The political scientist Liddle offers an alternative view to this class analysis. His study (1996) advances a political explanation focusing on the mechanisms of regime maintenance and intra-state conflict. His major claim is that ICMI should be regarded as a state corporatist organization designed and used by President Suharto for his own political survival. To explain Suharto's rapprochement to Islam since the late 1980s, the essay emphasizes the key political mechanisms that sustained Suharto's dominance: the armed forces and the state party, Golkar. The essay reveals that individuals appointed to the top positions of the armed forces and Golkar increasingly had *santri* (devout/orthodox Muslim) backgrounds and/or ICMI connections. Thus, Liddle contends, the formation of ICMI was part of Suharto's effort to co-opt—and cultivate support among—important segments of the Muslim community to balance the power of the military, which was led until 1993 by a Roman Catholic, General Murdani.

STATE-CHURCH RELATIONS AND DEMOCRATIC TRANSITION

Scholarship concerning state-Islam relations under authoritarian regimes is pertinent to the study of state-church relations and democratic transition. In particular, it provides insights about the conditions that allow religious organizations and actors to become viable oppositional forces against authoritarian regimes and thereby to aid democratic transition.

Scholars who adopt an institutionalist position focus on state-church relations from an organizational perspective, whereas civic culture scholars primarily focus upon cultural traditions in society. The institutional approach posits that the organizational and ideological character of clerical institutions and their relationship with the state affect processes of democratization.

Latin America scholars have focused particularly on the organizational and ideological character of the church. They have embarked on comparative analysis across Latin American countries to build and elaborate theories about the effects of state-church relations on popular protest against authoritarian regimes and democratization. Levine and Mainwaring, for example, seek to explain why the church empowers and legitimates protest in some cases and not in others. They focus on the varying nature of churches and on the varying degree of popular participation in community-based church activities to explain the variance (Levine and Mainwaring 1989).[27] Their comparative analysis of Brazil and Colombia highlights the central role that institutional churches play in stimulating and constraining popular initiatives, and in sustaining popular resistance to authority. Brazil, on the one hand, has been blessed with the most visible, intellectually forceful, and progressive Catholic church since the 1970s. This progressive church helped bring about popular mobilization and consequently provided the cultural underpinnings of Brazilian democratic transition. In Colombia, on the other hand, the church hierarchy has retained its own institutional strength, thus reinforcing the conservative nature of the predominant theology. As a result, popular groups in Colombia were largely unsuccessful in accumulating a critical mass of moral and religious legitimacy for social action (Levine and Mainwaring 1989: 234–236).

Southeast Asianists have similarly adopted an institutionalist approach that emphasizes the role of clerical institutions to account for political changes in the region. Youngblood, for example, highlights the crucial role played by the Catholic church in the fall of the Marcos regime (Youngblood 1990). Unlike in Thailand and Malaysia, where highly institutionalized and bureaucratized religious institutions remain intimately related to the state, the Philippine Roman Catholic church retained autonomy from the secular state. The formal institutional separation of state and church enabled the highly influential Roman Catholic church—alongside its Protestant counterparts—to offer moral leadership as well as sanctuary-cum-mobilizational structures to the opposition throughout the martial law period.[28]

Youngblood suggests that intra-church coherence against the regime was not always present. Organizationally, the churches in the Philippines were composed of a number of complexly related church associations. Ideologically, there was disagreement among clergy over the proper role of the church in society and the political activism of the clergy. What brought those religious leaders together to fight against the regime? Youngblood identifies two exogenous factors that served to reinforce the commitment of church leaders with different ecclesiological orientations to the ideals of social justice and to unite them against the regime: policy changes within the Holy See and the World Council of Churches in the 1960s, and deteriorating political and economic conditions in the Philippines.

Matthews's study on Burma, "Buddhism Under a Military Regime" (1993), similarly emphasizes the function of the ecclesiastic order in oppositional mobilization and shows that the same state-church institutionalist approach can be applied to different religious traditions. Specifically, the essay examines the military regime's attempt—and failure—to control the *Sangha* since the 1980s. What is striking about Burma's *Sangha* is its highly fractured and decentralized organizational structures. The monastic order was divided into various associations not only along sectarian but also along ethnic lines. This division was further reinforced by different political and ideological dispositions. In the 1980s, the government took historic steps to centralize and regulate the *Sangha*. However, the state's administrative control over the *Sangha* proved to be only partial, as is evident in the monks' significant involvement in the pro-democracy movement in the late 1980s and 1990s.

Institutionalist scholars have thus helped to fill the gap found in both the doctrinal and cultural approaches, which emphasize religion's timeless nature in discussions of the role of religion in politics. For example, Matthews's study demonstrates that the assertion that Buddhism promotes political compliance and negates political activism—in contrast to Islam—is not empirically tenable. The institutionalist approach also challenges the behaviorist approach that first looks into actors' religious beliefs and their disposition to explain political action.

This body of scholarship also raises intriguing questions about the autonomy and interests of nongovernmental religious organizations, and their role in democratization as civil society actors. It challenges the civil religion assumption that nongovernmental religious organizations always crave and pursue establishment of a democratic regime. For example, Kadir (2002) argues that mass-based nongovernmental religious organizations such as NU and *Muhammadiyah* played almost no significant role in the process of democratic transition in Indonesia. This is a puzzling observation given these organizations' mobilizational capacities among followers and some of the top leaders' reputation as democrats. This empirical observation evidently contradicts Hefner's claims about the significance of civil-minded pluralist Islamic associations that he asserts helped bring the authoritarian regime down. Can this weak commitment of nongovernmental religious organizations to democratic transition be fully explained by the state's coercive means? An answer to this question seems to lie in the way in which the government dealt with Islamic forces prior to the fall of the authoritarian regime.

In this respect, some important studies on nongovernmental religious organizations in Indonesia inform us that the stance of those organizations toward the authoritarian regime is not fully determined by their yearning to retain political autonomy as conventionally expected; in fact, their need to maintain religious autonomy and to maximize their immediate material interests and political influence counts for more than attaining a more democratic regime.

Feillard's study on NU, for example, suggests that NU's decision to withdraw from party politics—and to build an intimate relationship with the regime—in the mid-1980s was intended "to reduce tensions with the government and create a more peaceful environment in which the organization's social and religious activities could operate unencumbered" (1997: 136). NU schools, indeed, benefited significantly from this new relationship with the state; government subsidies for religious schools increased substantially, contributing to the recovery of membership (1997: 142). However, the NU's intimate relationship with the state cost it the loss of political independence, as this relationship engendered the organization's material and political dependence upon the regime.

For Feillard, the democratization question is not her prime concern. However, her study gives us critical information about the role of nongovernmental religious organizations in democratic transition. Moreover, it helps explain why prominent religious organizations such as NU were not willing (or were unable) to commit themselves to the process of democratization before and after the fall of the Suharto regime. One should not forget that Feillard's intimate empirical knowledge of the organization accumulated through her long ethnographic research is crucial to attaining such important theoretical insights.

Future Research Agendas

Three comparative research agendas warrant particular attention in the future. The first is the state's relationship to religious institutions. Case studies reveal that the manner in which states have interfered with religious institutions has varied across nations and across time. Why do some regimes employ a co-optation approach to control religious institutions whereas others employ a different strategy? Why do the same bureaucratic measures work in some countries but not in others? For example, Hedman's explicit comparative analysis of state-church relations and oppositional politics in Southeast Asia identifies varying patterns of oppositional mobilization, offering significant theoretical insights (Hedman 1997).

The political role of religious reformist movements also needs to be elaborated comparatively. Case studies on Indonesia, Thailand, and the Philippines have shown that new religious ideas and interpretations of religious texts and doctrines have greatly influenced the course of political activism. These cultural techniques and formulas have also enabled societal actors to offer an alternative vision of society and to challenge the legitimacy of ruling elites. This review reveals striking variations across nations in the scale and scope of religious debate and interpretation. Muslims in Indonesia are allowed considerable leeway and public space to interpret and express new religious ideas. In Malaysia, on the other hand, the space for doctrinal reinterpretations and religious debates seems rather limited. In fact, Islam played a crucial role in reinforcing intra-communal solidarity among Muslims. This was primarily (but not exclusively) due to the government's efforts to control religious dissent by administrative means. The actual impact of religious reformist movements in

Thailand also seems modest. Given the significance of religious ideas and cultural frames in mobilizing alternative political visions, comparative analysis of religious reformist movements is theoretically very important. In particular, causes of the varying influence of reformist movements across nations warrant further investigation.

Questions about religious authority also warrant comparative analysis: Who has the right to speak definitively about religious doctrines, and who is qualified to interpret them? Who has the ultimate right to authorize such religious qualifications? Scholars in other regions have grappled with these questions. In Egypt, for example, Islamist groups' successful appropriation of the authority to interpret sacred texts—an authority formerly monopolized by state-appointed *ulama*—paved the way for popular acceptance of their religious message (Wickham 2004: 239). This suggests that the possession of religious authority is a crucial quality for mobilizing the success of religious movements.

The studies reviewed here inform us that the function of religiously educated clerical actors in each of Southeast Asia's religious systems—*ulama*, monks, or priests—has not simply been limited to religious service; they have also been a vital political force. However, the level and the mode of their involvement in political activism vary considerably across place and time. This variation, as seen in case studies of Burma and Thailand as well as Malaysia and Indonesia, is not determined by religious doctrinal differences. Other institutional and structural factors appear to be more important. More specifically, the historical evolution of the state-church institutional formula seems to have had a considerable impact on the way in which religious authority structures are formulated and how clerical actors are involved in political activism.

Conclusion: Shortcomings in Existing Literature

Southeast Asian scholarship has considerably advanced our understanding of the relationship between religion and politics. At a broad methodological and theoretical level, this research has critiqued the classic-oriented dogmatic approach and the modernist assertion and moved beyond them. Southeast Asian scholarship has also challenged long-standing propositions about static culture.

Southeast Asian scholarship has mainly contributed to the accumulation of descriptive knowledge, although it has also advanced some important conceptual tools, such as civil Islam. Although the theoretical problems that many of these studies engage can be linked to broader debates outside the boundaries of a particular nation and religion, their theoretical and causal investigative pursuits are not always explicit.

Individual case studies provide important information about the interaction between religion and politics. Case studies of nation building, for example, demonstrate that religion has played an important ideological role in the forging of national identity and suggest that modern states cannot rely exclusively on coercive and secular bureaucratic mechanisms to integrate a religiously and ethnically fragmented nation. Governments manipulated cultural and religious forces to achieve their national development goals. Some governments decided to recognize a particular faith as the state religion, believing in the consolidating power of a national identity that is based on a single culture. Others followed this course to assert the cultural and political dominance of a particular group. The involvement of the state in the promotion of religion meant that the formation of religious doctrines was subject to secular political interests.

Southeast Asia scholars have revealed that the manner in which—and the extent to which—states interfere with religion significantly affects the formation of religious institutions and relationships between the state and the religious organizations. Studies of Thailand, for example, show that the state was fully involved in the organizational development of the ecclesiastical order. As a result, the state has exercised tight control over the *Sangha*, with a considerable effect on patterns of oppositional mobilization.[29]

The discussion of religious movements indicates that studies on Southeast Asia have flexibly adopted constructivist and instrumentalist approaches to offer a number of intriguing factors that explain the rise of religious movements, such as class and ethnicity. Consequently, we are now better informed about the causes of these movements. The studies reviewed here also show that social groups make use of religious symbols to further their political and socioeconomic goals. Many scholars now deploy instrumentalist and constructivist approaches not only to acknowledge changes in religious ideas and institutions but also to link them to the broader study of state institutions and social forces such as class and ethnicity.

Furthermore, research on religion and political transformations in Southeast Asia has advanced two theoretical perspectives to resolve the question of democratic transition and religion: the civic culture approach and the institutionalist approach. Taking up the Indonesian case, proponents of the former approach have contributed to broader debates about culture and democracy. They also challenge the conventional, static assertion that Islamic culture is not compatible with democracy. On the other hand, advocates of the latter position show that institutional form—especially the organizational nature of the church and its relationship with the state—has important effects on patterns of oppositional mobilization and the process of democratic transition.

Although Southeast Asian scholarship has contributed to social science, both theoretically and methodologically, three analytical weaknesses are painfully evident. The first, and perhaps most critical, shortcoming is the absence of comparative analysis—not only across various religious traditions and across regions, but also *within* the same religious system. Geertz stands out as an exception in this respect. His *Islam Observed* (1968) should be credited not only for his adaptation of the comparative method but also for being a rare instance of a comparison between a Southeast Asian case (Indonesia) and a non–Southeast Asian case (Morocco). Generally, however, Southeast Asian scholarship has not bridged national boundaries or built upon prior scholarship to search for and project common research agendas. Even after the retreat of the classical-oriented dogmatic approach and cultural essentialism, which emphasize the peculiarity of each religious tradition, only a very few studies have conducted inter-religious and inter-national comparative analyses.

The second major problem is the failure to engage broader theoretical debates. Many studies simply borrow an analytical tool to analyze one case, without seeking to make a theoretical contribution. There seems to be little interest in sharing theoretical concerns with studies outside their own territories. A third and final analytical weakness is the failure to vigorously pursue causal investigation and to elaborate causal findings.

Additional refinement and elaboration, in fact, will help resolve the limitations evident in many of these studies, and allow a closer dialogue with relevant literature. By adopting a comparative theoretical perspective, intriguing findings could be further elaborated, and viable research questions and testable hypotheses advanced. For example, Jackson's study on Thailand is unclear about the capacities of religious reformist movements to mobilize opposition against the government. Put in a comparative perspective, the political impact of these movements proves rather modest. As Jackson himself acknowledges, few religious leaders are willing to commit themselves to political activism in the conventional sense of party or oppositional politics. There is no religious-based political party led by clergies, for example. Moreover, we find that the ideological and political scope for the clergy to be overtly involved in political activities is highly restrained by secular statutes and religious codes.

Southeast Asian scholarship should not be held exclusively responsible for the low level of theoretical and comparative engagement with the literature outside the region. The scholarship on Islam, for example, has focused principally on the Middle East and has generally neglected Southeast Asia. This regional bias has been further reinforced by a methodological bias that emphasizes the classic-oriented doctrinal approach and the specificity of Islam. Southeast Asian Islam, from this analytical perspective, is a deviation from the orthodoxy and therefore is not regarded as important. Only recently has this attitude been modified,[30] as specialists on Islamic activism have attempted to bridge the gap between the study of Islamic activism and social science methods and theories (Wiktorowicz 2004). Such efforts to bridge Southeast Asian studies, social science theories, and other regions are badly needed.

Chapter Nine

The Study of Political Ethnicity in Southeast Asia

JAMIE S. DAVIDSON

Any essay on ethnicity in Southeast Asia will inevitably remark on the region's extraordinary ethnic heterogeneity. Less appreciated and acknowledged, however, has been the analytical richness of the study of this ethnic tapestry. Not only is this legacy reflected in its diversity of perspectives and voluminous contributions; it is also revealed in the influence its scholars have had on the social sciences. Political scientist Lucian Pye was a prominent proponent of the primordial paradigm and modernization theory, anthropologist Edmund Leach was a forerunner of the succeeding situationalist approach, and J. S. Furnivall of the plural society fame and Clifford Geertz were progenitors of the constructivist paradigm, which Benedict Anderson later helped to make mainstream. Moreover, institutional arrangements that have contained ethnic tensions have drawn the attention of noted comparativists. Malaysia, for instance, has been constructed as a critical case in the Lijphart-Horowitz debate over the merits of consociational democracy. The study of ethnic politics in Southeast Asia continues to draw productively on this fruitful lineage of interdisciplinary knowledge and perspectives.

However, this chapter argues that starting in the 1990s this tradition reached an impasse. Seemingly, the political study of ethnicity had run its course, having exhausted its three dominant paradigms. More specifically, it was forced to react to two developments that compelled scholars to rethink their approaches. One was the regional prevalence of ethnic and nationalist-related violence; the other was the penetration of international market forces, which precipitated a shift in some disciplines, especially anthropology, toward a focus on globalization, diaspora, and cultural studies. In response, two post-paradigmatic viewpoints emerged. One was a statist perspective. Despite claims to ethnicity's constructed or instrumental nature that implied an inherent superficiality, some scholars pointed to its stickiness—that as a real-world phenomenon it refused to be buried. In fact, the obverse was occurring, and ethnopolitics and ethnocentrism were rearing their ugly head in the form of violent separatist conflicts, ethnic expulsions, riots, and other types of aggressive political mobilizations. Therefore, given this apparent paradox— ethnicity's unstable foundations as viewed in the academy against worsening ethnic conflict—scholars sought explanatory recourse in studies of the state. They homed in on state policies and configurations of asymmetrical power relations embedded in a state to shed light on ethnicity's growing saliency. It was hoped that these insights would generate policy-oriented recommendations to aid conflict resolution.

Other scholars took a different track. Writing from a postmodernist viewpoint and in the context of globalization studies, they held that the hugeness and simultaneity of capital, informational, and cultural flows diminished the sovereignty of the state and the relevance of ethnicity.[1] Rising in its stead was an increasingly homogenized, new, consumerist cultural class. Simply put, whereas the above perspective zeroed in on the state, this one focused on the market and society. It was argued that Southeast Asia's growing wealth, middle-class lifestyles, and consumerist culture, not ethnicity, were what mattered, what gave people meaning and shaped identities under conditions of change and uncertainty. A neoclassist perspective, this method replaced relations of production with relations of consumption.

Adopting a wide-angle lens, this essay traces the intellectual unfolding of the study of political ethnicity in Southeast Asia, ranging from primordial, situational, and constructivist paradigms to the newer statist and neoclass, consumerist schools of thought. With regard to the studies selected, the politics of ethnicity figures prominently in the narrative, either as the phenomenon to be explained or as a significant contributing factor in the explanation of something else. I do not draw a sharp distinction between the two.[2] Furthermore, the works reviewed, methodologically qualitative in nature, are meant to be representative of the prevalent paradigm or perspective in question. In this way, despite exceptions, this essay tends not to assess critically the merits or demerits of each work. Rather, judgments are reserved for the paradigm within which they are situated.

Primordialism

The once-dominant view of ethnicity held by social scientists, primordialism embodied what for many years was deemed as commonsensical: Ethnicity is an innate characteristic of human society—it exists for its own sake. And given that one's ethnic identity and affiliation are irrevocably determined by birth, group boundaries are therefore immutable. Accordingly, what gives primordialism its emotional appeal, its strength, is the human and thus natural need to identify with or cling to something certain under conditions of rapid economic, political, and social change, which are capable of disturbing the way in which one views and relates to one's natural environment. As such, if this ethnic need constitutes one's most fundamental being, one's essence, political analysis must start from this point of departure; everything else is derivative.[3]

Writing in the 1960s, a bevy of scholars of Southeast Asia subscribed to this primordial conceptualization of ethnicity, which was particularly pronounced in a series of works devoted to exploring a country's "national political culture." What also made these accounts distinctive was their grounding of vital assumptions in an evident modernization framework. Broadly speaking, these authors sought to unlock the secret to the political culture—its timeless essence—that best explained why the countries in question lacked such attributes as rational bureaucratic norms; interest-based, political associations; functioning markets; and the rule of law, all of which were deemed necessary to develop along Western, modern lines.[4]

Five further characteristics draw these studies together. The first binding element is their unit of analysis, located at the level of the social structure or system. This is followed by their axiomatic assumption—and rarely empirically proven—that a dominant, national, political culture exists. Other ethnicities or competing alternatives are generally ignored or dismissed. Third, these studies seize on a single dimension that is believed to lie at the root of the political culture in question; as such, a great amount of discussion swirls about this core as the embodiment of the culture's mechanism of endurance. Their fourth unifying theme is the attempt to advance comparative political analysis by using a common vocabulary and standard set of variables and functions to describe the political system. In this way, such aspects as input/output functions, political communication, recruitment, political socialization, and political education are recurrent topics (Almond 1960). Finally, these exposés, implicated in the geopolitical polarization of the Cold War, are conservative in outlook. Typically, they aim to devise a cure for the illness that threatens to infect the body politic, which in these cases was susceptibility to mounting communist influence.

A noted scholar of this school, best encapsulated by his membership on the Committee on Comparative Politics of the Social Science Research Council, was Lucian Pye.[5] Exemplary is his 1962 book on the role of personality in Burmese nation building. Unquestionably condemning Burma's political system, debilitated by its utter instability and corresponding lack of associations predicated on rational interests, Pye casts the inadequacies of Burmese child-rearing practices not only as culprit, but also as that explanatory, primordial core of an ethnically Burmese political culture. By fingering the Burmese mother's maddeningly inconsistent attitude toward her children—ranging from periods of excessive doting to rash and sudden withdrawals of attention—Pye posits that the result is the Burmese boy's acute suspiciousness of human social relationships; he inculcates values and norms inimical to those necessary for the formation of predictable political groupings upon which a "transitional society" can firmly build. "The sum effect of these early experiences appears to be a peculiar blending of a perennial capacity for optimism with a diffuse, all-pervasive distrust and suspicion of others in any particular relationship" (1962: 185). Such gloom bodes ill for democratic politics or competitive markets.

Having laid the ethnic essence of Burmese political culture bare, Pye correspondingly fills his narrative with such categorical descriptors as the Burmese character, the Burmese attitude, the Burmese self of identity, and the Burmese outlook on life. On healing the ailing body politic, Pye concludes that, given the West's desire to contain communism, U.S. foreign aid should shift its emphasis from funding technical and economic programs to funding those that foster the political values, norms, and institutions within which a new national collective identity can take shape and grow.

The idea of a national political culture derived from an ethnic immutability was also brought to bear on Vietnam. In one such book, *The Vietnamese and Their Revolution*, McAlister and Mus posit the village as that essential ethnic element of Vietnamese political culture (and social structure): "Viet Nam is above all a way of being and living whose expression and means of expansion are the village" (1970: 50). In this way, to understand this peasant society's apparent paradox—its penchant for revolution combined with "patterns [of politics that] have remained virtually the same" (1) for centuries—one must analytically pierce the Vietnamese village that is "enclosed within a thick wall of bamboo and thorny plants . . ." (31). Behind this "bamboo screen," McAlister and Mus stereotypically find "energetic and tenacious workers" (6) with "a deep sense of spirituality" (4) who also possess high communalistic morals. These peasants are also inclined toward "instinctive reactions," while remaining naturally averse to "calculable elements" (66). Ultimately, as for Pye, for McAlister and Mus the central problem in Vietnam was how to create "a modern state out of a tradition-bound society" (2) with the least amount of violence possible. However, this modernity should not be of just any type—in particular, it must not be one "confused with communism" (6). The solution, as McAlister and Mus see it, lies in the successful integration of the village into the modern economy, which includes an increase of foreign-funded educational initiatives that will provide the Vietnamese peasant with the necessary tools to meet this challenge (143–144).

What faulty child-rearing practices were to Pye for Burma, and the village was to McAlister and Mus for Vietnam, smooth interpersonal relations were to scholars of this time writing on the Philippines. This "Filipino" ethnic essence, they proffered, accounted for a stable social structure and an attendant national political culture (Lynch 1968). Underlying this structure was the operating principle of *utang-na-loob* (debt of gratitude). Described as an "[a]ncient Filipino operating principle," *utang-na-loob* was deemed that essential something which "every Filipino is expected to possess . . ." (Hollnsteiner 1968: 28, 29). Functionally, this principle draws "big and little people" (Lynch 1984 [1975]) together in a web of putative reciprocity, which takes the form of distinctive patron-client networks. In turn, these networks explain the otherwise inexplicable outcomes of Philippine elections, when the patron calls on his client to cast a vote in his favor "regardless of the quality of the candidate involved or his party" (Hollnsteiner 1968: 39).

Although this overly personalistic feature of Philippine politics deviates from modern politics as predicated on rational interests and civic associations, with regard to healing the body politic these scholars differ from their primordial/modernization counterparts described above. Whereas the latter seek to instill new values and norms to effect fundamental change to ward off communism, the former do not. For them, reinforcing the status quo by deepening the mutually dependent web of reciprocity helped protect the Philippine body politic against the communist contagion that was the Huk rebellion of the 1950s (and early 1960s) in central Luzon. As these scholars saw it, curing a cold could invite a pandemic. In all, such natural and timeless conceptions of an ethnically rooted Philippine social structure influenced a generation of theorizing on the country's politics (Landé 1965; Wurfel 1988).[6]

Gordon Means's treatment of political ethnicity in Malaysia rounds out this section. In two important respects, however, Means's study diverges from the works reviewed above. First, unlike Burma, Vietnam, and the Philippines, Malaysia is lauded as that shining light where the judicious management of strained ethnic relations has instilled its political system with a stability conspicuously lacking in the aforementioned countries. In Means's own words, the 1963 formation of Malaysia was "a testimony to Malaya's progress toward a solution of its most vexing problems" (1970: 9). Second, Means does not configure a singular national political culture for Malaysia, yet his conceptions of the country's subnational counterparts along ethnic lines bring forth the work's primordial attributes.

Characteristically, like the authors examined above, Means lends credence to the notion that a singular, foundational dimension underpins Malaysia's social and political structure—in this case, its ethnic pluralism.[7] Regardless of the country's stability, adversarial communal relations have curbed the growth of a strong national identity in ways reminiscent of Pye's observations in Burma. To reflect the plurality of political cultures in Malaysia, Means devotes separate chapters to each major ethnic group, "the Malays," "the Chinese," and "the Indians" (and others), where ethnic essences come to the fore. In the Malay chapter, for instance, Means posits Islam as that natural cohesive that has intricately bound Malays together, providing them with a distinct ethnic homogeneity (1970: 17) and, over time, a discrete Malay political culture. Ultimately, the assumption that social divisions automatically translate into political conflicts is common to primordial conceptions of ethnicity.

Situationalism

For decades, primordialism held sway as the predominant paradigm through which to explore ethnicity and such related political phenomena as nation building, conflict, and voting patterns. Then, starting in the late 1960s, innovative scholarship conducted in large part in the new states began to challenge primordialism's preeminence. One leading cause of the latter's decline was the destructiveness and debacle that was the U.S. military involvement in Vietnam, where the teleological assumptions of modernization theory (and policies related to such) were torn asunder. New research was required that illuminated the great diversity of ways in which people were responding to the magnitude of the transformations their societies were undergoing. One critic of the time wrote: "As the experts' confidence in their constructs waned, their perspective changed. . . . The old paradigms . . . were refuted by history" (Kessler 1978: 18, 19). It was in this context that an alternative paradigm, an instrumentalist view of ethnicity, gained currency. Abner Cohen (1969), for instance, in his study of Yoruba towns in Nigeria showed how Hausa traders acted as an interest group that exploited ethnicity to maximize material gain.[8] Cohen's goal-oriented instrumentalism took aim at primordialism's view of ethnicity as a profound, psychologically held attachment that resonated evenly across time and space. Just as significant, in a seminal essay published in 1969 Fredrik Barth switched the focus of the study of ethnicity from such primordial favorites as culture and custom to the boundaries that distinguished one group from the other. For Barth, the significance of self-identity within a delimited set of borders, not culture, was what constituted the ethnic group. However, these boundaries were in constant flux and in danger of being breached. The need to continually defend, redefine, and renegotiate boundaries— all told, the conscious awareness of maintaining one's group structure— destabilized the fixed, rigid assumptions of ethnic identity to which primordial exponents subscribed.

Cohen and Barth—and later Brass (1991)—came to represent what became known as the situationalist paradigm, which privileged the shifting and mutable qualities of ethnicity according to circumstance.[9] Whereas primordial thinking sees a group's or a person's claim to ethnic identity as rooted in the allure of affective attachments, situationalism locates the instrumental manipulation of ethnicity for collective political and economic gain at the heart of its analysis. By loosening primordialism's rigid assumptions, this new school of thought also allows for individuals to significantly influence the way in which a society changes.

Anthropologist Edmund Leach was a forerunner of situational thinking, although he did not explicitly use the terminology that later came to be associated with this paradigm, such as interest group and economic maximization. Leach

(1954) studied the changing social structures of Kachin (and Shan) groups in the highlands of Burma.[10] The conclusions he drew were far-reaching; they dissolved the conventional assumption that social structure and culture/ethnicity were naturally commensurable and mutually supportive. Uncovering the fluidity with which individuals or cultural groups adapted to different social structures that over time are susceptible to the force of broad ecological or economic factors, Leach decoupled society from culture in such a way that the two could no longer easily coexist. Foreshadowing the situationalist school, Leach notes that "every individual of a society, each in his own interest, endeavors to exploit the situation as he perceives it and in so doing the collectivity of individuals alters the structure of the society itself" (1954: 8). Hence, anticipating Barth, Leach observes that structural oppositions, not cultural content, give rise to ethnic difference and that these structural oppositions oscillate over time—in this case, between what he calls Shan (valley) feudalism and Kachin (hill) democracy. It is simply foreign to primordial thinking that over time Kachins could "become Shans" (9).

Whereas Leach's work predated the rise of situational ethnicity, Judith Nagata's 1974 article on ethnic relations in Malaysia is exemplary of this paradigm. Here, Nagata demonstrates the dynamism of ethnic boundary expression and change among urban Malaysians in Georgetown, Penang. She works on the assumption that these boundaries are flexible, that the cultural features associated with an ethnic group are mutable, and that census-like ethnic categories and their social expression are incommensurable.

Nagata examines several situations of ethnic switching, particularly among Arabs, Indians, and Malays, who, as Muslims, share religious identifications. Social solidarity (and its obverse, social distance), expediency, social status, and social mobility all represent motivations for individuals to assume different ethnic identities according to context. For Nagata, it is critically important that this maneuvering be seen as a positive development to counter the conventional view that ethnic malleability reflects social marginalization, incomplete integration, or cognitive confusion. Nagata does note the limitations to ethnic adaptability in contemporary Malaysia, however. Pinpointing the dual role that Islam serves in this regard, she underscores the deep, cross-ethnic bonds of affection that Islam can stimulate while also widening cleavages in other contexts—in this case, the Chinese/Malay divide.

In Malaysia, the political discourse about ethnicity and the accompanying social sensitivity have been paramount in the country's short, post-independence history. Thus it is to be expected that Nagata and countless others have sought to grapple with ethnicity's social and political manifestations. In this regard, it is surprising yet no less significant that a signal contribution to the situationalist school came from the relatively ethnically homogeneous kingdom of Thailand. In two important works, anthropologist Charles Keyes furthered the idea of ethnic malleability, or what he calls "adaptation," among minority groups in Thailand (and Burma). A short yet influential monograph published in 1967, *Isan: Regionalism in Northeastern Thailand*, recounts the rise of Isan ethnic consciousness among this Lao-speaking minority. Two critical junctures stand out in Keyes's narrative. First was the late nineteenth century and King Chulalongkorn's (1868–1910) modernizing reforms that aimed to transform his kingdom into a strong, centralized, modern nation-state, complete with a professional bureaucracy and other Western technologies of governance and rule.[11] These reforms were the beginnings of thorough state penetration and incorporation of the northeast into Bangkok's realm. Second was the 1950s, when economic liberalization precipitated a boom in Bangkok's economy, thereby leaving other such regions as the northeast behind. Growing material regional differentiation also bore on social relations, and Isan who poured into Bangkok looking for work were stigmatized and denigrated as "northeasterners."

Importantly, Keyes concludes his study with a brief discussion of alternating ethnic identities. Loyalty to the king and to the Thai nation, for Keyes, is congruent with an Isan identity ploy of two "conscious models, one Isan, the second Thai" (1967: 60). In a 1979 essay, Keyes further elaborates his theme of "ethnic adaptation" and provides the following example: Northeasterners may be "Lao" when facing Thai government officials, "Thai" when visiting Laos, or "Isan" in other contexts (for example, in Bangkok) (1979: 4). In sum, these shifting "adaptive strategies" in the face of changing, short-term circumstances encapsulate the idea behind situational ethnicity.

The final situationalist work surveyed here is political scientist William Liddle's case study of ethnicity and political integration in northern Sumatra, Indonesia, published in 1970. Like Keyes, Liddle's work is situated on the periphery of the country in question. Due to Indonesia's great ethnic diversity, however, Liddle was forced to tackle a more complex regional, ethnic tapestry than Keyes faced.

Drawing heavily on Geertz's important article on primordial attachments in the new states (see below), Liddle is primarily concerned with the "integrative revolution" dilemma and the need to overcome what was for him a twofold gap: one horizontal (along racial, ethnic, and religious lines) and the other vertical (between the elites and masses). Liddle hypothesized that these gaps were in part surmountable through an effective, nationally oriented political party system.

At first glance, one might be tempted to highlight the primordialism that Liddle seemingly advocates. His account is dotted with references to primordial attachments and the strength of affective ties. Nor does he examine the colonial heritage of Indonesia's post-independence ethnic discourse. Yet, like Keyes, Liddle is attuned to the practices and policies of an external yet centralizing regime—in the case of Thailand, Chulalongkorn's reforms, and in Indonesia, the late colonial state—and the ways that they affect a local society. In northern Sumatra, the introduction of a plantation and a money economy, urbanization, and the imposition of world religions, especially the recent arrival of Christianity, figure prominently. Growing ethnic consciousness among social groups was one outcome of these transformations. Moreover, through the importance of party organizing and competitive elections, Liddle ascribes a critical agency to the ethnic entities under study to degrees greater than primordial accounts typically allow. These politics spur varying degrees of ethnic consciousness across groups, which further complicates primordial thinking. In the end, Liddle's conclusions echo those of Keyes's findings. Competing loyalties—one to the state and one to the ethnic group—need not be antagonistic. Instead, an individual's competence to adjust according to his or her needs and circumstances suggests that the two can be mutually supportive.

Constructivism

Just as Barth and Cohen, both of whom drew on Leach, brought situational ethnicity to the fore, scholars highlighted its shortcomings. Critically, if individuals freely oscillate between ethnicities, they queried, what then explains the tremendous passion that ethnicity seems to arouse in its adherents? This type of question confounds situational explanations. Situational ethnicity also problematically rested on radical transactional assumptions. That is, ethnic switching was described as occurring in situations that resembled unrealistic free-market conditions, where the forces of state formation, power, and dominance played no role. Historical processes were also bypassed, to the ire of skeptics.

Consequently, attempts were made to fuse insights from primordial and situational paradigms, with varying degrees of success (Keyes 1981; McKay 1982; Scott 1990). Here I want to focus on the last point mentioned above: the inattention that both paradigms paid to historical processes. Rectifying this gap in a Southeast Asian context meant revisiting colonial state formation and its impact on local societies—notably, on the origins of ethnic groups and cleavages.

Currently, mainstream political science has come to accept the notion that identities are socially constructed. This is taken to mean that people erroneously "believe that particular social categories are fixed by human nature rather than by social convention and practice." In this way, constructivism intends to show "how the content and even membership rules of taken-for-granted categories . . . have changed over time" (Fearon and Laitin 2000: 848–849). One popular method to advance constructivist arguments has been to investigate macrohistorical, economic, and social processes as crucial factors in the construction of social identities (Fearon and Laitin 2000: 852).

In the formerly colonized world, of course, this required delineating colonialism's role in these constructivist processes and outcomes. For instance, political scientist Daniel Posner (2003) has recently explored the colonial origins of ethnic cleavages, their relative sizes, and their geographic spread in present-day Zambia. African scholarship, as Posner recognizes, possesses a healthy lineage of this kind of historically oriented, constructivist methodology. Posner invokes research from the 1970s and 1980s by the likes of Crawford Young (1976) and Howard Wolpe (1974), along with the "invention of tradition" (Hobsbawm and Ranger 1983) and "creation of tribalism" (Vail 1989) projects. Had Posner conducted his research in Southeast Asia, he would have discovered a similarly fertile, constructivist heritage dating from the same time period that traces the origins of ethnic groups and cleavages to the political economy of colonial state formation.

However, it warrants mention that two scholars whose influence has resonated far beyond Southeast Asia helped to sow the seeds for the flourishing of this historical constructivism in the 1970s and 1980s. One was J. S. Furnivall, a renowned colonial civil servant–cum-scholar whose notion of the plural society remains one of the most enduring social scientific concepts to come out of Southeast Asia (Rex 1980 [1959]).[12] Coining the term to describe what he saw as the basic social structure in "tropical dependencies" (1956 [1948]: 303), Furnivall saw a plural society as "comprising two or more elements or social orders which live side by side, yet without mingling, in one political unit" (1944 [1939]: 446). Meeting and interacting only in the marketplace, Europeans, Indians, Chinese, and natives, taken together, lacked the organic cohesiveness found in European societies to produce the necessary social, and thus political, common will to cohere a free-market society. Famously, he observed, "[I]n Burma, as in Java, probably the first thing that strikes the visitor is the medley of peoples—European, Chinese, Indian and native. It is in the strictest sense a medley, for they mix but do not combine" (1956 [1948]: 304). Tellingly, for Furnivall the plural society did not arise out of timeless ethnic essences or out of the aggregation of choices made by individuals. Rather, it was shaped under the forces of colonial policy, which encouraged economic and social segregation for the sake of achieving stability and cost-effective rule. Thus, over time finer distinctions of "Chinese," "Indian," "native," and so on grew, and attendant identities gained currency.

Clifford Geertz, another important progenitor of constructivism, was a leading exponent of the interpretivist school of anthropology. This school advocated ethnographic "thick description" as an analytical methodology to delve into a people's worldview, culture, and, just as important, political action, attitudes, and behavior (Geertz 1973a). It is conventional to see Geertz as a primordialist. Attention is invariably drawn to his discussion of the problem that primordial attachments—race in Malaya, tribes in Nigeria, regionalism in Indonesia, for instance—posed for successful integration within the new states. In this essay, which was originally published in 1963, Geertz describes the power and essence of primordial attachments as the social entities that we take as "given," and that are "ineffable, and at times overpowering, coerciveness in and of themselves" (1973a: 259). Fingering Geertz as a primordialist for views put forth in this article misses the mark, however.[13] As has been recently argued, Geertz maintains that "peoples' beliefs in their primordial attachments rather than the inherent immutability of those attachments" was at issue; furthermore, these attachments manifest themselves in multiple forms, "none of them being a natural category" (Fearon and Laitin 2000: 849, n. 8). Instead, these categories, as Geertz notes, "are part and parcel of the very process of the creation of a new polity and a new citizenship" (1973a: 270).

Geertz's constructivism also stems from his analytical stress on the interpretation of people's thoughts and behavior—that is, a "method of describing and analyzing the meaningful structure of experience . . . as it is apprehended by representative members of a particular society at a particular point in time . . ." (364). As significant as what people think is *how* they do it: "All experience is construed experience, and the symbolic forms in terms of which it is construed thus determine . . . its intrinsic nature" (405). Thus, although our categories and forms are deeply meaningful and contain vital cores, they are not natural phenomena derived from ethnic immutabilities; they originate from the significance of the webs of meaning that we attach to them.

Geertz's studies on Java exhibit this kind of constructivism, tending toward its historical variant. In his seminal *Religion of Java* (1960), for example, he divides Javanese society into three subtraditions predicated on distinctive world outlooks: *abangan* (a kind of folk syncretism), *santri* (Islamic orthodoxy), and *priyayi* (the mystically influenced gentry). A close reading of the text reveals that the three groupings are not innate categories. Rather, they were generated in the colonial context of educational experience: the largely illiterate *abangan*, the *pesantren* or *madrasah*-educated *santri*, and the primarily Dutch-schooled *priyayi*.

Following Furnivall and Geertz, a leading proponent of historical constructivism has been Benedict Anderson.[14] One of his clearest statements on this approach comes from one of his less celebrated articles, an introductory essay to a 1987 volume on tribal groups and ethnic minorities in Southeast Asia.[15] Examining the formidable role that the colonial state had in creating majorities and minorities across Southeast Asia, Anderson grounds his constructivism in the essay's opening sentence: "It is easy to forget that minorities came into existence in tandem with majorities—and in Southeast Asia, very recently." He continues: "[Minorities] were born of the political and cultural revolution brought about by the maturing of the colonial state and by the rise against it of popular nationalism" (1987: 1).

Key for Anderson was the fact that, ideologically and politically, Europeans were the region's first rulers to think in majority-minority terms. In practice, this materialized in bureaucratic conventions and other aspects of state formation and colonial domination. Anderson singles out the case of the ethnic Chinese under the royal Dutch trading company (VOC) and the subsequent colonial regime. The VOC created a distinct juridical space for "Chinese," which included restrictions on habitation and travel that engendered a minority stigmatization. This contrasted starkly with the ease with which ethnic Chinese assimilated into mainstream Thai society, a country that was not colonized, thus illuminating how "unnatural" the situation in the Netherlands Indies had become.

Anderson also describes how "designated minorities" on the state's peripheries were strategically corralled into becoming ethnic groups to be pitted against troublesome "majorities." As colonial states came under the pressure of majority nationalism, Anderson observes, the colonial state leaned on "minority" partners—indigenous peoples in Malaya, mountain groups of Luzon, and the imagined "Papuan" people of the Indies' easternmost extreme. As such, motivated by the claims of popular nationalism, such "majorities" as Burmese, Javanese, and Vietnamese were denigrated by colonial elites as "unmanly, treacherous, aggressive, degenerate and feudal." In contrast, peripheral minorities were lauded as "honest, brave, truthful, sincere and loyal" (1987: 5). The residue of these colonial reifications remains salient today. All told, in Anderson's hands, ethnicity is a thoroughly modern yet historically contingent outcome of colonial state formation and domination.

Whereas Anderson brushes his constructivist strokes broadly across Southeast Asia, others have similarly reexamined colonial rule within single countries. Notably, in a 1982 essay Robert Taylor adopts a historical constructivist perspective to explore why or how politicized ethnicity has become an obstacle to national unity and integration in contemporary Burma. Taylor traces the lineages of politicized ethnicity to the origins of British colonial rule. Arguing that the British mode of governance fundamentally changed the way in which Burma's societies were ruled, Taylor underscores the simplifying classificatory schema that British imperial ideology championed to bolster its strategy of divide and rule. Besides lumping a great diversity of peoples under such crude ethnic umbrellas as the Burmans, the Chins, the Shans, and others, British colonial officials also exacerbated group difference. Prior to colonialism, "[I]t was not ethnic diversity," Taylor observes, "but cultural practice which [had] divided people socially, not necessarily politically" (1982: 13).

In essence, the British instituted a system of direct rule among valley peoples, thus imposing the restrictions congruent with a modern state administration. In the meantime, the hill areas were governed indirectly, whereby the British preserved the status quo by relying upon (and in fact significantly buttressing) a coterie of conservative petty princes or chiefs. This differential mode of rule reified hill-valley distinctions. The British ban on the Burmese national elite against organizing in upland areas further reinforced the divide, as did the importation of European ideas of ethnic/racial thinking and hierarchy. Taking a cue from colonial forerunners, the Burmese nationalist elite were taught to see ethnicity as determinative of social, economic, and political action. Nothing makes this clearer than the hierarchical ordering of the political economy of resource distribution: Europeans, Chinese, and Indians at the top, Burmese at the bottom. All told, it is this ethnic-think legacy, Taylor demonstrates, that has been bequeathed to post-independence Burma, and that, in turn, has greatly contributed to the prevalence of divisive ethnic politics that continues to fuel rebellions and endanger the country's existence.

Shortly after the publication of Taylor's essay, sociologist Charles Hirschman (1986b) examined similar British colonial legacies in the problematic "race" relations of Malaya/Malaysia.[16] Like Taylor, Hirschman holds that, despite the existence of ethnocentrism, pre-colonial ethnic boundaries were fluid, overlapping, and mutable. However, this changed, beginning in the late nineteenth century with the further institutionalization of British rule. Here, as in Burma, the ideological importation of social Darwinism, ascendant in European thinking, was crucial. Scientific racism and its attendant racial ideology justified the deepening of colonial rule, thereby worsening local social relations. The belief that ethnicities did not simply differ but constituted innately different capacities was reflected in the colony's changing political economy. Each group was slotted into its putatively natural place in this colonial capitalist economy: The British, as rulers, would protect Malays in their natural position as rice farmers; the Chinese would either work as tin-mine coolies or function as middlemen traders; and Indians, a more docile labor force, would ply the rail lines or toil on rubber plantations.

In a subsequent article, Hirschman (1987) applied this constructivist view to the history of census taking in Malaya/Malaysia, first conducted in the Straits Settlements in 1871. A crucial instrument in the development of modern governmentality, the census led to the British conceptual confusion. Whereas the original term, "nationalities," was used to classify social groups, it was later changed to "race," which, for the British, signified a more distinct categorization. More puzzling, however, was devising a classifying system to arrange and count all the "races" present in the colony. Census takers were confounded by the bewildering array of "Asian" peoples, including the colony's indigenous population, whose categories and labels underwent repeated and substantial change. some racial/ethnic categories came and went. Some were subsumed under other labels; some disappeared altogether. Hirschman further demonstrates that over time, census categories increasingly reflected strictly racial, rather than religious, categories.[17]

Crisis and the Start of Something (s) New

THE STATIST APPROACH

In the early to mid-1990s, the discrete attributes of the three paradigms began to give way as the study of ethnic politics in Southeast Asia entered into what can be called a post-paradigmatic phase. Two reasons in particular accounted for this transformation. One was increasing ethnic violence, the other the penetration of the market and the disciplinal reaction, especially that of anthropology, to this development, which sought recourse in globalization, diaspora, and cultural studies. We deal with the former before returning to the latter.

The historical constructivism described above left scholars who were grappling with the subject of ethnic violence unconvinced. To be sure, ethnic violence is only one issue among many in the study of ethnicity, but in today's world, it is particularly pressing. Conflict resolution required reliable yet rapid appraisal to produce effective policy recommendations. Uncovering the colonial origins of ethnicity or ethnic cleavages, no matter how intricately explored, seemed superfluous. For some, it simply lacked insight into resolving contemporary ethnic strife—let alone the years of painstaking research required to achieve this historical and analytical depth. Finally, the restricted scope of this research seemed to militate against generating comparative insights that might aid in ameliorating ethnic tensions across the region.

Primordialism was deemed equally problematic, if not more so. Its failure to explain the rise and fall of ethnic consciousness (and violence) across space and time, let alone the emergence of new ethnic constellations, was crippling. Nor could situational ethnicity explain the great passions that fed ethnic bloodletting, such as the horrendous, quasi-sadistic nature in which it was conducted (Horowitz 2001). If people could switch their ethnic identities at will, why were they killing others in the name of that identity? Confounded, scholars of Southeast Asia sought new approaches in order to understand contemporary ethnic dilemmas.

Ethnic troubles have been rife throughout Southeast Asia. Ethnic rebellions have wracked Burma and have flared on the fringes of Indonesia, Thailand, and the Philippines. Seemingly ubiquitous highland indigenous minorities have seethed with discontent due to decades of exploitation, marginalization, and stigmatization. Seeking to remedy the situation, scholars delved into studies of the Southeast Asian state. Delineating specific state policies and practices, it was believed, would not only uncover roots of ethnic tensions and help generate policy recommendations, but would also identify potential conflict areas. Another distinctive feature of this perspective was the attention it paid to comparative methodology, realizing that strained ethnic relations broadly conceived, and violence in particular, were regional issues that required regional solutions.

David Brown's comparative study of ethnic politics and the state in Southeast Asia is exemplary of this trend. At the outset, he establishes his focus to be on "how the development and political manifestations of ethnic consciousness are related to differences in the character of each of these [Southeast Asian] states" (1994: xi). Rejecting the extremes of both primordial and situational perspectives, Brown argues for a middle ground—or, in the words of this essay, a post-paradigmatic space. Inspired by such ethnic politics theorists as Walker Connor and Donald Horowitz, he seeks recourse in the social psychological literature to explain the multifaceted political manifestations of ethnicity. Accordingly, ethnicity is conceived neither as affective attachment nor as mere instrument, but as "an ideology which individuals employ to resolve the insecurities arising from the power structure within which they are located" (1994: 1).

To buttress his claim of conceiving ethnicity as an ideology, Brown applies a set of models to his respective cases: an ethnocratic state to explain Burma's ethnic rebellions, corporatism to study Singapore's effective management of ethnic relations, neo-patrimonialism to shed light on Indonesia's national integration, internal colonialism to understand ethnic rebellion in Thailand's northeast, and a class perspective to illuminate ethnic relations in Malaysia. In all, Brown's comparative approach highlights both case-by-base peculiarities and cross-case patterns. Brown concludes that ethnic relations mirror the strength of the state; a stronger state increases the chances of handling ethnic relations successfully. Ethnic diversity in and of itself is secondary.

Subsequent studies of political ethnicity in Southeast Asia have taken a cue from Brown's comparative focus on the state, as reflected in two edited volumes by Michael Brown and Sumit Ganguly (1997a, 2003). Both volumes underscore the saliency of state policy in exacerbating or alleviating ethnic relations, and the collection of case studies aids the comparative insights characteristic of this approach. What distinguishes Brown and Ganguly's work from David Brown's book is their unambiguous emphasis on policy. They anticipate that thorough, qualitative political analysis can generate recommendations for resolving conflict. For this they narrow their focus to government policy, which, they submit, "can push countries in the direction of instability, conflict and inequity, on the one hand, or stability, harmony, and justice, on the other" (1997b: 1). Accordingly, contributors were tasked with tracing the evolution of government policies, assessing these policies, and drawing a set of lessons and policy recommendations. Drawing on the case studies, in the volume's conclusion Brown puts forth a four-pronged prescription for national leaders: (1) accept a multicultural framework, (2) limit the use of coercion, (3) adopt proactive policies on ethnicity, and, finally, (4) implement policies—simply announcing them will not work (1997b: 514–515). A subsequent edited volume by Brown and Ganguly (2003) on state management of ethnic relations zeroes in on language policy, rather than exploring the breadth of government policies. Language policy is taken as a reliable indicator to assess a state's commitment to promoting quality ethnic relations. It is also considered an effective gauge of official attitudes toward ethnic minorities.[18]

In this context, Thaveeporn Vasavakul's chapter on Vietnam is illustrative. According to Thaveeporn, two competing features encapsulate what in actuality is a complex array of language and minority policies. On the one hand, minority languages are deemed "the cultural property of the entire nation" (2003: 211). Not only do the speakers of local languages enjoy the right to use their language; the government has also instituted writing programs designed to romanize minority languages. On the other hand, there are state policies that erode the benevolence of the first approach. Notable is the Vietnamese government's promotion of mass internal migration. In reality, this program is a continuation of French colonial policy, with the aim of buttressing state control by moving ethnically Viet populations from densely populated lowlands to less-dense, non-Viet upland areas.[19] This dynamic has been particularly pronounced in the country's central highlands, where demographic shifts have adversely affected highland minorities. Mounting land and natural resource pressures are but one result. With regard to language, as the number of Vietnamese speakers who inhabit the highlands grows, indigenous minorities are de facto forced to learn and read *quoc ngu*, the romanized Vietnamese script. Yet, as the number of Viet teachers unfamiliar with local languages increases, so too does the dropout rate of minority children. Some may celebrate the bilingualism or multilingualism of minorities in Vietnam, yet for these indigenous communities, as Thaveeporn underscores, it is a matter of survival.

Although indigenous-settler dynamics in upland central Vietnam can be described as tense, this region has not experienced the deadly ethnic conflict and separatist movements that peripheral areas elsewhere in the region have. One area rocked by ethnic violence stemming from a long-standing nationalist movement has been the southern Philippine island of Mindanao. The troubled national integration of the country's southern Muslim communities into the predominantly Christian nation-state has been a thorn in the side of Spanish, U.S., and Philippine administrations.

The conventional assumption holds that the recent unrest and rebellion are the latest manifestation of a 400-year-old Christian-Muslim conflict (Tan 1977; George 1980). According to this view, tensions have continued unabated since the arrival of Islam in the archipelago's southern reaches and subsequent Spanish attempts to quash it. Consequently, the contemporary rebellion, which in its present form dates from the early 1970s, is seen as inevitable and predictable, particularly given the inherently violent culture found among some of the ethnic groups that make up the Moro people (Kiefer 1972). As significant, it is submitted that a deeply held, transcendent Muslim identity has acted as a natural glue unifying these multiple ethnic communities (Gowing and McAmis 1974: x). The following observation exemplifies this primordial interpretation:

> For over 400 years, the Moros perceived their struggle as a fight to protect their religion, cultural identity and homeland against foreign invaders. . . . Over the centuries Islam has been important to the Muslim people . . . not only in forging the basis of their self-identity, but also as the cement between deep ethnic divisions that exist among the many cultural-linguistic groups that make up the Moro people. (Molloy 1988: 61, quoted in McKenna 1998: 80)

Besides conceptions of Islam as an innate magnet among Moros, another study draws on the narrative of universal Islamic warfare that proves the religion's inherently revolutionary and rebellious nature (Che Man 1990).

Two recent works take issue with the dominance of these primordial interpretations and the simplified history of local resistance and colonial bellicosity. Political scientist Patricio Abinales seeks to undermine the prevalence of what he calls "identity politics" (2000: 2), similar to what anthropologist Thomas McKenna dubs the "myth of Morohood" (1998: 45). Although both Abinales and McKenna admit that exploiting a radical Muslim identity to act as a mobilizing tool may have precipitated the outbreak of rebellion in the 1970s, they also demonstrate that this very same Muslim identity was used—and hence over time was sharpened—by Islamic elites for most of the twentieth century as a means of accessing state largess. In other words, Islamic elite integration into the body politic was real. Also, for both these authors, the swift decline of the primary secessionist organization—the Moro National Liberation Front—exposed this communal identity's fragility as both a primordial tie and a mobilizing symbol. As such, and in contrast to primordial viewpoints, Abinales and McKenna portray the origins of this pan-Muslim identity as a contingent outcome of colonial state formation, local elite co-optation, and center-periphery politics of the independent Philippine state—a mix of processes and perspectives characteristic of post-paradigmatic views on political ethnicity.

On the rebellion itself, by highlighting seven decades of acquiescence and elite accommodation under U.S. and Philippine regimes, Abinales fingers the breakdown of local elite-state relations during the increasingly centralizing and authoritarian Marcos regime. McKenna additionally notes the radicalizing effect that educational experiences in Manila had on select Mindanao Muslims, who then returned home to conceptualize the rebellion. Moreover, pervasive military harassment of Muslims, lethal anti-Muslim riots, and the affectual ties among subaltern networks that provided rank-and-file support for the separatist elite all aided in the outbreak of the revolt. More conceptually, McKenna champions a complex, multi-layered perspective of domination, accommodation, and resistance to grasp the ethnographic realities and competing narratives of nationalist movements and structures (1998: 4–5). Finally, by situating his case study in a rich, historically oriented society-state perspective, Abinales suggests that we as political scientists "need to examine exactly how the *state* affects the emergence and transformation of communal identities and how these, in turn, shape and reshape state-society ties" (2000: 4, emphasis added).

The concentration of ethnic and nationalist-related violence in the southern Philippines—and the studies thereof—contrasts sharply with similar violence in Indonesia. Viewed against the dominant case study mode of analysis, Jacques Bertrand (2004) has recently provided the most extensive account to date of the unrest that plagued the early post-Suharto state. By bridging the two principal categories of cases—the ethno-nationalist and the nonseparatist, communal variant—Bertrand constructs a singular explanatory framework that finds analytical purchase in the institutional makeup of the Indonesian state.[20] He advances the idea of a "national model" and its related formal institutional makeup shaping and influencing ethnic identities and inter-ethnic relations; these institutional relationships are what determine a nation's position regarding the state. For Bertrand, the New Order's constraining of the national model produced tensions and inequities in a way that would prompt intermittent ethnic violence under the regime, but would unleash great clashes, including a spike in nationalist movements, once it fell.

For Bertrand, the New Order's stranglehold over the national model led to the pervasive socioeconomic, cultural, and political marginalization of Dayaks on Kalimantan; at the national level, the subordination of political Islam; exclusionary practices toward and the resulting stigmatization of ethnic Chinese; and the late (and thus failed) integration of Papua (Irian Jaya) and East Timor into the nation-state. Once the regime succumbed to democratization pressures, acute politicizations and violence resulted from marginalized groups taking advantage of the uncertainties characteristic of rapid political transitions to make bolder claims for inclusion or greater access to state resources. Significantly, this was a moment—what Bertrand conceives as a critical juncture—when the New Order's national model cracked or was subjected to intense debate over its fundamentals. With the model's moorings unhinged, violent ethnic riots broke out on Kalimantan; scores of Indonesian women of Chinese descent were systematically raped in May 1998 in Jakarta; anti-Christian riots across Java increased in intensity and culminated in the ignition of three-year-long religious clashes in the Moluccan Islands; and East Timor, Papua, and Aceh experienced an increase in separatist demands and related violence. In all, as Bertrand explains, "these responses to the institutional evolution of the Indonesian *state*, and the particular national model it came to present, explain in large part why conflicts emerged in particular places and periods of time, while not in others" (2004: 8, emphasis added). Bertrand's productive mix of historical constructivist and situational approaches and attention paid to the role of the state and policy prescriptions—he sees decentralization as a possible ameliorative—makes his work exemplary of the post-paradigmatic study of ethnic politics.

The discussion of ethnic strife in the southern Philippines and Indonesia—the example of Burma or southern Thailand could as easily have been engaged—was not meant to overshadow those cases in the region where institutional arrangements have largely stymied deadly ethnic conflict. Malaysia is often judged as this positive counterexample. Here, the authorities' relatively skillful management of ethnic relations has also drawn considerable attention from nonspecialists, making the country an important case in the broader comparative literature to degrees greater than its Southeast Asian neighbors. However, comparativists have been at odds as to what accounts for the country's stability.

In particular, the case of Malaysia has figured prominently in the Lijphart-Horowitz debate on the efficacy of consociationalism in reducing conflict in deeply divided societies (Montville 1990). Conceived by Lijphart as an accommodative model of government, consociationalism at root comprises an elite-run, grand coalition that provides each major ethnic group the protection of minority interests, proportional political and administrative representation, and internal autonomy (1977: 25). With respect to Malaysia, Lijphart traces its consociational achievement to the formation of the Alliance Party. This was the electoral coalition negotiated between the elites of the United Malays' National Organization, the Malayan Chinese Association, and the Malayan Indian Congress that undergirded the country's stability from 1955 to 1969— that is, until lethal ethnic riots erupted in urban Penang, Kuala Lumpur, and elsewhere over increasing political competition and worsening economic conditions. Although Lijphart admits that institutional arrangements reconstituted in 1971 fell short of the consociational ideal—they overly favored Malays—he does nevertheless consider Malaysia as "a reasonably successful consociational democracy in the Third World . . ." (1977: 150).

In contrast, casting doubt on this characterization of Malaysia,[21] Horowitz maintains that the alliance never constituted a genuine, grand coalition. That each major ethnic group lacked a single set of leaders was reflected in its lukewarm electoral results: a high of some 58 percent in 1964, and several showings of about 50 percent. More tellingly, the 1969 killings exposed the alliance's fragility (1985: 575).

Still, Horowitz's analysis agrees with Lijphart's observations to the extent that electoral democracy helps to explain Malaysia's impressive stability. Horowitz (1990b) lauds its promotion of a centrist coalition that requires winning votes across ethnic divides, an electoral design that stands in marked contrast to Sri Lanka's framework, which prompted ethnic outbidding and thus intense polarization. Horowitz's conclusions have been critically scrutinized by another comparativist, however. Jack Snyder, in his book on democratization and nationalism (2000), considers that, rather than the encouragement of democracy, its obverse, the curtailment of democracy, saved Malaysia in the late 1960s and early 1970s from heading down the Sri Lankan path of prolonged civil war. The restriction of press freedoms and democratic rights, according to Snyder, helped to reduce ethnic tensions, which, in turn, created conditions that allowed this communally divided society to survive and economically thrive (2000: 274–275, 280–287).[22]

THE CULTURAL, CONSUMPTION APPROACH

As may be gleaned from the above discussion, this state-oriented view has engendered a prolific literature that has enabled scholars and policy makers to obtain a fresh approach in dealing with ethnic relations as broadly conceived. Not all scholars subscribe to this statist view, however. In fact, the stands that they have taken sharply diverge from the state-oriented perspective. Attuned to the burgeoning globalization and cultural studies literature, these observers have emphasized the demise of the nation-state under capitalist market forces and, just as significantly, the decrease in the salience of ethnicity as empirically real and analytically liberating. For them, there is no doubt that the qualitative condition of state sovereignty and power has been altered by the immense global flows of people, trade, and cultural forces that even the strongest states cannot dam. With regard to the state, however, the works reviewed below take a moderate stance; all attest to the crucial role that state-business relations have played in fueling the rapid growth necessary to create the structural conditions within which the "the new rich" and a "global, consumerist culture" can flourish. More controversial are their views on ethnicity. Generally, it is held that this middle-class, consumerist lifestyle crosscuts and overwhelms vertical ties of ethnic sentiment. Instead, relations of global consumption have become dominant, shaping new identities and imbuing others with fresh meaning. Representative of this view has been the "New Rich in Asia" series, edited by Richard Robison, a political economist then at Murdoch University in Perth, Australia. Its inaugural title was published in 1996 (Robison and Goodman 1996).

In one way, the "New Rich in Asia" series is a recent manifestation of a long and valuable heritage of writing on the ethnic Chinese diaspora of Southeast Asia. The country study has been the dominant narrative, although a number of comparative explorations have also been skillfully attempted.[23] Observers have pointed to the dominant religion of the host country and state colonial policies as determinative factors in explaining the different degrees of assimilation and economic positions of the ethnic Chinese across the region.[24] However, the "New Rich in Asia" series has sought to take "Chinese" out of the "Chinese problem" altogether.

In his 1999 contribution to the series, Ken Young examines four Southeast Asian cases—two where ethnic Chinese populations form a minority (Thailand, Indonesia) and two where they are more dominant (Singapore, Malaysia)—through this cultural, consumerist prism. The newness of this middle class and its attendant lifestyle, for Young, is both learned and continually evolving in the shopping mall, the ubiquitous consumerist paragon that clutters the region's metropolitan cityscapes. Nor, however, are workplaces, housing estates, and places of worship immune from this global deluge of consumerist signification. Although noting the strong business-government relations that make all this possible, Young also examines the special position of ethnic Chinese in this dynamic from the viewpoint of the Chinese themselves. To be sure, ethnic Chinese quantitatively dominate Southeast Asia's middle class, but Young challenges the view that there is anything firm, unifying, or essential to what it means to be "Chinese" today. Variations within and across societies and countries forthrightly confound any simplifying schema. Just as critical, however, is the other side of the equation, namely, the gradual "Chinese-ization" of state and society that is the very stuff of this push toward middle-class consumerism. One example that Young provides is the reconceptualization of state ideologies to justify the preeminence of a capitalist economy. This in turn enables civil servants and ordinary citizens alike to feel at ease regarding their increasingly homogeneous, consumerist desires.

In two similar articles, anthropologist Ariel Heryanto (1998, 1999) situates late New Order economic, ethnic, and state-society relations within this analytical framework. Growing attention to lifestyle and consumption, Heryanto argues, has led to the slow yet perceptible erosion in Indonesia of the stigmatization of the Chinese as the cultural/economic/political Other. In other words, as more and more Indonesians become structurally "Chinese," "Chinese" itself has gained acceptance and thus become mainstream. Besides the growing affluence of non-Chinese Indonesians, the waning of the communist threat has also aided this development. So, too, has the retooling of the state ideology of Pancasila to rationalize the increasing starkness of government-supported capitalist policies. In the cultural realm, for Heryanto, the mounting prominence of Indonesians of Chinese descent in the country's public sphere signifies society's comfort with things Chinese. Heryanto also singles out a series of incidents that in the past might have had detrimental consequences for Chinese communities, but in the late New Order period passed without incident—the killing of the labor activist Marsinah (who worked in a Chinese-owned factory) and labor unrest in Medan, to name just two.

Finally, sociologists Chua Beng Huat and Tan Joo Ean (1999) bring this culturalist, nonethnic approach to bear on Singapore, Southeast Asia's globalization hub *par excellence*. Chua and Tan aim to counter the conventional view of Singapore as a society based on ethnic demarcations. Noting worsening economic stratification, they find a neoclass perspective helpful in illuminating this city-state's contemporary social landscape. For Chua and Tan, its main ethnic groups—Chinese, Indian, and Malay—share what has typically become a Singaporean consumerist-driven lifestyle where the imperative to own a car or a private condominium outstrips intra- or inter-communal concerns. To bolster their claims, Chua and Tan provide such evidence that family characteristics—the educational attainment of parents, for instance—are more accurate as indicators of poverty than ethnicity. By also highlighting the quantitative growth of the Malay middle class, these authors stress the identity formed in the consumerist practices of this globalizing middle-class culture that create affinities across ethnic groups. In all, Chua and Tan champion the cultural construction of class, predicated on obtaining and displaying material goods, in which "ethnicity plays an insignificant part in such constructions" (1999: 139).

The region's recent economic crises have provided skeptics of the cultural, consumerist approach with ample ammunition to launch their critiques, which have elicited responses from the approach's defenders (Chua 2000). Here, I bypass the economic argument to assess critically the increasingly nonethnic realities to which this view attests. Consider Singapore, the place where the "new rich in Asia" perspective should work best. In no other country in Southeast Asia does the cutting edge of market-driven, global, capitalist cultural trends make greater inroads than on this island. Globally, also greatly affecting the island has been the recent yet radical transformation of its (and the region's) security environment. Singapore had been a hub for the Jemaah Islamiyah (JI), the militant Islamist regional network that was allegedly behind a series of terrorist attacks in Indonesia, including the October 2002 and 2005 Bali bombings and the August 2003 Marriott Hotel bombing in Jakarta. In December 2001 and in January 2002, Singaporean authorities arrested scores of JI members, many of whom have been held indefinitely under the city-state's draconian Internal Security Act. It was revealed that plans included domestic attacks against U.S., Australian, and Israeli interests.

How does this relate to the issue of depoliticized ethnicity in Singapore? For one thing, the mounting prominence of and pressure on Islam in the region bear directly on the country's Malay population. Distressed as the result of the unwanted attention focused on its community, Malay leaders have been forced to repledge and redemonstrate public loyalties to the state and government. Recent events only exacerbate what continues to be a concern toward and social stigmatization of Islam and ethnic Malays in Singapore. The "new rich" approach undoubtedly remains a fruitful avenue for further exploration, but it is premature to hail ethnicity's disappearance under the weight of consumerist culture. This is particularly so as long as the specter of terrorism continues to haunt this city-state, sentiments idiosyncratically captured by the city-state's elder statesman, Senior Minister Lee Kuan Yew. Days following the 9/11 attacks in the United States, Lee explained in the local papers: "If for instance, you put a Malay officer who's very religious and who has family ties in Malaysia in charge of a machine gun unit, that's very tricky business. . . . [I]f today the Prime Minister doesn't think about this, we could have a tragedy" (quoted in Mutalib 2000: 43). It is hence no exaggeration to say that Singapore's defense policy will continue to be infused by ethnic considerations—in particular, the denial of strategic positions to Malay soldiers on account of their ethnicity.

A second example comes from Singapore's much larger and imposing neighbor, Indonesia. As in the Singapore example, recent events—in this case, the anti-Chinese riots of May 1998 that anticipated the resignation of the country's long-time authoritarian ruler, Suharto—undermine a cultural, consumerist perspective that suggests a successful decoupling of ethnicity and capitalism. These riots have exacerbated the country's "Chinese problem." To be sure, evidence points to the organized characteristics of the violence, including military involvement. As such, this unrest was not a mass outburst from below; neither was it geographically widespread. Yet these grave human rights abuses, particularly the gang rape of scores of women of Chinese descent, reverberated throughout the country (and region). Thousands of ethnic Chinese sought safer locales in parts of Riau, West Kalimantan, and Bali, but also abroad in Singapore, Australia, and Hong Kong. Capital flight valued in the billions followed. Moreover, following the May 1998 disturbances a series of smaller yet significant food riots afflicted cities across the country. Rioters primarily targeted Chinese-owned property and warehouses. All told, these developments call into question claims that "Chinese" as an ethnic other has died away. In the early post-Suharto state, many of the restrictive regulations on ethnic Chinese have been lifted. Notable is state recognition of Confucianism as a religion. Yet the "Chinese problem" still lurks. It will require more than an infusion of global, consumerist culture coupled with market-driven, economic growth to cleanse the Indonesian state and society thoroughly of this disquieting blemish.

Conclusion

This essay has sought to sketch the intellectual evolution of the study of political ethnicity in Southeast Asia. It began in the 1960s with works steeped in modernization theory that saw the "national political culture" of the country in question rooted in primordial ethnic essences. Moreover, such timeless immutabilities were held accountable in part for the disappointing development performance of these countries. Given the severely limited ability of primordialism to explain significant change and the demise of modernization theory under the weighty failure of the U.S. war in Vietnam, scholars soon switched emphases and began to conceive of ethnicity as a transactional mode of being, where fluid and malleable identities shifted according to circumstance. The advent of situationalism resonated across disciplines, as evidenced by the survey of works by anthropologists Judith Nagata and Charles Keyes and political scientist William Liddle. Then, like the primordialist paradigm before it, the situationalist school—while never entirely discarded—was challenged by scholars such as Benedict Anderson, Robert Taylor, and Charles Hirschman who, discomforted by the inattention paid to historical processes, sought to shed light on the construction by colonial regimes of ethnic categorization and the inherent power asymmetries embedded in the relations of such categories.

Finally, this chapter showed how, beginning in the 1990s, this multidisciplinary lineage reached an impasse. Spurred by pervasive ethnic violence and the consequences of market-driven globalization, scholars developed two post-paradigmatic approaches to political ethnicity in order to fill analytical gaps left unexplained by the three paradigms. Underscoring a statist perspective, some aimed to produce policy-oriented recommendations to help ameliorate the many ethnic conflicts afflicting Southeast Asia. In contrast, others deemphasized the state and ethnicity by concentrating on the rise of a homogenizing, consumerist class, controversially believing that the identity produced as a result of this change has supplanted affective ties of ethnicity. All told, it is in this context that future studies of political ethnicity in Southeast Asia will evolve and continue to develop.

Chapter Ten

Southeast Asia and the Political Economy of Development

REGINA ABRAMI AND RICHARD F. DONER

Introduction

This chapter assesses the contribution of contemporary qualitative research on Southeast Asia to the field of political economy. Specifically, we examine Southeast Asian research on the origins of economic institutions and their influence on economic performance. Institutions often account for persistent and puzzling divergence in economic performance over time and across countries, but their roles and origins defy easy explanation. Similar institutions vary in their impact and are influenced by local contexts. Institutional analysis must therefore consider sociopolitical variables in addition to the efficiency considerations that economists emphasize. Analytic methods should allow for systematic comparison. Southeast Asia's social, economic, and political variations are ripe for such analysis.

The rest of this section is a critical review of Southeast Asia–related research on the political economy of development. The next section focuses on the consequences of institutions in the region's market-based economies. We then explore the origins of several institutional arrangements and examine the origins and impact of institutions from the less-studied experience of the region's post-socialist economies, especially Vietnam.[1]

INSTITUTIONS AND DEVELOPMENT PUZZLES

Academic interest in the relationship between institutions and economic growth emerged from a puzzling divergence in economic performance, both within the developing world and between developed and developing countries. Although the sources of this divergence remain deeply contested (Temple 2003, 152–183), scholars appreciate that the less-developed world almost universally suffered from weak or ill-suited institutions, ranging from the "big states" of Africa to the bureaucratic behemoths of state socialism.[2] In response, economic development was recast, especially in New Institutional Economic accounts, as a matter of organizational change, lowered transaction costs, and capital accumulation—all with an emphasis on the role of the state (Meier and Stiglitz 2001; Rodrik 2003; Harriss, Hunter, and Lewis 1995). However, politics, unlike economics, concerns tough, inter-elite maneuvering rather than welfare-enhancing choices by private individuals (Bates 1995; Knight 1992).

The inherently comparative requirements of institutional analysis also emerge from the empirical growth record. Successful developers have combined "sound money/free market" policies with more heterodox measures, and implemented these measures through decidedly homegrown institutional arrangements (Rodrik 2003). Further, the utility of various institutions appears to vary by stage of development, with countries often failing in the transition from one set of institutions to another (Temple 2003; Meier and Stiglitz 2001). Institutions that initiate growth may not sustain it. Institutions that aid economic diversification ("structural change") may not promote movement from lower-value to higher-value activities within global commodity chains.[3] Institutions that promote expanded economic activities may pose redistributive political challenges without improving people's welfare outcomes. In sum, knowing that certain institutions are strongly associated with economic growth compels students of development to look beyond their efficiency or lack thereof, and to consider their comparative origins, sustainability, and redistributive impact.

SOUTHEAST ASIA AND INSTITUTIONALIST ANALYSIS

Southeast Asia offers significant opportunities to investigate such matters. Variation in development outcomes and in potential causal factors, combined with commonalities in other causal factors, allows both "most similar" and "most different" research designs. For example, the region's impressive overall growth is reflected in the emergence of the "high-performing Asian economies" during the 1980s and 1990s and in the region's relatively healthy emergence from the 1997 Asian financial crisis (World Bank 1993, 2005). Vietnam and the Philippines illustrate the different challenges of initiating growth out of a poverty trap and sustaining growth (Pritchett 2003). Differences between successful structural change and upgrading can also be seen in the contrast of Singapore with Southeast Asia's industrializing "ASEAN-4" (Malaysia, Thailand, the Philippines, and Indonesia) and of Penang with the rest of Malaysia.[4] Finally, there is cross-national and temporal variation in the challenges of combining economic expansion with improvements in health care, education, income equality, and environmental protection.

Independent variables such as marketization, bureaucratic strength, private-sector organization, ethnic heterogeneity, factor endowments, political coalitions, regime types, and electoral rules also vary across Southeast Asia. Religious beliefs, nationalist sentiment, and constructions of gender vary as well. Yet these countries also share important features, such as pervasive minority entrepreneurs, a history of U.S. security involvement, and participation in Northeast Asian–led trade and investment.

Clearly, this is a region where qualitative scholarship can make important contributions to core questions of political economy. Yet political-economic research on Southeast Asia has so far yielded fewer theoretical breakthroughs and less systematic analysis than scholarship on Latin America or Africa (Doner 1991a). The emphasis has been on "anomalies that compel theoretical examination" rather than on building or testing theory (Johnson 1975, cited in Doner 1991a: 819).[5]

This is changing. Southeast Asianists have made progress in showing the theoretical significance of regional anomalies and in generating and evaluating new hypotheses. Indeed, the subfield's future impact on political science depends on the current generation's embrace of "big questions" and its openness to more systematic and explicit methods recently developed by qualitative scholars.[6] Differences between probabilistic and deterministic explanations, and between variable-based and process-based accounts, illustrate how causal variables differ from the mechanisms linking explanatory factors with outcomes. For example, causal processes are often shown as unintended and thus unconnected to the goals of actors. Likewise, different factors may lead to similar outcomes, suggesting that theories may be valid for a limited set of cases.

The institutional diversity of Southeast Asia is a natural laboratory for testing theories of comparative economic development through these methods. In what follows, we discuss contributions already made and work that remains to be done.

Institutions and Economic Development

Here we examine research on institutional arrangements identified by scholars as potentially significant for economic performance. We begin with two explicitly political arrangements: regime types and veto players. We then address research on the impact of "governance" institutions—states, private-sector organizations, and public-private sector linkages—on Southeast Asian market economies.

REGIME TYPE

The literature on the importance of regime type for economic performance is extensive but inconclusive. Some scholars assume that democracy encourages economic growth because it is better than authoritarian systems at guaranteeing property rights and avoiding the predation of authoritarian rulers. Others suggest that authoritarian regimes, more insulated from particular interests, exhibit longer time horizons, enabling dictators to better mobilize savings and generate growth. But several books in the 1990s suggested the indeterminacy of regime type for economic growth. They implicitly questioned the value of "state autonomy" by demonstrating the importance of elite motivations and coalitional bases in shaping economic outcomes (Bertrand 1998).[7] A review of the statistical evidence also concluded that "there is no reason to think that the regime type affects the rate of growth of total income" (Przeworski, Alvarez, and Cheibub 2000: 156).

These studies have provided the empirical basis for going beyond regime type to a deeper analysis of institutional causes of divergent economic outcomes, anticipating the subsequently important arguments that (a) growth-promoting institutions are a result of political calculations and (b) "growth-producing policies are not necessarily incompatible with distributive imperatives" (Bertrand 1998: 363).[8] Nonetheless, their theoretical impact outside Southeast Asian studies has been limited, perhaps because they were methodologically designed to explain single-country cases with existing theory and/or to highlight weaknesses in the prevailing literature, not to generate new hypotheses or to provide comparative assessments of existing arguments.

The above research also offered limited analysis of the impact of specific political institutions. But more recent theoretical scholarship suggests that although democracy might not lead to economic development, its competition-promoting rules aid in the provision of public goods useful for development, such as education, and also encourage political elites to function as more "regulated" monopolies, whereas authoritarian rulers are freer to garner and distribute monopoly rents to themselves and their supporters (Lake and Baum 2001). Recent comparative work on Southeast and Northeast Asia also suggests that constraints on elite actions do not only co-vary with democracy (Doner, Ritchie, and Slater 2005). For example, elites in authoritarian Singapore have acted more as "regulated" monopolists, whereas those in the Philippines have developed such a grip on power that they win elections without delivering significant distributive benefits (or side payments) to constituents.

VETO PLAYERS

Recent scholarship has also explored political institutions as "mechanisms of preference aggregation," looking to the origins and impact of electoral rules, federal versus unitary systems, party structures, and coalitional cabinets (Gourevitch 2003: 108). The importance of these institutions for economic performance lies in the degree to which they are hypothesized to generate "veto points." Functionally defined by a capacity to block policy, veto points affect the credibility and decisiveness of state actions. Numerous veto points is thought to increase both credibility and the probability that policies will last a long time. Fewer veto points, or higher centralization, in contrast, is said to promote decisiveness or the ability to change policies quickly in response to new demands (Tsebelis 1995).

Andrew MacIntyre (2003), applying the veto player approach, argued that countries at the institutional extremes—with either many (Thailand) or few (Indonesia) veto players—were the most vulnerable to exchange rate pressures. His conclusion, at least with regard to exchange rate pressures, is that institutional arrangements providing a median position are the most helpful in confronting exogenous shocks. Relying on cross-national comparison,

MacIntyre's work provides a test of the veto player arguments but uses regional expertise to amend the literature in an intriguing way. He has thus contributed to broader debates in both political science and economics on divergent regime responses to exogenous shocks.

Other Southeast Asianists have questioned the assumptions of the veto player argument. Allen Hicken and Bryan Ritchie (2002) find that even where multiple veto players might undermine policy decisiveness, investors can count on some certainty through the creation of "pockets of efficiency" that delegate jurisdiction over a particular issue area to a set of actors operating along more bureaucratic lines.[9] Conversely, even in cases with few veto players, governments may signal credible commitment to a particular policy agenda by tying their hands through measures such as opening their capital accounts.[10] Hicken and Ritchie (2002: 5) therefore argue that the "dichotomy between decisiveness and credibility is drawn too starkly."

To make their case, they explore the institutional challenges of human resource development, which requires more actors and longer time-to-payoff than the macroeconomic policies addressed by MacIntyre.[11] Taking Singapore as a crucial case and then extending their analysis to Thailand, they argue that success in tougher development tasks requires centralized veto authority *and* participation by a broad range of public and private parties throughout the entire policy process. Policy credibility is thus not reducible to the number of veto players.

NATIONAL SYSTEMS OF ECONOMIC GOVERNANCE

Scholars of "varieties of capitalism" have extended the veto player literature, arguing that degrees of credibility or decisiveness affect economic growth indirectly (Hall and Soskice 2001). Governments with more veto players exhibit greater policy stability and are more likely to establish coordinated governance institutions. Such "coordinated market economies" also display incremental forms of economic innovation. Conversely, governments with smaller numbers of veto players are prone to policy instability and thus more arms-length governance institutions. Such "liberal market economies" display more radical economic innovation.

Generally limited to the industrialized world, the "varieties of capitalism" approach can be compared to work on Southeast Asia. Largely by way of "most-similar" research design, Southeast Asianists also examine how different countries address similar economic challenges. Some examine economic performance in multiple sectors or issue areas in one county.[12] Like the "varieties of capitalism" scholarship, these studies presume that a country's institutions affect its growth by shaping the incentives and organizational tools available to firms and public officials (Felker 1998: 12). But at present, most of this literature has focused on three specific sets of arrangements, the first of which is the state itself.

THE STATE

A key impetus for comparative research on the state came from evidence that the striking economic performance of the newly industrialized countries (NICs) was associated with sector-specific politics backed up by highly capable state institutions.[13] Yet long prior to the idea of the "East Asian" model of development, Southeast Asia scholars were examining the relationship between the state and economic performance. But the region was initially portrayed as a failed case of development.

Ruth McVey forcefully argued that such skepticism was a function of Fred Riggs's emphasis on the bureaucratic polity to explain economic outcomes (McVey 1992a; Riggs 1966). Riggs had argued that Thailand's economic development was bogged down by military-bureaucratic elites pursuing inter-elite rivalries rather than economic transformation. As a result, the Thai state had few if any Weberian-type attributes of rational bureaucracy. Riggs's account had a broad impact on development studies in part because it confirmed existing assumptions about the developmental necessity of independent entrepreneurship, the rule of law, and property rights. Its prediction—that Thailand would stagnate and the Philippines would prosper under private-sector-led growth—failed, however, only stimulating further research on Southeast Asian states and institutions.

McVey argued that the bureaucratic polity was less "a developmental bog than a container for fundamental transformation" (1992a: 23). She usefully relaxed the assumption that (bureaucratic) patrons determine the nature of clientelism. Even if business (merchant) clients needed political protection, she argued, they also had leverage of their own. As a result, officials not only needed to acquire sufficient business knowledge to oversee the handling of the economy; they also had to impose "effective legal guarantees for private property, so that political misfortune could not sweep it all away" (1992a: 23). McVey implicitly relied on comparative-historical analysis of the incentives and constraints facing political elites to explain the origins of a (relatively) secure property-rights regime in capitalist Southeast Asia.

The bureaucratic polity literature and responses to it also generated useful work on corruption and its impact on growth (Scott 1972a). McVey's attention to the vulnerability of military-bureaucratic elites can be linked to later research into variation in growth rates under conditions of rampant corruption. Recent work, more engaged with the broader theoretical literature on rents and rent seeking, has shown that some structures of elite politics raise bribery costs and market entry barriers, whereas others lower market entry costs, encouraging the development of competitive markets as well as secure property rights.[14] Corruption research has also begun to inform more theoretically driven analyses of bureaucratic inefficiencies in Southeast Asia, including the politics of administrative reform in Thailand, "booty capitalism" in the Philippines, patronage in Malaysia, and "rent seizing" in resource-rich Southeast Asian countries.[15] Collectively, this research suggests that although property rights and competitive markets are important for economic growth, they often emerge under conditions unanticipated by neoclassical economics.

Southeast Asianists have gone beyond neoclassical analyses in other ways. Earlier work on the Northeast Asian NICs showed that Southeast Asian countries assumed to conform to neoclassical prescriptions have in fact also pursued decidedly heterodox economic policies.[16] While some interventionist policies have yielded positive economic outcomes, others have become mired in failure and corruption.[17] Southeast Asia scholars have begun to specify the challenges inherent in policies such as financial intermediation, human resource development, revenue collection, and the management of foreign investment for upgrading (e.g., Hamilton-Hart 2002), confirming that many policies, especially those promoting catching up and upgrading, require significant formal institutional capacities.

To identify such institutions, scholars have drawn on the concept, first seen in the analysis of Northeast Asia, of developmental states distinguished by their capacity to promote information flows, provide credible commitments, and coordinate the interests and behavior of multiple actors for long-term development.[18] There are few such cases in capitalist Southeast Asia other than Singapore. The developmental state concept nonetheless offers benchmarks with which to compare and contrast countries. For example, Thailand and Malaysia are closer to what Peter Evans labels "intermediate states," having bureaucracies with some organization—including significant "pockets of efficiency" resembling the developmental state model—yet without the overall organizational coherence of the developmental state (1995: 60).

The developmental state and its "intermediate" counterpart have given scholars a tool with which to disaggregate the bureaucratic polity and its successors. Scholars now look for government agencies with uncommon levels of coherence, expertise, and organized linkages with private business and civil interests—that is, with apparent autonomy from political interference. Much of this newer research has been on macroeconomic agencies, especially central banks, but some has explored agencies responsible for agriculture and industry, helping to account for inter-regional and intra-regional variation in economic performance. Again, the theoretical leverage of these studies depends in part on how systematically comparative their analysis is.[19]

BUSINESS AND ETHNIC ENTREPRENEURSHIP

Although the Southeast Asian literature on the state was heavily inspired by earlier work on Northeast Asia, its contributions to our knowledge of entrepreneurship in the developing world—particularly ethnic entrepreneurship—were pathbreaking. These studies countered both dependency theory portrayals of local capitalists as subservient to foreign capital and bureaucratic polity assumptions of local firms as dependent "pariah entrepreneurs."[20] Instead, they nested analysis of business development within national political contexts, stimulating important research on the culture and organization of Southeast Asian business.

Scholars of Southeast Asia have shown that institutions of ethnicity brought economic relief from the transaction costs and insecurity of doing business in an environment of weak formal property rights.[21] Under conditions of "missing markets" for capital, labor, and information, ethnic-based institutions helped fill the institutional and informational voids that can make transactions costly. These institutions vary. Ethnic trading networks may provide market information, matching and referral services, or "collectivist" contract enforcement that deters opportunistic behavior (Landa 1991).[22] Business groups can benefit from being based on patriarchal family structures and/or relying on horizontal networks among families (e.g., Ammar 2000). More recent scholarship also views ethnic-based entrepreneurship as proof that norms of trust constitute a form of "social capital."[23]

This literature addresses a core puzzle in comparative development: Why, despite weak formal property rights, has the private sector thrived in Southeast Asia, sometimes even playing a key role in economic development and policy reform? By focusing on the "efficiencies of ethnicity," for lack of a better phrase, these studies showed that many ethnic Chinese entrepreneurs developed, within a generation, from low-status peddlers and shopkeepers to captains of multinational businesses by combining internal group solidarity with extra-group ties throughout the region.

Emphasis on the transactional benefits of ethnicity can hide important contributions. For example, an emphasis on the social capital of the Chinese in Thailand, although certainly correct, diverts our attention from one of the earliest Thai business groups explicitly focused on economic transformation, the Crown Property Bureau's Siam Cement Group (Brown 1988). Also, it has been assumed that ethnic Chinese business strengths were in commerce, not manufacturing or technology (Yoshihara 1988). But as William Skinner (1958) showed, Chinese engineers in early-twentieth-century Thailand not only pioneered novel rice-milling processes but also replaced Western milling equipment with their own designs.

Other questions concern the "fit" between ethnic-based business institutions and more "advanced" development tasks. To what degree are ethnic institutions second-best alternatives, destined to become obsolete or even counterproductive once the market imperfections they resolved are "modernized" away? Are family business groups less useful in promoting technological competence? Or are ethnic groups actually well suited for the future by virtue of their flexibility, transnational linkages, and ability to internalize research and development gains? Studies on the evolution of multinational electronics networks in Northeast and Southeast Asia find that Chinese firms become important players not simply because they enjoy close ties (*guanxi*) with other Chinese firms but also because they are part of "local" concentrations of technological and production capability.[24]

The growing recognition that ethnicity is not everything when it comes to explaining the role of nonstate actors in national economic performance has led to research on other forms of social capital and networking, such as business associations and clusters, or "industrial agglomerations."[25]

PUBLIC-PRIVATE SECTOR LINKAGES

The developmental contributions of public-private "deliberation councils" in the Northeast Asian NICs spawned lively interest in the question of whether, and under what conditions, collaboration engenders efficiency as opposed to corruption.[26] In Korea's early postwar development, the "mutual hostage balance" between business and government "kept corruption from swamping growth," but in the Philippines, power imbalances in the business-state relationship allowed economic elites to capture as much "booty" as possible (Kang 2003: 183).

Related research reveals a significantly more clientelistic and fragmented set of public-private linkages in the ASEAN-4 than was the case for Singapore and the East Asian NICs.[27] In a "most similar" research design comparing the impact of clientelism in Taiwan and the Philippines, Kuo Cheng-Tian attributes Taiwan's economic success to its shift "from clientelism to state corporatism," whereas the Philippines went from "clientelism to authoritarian clientelism" (Kuo 1995: chapter 3). Scholars have argued that it was precisely the centralized nature of clientelism under Marcos that led to monopoly and inefficiency. Thus, the contrast with Thailand is not that Thailand lacked clientelism and corruption but that Thai clientelism was competitive enough that "no single firm or group of firms could block competition from new entrants" (Unger 1998: 125).[28]

LABOR AND ECONOMIC PERFORMANCE:
NOT ALWAYS A SILENT ENGINE OF GROWTH

We now turn to labor's role in economic performance. Although East Asia's labor regimes in general "have been politically exclusionary from the very onset of industrialization" (Deyo 1989: 110),[29] there is evidence that this picture is not complete. Labor's weak voice in key development issues seems to contribute to the low level of indigenous technological diffusion found in the region, raising the important issue of just how "good" the exclusion of labor can be for economic development.[30] Further, labor's involvement in many Southeast Asian states need not take a political form to improve economic performance. The Singapore government's successful initiatives to improve productivity after the problems of the "Second Industrial Revolution" involved labor and business jointly designing, implementing, monitoring, and evaluating training programs (Ritchie 2001). Political mobilization was not part of the initiative, however. Instead, Singapore's involvement in labor training recalls Japanese "corporatism without labor" as well as some of the institutional bases of incremental innovation identified in the "varieties of capitalism" literature.

Still, the Southeast Asia political science literature has been deficient in developing cross-national accounts of divergence in labor regimes. Instead, much of this work has been done outside the political science discipline.[31] But globalization, China's increasing competitiveness, and the need to improve productivity through new technologies, skills, and training will stimulate more research interest in labor as an institutional participant.

The Origins of Institutions

So far, we have identified a number of ways in which research on Southeast Asia has advanced theoretical knowledge on the relationship between institutions and economic performance. But understanding the political economy of growth also requires a better grasp of how these institutions emerge and evolve.

Institutions are typically homegrown. Our comparative understanding of how they grow has remained fairly rudimentary, hampered by the obvious complexity of their creation and evolution and by the economistic assumption that they "represent agreements or conventions chosen by voluntarily transacting parties in efforts to secure mutually welfare-enhancing outcomes" in the face of changes in relative prices (Bates 1995: 46). This reflects "thick" rationality assumptions in which preferences are given ("exogenous"). It not only presumes that actors use the most efficient means to pursue their goals but also that "agents in a wide variety of situations value the same sorts of things; for example, wealth, income, power, and perquisites of office" (Ferejohn 1991: 282).

Scholars in several disciplines have challenged the rationality assumption by "endogenizing" preferences, identifying instead a range of constraints and processes influencing how and why people create institutions.[32] According to the power-distributional account, institutions emerge and evolve not out of a search for joint gains but through strategic bargaining and political conflict (Knight 1992). Cultural-sociological perspectives argue that institutions are the creation of people driven by neither efficiency nor power but rather by socially enforced norms of legitimate behavior (Beckert 2002). Meanwhile, the cognitive science concept of "bounded rationality," although typically interpreted as a matter of missing information or imperfect calculative ability, is partially consistent with a nonobjectivist perspective in that it accepts that individuals process information about their world into socially derived mental schemas or cognitive maps. Historical institutionalists, rather than viewing institutions as the result of one causal process, argue that preexisting arrangements influence the options and preferences of those creating new institutions or modifying old ones.[33] This approach assumes that change is path-dependent but allows that outcomes are the unintended consequences of competing preferences.

STATE ORIGINS

We have seen that political conflict, power differentials, social norms, and identity can all be mechanisms of institutional development and change. We will now examine how these factors have contributed to our knowledge of the origins of developmental states and the organization of ethnic entrepreneurship in Southeast Asian market economies.

Perhaps nowhere has the disjuncture between our understanding of the *economic impact* of institutions and their *political origins* been greater than with regard to the origins of state strength. This has been exacerbated by a tendency to attribute state capacities to some core motivation, whether benign or predatory, or to some hard-to-operationalize term such as "state autonomy," which always seems more readily known after the fact than beforehand. But what factors drive political leaders to develop effective state institutions in some cases, to cannibalize the state in others, or to promote a mixture of capacities and strengths in yet others? We now assess four possible single-variable explanations—colonial legacies, political coalitions, external security threats, and resource endowments—and the more combinatory condition of "systemic vulnerability."

One strand of scholarship on both Northeast and Southeast Asia argues that colonial legacies offer the best explanation for divergent development. Atul Kohli has argued that "Japanese colonialism [of South Korea], as brutal as it was," created new "state structures" and "patterns of state-class relations" that helped post-colonial ruling elites (1999: 95, 133). Conversely, Paul Hutchcroft's work demonstrated that Spanish and U.S. colonialism in the Philippines led to the growth of a socioeconomic elite whose economic base lay largely outside the state. The result was a "national oligarchy" with "powerful—yet particularistic—control over elements of the state apparatus" that remains in command (1998: 218).

Similar colonial inheritances in Singapore and Malaysia nonetheless did not result in similar post-colonial state capacities. Initial conditions also cannot explain why postwar Philippine leaders squandered the colonial legacies of a well-educated population and a bureaucracy with impressive pockets of expertise. Clearly, we need tools for understanding what factors encourage leaders to reproduce and reinforce or abandon such legacies.

Some scholars have turned to political coalitions to account for variation in state strength. For example, Greg Felker attributes the different industrial trajectories of Malaysia (high upgrading, weak indigenous presence) and Thailand (weak upgrading, strong indigenous presence) to variation in elite coalition structure, which gave rise to a fragmented state and a politically influential business class in Thailand and a cohesive state elite able to impose more economic coordination in Malaysia (Felker 1998). This line of research is critical to shedding light on the institutional impact of varying distributional interests, although it may be less useful in accounting for within-state variation across sectors and over time. Underlying this weakness is a lack of focus on political leaders' willingness and ability to modify their relationships with powerful private interests. Yet this factor may have some effect on whether or not core institutions dating from the colonial era remain entrenched.

Other scholars have addressed this very issue by asking whether elites choose to widen or narrow their coalitions in response to the challenges of managing economic transition, redistribution, and extraction. David Waldner, comparing Middle Eastern and Northeast Asian cases, found that the redistributive policies underpinning the creation of broad coalitions led to clientelistic relationships between business and government that thwarted innovation and export-led growth (Waldner 1999). In direct contrast, Campos and Root argue that broad coalitions are the very key to economic growth in both Northeast and Southeast Asia, as these coalitions demanded that the state "learn" to extract and redistribute resources efficiently (Campos and Root 1996).

All these findings beg the question of why some political leaders can respond to increased popular demands—without state collapse, coups, or revolution—whereas others cannot. One answer may involve the sources of elite cohesion. Dan Slater (2005) argues that when urban class protest exacerbates communal tensions, elite coalitions can be strengthened in ways that promote state fiscal capacity. Meredith Woo-Cumings (1998) has argued that "economic growth" became "indispensable for military security" and regime survival in Korea and Taiwan, and Campos and Root (1996) contend that external threats compelled leaders to create strong institutions to promote growth and implement wealth-sharing mechanisms for popular sectors. Yet other research has shown that external threats are not always associated with growing institutional capacity (Centeno 1997).

There is now a substantial literature, ranging from "resource curse" to "rentier states," suggesting that a state's ease of access to revenue deeply influences patterns of institutional development.[34] Michael Ross's (2001) comparative study of resource-rich Southeast Asian countries finds that "resource curses" do far more harm than "simply" stalling institutional development. They actually encourage politicians to dismantle state institutions as a way to "seize" rents. Rajah Rasiah (2003: 66) similarly argues that easy revenues from natural resource exports left the ASEAN-4 under little fiscal pressure to encourage the kinds of "complementary institutional and linkage development" that occurred in the East Asian NICs.

But how are we to explain the institutional differences between countries with relatively similar resource endowments—between resource-rich Malaysia and Venezuela or between resource-rich Botswana, with its strong institutions, and its resource-rich but predatory neighbors?[35] Underlying these limitations is, as Ross notes, an assumption that states are revenue "satisficers," not revenue maximizers (1999: 313). Ross contends, however, that whether a state seeks the maximum possible or least minimum revenue (i.e., "satisficing") depends on its coalitional and geopolitical context. As such, an assumption of "satisficing" alone is insufficient for understanding outcomes.

In sum, we have argued that each of the preceding variables is useful but perhaps insufficient to explain institutional strength, especially the exceptional capacities of developmental states. An alternative approach argues that the high levels of institutional strength embodied in developmental states arise only when political elites are faced with three of these variables: popular pressures, external threats, and resource constraints (Doner, Ritchie, and Slater 2005). Such a state of "systemic vulnerability" pushes leaders to develop institutional capacities to extract and redistribute resources.

Yet even the vulnerability account requires further assessment. To what degree does it apply outside Southeast Asia, in countries that were not exposed to Southeast Asia's particular combination of U.S. security interests and a vigorous regional economic dynamic stimulated by Japan? Is it useful for explaining institutional changes in the one-party, socialist states of Vietnam and Laos or the region's other market economies? How useful is it for explaining institutional changes well after state institutions have been formed?

THE ORGANIZATION OF ETHNIC ENTREPRENEURSHIP

Research on Southeast Asian ethnic entrepreneurship has shown that ethnic minorities, especially the Chinese, contributed to economic growth. But why did "ethnic" entrepreneurship arise in the first place? Why did its form vary throughout Southeast Asia?

The pervasiveness of network-based Chinese businesses throughout the region encouraged cultural explanations of their success. The inner workings of family firms, networks, and business groups have been linked to Confucian values (Numazaki 2000; Landa 1991; Hamilton 1991),[36] establishing that norms as a kind of informal institution can influence the structure and operation of formal private organizations. But taking Confucian values as primordial unchanging representations of "Chineseness" often results in a static account of how culture affects preference formation, economic organization, and economic development.

Other studies of Southeast Asian political economy have instead contributed to our understanding of ethnic entrepreneurs by focusing on the strategic interests of both state and nonstate actors. In turn, political marginality has been shown to provide surprising advantages to both private and public actors. For example, as Chinese entrepreneurs sought protection through patronage, sponsors in the state bureaucracy and military acquired allies for import substitution policies and capital accumulation (Lim 1996). In turn, the political economy literature refuted the long-standing idea of the Chinese as "pariahs," recasting their economic relationship with government from unequal clientelism to mutual gain.

Variation in government policies toward ethnic Chinese also sheds light on the legacy of colonialism.[37] Arguably, the absence of colonialism and the existence of indigenous bureaucratic elites mean that Thailand could accommodate Chinese assimilation more easily. But the memory of Chinese "middlemen" pitched between colonial rulers and the indigenous population undermined peaceful ethnic relations in postwar Indonesia and Malaysia (Mackie 1992;

McVey 1992a). To this day, the "ethnic card" can be invoked whenever inter-elite struggles threaten entrenched political bargains.

Clearly, then, private-sector institutions exist in sociopolitical contexts. Specification of state interests and how they influence the norms and organizations of private actors is an important and fruitful area for comparative research. Recent analysis of cross-national variation in Latin American business associations is a useful point of reference.[38] Explaining variations in the development and impact of private-sector institutions is sure to grow in theoretical and topical importance as trade and investment liberalization and the pervasiveness of global value chains compel all of Southeast Asia to operate as more open economies.

Post-Socialist Southeast Asia: Old Lessons, New Interpretations

The economic liberalization of Vietnam, Laos, and Cambodia has offered a natural test of claims about the relationship between institutions and economic performance, along with the chance to compare a range of regime types within Southeast Asia. As a result, the field has moved a step closer to making significant contributions to leading political science debates about the legacies of state socialism and about the impact of global economic integration on institutional continuity and change.

These cases also address key debates within the regional literature: How well do explanations of the origins and nature of state-business relations in nonsocialist Southeast Asia apply to the emerging markets of Vietnam, Cambodia, and Laos? Are patron-client relations as mutually beneficial in the post-socialist cases as McVey claimed for the nonsocialist cases? How do socialist legacies affect institutional opportunities and constraints in post-socialist Southeast Asia? Are these legacies rooted in organizations, norms, expectations, or some combination thereof?

POST-SOCIALIST RESPONSES TO ECONOMIC LIBERALIZATION

When these countries began to emerge from socialist planning systems, all economic actors were imagined as deeply embedded in, and largely dependent upon, networks of patron-client relations, unable to break free to design alternative paths to prosperity.[39] Given this, even the smallest degree of economic autonomy was predicted to bring an "economic revolution," "great transformation," or the like.[40] This betrayed an implicit faith in a single-trigger theory of change, the trigger being the end of dependency on state redistribution and its channels of social mobility.

The introduction of market-based economic exchange, growing international trade, and foreign investment was expected to stimulate wide-ranging and fundamental shifts; some economists advised full economic and political liberalization—"shock therapy." Gradual policy reform, having made people and prices only partially unfree, was not expected to generate economic prosperity (Kornai 1990). In light of the experiences of China, Vietnam, and Laos, however, it is now widely appreciated that the steps by which a state manages economic liberalization affect economic outcomes.

Gradualism remains the preferred government strategy in China, Vietnam, and Laos. But its composition has varied widely, especially in price liberalization, privatization, and global economic integration policies. Moreover, gradualism did not bring down the Communist Party, even in cases where economic performance did not support regime legitimacy. There has also been considerable variation in the degrees and forms of economic change in these cases. As elsewhere, however, students of Vietnamese political economy were quick to build on the idea that *any* form of economic freedom would lead to greater agency and power at the subnational level. Accounts of everyday resistance in Vietnam, for example, suggest that economic liberalization policies were driven from the bottom up: The Vietnamese people faced hardships under the economic planning system, and the regime had to respond.[41]

Research on relations between central and local levels of government in Vietnam also supports resource-based accounts of preference formation, and political economic change, more generally. For example, Edmund Malesky's work shows how access to foreign direct investment allowed Vietnamese provincial leaders to expand their power in terms of the center and to pursue policy experiments (Malesky 2005). Foreign investors are also important in pushing for deeper economic reforms, yet in Vietnam, it seems, only under the credible threat of resource exodus. In the mid-1990s, the loss of foreign investors in response to the Vietnamese government's intractability on key foreign investor issues seemed insignificant in light of foreign aid inflows. By the late 1990s, however, and partly in recognition of China's pending entry into the World Trade Organization, the Vietnamese government engaged more with the foreign investor community. Foreign firms increasingly engage provincial and national officials about the policies needed to create a viable investor environment (Malesky 2004, 2007).

Abstracting from this, at least one effect of economic liberalization is the introduction of new, often powerful players into the national political arena. Others have also looked at how economic liberalization more generally shifts coalitional politics, even within the Vietnamese Communist Party. Provincial leaders who supported economic reform in the 1980s opposed it once pressures increased for equitization of firms over which they had some control or interest (Riedel and Turley 1999). They were joined by state enterprise and ministerial leaders who also stood to gain from an economic system left only partially changed. In turn, the re-division of Vietnamese provinces, beginning in the late 1990s, has been interpreted as an effort by reform and anti-reform coalitions to expand their membership base and power (Thaveeporn 1997; Riedel and Turley 1999; Malesky 2005). It seems that veto player dynamics come into play in nondemocratic systems as much as they do in the nonsocialist cases.

Resource-based claims of diminishing central state power have also focused on rising corruption. But Martin Gainsborough suggests that anti-corruption campaigns, rather than indicating state weakness, signal continued (and possibly growing) strength. Here, he moves away from resource-based accounts of power and agency to focus on the signaling effects of government campaigns for ongoing legitimacy (Gainsborough 2003a, 2003b).

In Vietnam, anti-corruption cases are given wide play in the media, and crowds are often tolerated outside courthouses. Moreover, given the speed with which the Vietnamese government moves against individuals fighting for more political and religious freedoms, it seems that spontaneous gatherings ought not be seen as a sign of state incapacity. They may simply be well-crafted opportunities for the Communist Party and the government to demonstrate support for "the people." In this regard, the appearance of new economic actors, especially private entrepreneurs, seems not so much to diminish state and Communist Party power as to ensure its durability through ideological shifts and the co-opting of new groups.

For example, research on Vietnamese business associations shows close public-private collaboration, particularly in drafting enterprise- and investment-related laws (Stromseth 2003). Other associations—such as those for laborers, farmers, and small-scale industry and cooperatives—are also undergoing considerable revival.[42] Nonetheless, it would be a mistake to cast these relations simply as old-style socialist-era corporatism. Jonathan Stromseth's detailed research on business associations shows that the state is often willing to act on outsider recommendations that further economic development, create employment, or enhance Vietnam's international competitiveness. We have seen similar public-private partnerships elsewhere in the region. Just as McVey (1992a) warned against accepting the bureaucratic polity framework, Vietnam today warns us against static portrayals of patron-client relations in Leninist regimes.

If anything, the "strong versus weak state" dichotomy that once dominated the literature has been replaced with research on how economic liberalization creates power in new ways. Socialist-era managerial and administrative elites, once predicted to be weakened under market conditions, remain important in the more liberalized economic system, often by means of the very laws intended to rein them in and level the playing field for all economic actors.[43] But as Fforde's work on "real" property rights in reform-era Vietnam shows, state equitization can be accompanied by "rent-switching," allowing enterprise managers to maintain a good deal more economic power and autonomy than the government may have intended (Fforde 2004).

This fits what we know from other post-socialist transitions from plan to market. A growing number of studies also reveal that state-led efforts to develop the private sector through business registration and the rule of law are weakening the informal private economic networks that were critical to economic survival for many households during the socialist era (Abrami and Henaff 2004; DiGregorio 2001; Leshkowich 2000). Increasing social inequality partly reflects the interaction effects between social location in preexisting networks and new policies and laws of economic engagement. Related arguments have been made for the Chinese diaspora in Southeast Asia, whose opportunities were no less differentiated by local economic networks.

The need for foreign investment and international markets also means that the governments of Vietnam, Cambodia, and Laos are somewhat constrained in how they can manage growth with equity. The desire to secure membership in the World Trade Organization necessitates a more open and genuine embrace of foreign direct investment, private-sector development, and trade, thus narrowing the scope for national industrial policy.

Although Cambodia, Laos, and Vietnam underwent dramatic transformation of property relations after the Communists came to power, few would depict these countries as successful cases of state socialism, particularly if we take redistributive capacity and economic control as measures. Not only did they remain largely unindustrialized, but they were also heavily dependent on foreign aid and increasingly dominated by informal economic exchange. How the political leadership of each state sought to mobilize resources also varied considerably, with Cambodia and Vietnam offering the sharpest contrast.

Such variation raises the question of the direction of causality between strategies of socialist state consolidation and control over resources. Much of the literature presumed that significant grassroots economic compliance could be traced to the redistributive economy. But its later absence has not done away with the economic and political power of existing elites, suggesting that high economic compliance (or lack thereof) owes its institutional origins to something other than state economic organizations (or formal institutions) alone.

Regina Abrami (2002) looks instead to state strategies of political mobilization, identifying their relationship to what the political leadership of a given socialist regime understood as the dangers facing regime consolidation. Political mobilization not only affected economic monitoring, but also expectations of credible state signaling that linger today. This explains why Vietnam and China became dynamic emerging markets while lacking many seemingly necessary institutions. The argument, initially made in relation to Vietnam and China, might as easily have been made about the Southeast Asian cases of Vietnam and Cambodia alone.

More generally, the study of Asian post-socialist regimes suggests that institutions as strategic, normative, and socially constructed rules simultaneously create and constrain opportunity. Yet if we refrain from treating institutions as rules for sense making, we may miss a chance to explain divergent responses to similar structural pressures and policy incentives. For example, emphasis on institutions as rules for sense making could add a helpful layer to Doner, Ritchie, and Slater's (2005) account of the origins of developmental states; Vietnam, China, and Cambodia suggest that how external and internal threats are understood, rather than their objective existence, can determine whether developmental state institutions are put in place.

A "rules for sense making" framework might also be applied to explain wide variations in each country's emerging private sector, in policies toward ethnic Chinese, and in government responses to labor activism. The indigenous business class, including ethnic Chinese, had all but disappeared from the Asian socialist states during the planning era. Their reemergence and relative power in these countries nonetheless continue to vary considerably. In Cambodia, for example, the industrial business sector includes many overseas Chinese foreign investors, who frequently threaten to leave in order to insist on sound business practices. In contrast, the drive to keep state-owned enterprises alive in Vietnam led similar appeals to fall on deaf ears. But is this difference just a matter of pragmatism, or might it be traced instead to different accounts of the national interest and its sociopolitical and economic contours? For now, we recommend only an appreciation of how social rules for sense making shape the impact of seemingly objective phenomena.

THE INTERPRETIVE TURN: A BRIDGING-LEVELS TECHNIQUE LINKING ORIGINS AND ENDS

Institutions necessarily embody far more than the "rules of the game" (Woodruff 2006). They stipulate who is a "player" and in what way, as we see clearly in constructions of the "Chinese" in Southeast Asia. By focusing attention on the social origins of rules for sense making, we also might shift away from the growing emphasis on "mental models" as the origins of preferences (Denzau and North 1994) and look instead to how rules for sense making construct the very categories by which people organize, classify, and weigh information (Herrera 2004; Woodruff and Abrami 2004; Woodruff 2000a).[44] The point is not to do away with individual agency or even strategic interests, but to locate them in socially situated forms of knowledge and learning and in the contentious politics around them. Only in this way, we suggest, can path dependence substantively coexist with unintended outcomes. Anything less leaves the micro-foundations of decision making disengaged from social life and based only on cognitive capacity, generic human nature, or an exogenous shock yielding a shift in preferences. Of course, general acknowledgment of "rules of the game" does not preclude battles over their interpretation and application.

Work on Southeast Asian political economy can thus include an interpretive perspective, yet the connection between distributive outcomes and institutions as rules for sense making remains mostly implicit in the literature.

For example, early battles shaping industrial relations and employment policy were precisely related to making decisions about the meaning of different types of citizens and their status. "Being Chinese" was not the same in Thailand, Singapore, and Indonesia. Now that Vietnam, Cambodia, and Laos are again welcoming overseas and domestic investment, a fruitful topic of inquiry is whether old social constructions of the Chinese as a "comprador class" are affecting investment and other economic-related patterns there.

An account of institutions as rules for sense making also allows us to escape static depictions of culture as "individualist," "collectivist," or "hierarchical" (Greif 1994). Essentialist descriptions of Southeast Asian culture once dominated the field, making political economists hesitant to treat culture as an explanatory variable. So it was with work on the origins of developmental states. These states had similar achievements, yet public-private partnerships vary considerably within and across them; the variation cannot be explained by differences in objective conditions alone. Rather it seems that different social constructions of class, ethnicity, and gender—and perhaps national purpose—bring about different understandings of material interests, profoundly shaping patterns of cooperation and conflict.

Conclusions

Qualitative methods have taught us much about aspects of the political economy of development in Southeast Asia, including the origins and impact of ethnic entrepreneurs, the developmental consequences of regime type, the varying nature and impact of corruption, and the role of labor in rapid development. Increasingly, Southeast Asianists are moving beyond "merely" addressing anomalies that, in fact, demand theoretical examination (Johnson 1975). The challenge remains to continue broad comparative analyses without losing a deep familiarity with regional contexts. Overcoming this challenge involves (1) identifying key areas for future research, (2) striving for generalizability while recognizing the inherent complexity of social phenomena, and (3) being more rigorous and explicit about our methods and their costs and benefits.

The varying levels of economic development within the region, the movement toward political and economic liberalization, and increasing access to the region's post-socialist economies offer important opportunities to investigate the political economy of growth. Political shifts, such as the emergence of party competition in post-Suharto Indonesia, allow a deeper understanding of the impact of specific political institutions, such as veto players and electoral rules, on policies and implementing institutions. Evolving relations between the central and provincial levels of government in Vietnam allow a deeper understanding of how norms of interest articulation shape economic outcomes. The broader significance of such center-periphery relations will grow as decentralization pressures increase throughout the developing world.

Southeast Asia also offers opportunities to assess the interactions between proximate political institutions and broader structural pressures on political elites. It is one thing to note the weight of hard or soft budget constraints, external security threats, pressures from restive popular sectors, and external actors such as Japan and China. It is quite another to understand how such pressures are mediated by shifting electoral rules, party structures, legislative arrangements, or central-provincial relations, not to mention competing interpretations of them. The region's varying sociopolitical legacies challenge scholars to go beyond claims that culture matters and develop more systematic accounts of how and under what conditions it matters.

The real-world implications of these theoretical questions are expanding. Growth depends more than ever on national capacities to address external competitive pressures *and* domestic pressures to maintain political legitimacy through employment growth and economic dynamism. An understanding of the institutional and political bases of economic upgrading, especially the growing importance of labor and technical skills, will be critical. Thailand's textile industry has become a major source of employment and foreign exchange due to sound macroeconomic policies and efficient networks of Sino-Thai firms, associations, and banks. But if Thai producers are to sustain growth in the face of stiffer competition, they must expand intra-industry linkages and improve the technical capacity of their personnel. Similarly, the success of Vietnam's catfish export industry reflects astute policies and innovative institutions based on mutually empowering center-provincial and public-private linkages. But sustaining growth will require improving operational efficiency and managing protectionist resistance from U.S. catfish interests (Abrami 2005a, 2005b).

That is to say, we can strive for generalizability and parsimony without doing injustice to local complexity, in part by making explicit use of Southeast Asia's variation and its usefulness in cross-regional analysis. Much recent work on successful institutions and growth has drawn on the Northeast Asian NICs, whereas more negative lessons have often been drawn from other regions, especially Latin America. The challenge is to find what Collier and Mahoney call good "contrast spaces"—sufficiently similar to the NICs in terms of their (export-led) development strategies and geographical position but differing in institutional capacities and development outcomes. Southeast Asia, by and large, occupies just such a "contrast space" between Northeast Asia and most of Latin America.[45]

The effort to reconcile generalizability and local complexity can apply the more sophisticated understanding of causal processes and related methodological issues proposed by scholars of qualitative methods. Causal relationships do not necessarily conform to a political world "governed by immutable causal regularities based on a few forceful causal variables" (P. A. Hall 2003: 387). Political outcomes are often a function of complex processes of strategic interaction and path dependence; this has encouraged scholars to study mechanisms linking causal factors to outcomes, to develop a better grasp of interaction effects, and to explore "multiple conjunctural causation," meaning situations in which the same outcomes arise from different variables operating in different cases.

Such scholarship requires the kinds of knowledge—a deep understanding of history, of actors' beliefs, and of the sequences and practices by which "context" unfolds—through which Southeast Asianists have made some of their most important contributions. It also requires engagement with comparative theory. Scholars must analyze individual "cases" through multiple "observations," using alternative methodologies when appropriate. Scholars of the region are developing and gaining access to large-scale data sets required for statistical analyses, game-theoretical formulations for exploring strategic interactions and collective action problems, and mathematical tools for capturing complex causation. Such methods, combined with deep contextual knowledge, allow the development and testing of "typological" or "middle-range" theories that shed light on the region and broaden our understanding of political economy.

Chapter Eleven

The Missing Countryside
The Price of Ignoring Rural Political Economy in Southeast Asia

ARDETH MAUNG THAWNGHMUNG

Southeast Asia is predominantly an agrarian region. Rural residents constitute 42 percent and 43 percent of the populations in Philippines and Malaysia, respectively, and 75 percent, 80 percent, and 84 percent in Burma/Myanmar, Vietnam, and Cambodia, respectively. Although the region's rural areas have attracted considerable scholarly attention and have generated a rich stream of literature, "rural political economy" per se has been of little interest to political scientists. For example, articles in the *Journal of Peasant Studies, World Development*, and the *Journal of Development Studies* that focus on rural Southeast Asia are predominantly the works of historians, economists, and anthropologists. This is very much the case with the authors found in one of the most widely read edited volumes on Southeast Asian rural economy, *Agrarian Transformations: Local Processes and the State in Southeast Asia*; these are mostly anthropologists, agricultural economists, and sociologists. Of all the articles that have appeared since 1987 in *Comparative Politics*, there is only one political science effort (by Bill Liddle) that briefly touches upon the agricultural sector of Indonesia. This chapter will demonstrate how and why the political science discipline is hindered by its failure to engage in a field that offers rich empirical discovery and innovative theoretical scholarship.

The first part of this chapter will shed light on why this topic has attracted little attention from political scientists. The second part of this chapter will demonstrate how political science can use Southeast Asia as an important empirical source for confirming, challenging, and/or reformulating conventional analyses. I will argue that failure to explore the field or to incorporate findings that have been generated by it has resulted in a discipline limited in its focus and approaches. The concluding section provides suggestions on how to raise the profile of Southeast Asia's rural economy within the political science discipline.

Defining Rural Political Economy

No separate mention has so far been given to the field of rural political economy as an important topic of study in any social science or political science encyclopedia. In this chapter, I define *rural political economy* as the study of the nature and dynamics of power relationships that emerge from economic activities in rural areas (Caporaso and Levine 1992: 220).[1] The rural sector is generally characterized as localities of fewer than 5,000 inhabitants who engage mainly in the production and marketing of plants, animals, and other raw materials (Larson 1968; Long 1996). These residents may simultaneously engage or specialize in nonfarm occupations such as processing, manufacturing, craft, trade, commerce, construction, transportation, teaching, and government services, or rely on remittances from other family members in urban areas. There are important works available that look at agrobusinesses, rural entrepreneurships, and plantation economies (Abrami 2002; Stoler 1995; Pelzer 1978), but this chapter focuses mainly on issues related to small landholders and poor peasants, and to the production and distribution of agricultural crops.[2]

The issues stressed in this chapter to some extent overlap with those in Ben Kerkvliet's chapter on agrarian politics in Southeast Asia. Whereas Kerkvliet's chapter covers the political aspect of agrarian studies and focuses more narrowly on the topics of revolution and patron-client relations, this chapter attempts to cover broader issues that deal with the varied economic aspects of rural Southeast Asia. However, the review in this chapter is obviously not comprehensive, given the vast volumes of literature on rural political economy in the region.

Where Are the Political Scientists?

There are six potential reasons that political scientists from U.S. universities are generally not found in this field and why the field has made such a small dent in political science. First, compared to Latin America, East Asia, or the Middle East, the Southeast Asian area as a whole is less strategically, economically, and politically situated in the minds of the U.S. public and government. Anthony Reid observes that "Southeast Asia lacked the weight in global affairs and American strategic thinking of China, Japan, or the Middle East; it also lacked the interest of Africa and Latin America to strong segments of the US population" (2003a: 4). Academia is no exception, because resources for social science research often specify the research question in terms of national priorities or problems (Hirchman 2003: 162). Specifically after the U.S. withdrawal from Vietnam, political science was replaced by anthropology as the most popular discipline for those working on Southeast Asia. Not surprisingly, "of all the regions affected by the turn against area studies, South and Southeast Asia were the two regions most vulnerable to being completely marginalized in American universities" (Reid 2003a: 5).

In addition, rural political economy is an interdisciplinary study, and findings from the field are more likely to appear in interdisciplinary journals than in political science journals. Out of a quite small universe of political scientists who specialize in Southeast Asia, there are even fewer who study rural political economy, at least in comparison with those who specialize in more popular topics such as democratization, state building, ethnic conflict, and industrialization. In fact, rural political economy has never been treated as a separate field that deserves special attention; it remains at the margins of the subfield of political economy or gets lumped into a broader category of peasant studies or agrarian studies.

The third reason that very few political scientists are found in this field lies in the difficulty of accessing data in remote rural areas. Working in rural areas, whose daily activities can be assessed only superficially from a distance, usually requires long, exhausting ethnographic work in one specific location—a methodological approach that is not favorably received by mainstream political science. Reid laments that "scholars focusing on a single Asian country are even less likely than thirty years ago to be employed in major social science departments" (2003a: 3).

Fourth, a majority of works on the region's rural economy have not been concerned with developing theoretical generalizations and broadly applicable analytical concepts, or with addressing important debates. With the exception of Scott's and Popkin's works on peasant behavior and practices, there has been no noteworthy effort to develop theoretical and analytical generalizations to push Southeast Asian rural economy beyond the periphery of political science concerns. For example, Tom Brass, an editor of the *Journal of Peasant Studies*, comments that the main reason, broadly speaking, that Southeast Asia has lagged behind Latin America and India in this sphere is that Latin America and India featured in important debates about Third World development from the 1960s (the development decade) onwards. Dependency theory made its impact in the case of Latin America, and the mode of production debate plus the subaltern studies project were important cases for Indian studies.[3]

Fifth, there is a general tendency among Southeast Asia scholars on rural economy to confine their findings to a specific country. This not only hampers the development of theoretical or analytical generalization but also makes it less likely to generate interest in scholars involved in other regional studies. Occasionally, one may come across comparative rural studies that cut across regions. For instance, the Philippines has been compared with Latin America or South America on land reform issues, and Vietnam has been occasionally paired with other transitional Asian economies such as China and Russia in the areas of communist and post-communist economies. More works on intra- and inter-regional comparisons are needed to analyze common issues confronted by Southeast Asian countries and to raise the profile of the field beyond Southeast Asian boundaries.

Sixth, the field itself covers a wide range of issues that make it difficult to develop a more coherent theoretical and analytical set of questions that can broadly address various aspects of rural political economy. Topics range from rural situations in pre-colonial and colonial periods to state intervention in the post-independence era, among which are land reform and collectivization, the Green revolution, liberalization, and sustainable development. In fact, there are a host of important topics that can be broached: rural entrepreneurship, agribusinesses, the plantation economy, forced migration, price and subsidy programs, and agricultural export policy. And one consequence of this very broad universe is that many scholars who study rural economy in Southeast Asia end up talking past one another.

What Have We Missed?

There are a few works on Southeast Asian rural areas that have managed to make a long-lasting impression within the political science discipline. Examples are James Scott's *The Moral Economy of the Peasant* and *Weapons of the Weak: Everyday Forms of Peasant Resistance*, and Samuel Popkin's *The Rational Peasant* (Scott 1976; Scott 1985; Popkin 1979). These works have introduced innovative analytical concepts and addressed larger theoretical questions that can be applied beyond Southeast Asia, making them stand apart from the broader body of studies devoted to Southeast Asian rural economy.

Except for these studies and a few others, the remaining body of studies on Southeast Asian rural areas remains marginal to the majority of political scientists. I propose here to shed light on how the political science discipline has missed opportunities from failing to use the region as a deep well of empirical resources. First, the field serves as a natural laboratory to replicate works and findings that are well known within the political science discipline. Second, the region has provided and potentially can provide valuable empirical cases for confirming, challenging, and reformulating dominant theories and paradigms in political science. Third, Southeast Asia can serve as a set of cases for comparison with countries from other regions that share common political, economic, and social problems. Last but not least, rural Southeast Asia can be used as a locale and source for generating new theoretical concepts while improving qualitative data collection and analysis.

A NATURAL ENVIRONMENT FOR REPLICATION

To understand how the idea of the moral economy of the peasant has been developed, one must examine Scott's work in light of earlier works on Southeast Asia that influenced his thinking. Long before Scott's work made an appearance in the political science literature, the well-known anthropologist Clifford Geertz introduced a concept called "agricultural involution" to demonstrate how Javanese peasants responded to rapidly growing population pressures under Dutch rule (Geertz 1963). Geertz found that the labor-intensive nature of wet-rice technology was able to absorb additional numbers in the labor force to feed the growing populations in colonial Java. However, what is unique in his analysis is the "poverty-sharing" aspect of Javanese culture (96–97). Geertz found that under the pressure of limited resources, Javanese villages "maintained a comparatively high degree of social and economic homogeneity by dividing the economic pie into a steadily increasing number of minute pieces" (97).

James Scott's *The Moral Economy of the Peasant* is very much a product built on the ideas of Geertz, and it has spurred studies that confirm, challenge, and reformulate Scott's idea within Southeast Asian contexts. Scott argues that the precarious nature of their existence led *poor* peasants in pre-colonial Southeast Asia to be mainly preoccupied with maintaining their "subsistence" and with minimizing risks. Accordingly, peasants perceived a "just lord" to be someone who recognized peasants' rights to subsistence and regulated the timing and size of his rent or revenue demands to ensure that the cultivator would retain enough food to support himself and his household. These principles of the "moral economy" were destroyed by the introduction of a capitalist economy that subjected peasants to new economic practices and social customs.

Kerkvliet's much-acclaimed work on the Huk rebellion echoes the thesis of a moral economy of the peasants as a basis for rebellion in the Philippines (Kervliet 1977). Robert Hefner studies the economy of Tengger in the Javanese highlands, where the society remained relatively "small and undifferentiated" despite early commercialization in the colonial period (Hefner 1990). It was not until after the peasants adopted a Green revolutionary crop package and were exposed to a flood of urban consumer products in the late 1970s that class division became accentuated. However, others find the presence of severe socioeconomic inequality in pre-colonial Indonesia (Hart 1986; Booth 1988: 7). Many concur that pre-capitalist societies were no more protective or humane than those that came in contact with the market economy (Popkin 1979; Rigg 1994: 123; Bowie 1992: 815).

Therefore, controversies abound over whether pre-colonial villages were egalitarian or stratified, and over whether peasants were self-interested or constrained by a supposed normative view of the world. Given the relatively scanty and patchy data on Southeast Asian villagers in the past and the wide variety of interpretations and findings, it is not clear whether these debates have been settled. However, in the efforts to reevaluate Scott's work, a great deal of new information about villages in pre-colonial and colonial societies has been generated. We learn from these debates that rural behavior and economic practices depend on the socioeconomic and political contexts within which the village is situated (Hayami and Kikuchi 1981; Brocheux 1983; Adas 1998;

Husken and White 1989). Scott has actually cautioned that subsistence ethics and norms of reciprocity were strongest in some areas, such as the Tonkin and Upper Burma, and weakest in recently settled areas, such as Lower Burma and Cochinchina (Scott 1976: 40, 83).

Scott's analysis has had relevant implications for previous studies, and it has generated further research with respect to various foundations of peasants' political values and attitudes. These studies range from moral and ethical (Kerkvliet 1977), cultural or religious (Adas 1982; Wiant and Steinberg 1988; Aung-Thwin 1989), instrumental (Nash 1965; Migdal 1974), and institutional (Shue 1988; Scott 1976; Adas 1981; Taylor 1987) to locally specific explanations (Migdal 1988: 94; Anek 1996; Kerkvliet 1998; Thawnghmung 2004).[4] Some of these explanations respond to earlier works and thereby attempt to challenge and reconceptualize the conventional wisdom (e.g., Adas's response to Scott and Thawnghmung's reviews of all the above authors' works), whereas others mainly talk past one another. Quite a few of them have in fact overlapped; for instance, Scott's moral economy emphasizes moral as well as institutional bases of peasants' support for authorities. Kerkvliet's works at various points in time acknowledge both the importance of moral principles and the nature of interpersonal relations between local authorities and local residents as a key to understanding political legitimacy in rural areas (Kerkvliet 1982, 1998).

Two observations that emerge in response to Scott's analysis deserve attention because they provide different perspectives on the study of rural political economy and open up opportunities for new research agendas. First is Rigg's criticism of "village" as a discrete, identifiable entity. According to Rigg, villages as we know them in a conventional sense may not even have existed in pre-colonial societies because "there is considerable evidence to indicate that villages were creations of the colonial period, designed to facilitate administration and control" (1994: 124). A second noteworthy observation comes from *Shadow of Agriculture: Non-Farm Activities in the Javanese Economy*, whose authors contest previous scholars' tendencies to equate the rural economy with a peasant economy and to overlook the significance of nonfarm income (Alexander et al. 1994). Both observations not only initiate a shift in analytical focus but also spur the development of works that examine nonfarm activities in rural areas (Mai 1990; Rutten 1999; Abrami 2002).

Thanks to the concept of the "moral economy of the peasant," which has generated new studies within the context of Southeast Asia, we now have a more comprehensive understanding of the variation in the nature of peasant villages and economies and a wide variety of perspectives in analyzing the village economy.

A CASE FOR TESTING DOMINANT POLITICAL SCIENCE THEORIES

Rural Southeast Asia provides valuable empirical data for testing dominant theories in the political science discipline. One example is the contributions made to the urban-bias literature. The urban-bias analysis was introduced by Michael Lipton and Robert Bates, whose primary research was on Africa and who demonstrated that Third World countries' developmental policies are biased in favor of the urban sector (Lipton 1977; Bates 1981; World Bank 1986). In his widely read *Why Poor People Stay Poor*, Lipton argues that the most important conflict in poor countries is "between rural classes and the urban classes. . . . The urban sector contains most of the articulateness, organization and power. So the urban classes have been able to win most of the rounds of the struggle with the countryside" (1977: 13).

Southeast Asian studies shed light on a diverse array of government strategies and offer a more nuanced understanding about the causes and consequences of urban-biased policies. For instance, Judy Ledgerwood concurs with urban-bias theory by arguing that there has been an urban-rural disparity in development assistance in Cambodia, where 85 percent of the population live in rural villages (Ledgerwood 1998). Ardeth Thawnghmung's article on rural Burma (1998) also discerns the trend of urban-biased policies in post-independent Burma.[5] In *Agrarian Transformation*, Hart, Turton, and White use urban-bias theory as a framework of analysis to examine the agricultural sectors in Malaysia, Indonesia, Thailand, and the Philippines (Hart et al. 1989). They found that whether Southeast Asian governments will pursue urban- or rural-biased policies depends on their macroeconomic environment. In this case, Southeast Asian experiences confirm the findings from other regions on the importance of macroeconomic environments and the nature of party coalitions in determining the types of development priorities.[6] The authors explain that rural-biased strategies in Malaysia are rooted in (1) the small size of the rice sector, (2) Malaysia's relative wealth, and (3) the attempt of the state party (United Malays National Organization, or UMNO) to build political support within rural society. Thailand's economy, on the other hand, is still heavily dependent on extracting resources from agriculture, for rice provides a large proportion of its revenues. In Indonesia, the growth of oil revenues during the 1970s explains the shift from extraction to subsidization, whereas the deterioration of the Philippine economy over the same period led to the reduction of subsidies for rice producers.

One of the main criticisms directed against urban-bias theory is that it is based on the assumption of a clearly defined boundary between urban and rural areas. Among these critics is Jon Rigg, who observes that it has become increasingly difficult to apply the urban-bias concept because the scope and level of industrial activity are fast expanding in some Southeast Asian rural areas (Rigg 2001). Therefore, urban-bias theory serves as a springboard for the discovery of new empirical and theoretical studies, for they question the utility of an urban-rural dichotomy and stress the emergence and increased significance of nonfarm, nonagricultural employment (Koppel et al. 1994). Political scientists can benefit from probing further into the issue of the blurring line between urban and rural sectors, and explore how these new findings can transform understandings about the nature of economic development in Third World countries.

Two other issue areas in which Southeast Asian rural regions serve as a case for confirming, challenging, or reformulating mainstream political science hypotheses or theories are the debate over (1) the relationships between the size of land tracts and agricultural productivity, and (2) the relationships between the types of government on the one hand and performance on the other. Some of these works do not directly address these debates, but their findings have relevant implications. However, scholarly consensus over these debates has yet to be achieved.

Consider the debate over the relationship between the size of land and agricultural productivity, which goes as far back as the early 1900s. Some Marxists and liberal economists, for instance, emphasize the development of large-scale units of production as the key to transforming agriculture or improving the lives and productivity of rural producers and diversifying a rural economy. This is one of the main ideological forces, along with the need to mobilize peasants' support, behind agricultural collectivization in communist countries. The other side of the spectrum is occupied by the "populists" or "neo-populists," who argue that small-scale farms are more productive than large farms (Harriss 1982: 37; Bray 1983: 3–33).

Therefore, scholars disagree on whether the size of land matters in determining the level of economic development at all. For instance, Salim Rashid and M. G. Quibria argue that history shows that "land reforms in many countries have contributed little to equity, and even less to efficiency" (1995: 128). Both the Indonesian and Thai economies remained impressive despite the discontinuation of land redistribution programs in the former and the implementation of land reform that had effects only on marginal farmers in the latter (145). Likewise, there is a disagreement on whether tenancy systems should be based on share rent, fixed rent, or wage labor (127–153).[7] To my knowledge, we are left with no definitive findings about the relationship between the size of land ownership on the one hand and rural growth and productivity on the other. However, it is to the advantage of political scientists to use these already existing data to analyze how other regions have fared in comparison with Southeast Asia and to examine the roots of success and failure in land reform implementation.

Rural Southeast Asia also contributes to the debate over whether an authoritarian or a democratic government will do a better job of implementing agrarian reform (Riedinger 1995). For instance, some scholars argue that there is no relationship between type of government and economic performance. Ben Kervliet's work on the Philippines (1979) implies that neither democratic regimes nor authoritarian regimes brought significant improvement to the peasantry because of their limited goals. Likewise, Gary Hawes looks at three main agricultural export industries (coconut, sugar, and fruits) under Marcos and articulates that "change, if it is to have a significant impact on the lives of the millions of Filipinos who produce the agricultural exports of the nation, must come not just at the level of the regime but also at the level of the state" (1987: 164). In the same manner, Linda K. Richter, who looks at policy-making processes in tourism and land reform in the Philippines, finds that authoritarian rule does not necessarily make policy more cost-effective, consistent, development-oriented, disciplined, independent of foreign control, or productive (1982: 5). Her study is a response to previous studies in the 1960s and 1970s that suggested that "authoritarian rule might have a place in national development if it were to facilitate economic and social processes such as land reform or other policy areas in which entrenched interests might otherwise prevent or delay reforms."[8] To the contrary, Jeffrey Reidinger, who compared the situations under Marcos and Aquino, finds virtue in democratic government: "[H]owever flawed and incomplete, the new Philippine democracy has proven more conducive to redistributive reform than its authoritarian predecessor" (1995: 233).[9]

The debate over the impacts of different forms of government on economic development has continued to occupy mainstream political science. But mixed reviews from rural Southeast Asia have demonstrated that scholars must move beyond this dichotomized approach and explore the various types of authoritarian/democratic governments and the nature of policies that are particularly conducive to land reform in particular and economic development in general. In her attempt to explain the Burmese government's failure to promote the agricultural sector, Anne Booth, for instance, does not discredit the instrumental role of military-led governments in achieving rapid economic growth. However, she argues that the Burmese government's failure to promote the agricultural sector is not because of the dominance of the military per se, but rather because "the military have been either unwilling or unable to share power with other groups, whether technocrats in the civil service or private entrepreneurs, who could place the economy on a secure and sustainable upward path" (2003: 14).

A CASE FOR COMPARISON

Rural areas in Southeast Asia are also sites for comparing issues or problems that are commonly confronted by countries with similar levels of economic development. For instance, policies or strategies such as land reform, Green revolution, and liberalization are implemented in almost all developing countries. It is difficult to imagine how Southeast Asia can be left out in comparative studies if we are to understand the causes and consequences as well as the variations in the level of success and failure of specific strategies. The majority of works that focus on these issues in Southeast Asia are single-case studies, but they uncover rich descriptions and causal relationships that can be used as secondary resources for comparative research that transcends Southeast Asia. Also, they produce new analytical and theoretical ideas.

Land reform (land redistribution and tenancy reforms) and agricultural collectivization (the pooling of resources such as land, labor, and agricultural inputs to maximize efficiency in agricultural growth and productivity) were topics of concern in the late colonial and early independence eras in Southeast Asia. Colonial policies, in particular, were held responsible for widespread poverty among landless peasants and extreme income disparities between the landed and the landless. In the Philippines, piecemeal efforts were undertaken during the U.S. colonization to prevent agrarian unrest (Hayami and Kikuchi

1981: 74). In Burma, Vietnam, Cambodia, and Laos, nationalist and communist leaders launched a variety of land reform programs immediately after obtaining independence from the colonial powers (White 1981; Hayami et al. 1990).

There are a few comparative studies that examine the roots of the varying levels of success of land reform implementation in Vietnam, China, and Russia. For instance, Edwin Moise uses archives and newspapers to compare Chinese land reform in 1947–1953 with that of North Vietnam in 1953–1957 (Moise 1983). Moise attributes the more satisfactory results in China to the Chinese party's longer experience in transforming Chinese villages. Andrew Vickerman's work is a comparative study of land redistribution and collectivization in Vietnam, China, and the Soviet Union (Vickerman 1986). His pessimism about development policies in these countries was based on their "anti-peasant bias" and reliance on agriculture to finance industrialization.

However, the majority of studies on land reform in Southeast Asia are single-case studies. Nonetheless, these in-depth studies offer us illuminating findings that can be used as secondary data for comparative studies and statistical analyses (White 1981; Truong 1987). For instance, although history has shown that the Marxist notion of agricultural collectivization is not economically feasible in the long run, some single-case studies on land reform and agricultural collectivization in Southeast Asia offer alternative explanations as to why the policies failed to achieve their objectives. Quang Truong attributes the roots of failure to the Vietnamese Communist Party's attempt to impose a one-size-fits-all package in diverse ecological, sociocultural, and politico-economic climates (Truong 1987). Adam Fforde sees the collectives as a relatively efficient means of using scarce resources, mobilizing manpower, and providing a safety net for poor peasants, but he identifies rigid adherence to Leninist ideology as the cause of the failed experiment (Fforde 1989). These studies have larger implications because they challenge the blanket discrediting of Marxist ideologies and generate interesting findings that can be explored in other regions.

Some studies that deal with land reform also reveal interesting findings challenging conventional understanding. For instance, works on decollectivization in Vietnam seriously question the top-down approach to decollectivization that was originally accepted by the scholarly community. Fforde, one of the first Western scholars permitted to undertake long-term research in North Vietnam after 1975, found that, contrary to popular assumption, there was peasant opposition against collectivization through noncompliance with official regulations (Fforde 1989). He wrote that by the early 1970s, three-quarters of the collectives in North Vietnam were only nominally socialist. Kerkvliet elaborated in detail how the Communist Party's authorization of long-term land use rights for peasant families in the north has been the result of the "everyday forms of resistance" by peasants who found collective farming and cooperatives inefficient (Kerkvliet 1995a: 67; Kerkvliet 2005). It should be noted that such a bottom-up approach has also been discerned by research on rural China (Kelliher 1992). It will be interesting to take this finding as a reference point of analysis to compare and contrast the roots, nature, and processes of decollectivization in other former communist regimes in the Soviet Union, Eastern Europe, and Latin America.

Another strategy that was applied across the region is the Green revolution, or, much more broadly, the application of science and technology as an alternative to address agrarian problems. The "Green revolution" incorporated intensive use of high-yielding varieties, irrigation, chemical fertilizers, pesticides, and multiple cropping. The application of the Green revolution increased world food production by 7 percent and per capita food production in Asia by about 40 percent since its inception in the mid-1960s (Pretty 1995: 3). In Indonesia, the Green revolution was fueled by an increase in oil revenues. During the 1970s about 20 percent of the development budget was allocated to agricultural development, and equally impressive amounts were channeled to infrastructure development programs in rural areas.

However, the Green revolution was not sustainable in the long run: "[A]ll countries where the Green Revolution has had a significant impact have seen average annual growth rates in the agricultural sector fall during the 1980s, compared with the post-revolution period of 1965–1985" (Pretty 1995: 7). In addition, "many poorer farming households simply cannot adopt the whole package" to achieve high yields (4). Nonetheless, studies on the socioeconomic, political, and environmental consequences of the Green revolution provide mixed reviews. Most of the literature found that the new technology tended to be monopolized by large commercial farmers, and therefore had polarized agrarian communities. For instance, Hart and his colleagues found that the Green revolution exacerbated rural inequality in Thailand, Malaysia, Indonesia, and the Philippines because large farmers were the main beneficiaries of the policy package of subsidized credit, inputs, licenses, and guaranteed prices (Hart et al. 1989: 31). Their privileged position in turn aided the replacement of traditional open labor markets by exclusionary practices. In

Thailand and Java, for instance, "tied" workers, though not as well paid during peak season, had secure employment and a higher annual income and had to work hard to ensure renewal of their contracts. Therefore, tied labor arrangements denied opportunities to workers who were outside of such arrangements; ensured employers of reliable, hardworking laborers; and enhanced social control of the village upper stratum (Hart 1986). In turn, this state-favored group helped assist the state's control in rural areas by monitoring labor discipline and enforcing law and order.

However, Hayami and Kikuchi argue that a statistical analysis of thirty-six Asian villages that adopted new rice technology shows that the Green revolution did not promote polarization. They contend that "we see a real danger of polarization not because of new technology but because of insufficient progress in technology" (Hayami and Kikuchi 1981: 59). Again, works on rural Southeast Asia offer us some interesting insights on the consequences of the Green revolution that can be compared with experiences from other regions.

The third state development strategy that became a dominant development paradigm in the Third World by the 1980s was liberal-oriented ideology. Former communist and socialist economies in Eastern Europe and Asia, including Burma and Vietnam, have embarked on various reforms to address poor and worsening conditions in rural areas (Tri 1990: 190–192). Generally, the implementation of market policies was treated as a consequence of top-down initiatives that emerged as a response to externally stimulated crises as well as failures in domestic policies (Naya and Tan 1995; Marr and White 1988; Than and Tan 1990). These include failures in import substitution industrialization and collectivization, excessive state intervention in the economy, debt and currency crises, the remarkable achievements of the export-oriented policies of the newly industrializing countries, the unwillingness of the "North" to accede to the demands of the "South," and pressure from the "North" and international organizations leveraged through "structural adjustment," "conditionality," and "shock therapies."

Southeast Asian areas have produced works that look at the socioeconomic consequences of market reforms in the former socialist and communist economies (Selden 1993; Kerkvliet and Porter 1995; Henin 2002). Most of them are single-country studies, but quite a few use inter- and intra-regional comparisons to assess the similarities and differences among these countries and to explain their performance variations (see, for example, Leonard and Kaneff 2002; Pryor 1992). In Vietnam, market reform has promoted economic growth and raised the standard of living, but it has also led to increased socioeconomic differentiation and poverty, a rise in unemployment and rural-to-urban migration, declines in social services, and environmental deterioration (Henin 2002). In Burma, the relaxation of control over rural areas provides numerous opportunities for local corruption and rent-seeking activities (Thawnghmung 2004). Because there are many post-communist countries that are treading along this liberal-oriented trend line, comparative research that examines the nature of different reform strategies, the various roots and outcomes in achieving aggregate growth and socioeconomic equity, and the socioeconomic consequences of these different reforms will significantly add to our existing knowledge about market operations in developing countries. A large number of works compare the varying levels of success or failure of market reform in post-communist countries in the former Soviet Union, Eastern Europe, and China. Thus, new studies that incorporate Vietnam, Laos, Burma, and Cambodia can offer us important theoretical as well as policy implications on how to alleviate the negative and unintended consequences of market reform.

The periods of liberalization have also witnessed a surge of activities in two interrelated issue areas. First, there is a growing concern for environmental preservation and sustainability, which in part is a response to the detrimental environment impacts of the Green revolution, which stresses intensive use of pesticides, chemical fertilizers, and large-scale irrigation projects. Sustainable development emphasizes the use of regenerative and resource-conserving technologies that can bring both environmental and economic benefits for farmers, communities, and nations.

The second issue deals with rural industrialization, rural enterprise development, and the establishment of agricultural-nonagricultural linkages. This new paradigm develops strategies to supplement peasant income and ultimately transform the peasant economy through community development, resource management, and participatory development (Koppel et al. 1994: 2). Both sustainable development and the promotion of rural industrialization emphasize greater use of local resources and knowledge, capacity building, people-centered (rather than state-centered) initiatives, good governance, and popular participation (Pretty 1995: 8).

The actual implementation of both strategies has become a subject of scholarly scrutiny and has generated many worthwhile findings (Weiss et al. 2004: 264). I will elaborate on a few case studies, but I recommend Peluso, Vandergeest, and Potter's excellent review of works on Southeast Asia's forestry for a more comprehensive understanding of the nature of academic works on this debate (Peluso et al. 1995).

Nancy Peluso sees serious limitations in state intervention in the agrarian economy in the name of environmental preservation (Peluso 1992). Peluso demonstrates that colonial and contemporary states have often replaced traditional systems of land rights with new land use laws by appropriating large tracts of land "in the common interest for the greatest good." But these large-scale forestry projects have done very little to change the existing structure of power relations in the local areas. Peluso explains first that typical foresters tend to establish links with villages through influential village elites who helped these foresters implement their projects. Field foresters then feel pressure to return favors back to these patrons. Second, the poor are less likely to become or remain involved in social forestry projects because of a lack of initial capital and financial support from the government. In the end, this well-intentioned social forestry program has been undermined by its failure to incorporate the needs of the local populations (see also Casson and Obidzinski 2002: 2133–2151).

Philip Hirsch's studies also uncover how state development plans to encourage local participatory development ultimately serve as a means of establishing control over rural people's lives (Hirsch 1990: 6). He looks at the implementation processes of "development" programs in rural Thailand that attempted to integrate peripheral regions into national economic and political space. Hirsch shows that "development," which was associated with "prosperity, or civilization," and the need to develop values "such as diligence, punctuality, and honesty among other civic virtues" simply turn out to be "paternalistic watching over" and potentially repressive by "keeping an eye" on those living in previously autonomous areas (13–14). Along the same lines, the study by Craig Johnson and Tim Forsyth on watershed forests and mangroves in Thailand finds how efforts to conserve forests through community participation and decentralization of power have been undermined by a state that has frequently supported commercial interests (Johnson and Forsyth 2002). Likewise, findings on the impacts of rural industrialization dispel myths about the supposed potential benefits. Jon Rigg argues that in Southeast Asia there are cases in which rural industrialization has undermined agricultural growth because many traditional rural industries are poorly paid and provide little chance for upward mobility and skill acquisition (Rigg 2003: 151).

The findings by these studies as a whole seriously question the utility of a concept that has become popular in recent development discourse. Case studies in rural Southeast Asia demonstrate that the terms "local participation," "decentralization," and "sustainable development" have various ramifications at the local levels and do not necessarily bring benefits to underprivileged people. They should not be taken at face value.

The last topic that has been the concern of many developing countries and is worthy of research is the issue of agricultural transition. As late as the 1980s, scholars emphasized the essential role of agriculture in economic development (Mellor 1986). According to this view, rising agricultural incomes create a demand for consumer goods and services. This spurs the development of nonfarm activities such as motorcycle shops and watch repair shops, which help to absorb surplus farm labor. This in turn further boosts demand for farm output while contributing cash for investment in agriculture, thus stimulating additional increases in agricultural production. At the same time, withdrawal of labor from the agricultural sector leads to increased commercialization of agricultural systems (Fei and Ranis 1964; Pingali 1997). Commercialization of agricultural systems involves greater market orientation of farm production; increased substitution of nontraded inputs with purchased inputs; gradual replacement of integrated farming systems with specialized enterprises for crop, livestock, poultry, and aquaculture products; and large proportions of income from nonagricultural employment.

As the 1990s proceeded, studies tended to demonstrate uncertainty over whether Third World countries would take transitional paths similar to those that had been followed by industrialized countries. T. J. Byres (see Bernstein [1996] and Bernstein and Brass [1996]) shows that even industrialized countries—England, Prussia, the United States, France, Japan, and Taiwan/South Korea—took varying paths to industrialization. Rigg also disputes the wisdom of regarding agrarian transitions in Japan, South Korea, and Taiwan as indicative of the path(s) that other countries in Asia will follow over time (2001: 13). Bernstein concurs that Third World countries are presented with different agrarian questions and that the prospects and problems in contemporary poor countries must be analyzed within the context of their location in world development (Bernstein 1996: 39).[10] For instance, the question of agrarian transition/industrialization in Third World countries was not only delayed until the moment of their independence, but these countries also confronted an already existing world market dominated by the more advanced capitalist powers. One the other hand, external capital was made available through foreign investment and aid.

The processes of agricultural transitions have been the least-studied subject in rural political economy in Southeast Asia. Malaysia, Indonesia, and Thailand are currently witnessing rapid transformation of agricultural systems; income and expenditure surveys as early as in the 1980s reveal that the proportion of off-farm income was as much as 40 percent in Indonesia, Thailand, and the Philippines (Koppel and Zurick 1988). Eighty percent of the fifteen-to-twenty-five-year-old age group in central Thailand worked in the cities in the mid-1990s (Pingali 1997). However, agricultural commercialization is by no means a "frictionless process," and it entails, at least in the short to medium term, significant costs in learning new skills, family dislocations, socioeconomic differentiation, and environmental and health costs (Bernstein 1996: 10).

Some single-country studies assess particular aspects of problems that accompany agricultural transformation and commercialization. A few comparative studies have also established common analytical and theoretical questions in order to understand diverse local transitional processes. In the early 1980s, Hamayi and Kikuchi significantly identified two possible trends in Asia: first, a polarization between large commercial farmers and a landless proletariat, and second, "peasant stratification," which includes a spectrum ranging from landless laborers to noncultivating landlords, tied to one another in "multi-stranded personalized relations, where all community members have some claims to the output of land" (Hayami and Kikuchi 1981: 60). However, these authors were not sure about which directions the Asian village economies were heading: "The Asian village economy is at the crossroads" (62). Further research on regional and cross-regional comparisons has yet to be analyzed.

One new development that presents a stark contrast with the experiences of earlier developers is the growing "internationalized integration of national agricultures in the patterns of world production and consumption" (Bernstein 1996: 46). The globalization of the world food economy mainly refers to the growing private (corporate) regulation of agricultural production, trade, processing, and consumption on a global scale (Bernstein 1996; Carter et al. 1996). Its main emphases are nontraditional exports and the contract farming of smaller-scale producers (White 1997; D. Hall 2003). According to White, contract farming is a particular way of linking commercial agro-production and agro-industry in which primary production (of annual or tree crops, livestock, dairy, poultry, eggs, fish, shrimp, etc.) remains in the hands of small holders. It is linked institutionally through contracts to a larger nucleus enterprise that handles one or more of the upstream and downstream activities such as input supply, output processing, and marketing (White 1997: 102).

The central concern with the issue is whether this type of agro-industrial development has improved rural welfare. Because contract farming incorporates a variety of situations and processes at work, scholarly findings on this type of agrarian arrangement vary. In his study on the experiences of dairy and hybrid coconut contract farmers in the hilly southern region of West Java, Ben White finds that profits and enrichment are possible in both schemes but that the "prevailing structures of local power and privilege, institutions which on paper appear to foster participatory, egalitarian forms of development tend in practice to be dominated by the wealthy and powerful and are subverted to their interest" (White 1997: 132). However, Jasper Goss, David Burch, and Roy Rickson discern that the shrimp industry in Thailand has fostered "participatory control of social resources" (Goss et al. 2000). Unfortunately, although contract farming has marked a "watershed in the transformation of rural life and agrarian systems in the Third World," it has been "relatively neglected in research in Asia," and very few have "attempted to integrate analysis of the social, cultural, political and economic aspects of contract farming and the specific forms of social change which it implies" (Goss et al. 2000).

There have been, all the same, quite a few single-country studies that analyze how transition processes in Southeast Asian countries transform the nature as well as the understanding of rural political economy (Eder 1993; Dearden 1996; Henin 2002; Goss et al. 2000). Some studies challenge the analysis of household, village, or rural sectors as units of analysis, and show how the larger national and global trend affects demography, socioeconomic status, power relations, and gender issues in Southeast Asian villages (Goss et al. 2000). One comparative study that deserves our attention is the work of Jon Rigg (2001), which identifies general trends, common issues, and problems that are facing contemporary Southeast Asian countries. Rigg points out that in Southeast Asia, the household as a single, welfare-maximizing, decision-making unit is breaking down because of recent transformations in rural areas. First, household members live far away from home, sometimes for extended lengths of time, but remain a component part of the household. Second, factory work accentuates divisions within the family because it confers on young women a higher status, greater spending power, financial autonomy, greater assertiveness, and independence (Rigg 2001: 86). Third, richer and poorer households use farm work differently and engage in nonfarm work for different reasons. Fourth, rural spaces have been penetrated by urban activities, such as small-scale capitalist industrial enterprises, cottage and craft-based manufacturing, and large-scale, capital- and technology-intensive factories, significant numbers of which are foreign invested and export oriented (26). Finally, there is also a growing lack of interest in agriculture among younger generations, which Rigg refers to as "de-agriculturalization," because of the abundance of nonfarm work and the income that the younger workers generate (121).

Rigg's powerful comparative analysis, which sheds light on new agrarian questions that emerged out of new global, regional, and local contexts, as well as recent scholarly emphasis on the significance of nonfarm agricultural activities, opens up new fields and research agendas for scholars across disciplines and regions.

A CASE FOR GENERATING THEORETICAL CONCEPTS
AND IMPROVING QUALITATIVE METHODOLOGY

The opportunities for using rural Southeast Asia as an empirical base to generate new theoretical and analytical concepts are limitless, given the diverse array of issues that can be explored in the region. Many problems and strategies that are commonly confronted and implemented by Third World countries—deforestation, environmental degradation, decollectivization, sustainable development, rural industrialization, resource management—can be studied in Southeast Asia through in-depth case studies, intra-regional and inter-regional comparison, and statistical analysis. Rural Southeast Asia can be used as a tool to address other, broader theoretical questions such as issues of religion, ethnicity, globalization, governance, decentralization, and democracy (McCarthy 2004). However, the prospect of rural Southeast Asia becoming a magnet for the production of theories and analytical concepts in political science depends very much on the creativity of the scholars and how they make use of the available data and address immediate, pressing, and broader theoretical issues.

Michael Ross's work is an excellent example of how the study of rural economy in Southeast Asia can have broader theoretical and empirical implications and policy prescriptions (Ross 2001). Although he undertakes a comparative study of forestry institutions in the Philippines, Malaysia, and Indonesia, his work addresses larger concerns of developing countries, especially the three-quarters of those developing states that rely on natural resource exports for at least half of their export income. Ross situates his question within the framework of the international political economy literature by asking why commodity-exporting governments have responded so poorly to positive shocks in commodity prices. He shows how international economic forces influence domestic political institutions and introduces a new concept called "rent seizing," in which state actors seek rents that are held by state institutions.[11] He argues that international markets can harm developing states by creating positive economic shocks that lead to rent seizing and institutional breakdown. Ross skillfully uses case studies in rural Southeast Asia to engage in a larger theoretical debate that is central to political economy.

Last but not least, fieldwork in rural Southeast Asia region can be used as a guide to improving qualitative research methodology in the social sciences. Ben Kerkvliet's chapter has eloquently shown us how in-depth studies in rural Southeast Asia have enhanced our understanding of politics in Southeast Asia. However, the processes through which these data are collected and analyzed for these widely acclaimed works are less well known in scholarly circles. Although most works on rural Southeast Asia are by no means based on ethnography, quite a few of them are based on anthropological research, which could offer illuminating insights on data collection and analysis. In particular, a majority of Southeast Asian countries are authoritarian and semi-authoritarian societies, where the complexity of political and social phenomena cannot be easily understood without engaging in field research inside the country (Thawnghmung 2004; Antlov 1995). In addition, existing textbooks on qualitative methods are of little use when scholars have to conduct research in politically restrictive environments, where politically sensitive questions have to be eschewed, where communication and transportation are poor, and where messy data do not lend themselves readily to "scientific research methods" that emphasize standardized approaches such as randomization or statistically significant case studies.

The field experiences from rural Southeast Asia will shed light on a host of unresolved issues that arise during the course of fieldwork in authoritarian countries. These include how to improve the validity and reliability of the findings, how to compile data and frame questions, and what the costs and ethical consequences are of interviewing citizens in nondemocratic countries. These findings can add significantly to the small volume of existing work on qualitative methodology and offer an opportunity to explore whether current scholarship, largely derived from research in open political environments, applies in nondemocratic contexts (Seidman 1998; Yin 2003; Mahoney and Rueschemeyer 2003).

Conclusion: Future and Prospects

This chapter has shown the potential contributions that Southeast Asia can offer political science. However, the question remains: How can we raise the profile of rural economy in Southeast Asia and get the attention of political scientists? This is definitely a daunting task. Some of the answers to this challenge—such as situating Southeast Asia within any number of prominent strategic and geographic concerns—are beyond our control. On the positive side, it is expected that the demand for Southeast Asia studies will increase as a result of the rising numbers of second-generation Southeast Asian immigrant populations at U.S. universities and colleges who are eager to retain or rediscover their culture in a more determined way than were earlier generations of migrants. In the meantime, we can attempt to raise the profile of Southeast Asia by situating our empirical studies in broader theoretical contexts, addressing pressing and immediate development concerns, making inter- and intra-regional comparisons, and confronting methodological issues. To appeal to a wider audience, we can also choose topics that cut across subfields—for example, by connecting issues of democratization, ethnicity, religion, governance, and political legitimacy to rural political economy in Southeast Asia. We should attempt to publish our findings not just in interdisciplinary journals but also in political science journals. The prospects for this field of study may not be so bleak if we are able to open up awareness of the region to achieve these goals.

Chapter Twelve

Southeast Asia and Globalization
The Political Economy of Illiberal Adaptation

GREG FELKER

Introduction

This chapter analyzes the contributions of research on Southeast Asia to the study of globalization, focusing specifically on political economy debates.[1] The region's dramatic late-twentieth-century boom and bust seemed a graphic illustration of globalization's power both to transform developing economies and to trigger vast economic disruption. In the wake of the Asian financial crisis (AFC), Southeast Asia thus became newly prominent in globalization debates. It does not follow, however, that regionally focused research per se has had much influence on the study of globalization.[2] One might suppose that the rationales for traditional regional specialization are weak in the field of globalization studies, which is concerned with distinctly global dynamics.

In fact, research on globalization in Southeast Asia *has* engendered a significant accumulation of theoretically relevant knowledge. Regional specialists have increasingly deployed concepts and hypotheses taken from the wider discipline to illuminate their observation and historical knowledge of the region's international political economy (IPE) dynamics. In turn, the shared historical and contextual knowledge at the heart of Southeast Asia area studies has also informed efforts to transcend current impasses in globalization debates, to create new typologies, and to offer new causal hypotheses.

One such theoretical debate considers whether the structural pressures of global markets have rendered obsolete distinctly *national* variation in patterns of capitalist governance ("varieties of capitalism") or development ("comparative development strategies"). Many Southeast Asia specialists view the relationship between globalization and state authority in less binary terms. Nation building and economic development in Southeast Asia have been highly contested and incomplete historical projects, and ones always powerfully shaped by extra-regional forces. Perhaps more than in other regions, national and transnational dynamics have operated jointly and simultaneously in economic transformation, rather than in the sequential, zero-sum relationship explicit in many globalization analyses (Loh 2005: 19). Work on Southeast Asia thus highlights the importance of local-cum-national *agency*, even on the part of comparatively weak nation-states, in shaping patterns of change *within* transnational systems' unfolding dynamics of integration and contestation.

Regional specialists typically augment historically informed study of particular national cases with relatively deep knowledge of regional comparators. This is particularly important insofar as national and regional responses to globalization continue to display important variation that challenges expectations of neoliberal convergence (Loh and Ojendal 2005; Hewison and Robison 2006). How can such variation best be conceptualized and explained? A provocative typological theme in Southeast Asian research is the growing evidence in some cases of purposive strategies of *illiberal adaptation* to globalization dynamics. Such strategies are distinct from, and challenge, the typical binary or polar classification of responses as ranged between neoliberal reform, which gives international market forces free rein to restructure domestic systems, and resistance, which seeks to reassert national or regional political limits on global market integration. Examination of illiberal adaptation in turn prompts important causal questions with rich theory-building implications. How, for example, do state elites and societal actors operating in different national contexts try to secure advantages of power and wealth *within* transnational hierarchies constituted by systems of production, investment, accumulation, trade, and migration?

Structure and Agency in Globalization Debates

Asia's devastating crisis of 1997–1998 seemed to many an emphatic demonstration of the claim at the core of globalization debates: that transnational markets have made nation-states' role in governing economic affairs substantively obsolete. Many foresaw (for good or ill) the dismantling of Asia's distinct national systems of political economy, whether characterized as developmental or clientelist (Robison et al. 2000), and an imminent shift toward a much more free-market form of capitalism. Others predicted that the economic pain wrought by global market forces, and the coercive imposition of liberalizing reforms by the International Monetary Fund (IMF), would provoke disillusionment with, and active resistance to, further globalization.

Malaysia soon emerged as a key test of these projections. After loudly blaming "moronic" international currency speculators and neocolonial Western powers for undermining Asia's successful development model, Prime Minister Mahathir Mohamad authorized capital account controls, trapping $10 billion in foreign funds in the Kuala Lumpur Stock Exchange. International market players reacted by downgrading the country's credit ratings and removing it from international investment indexes. In colorfully worded client advisories, the investment brokerage Credit Lyonnais predicted a global investment strike: "This is one country that investors can safely delete from their investable universe. . . . Now to foreigners you [Malaysia] are like your much-misunderstood durian—prickly on the outside and stinking in the middle. . . . Malaysia's flirtation with an economic miracle is now just a footnote in history. . . . So farewell then, Malaysian equity market, may we meet again—when the current generation of global investors has retired or is bullish on Bangladesh."[3]

Something odd happened, however, on the way to the "clash of capitalisms." The putative antagonists in this globalization drama quickly reached accommodation. "We are not going to cut ourselves off from the global economy," Mahathir assured a meeting of twenty-eight foreign fund managers in January 1999, shortly before relaxing the ban on withdrawals.[4] Gainsaying his own analysts' apocalyptic threats, Credit Lyonnais's CEO Gary Coull affirmed that foreign investors would return if the market looked promising. And what of Malaysia's capital controls heresy? "The market has a short memory."[5] His assessment proved astute. The KLSE main index had nearly tripled in value by the time the exit controls expired on their first anniversary, and net capital outflows were small.

What did this peculiar episode signify? Had Malaysia, recognizing its unalterable dependence on internationally mobile capital, bowed to the inevitability of neoliberal reform and begun dismantling its patrimonial-clientelist variant of "Asian capitalism"? Or had its successful defiance of neoliberal orthodoxy signaled the dawn of a wider revolt against globalization and exposed the "powerless state" to be an overblown myth?[6] Answering such questions requires assessing how domestic and international forces interact in driving trajectories of change at the national level. Regional specialists are particularly well equipped to undertake such analysis (McVey 1998). However, exploring the international-domestic nexus entails more than using richer empirical data to test globalization hypotheses against particular cases. It involves problematizing and reconceptualizing the complex structure-agency relationships that lie at the heart of globalization arguments.

Contending perspectives on globalization and the nation-state draw implicitly or explicitly on varying models of structure and agency. Hobson and Ramesh (2002) observe that both globalization exponents and skeptics frame their arguments in "hard" (structuralist) or "soft" (agent-centered) terms. "Hard"- or "hyper"-globalists such as Strange (1996) portray the contemporary global marketplace as an aggregation of structural pressures that emanate from trans-territorial markets and nonstate governance systems such as corporate networks and international credit ratings agencies. Market actors operate on a global scale and bypass uncooperative states; ineluctable competitive pressures thus force governments to abandon active macroeconomic policies, trade protection, and capital account regulation. Attracting and retaining mobile capital demands not only external opening, but also internal liberalization in the form of radical privatization and deregulation. By contrast, hard globalization skeptics emphasize the enduring importance of state power in global economic integration (Krasner 1999). Neorealists argue that globalization reflects hegemonic states' interests and thus that such trends might be countered by politically determined resistance or counter-hegemonic movements (Wade and Veneroso 1998).

In recent years, globalization debates have featured more sophisticated conceptualizations that blend structural and agent-centered logics. Proponents of "soft globalization" arguments accept that national governments remain a primary locus of authority in the contemporary global economy. Structural pressures, however, mean that states may adapt only more or less efficiently to the dictates of global markets and thus become mere instruments of the latter's reproduction. Neoliberal institutionalism anticipates the emergence of neutral, market-supporting "regulatory states," whereas a more critical literature describes how globalization transforms nation-states from civic associations orchestrating and distributing public goods into a more limited enterprise association that Cerny (1999) calls "the competition state." "Soft skeptics," for their part, maintain that globalization does not entail the ascendance of wholly disembedded global markets but is constituted by the *political interdependencies and interactions* of states and societal groups, with structuring influences flowing "up-scale" as well as "down-scale." Distinctly supra-national economic forces impinge ever more deeply on national systems, yet globalization also offers states new opportunities to enhance their domestic authority and to pursue distributional or developmental goals (Weiss 2003a).

Southeast Asia is an especially promising empirical field within which to evaluate these competing arguments and to build new theory. Compared to most parts of the post-colonial world, Southeast Asia's industrialization involved a relatively early and progressively deepening embrace of key globalization phenomena—in particular, private foreign direct investment (FDI) for global manufactured exports and, in the 1990s, private financial investment flows (Lim 1995). This offers a unique opportunity for macro-historical process tracing in testing globalization arguments.

According to many accounts, Southeast Asian governments' choice of a more liberal development strategy was heavily determined by the fact that the region's states were weak both internationally and domestically (McVey 1992a: 14). Southeast Asian states' political autonomy, bureaucratic expertise, and policy capacities differ greatly, but with the important exception of Singapore, none approximate the Weberian strong-state template (Crouch 1984; Hamilton-Hart 2002). Nationalist economic programs that use strategic industrial policies to nurture indigenous infant industries were intermittent and ineffective (MacIntyre 1994c).

Southeast Asia's combination of highly internationalized economies and relatively weak states makes the region a strong test of "hard" globalization arguments. These are undermined to the extent that even the less-capable governments in this region have defied global pressures for ever-deepening economic and political liberalization. For their part, "soft" globalization arguments do not presume that global structural pressures overdetermine national responses. However, states must have a minimum of institutional coherence if they are to wield agential power in the face of globalization dynamics. Wholly incoherent or corrupt states, then, fall outside the relevant sampling domain for soft globalization hypotheses. Likewise, very powerful or societally embedded states might mask globalization's effects by paying the price of resistance or otherwise postponing inevitable reforms. *The likelihood of state trans-*

formation or adaptation might thus be greatest in political economies with middling levels of institutionalization and policy capacity. In this regard, Southeast Asia is particularly well placed as a regional frame of inquiry. Its constituent states differ in their governance capacities but are neither too powerful to defer adjustment to globalization nor, with some exceptions, too fragmented to avail themselves of whatever scope it might afford for deliberate adaptation to sustain nation building, development, or political monopoly projects.

Globalization and Southeast Asian States
Before the Asian Financial Crisis

"WHEN THEY WERE DOMINOS": TRANSNATIONAL INFLUENCES ON EARLY POST-INDEPENDENCE DEVELOPMENT

Southeast Asia's early embrace of foreign trade and investment should have made it prominent in an intellectual precursor to globalization debates—namely, dependency theory. Like hard globalization arguments, *dependencia* also posits that global market forces vitiate developing countries' policy autonomy and make self-directed national development strategies untenable. Most of Southeast Asia's capitalist economies remained heavily reliant on colonial-era resource exports for several decades after independence. In the early 1970s, many governments relaxed foreign investment restrictions, provoking popular nationalist reactions in Indonesia and Thailand. Not coincidentally, several English-language studies appeared around this time employing dependency frameworks to explain both Southeast Asia's relatively modest industrial achievements and the growing role of foreign corporations in these countries (e.g., Wolters 1976). Dependency analysis was even more influential in studies of the Philippines (Broad 1988).

Despite persistent quasi-colonial economic structures and faltering nationalist industrialization projects, such work did not reflect a wider consensus among regional specialists that dependency theory could explain the salient features of Southeast Asia's development. Doner's comprehensive survey (1991a: 820–823) attributes this issue in part to the shallowness of import-substitution industrialization (ISI) and the consequent weakness of a bourgeois-nationalist constituency for criticism of the international constraints on development. Especially after Sukarno's fall in Indonesia, economic nationalism was weaker in Southeast Asia than in many parts of the developing world. Because industrial policies were desultory and often incoherent, it was largely moot whether their limited achievements could be blamed on foreign trade and investment.

Indeed, much of the literature of this era found that transnational political economy dynamics complemented, rather than undermined, state building and development projects in Southeast Asia. Crone's (1982) study of ASEAN's economic diplomacy argued that Southeast Asian states sought to mitigate their dependency through a "defensive regionalism"; that is, coordinated efforts to diversify the region's external investment and trade linkages, thereby enhancing member states' bargaining leverage and autonomy in domestic economic governance. Bowie and Unger (1997: 28–29) observed that regionalism in the 1970s owed much to external great-power politics, as the United States encouraged an enlarged Japanese presence in Southeast Asia as part of its own hegemonic retrenchment following the second Indochina war. More generally, Anderson (1988) describes how U.S. and later Japanese economic, military, and political support bolstered Southeast Asia's conservative regimes, even after left-wing insurgencies were contained and the Sino-U.S. alignment removed the only real external threat. Stubbs (1989a, 1999, 2005) likewise argues that these geopolitical conflict imperatives served to consolidate state authority, encourage developmental intervention, and subsidize export-led growth in Southeast Asia, in a dynamic similar to that which produced Northeast Asia's developmental states. This conclusion stands in partial tension with the prevailing view of Southeast Asian states as conspicuously weak and ineffectual, and their industrialization as historically ephemeral (Anderson 1998a). Yet Stubbs's analysis seeks to account for a template of domestic state-society *patterns* across East and Southeast Asia rather than to explain identical "manufacturing miracles" with reference to a singular economic development model per se. His argument might easily be read as an IPE explanation of why state-building and developmentalist projects achieved as much as they did *despite* tremendous internal conflicts and external challenges facing Southeast Asia's newly independent polities.

BEFORE THE FALL: TRANSNATIONAL AND NATIONAL DYNAMICS OF SOUTHEAST ASIA'S INDUSTRIAL BOOM

Attention shifted in the late 1980s from Southeast Asia's development failures to its striking industrial dynamism. Many explanations focused on domestic politics, comparing statist with business-centered explanations of successful liberal reform and export-oriented industrialization (Hawes and Liu 1993; Higgott and Robison 1985; McVey 1992b; MacIntyre and Jayasuriya 1992). Regional and global factors often figured in these comparative approaches as condition variables that altered the incentives for liberalization or else as exogenous stimuli of policy change. For example, Bowie and Unger's (1997) comparative study of the ASEAN-4 (Thailand, Malaysia, Indonesia, and the Philippines) frames international-domestic interactions as a series of shock-and-response episodes prompted by global economic shifts such as the global oil price spike of the early 1970s, the mid-1980s collapse of commodity prices, and the surge of inward FDI later in that decade.

While recognizing the importance of international factors in prompting liberal reform, most such comparative studies emphasized the determining role of domestic variables and rarely explicitly theorized the dynamics of the international political economy into which Southeast Asia had become integrated.[7] Winters's (1996) book on Indonesia, by contrast, takes as its chief independent variable the archetypical globalization phenomenon. In his framework, enhanced capital mobility "de-nationalizes" capital and pressures state officials to enhance the national investment climate by replacing discretionary resource allocation with markets. Various domestic and international factors can mediate this structural pressure for liberalization, and states can resist, particularly if they control alternative sources of investment capital. Yet the controllers of mobile capital are strengthened politically as reform progresses, and competition among national governments to attract FDI also raises the opportunity costs of resistance.

In this model, as in most of the comparative literature on Southeast Asia's turn to export-oriented industrialization (EOI), the global economy is conceptualized as a domain of ungoverned markets that exists in tension with domestic clientelist or developmentalist state-society patterns. While explaining Southeast Asia's economic internationalization as the product of deliberate, domestically driven choices, most such treatments also hold that a subsequent liberal transformation of domestic governance was inevitable as the region became more deeply integrated into transnational markets. In this respect, much of the boom-era comparative literature conforms to a "soft globalization" model.

In light of such assumptions, Singapore seemed a striking anomaly. How was it that state-corporatism and discretionary interventionism remained firmly entrenched in *the most globalized* of Southeast Asia's political economies?

In addressing this paradox, Rodan's (1989) work portrayed a more complex international economy than the one described in most globalization accounts. Compared to a global economy made up of arm's-length transactions, a division of labor shaped largely by transnational corporations' (TNCs') proprietary networks entailed not just dependency constraints, but also crucial opportunities for positive-sum bargaining, particularly for "first movers" such as Singapore. After an initial, failed attempt in the late-1970s to use non-selective ("market-conforming") wage policies to induce structural upgrading, the government redoubled its efforts to influence TNCs' locational decision making by making selective investments in sector-specific infrastructure and skills and positioning Singapore as the hub of expanding transnational corporate networks (Rodan 1993, 1997b: 161–170). Rather than progressing toward a neutral regulatory state, boom-era Singapore thus resembled a "competition state" as it orchestrated its own deepening internationalization while preserving the discretionary authority that secured its domestic political monopoly.

In a similar way, much of the IPE literature on Southeast Asia's boom portrays the evolution of a regional political economy in more complex, agent-centered terms than the structuralist logic of neoliberal accounts of globalization. Neoliberals explained East and Southeast Asia's deepening integration into the global economy as a natural market process. Indeed, the fact that trans-border private investment outpaced formal regional cooperation seemed a clear confirmation of neoliberalism's causal ontology: Initial experiments with market opening were politically self-reinforcing, strengthening internationalist coalitions and prompting governments toward further openness, deregulation, and privatization. In this view, the subsequent rise of formal regional economic cooperation initiatives, most notably the ASEAN Free Trade Area (AFTA) and the Asia-Pacific Economic Cooperation Forum (APEC), reflected the functionalist logic of neoliberal institutional change.

Many specialists on Southeast and East Asian political economy, however, observed quite visible corporate and political hands at work in regional integration. The Japanese government worked closely with private-sector organizations such as the Keidanren in shaping the scale, direction, and content of investment and intra-firm trade in Southeast and East Asia (Unger 1993; Machado 1995). TNCs brought trans-regional flows of goods, capital, technology, and labor under managerial governance by extending proprietary networks of subsidiaries, affiliates, and subcontractors (Borrus et al. 2000).

The literature on network-based regionalization contains a spectrum of analyses closely linked to the globalization debate. The popular metaphor describing East Asian economies as a flock of geese flying in formation served to naturalize the emerging regional division of labor as the outgrowth of a self-governing international product cycle working through FDI flows (Yamazawa 1995; Ozawa 1999). By contrast, more realist (or neomercantilist) perspectives saw Japanese and U.S. business networks as instruments of either TNCs' global oligopolistic competition strategies or their home countries' international strategies of cooperation, competition, and hegemonic control (Borrus 1993, 1999; Encarnation 1992). A chief claim in this literature was that Southeast Asia had been incorporated into a Japan-centered regional hierarchy (Machado 1999; Beeson 2001). Hatch and Yamamura (1996: 31) put the case in its starkest terms, arguing that Japanese corporations, supported by Japanese state agencies, had transposed the hierarchically ordered institutions of Japan's domestic political economy to the wider region in order to secure the home country's dominant position in the international division of labor.

Others viewed the extension of Japanese business networks into Southeast Asia as embedded in a somewhat more consensual or at least open-ended set of regional political dynamics (Doner 1993, 1997; Rix 1993). In Rix's phrase, Japan sought to exercise "leadership from behind" through positive inducements to Southeast Asian governments to promote integrated regional production. Despite their hierarchical features, Japanese competitive strategies led state aid agencies and private businesses to bolster host countries' infrastructure, supplier bases, and skills.

In Katzenstein's work (1997, 2000, among others), by contrast, Asia's "soft regionalism" of business-network integration and informal inter-governmental consultation reflected the *absence* of a clear hegemonic center or regional hierarchy. Regional integration was realized in multiple, overlapping social networks, each of which bore the distinct institutional hallmarks of home country systems—Chinese family capitalism, Japanese *keiretsu*, Korean *chaebol*—rather than statist logics of regional domination.

This array of perspectives on the extra-market determinants of "network regionalization" had similarly diverse implications for the scope for Southeast Asian host economies to pursue deliberate strategic responses. Bernard and Ravenhill (1995) argued that regional networks expressed TNCs' growing ability to de-territorialize control over investment, production, and technological innovation. With TNCs deploying and integrating technology, skills, and capital through flexible regional production networks, FDI increasingly *substituted* for local inputs of skills and technology. Opportunities for local learning and decision making in their host Southeast Asian economies were crucially limited. Hatch and Yamamura (1996) likewise argued that Japan's mercantilist network strategy had drawn Southeast Asian economies into a form of "captive development" that conferred short-term growth benefits but precluded autonomous development strategies based on national industrial dynamics.

In Katzenstein's analysis, however, Asian business networks reflected not only home-country influences but also enduring business practices arising from broadly similar state-society relationships across Asia. These include non-Weberian systems of rule, in which spheres of public and private authority are blurred, as well as the exercise of flexible, informal influence across both formal institutional and national political boundaries. Crucially, then, network-based regionalization did *not* fundamentally challenge, or promise to transform, Southeast Asia's domestic political economy regimes. Rather, by forging investment partnerships with local elites, and relying on local ethnic Chinese subcontracting intermediaries, the regional interdependence created by the FDI boom conformed to preexisting, illiberal state-society relationships. Indeed, according to Hamilton-Hart (2005), transnational business networks in Southeast Asia have adapted their inter- and intra-firm managerial practices over time to better match the incentives of particular host-country institutional environments, including varying degrees of clientelist corruption. For their part, meanwhile, Southeast Asia's governments were far from passive objects of externally driven network regionalization projects. They actively promoted, screened, and targeted FDI inflows, seeking to guide them toward particular sectors, activities, and locations (Felker and Jomo 2003).

Jayasuriya (1999, 2003) conceptualizes the boom-era relation between regional integration and national political economy systems as a model of "embedded mercantilism."[8] Southeast Asia's national economies were segmented between highly internationalized manufacturing sectors and protected nontradeable sectors. Export revenues allowed incumbent rulers to patronize new, politically connected business groups in finance and banking, construction, transportation, retailing, and media. Policies of domestic privatization and deregulation, ostensibly reflecting Southeast Asia's embrace of the neoliberal Washington Consensus, instead gave rise to oligopolies in nontradeables through investment subsidies, no-bid privatization deals, preferential lending and licensing, public contracting, and manipulated finance (Gomez 2002). Across the region, financial markets remained underdeveloped relative to banking systems, which in turn were largely government-controlled and generally subordinated to the interests of these new business empires. "Open regionalism," with its recipe of weak institutionalization and unilateral reforms rather than supranational regimes, allowed Southeast Asian states to position themselves at the turnstiles of their economies' internationalization.

In sum, "nonregionalist" scholarly literature often superficially cited East Asia's pre-crisis regional political economy as an example of neoliberal globalization in action. Many regional specialists, though, portrayed regional integration as powerfully shaped by the institutions and strategies of both states and corporate actors, who bargained at multiple levels—subnational, national, and regional—as often in collusion as in rivalry.

THINGS FALL APART: GLOBAL AND NATIONAL
DYNAMICS OF THE ASIAN FINANCIAL CRISIS

The claim that Southeast Asian political economies remained essentially neopatrimonial or clientelist in the midst of the region's globalization boom became suddenly less contentious after the financial disaster of 1997–1998. Debate about "what went wrong" often turned on the relative importance of domestic-national versus global factors, but at a meta-theoretical level, many observers agreed that the crisis signaled the ripening of previously latent contradictions between the forces of globalization and Southeast Asia's national systems of political economy. The rise of a new, financialized, informationalized "postmodern" form of globalization provoked a structural crisis in Southeast Asia's patrimonial-developmentalist regimes (Loh and Ojendal 2005: 4–6). According to Jayasuriya (2003), financial globalization gave the new, politically influential nontradeables business empires erected during the boom direct access to global capital markets to finance their speculative growth. By displacing national systems of "financial repression," globalized financial markets swamped weak states' limited capacities to monitor and steer investment flows in domestic markets. Although the prior reciprocal accountability between state elites and their domestic business clients was always more clientelist or rentier than developmental, its breakdown nonetheless had disastrous consequences, unleashing a flood of unhedged foreign borrowing and inflating domestic asset-price bubbles.

Why had this change occurred? In hard globalization models, global dynamics create structural pressures that make national-level changes inevitable. In Asia, export-manufacturing capacity became a globalized commodity as China became the world's latest and greatest workshop. Only full participation in the new "strategic sectors"—financial intermediation, information technology, multimedia production, and other information-intensive services—could sustain Asia's growth momentum, and these were incompatible with existing political arrangements (Ozawa et al. 2001; Masayuma and Vandenbrink 2001).

Realist skeptics, by contrast, located the core dynamics of the crisis in the tectonics of hegemonic transition, which presented Southeast Asian states with a suddenly less-accommodating external political environment. Financial globalization reflected the decay of an incipient Japan-centric order and the recrudescence of U.S. hegemony after its Cold War victory. With the United States relieved of the geopolitical need to support erstwhile client states, the IMF–Wall Street–U.S. Treasury complex sought to remake the world economy through, and for, the transnational leverage of U.S. financial power and intellectual property interests (Beeson 1999; Beeson and Robison 2000; Wade 2001; So 2001). Southeast Asia's state elites remained largely helpless in the face of great powers' reshuffling of the rules of the global economic game (Beeson 2003a: 367).

Winters's (2000) treatment of the crisis exemplifies a "softer" globalization analysis. He also cites post–Cold War hegemonic shifts as enabling factors but insists that recent trends made transnational market actors vastly more powerful and thus independently significant causes of changes in Southeast Asia. His question is why global financial investors tolerated Southeast Asian states' corruption for so long, only to stampede for the exits in a destabilizing rush. Winters points to the irrationalities arising from the social organization of global finance. The recycling of investment capital from developed country savers to emerging market borrowers "funnels" capital through a community of some 100 poorly informed, reactive fund managers (see also Beeson 2003b).

Other students of Southeast Asia saw national-level dynamics and policy choices as far more consequential in setting the stage for crisis through incautious financial liberalization. After all, in some Southeast Asian economies, national savings rates were high, and in Indonesia official development assistance had long provided a stable source of investment capital, so capital account liberalization was hardly a survival exigency. In a collection of essays titled *East Asia and Globalization: Crisis and Response*, chapters on Thailand (Hamilton-Hart 2000b), Malaysia (Welsh 2000), and Indonesia (Murphy 2000) portray national authorities as eager partners of the United States and the IMF, or indeed as clear initiators, in lifting barriers to global financial inflows during the 1990s. A puzzle is thus suggested: Why would Southeast Asia's rulers abdicate their lucrative "gatekeeping" roles between their domestic big-business clients and the global economy by lifting restrictions on private foreign borrowing?

Some explanations focus on politics within the state. Neoliberal reform factions, composed variously of technocrats or politicians representing urban middle classes, gained increasing sway over the policy agenda (Weiss and Hobson 2000). Trusting in the salutary effects of greater competition from abroad, they sought to use liberalization to pry apart the nexus of state-influenced finance and big domestic business. Yet they did not adequately account for the risks of international financial volatility or for the inevitable domestic manipulation of liberalization policies. Instead of producing gains in competition and efficiency, the mix of domestic oligopoly and footloose international finance proved downright combustible (Wade and Veneroso 1998).

A major objection is that this argument is voluntarist, hinging on the short-sightedness of East and Southeast Asia's state elites and officials, a grand policy blunder that somehow occurred in multiple countries simultaneously. Instead, many attribute attention to the shifts in social and political power that underlay these policy choices (Jayasuriya 1999: 151). Those employing class-based and interest-group coalitional analyses argue for variants of a "policy capture" argument (Haggard 2000). In these accounts, policies of reckless financial liberalization, as well as the maintenance of exchange rates quasi-pegged to the U.S. dollar, were driven by their immediate beneficiaries: ascendant business interests or capitalist classes, concentrated in domestic nontradeables and exercising newfound political clout. Upending the previous power balance within clientelist networks, such groups escaped the control of their erstwhile bureaucratic or military patrons and pursued highly leveraged growth. In contrast to their progressive image in first-generation accounts of Southeast Asia's economic boom (McVey 1992a), rising bourgeoisies sought policy changes that would bolster private control over domestic finance and foreign borrowing *without* inaugurating competitive domestic markets. In breaking the patrimonial state's gatekeeping, however, "crony" businesses exposed themselves to far more powerful market pressures, thus sowing the seeds of their own downfall.

In fact, the empirically rich case studies in *East Asia and Globalization* make a plausible case for strategic misjudgment on the part of Thai, Malaysian, and Indonesian political leaders, regardless of the political clout of their private business clients. Since the early 1980s, globalization had proved an unalloyed good from the standpoint of incumbent elites. The surge in private financial flows into emerging markets during the 1990s appeared as simply yet another chance for Southeast Asian governments to harness global capitalism's ongoing de-territorialization, this time by promoting financial service industries and positioning themselves as regional financial hubs. Booming local stock markets at first bolstered, rather than threatened, the patronage mechanisms (such as special share-allocation schemes) that cemented the coalitional relationships at the heart of "embedded mercantilism." Obliviousness to the concomitant growth in risk exposure proved costly.

Globalization and Change in Post-Crisis Southeast Asia: Convergence, Resistance, Adaptation

Southeast Asia's crisis of 1997–1998 offers a natural experiment by which to assess contending theoretical perspectives on globalization. First, its proximate trigger was the quintessential globalization phenomenon: massive, instantaneous trans-border capital flows. Second, its very enormity signaled that Southeast Asia had entered a "critical historical juncture" that would make structural forces clearly visible, undermine established power relations, and accelerate changes in basic institutions. Most observers expected either a systemic transformation of the region's political economies in the form of neoliberal convergence or a vigorous nationalist counterreaction against globalization. Given the awesome scale of the turmoil, seemingly the least likely outcome was incremental adaptation and mutual accommodation between global markets and incumbent regimes.

CONVERGENCE: PARADOXES AND TRIBULATIONS OF REFORM

A chief corollary of the "hard" globalization hypothesis is the inexorable narrowing of national differences in the organization of capitalism around a universal norm of neoliberal economic policies. In this vein, scholars who previously disagreed about the efficacy of a distinct Asian model of capitalism shared a belief that the crisis had dealt a fatal blow to Southeast Asia's clientelist and patrimonial-developmental systems (Beeson and Robison 2000; Moon and Rhyu 2000). When financial panic made Southeast Asia's corporate economy insolvent, a prostrate region had no choice but to embrace market-strengthening institutional reforms, including independent central banks combating inflation, independent judiciaries implementing bankruptcy codes, securities commissions policing financial markets, and anti-corruption, electoral, and human rights commissions checking patrimonial political networks. The bolstering of autonomous institutions would protect the central resource-allocation role of free markets against systemic political manipulation (Haggard 1999). Incumbent elites might resist, but the crisis had unleashed structural imperatives so compelling that the elites' desires and strategies, regardless of whether they had helped or hindered boom-era growth, were now irrelevant.

Early analyses of post-crisis reform in Southeast Asia suggested that political and economic liberalizations were, in fact, proceeding in tandem, particularly in the worst-impacted countries (Emmerson 1998). In Thailand and Indonesia, incoming governments accepted IMF agreements that required the nationalization and liquidation of bankrupt corporate assets as well as the lifting of barriers to foreign acquisitions. In those countries as well as in Malaysia, the downturn galvanized reform movements whose protests focused attention on the collusive ties between state leaders and their big-business clients (Connors 1999). Significantly, even Singapore, which faced little obvious pressure from below, felt compelled to pledge new measures to enhance policy transparency, strengthen corporate governance, ensure competition, and permit greater foreign participation in formerly protected sectors (Rodan 2001).

Similar evidence of neoliberal convergence could be found at the regional level. Previously, Southeast Asian elites and scholars had boasted of the "ASEAN Way" as a culturally embedded mode of international economic cooperation distinct from Western models. Instead of building supra-national institutions to ensure cooperation, ASEAN regionalism relied on socialization processes, such as consultation and consensus, leading to mutual empowerment among sovereignty-conserving states. The crisis punctured these claims and confirmed criticism that regional cooperation was neither substantive nor robust (Acharya 1999; Narine 1997). However, post-crisis liberalization enabled a deeper, more participatory form of regional interaction based on shared democratic values and procedures (Acharya 2003; Solingen 1999). The long-standing aversion to formally institutionalizing regional free trade and investment also seemed to be falling by the wayside. In 2003's Bali Concord, the region's leaders dedicated themselves to the goal of achieving a full-fledged "ASEAN Community," inspired in part by the European Union (which, ironically, was the foil for earlier claims of a unique ASEAN way of regionalism).

However, more recent research has documented the decidedly mixed record of liberal reform in Southeast Asia (Hewison and Robison 2006; Rosser 2002; Robison and Hadiz 2004). Across Southeast Asia, the policy and institutional landscape has been reconfigured to varying degrees by the opening of formerly sheltered industries to foreign investment, the strengthening of corporate and financial regulation, and the adoption of freer trade (e.g., under the ASEAN Free Trade Area). Yet neither the reform process itself nor its outcomes in various Southeast Asian countries conform clearly to the neoliberal template.

In the region's more weakly institutionalized states, the greater severity of the crisis and the temporary loss of policy autonomy meant that initial reforms were far more sweeping, but implementation has been more sporadic and compromised. In Indonesia, efforts to strengthen the central bank and judiciary system, as well as corporate governance regulations, met with acute difficulty (Rosser 2003; Robison and Hadiz 2005). In a dark irony, corrupt officials operating within these institutions have appropriated the neoliberal rhetoric of "independence" from political interference to rebuff oversight and accountability. In Thailand, the post-crisis government of Chuan Leekpai conscientiously implemented a series of key governance reforms, chief among them the lifting of barriers to foreign corporate takeovers, the raising of capital adequacy and other prudential standards for the finance sector, and the creation of a new bankruptcy system. Although Chuan's technocrats were unable to enforce new standards and creditor rights vigorously, and strategic defaults became widespread, the parlous finances of many business groups eventually led to a winnowing of Thailand's top business families. As Hewison (2000) describes, though, a new set of powerful business elites, based in highly regulated sectors such as media and telecommunications, has leveraged political power to extend oligopolistic control over large areas of the publicly listed corporate realm.

It is striking that corporate-sector reforms were more sustained and consistent in the "strong state," non-IMF-supported cases of Malaysia and Singapore (Felker 2004; Rodan 2002, 2003). In those countries, reforms to financial systems, capital markets, and government-linked companies (GLCs) have been clothed in the language of neoliberal ideology: transparency and responsiveness to minority shareholder interests, especially including the international investment community. Yet corporate restructuring has not occurred primarily by neutral market processes, such as bankruptcy proceedings, voluntary mergers, or foreign acquisition. Rather, state authorities have wielded discretionary power to mandate mergers or broker takeover deals and, in Singapore's case, to guide the regional expansion of government-linked service and technology companies. In Malaysia, corporate restructuring has entailed the re-nationalization of distressed private companies by government-linked investment vehicles, and their re-staffing with handpicked managerial proxies.

Close to a decade after the crisis erupted, the chief lesson to be drawn from Southeast Asia's experience of economic reform is *a surprisingly high degree of continuity* in underlying political-economy institutions and practices. Despite important discrete policy changes, particularistic networks and rule-by-law discretionary authority appear far more resilient than most observers anticipated (Robison and Hewison 2005): party-state control in Singapore, party-business networks in Malaysia, family-oligarchic business structures and business-backed political parties in Thailand and the Philippines, and political-oligarchic business groups in Indonesia's transitional democracy. To the extent that market-strengthening reforms have advanced, they have involved exercise of tremendous government discretionary authority; the role of pro-liberalization societal coalitions appears limited. This "orthodox paradox" could be seen as merely a transitional phenomenon, a midwife to the remaking of Southeast Asian economies as more thoroughly market-based systems. With plausible expectations of systemic transformation thwarted, however, neoliberal teleology itself must come into question.

RESISTANCE: POPULAR, STATIST, REGIONAL?

In globalization debates, "convergence failure" is usually linked to local-cum-national *resistance*. Echoing Karl Polanyi's (1944) dialectical theory of market disruption and societal countermovement, a large academic literature has focused on new agents, sites, and modes of resistance to the encroachment of global markets. The social pain inflicted by the crisis led some to anticipate that resistance movements would strengthen across Southeast Asia and begin to shape the reconstruction of the region's political economies (Higgott 1998; Bernard 1999).

A flourishing body of research analyzes the growth of civil society actors who challenge Southeast Asia's neopatrimonial political regimes (Heryanto and Mandal 2003a). The shock of the crisis promised, and seemed, to draw together reform coalitions composed of the urban middle classes, nongovernmental organizations, and some small and medium business interests. Yet these people-power and *reformasi* movements were typically ambivalent regarding deeper economic internationalization. In fact, their indictment of government corruption and cronyism often blamed elites for auctioning national autonomy to global bidders, and this made pro-reform movements susceptible to nationalist appeals, resulting in complex and contradictory pressures on existing political economy institutions.

Hewison (2001) analyzes the political agendas of several leading nongovernmental organizations (NGOs) in Thailand and Malaysia that opposed the IMF's crisis prescriptions and advocated the repudiation of FDI-EOI growth strategies. He argues that these appeals, rather than realistically apprehending contemporary global capitalist dynamics and suggesting viable alternative models, often come down to an archaic de-linking policy little different from the *dependencia* rhetoric of the 1970s. Their popular variants typically invoke a romantic localism expressed in profoundly conservative lexicons, yet nationalist populism did not create a durable political impetus for systematic programs to fundamentally change internationalist development strategies.

Laborers, the urban poor, and farmers often figure prominently in anti-liberal or anti-globalization movements in various parts of the world. Deyo and Agartan (2003) suggest that the crisis, by exposing the lack of competitiveness arising from low work-force skills, has caused some Southeast Asian governments to begin to renovate labor regimes to enhance human capital investments. Yet even these tentative measures do not arise primarily out of resistance from below. Hadiz (2002) argues that despite important successes in delaying privatization in Thailand and the Philippines, labor movements have been unable to strike cross-class alliances to decisively affect reform processes.

In contrast, then, to examples from other world regions that feature subaltern revolts, resistance to neoliberal reforms in several Southeast Asian countries was driven more often by entrenched business classes. In Hewison's (2005) account, Thailand experienced a decidedly skewed version of Polanyi's "double movement." Post-crisis reforms posed an existential threat to the domestic business elite, but "the economic crisis and strident opposition to neoliberal policies resulted in processes of reorganization that galvanized and eventually enhanced [domestic capital's] power." Thailand's earlier democratization allowed a reconstituted business elite to capture state power by backing Thaksin's electoral machine (Pasuk and Baker 2004), which in turn co-opted the conservative nationalist lexicon of the NGO- and middle-class "localist" movement (Glassman 2004). In Indonesia, a similar dynamic saw the reconstitution of a politico-business oligarchy through parliamentary democratic politics, as politicians raised campaign financing by selling debt-cleansed assets back to their former owners (Robison and Hadiz 2004, 2005: 229). Case (2005) likewise argues that rentier business interests have contested reform measures in Malaysia, although, in contrast to Indonesia, the government proved capable of accelerating reform when this was deemed important to maintaining broader political support. In comparative terms, however, it is notable that changes to the government-linked corporate establishment have gone further, even though the pre-crisis political regime remained firmly in place and initial reforms were less decisive (Felker 2004).

A large literature suggests that beleaguered national governments often seek to use regional cooperation to avoid a competitive "race to the bottom" as transnational capital arbitrages differences in national taxation and regulatory standards. In Southeast and East Asia, although the failure of regional solutions to the economic crisis punctured exalted claims of a distinct "ASEAN Way," regionalist projects quickly resumed within ASEAN and in the form of the ASEAN Plus Three (APT) and the East Asian Summit (Stubbs 2002; Thomas 2002). According to some regional observers, this renewed East Asian regionalism represents a resurrection of regional resistance to Western-style neoliberal globalization, this time based on a more realistic appreciation of the need to build genuine institutions of regional cooperation (Higgott 2000; Bowles 2002). Other observers are skeptical. Beeson (2003c), for example, argues that defensive or "reactionary regionalism" is likely to amount only to a gloss on the region's underlying dependence on the complex of U.S. hegemonic power, global international financial institutions, and nonstate governance systems operated by financial and corporate market actors. Meanwhile, the locus of enhanced economic cooperation has been bilateral negotiations, many with partners outside East Asia, hardly consistent with a bid to defend a distinct regional political economy model (Ravenhill 2003).

In short, if Southeast Asia's recent crisis and recovery cast the region into a "globalization crucible," the result was a very mixed alloy. Although exposing intra-regional variation, research by Southeast Asianists points to a regional meta-pattern of change but not convergence, and resistance but no clear countermovement. Once again, one might argue that despite the epic scale of the economic disaster, the resulting systemic changes—whether a convergence with or abandonment of neoliberal globalization—are unfolding only incrementally. Some research into Southeast Asia's post-crisis political economy points instead to the possibility of deliberate *illiberal* adaptation.

ILLIBERAL ADAPTATION: "CAPTURING" GLOBALIZATION

Southeast Asian polities' historical experiences of state building and economic development have always been prompted and constrained by powerful external actors and structures. With some major exceptions, the regional record features a pattern of effective adaptation to the forces of global economic integration and trans-territorial structures of political authority. Recent work on globalization and Southeast Asia has begun to address the theoretical implications of these patterns of purposive adaptation. This literature examines four broad issues or themes: how state power, if it is not simply eroding, is *changing* in the midst of globalization; how illiberal regimes might reach *accommodation* with new pressures in the global political economy; the *prerequisites* for successful illiberal adaptation; and the *implications* of illiberal adaptation for theoretical debates about globalization and the nation-state.

According to proponents of hard and soft globalization arguments, developing countries surrender the capacity to pursue redistributional or developmental agendas when they embrace global markets to avoid the worse fate of economic marginalization (Wade 2003). However, evidence of deliberate adaptation in Southeast Asia supports a different theoretical critique of hard globalization arguments, one that challenges such zero-sum conceptualizations of the relationship between global forces and nation-state power and agency (Weiss 2003a). Mittelman and Othman, for example, propose a conceptual framework centered on the concept of "capturing globalization," which focuses attention on the "interactions of globalizing structures with a multiplicity of agents" (Mittelman and Othman 2001). The global economic system depends upon the exercise of power for its reproduction, including at lower levels; thus, national governance continues to matter crucially both to particular national patterns as well as to global dynamics.

What is novel, however, is the way that globalization causes actors to conceive of their goals. Faced with powerful structural economic changes over which they have little control, states and societal groups do not simply try to conserve instrumental power by defending or enhancing their autonomy—that is, by resisting globalization processes. Rather, they respond to globalizing trends by maneuvering to secure advantageous structural positions *within* emerging transnational hierarchies (Othman and Kessler 2000). By fully embracing FDI-EOI strategies in the 1980s, for example, Southeast Asian governments foreclosed more autonomous development strategies based on locally integrated industrial structures. Yet this did not mean that Southeast Asia's states had simply retreated to neutral regulatory roles. Rather, this form of globalization often actually bolstered Southeast Asian states' uneven, contested domestic authority by positioning them as the *arbitrageurs* of new linkages and exchanges between local and international actors and resources, especially through FDI promotion and domestic investment regulation. In this way, Southeast Asian state elites traded autonomy-cum-sovereignty for enhanced control over the domestic political economy.

Hobson and Ramesh (2002), articulating a concept of "spatially promiscuous" states, likewise challenge the notion that the trans-nationalization and de-territorialization of markets, by undermining nation-states' economic *sovereignty*, necessarily undermine their economic *agency*. States, like capital controllers, can project power trans-territorially. Rather than simple conformity or resistance, their strategies involve a mix of measures aimed at adapting to structural dynamics and, if possible, influencing emerging structures in favorable ways. In the 1990s, for example, Singapore forged new governance relationships with neighboring subnational governments and multinational and local businesses to create an integrated local transnational economy, the Singapore-Johor-Batam growth triangle (Parsonage 1997). Since the AFC, government-linked companies have expanded regionally in a simultaneous pursuit of strategic and economic goals. Singapore's state is thus involved in externalizing its domestic political economy institutions in much the same way that Japan's had done during an earlier era.

Similarly at the regional level, Nesadurai (2003) maintains that Southeast Asian governments' enhanced cooperation does not represent "defensive regionalism," but an example of "developmental regionalism," a deliberate adaptation designed to give partial and temporary help to local firms as they prepare for intensified global competition. Likewise, the bilateral free-trade negotiations under way between Southeast Asian governments and with extra-regional partners, crucially China, feature sector-specific bargaining and the exclusion of "sensitive" products. Ravenhill (2003: 307) refers to this as "liberalization without political pain" and speculates that it might reduce incentives for deeper, more institutionalized free trade and investment. In other terms, these new regionalist projects could be said to reflect the search for a new equilibrium between transnational integration and illiberal domestic regimes, one that is analogous to the "embedded mercantilism" of the boom era. Southeast Asia's rulers do not hope to sequester a distinct national or regional capitalist model against deepening global market integration. Rather, they seek to conserve their states' capacities to manage economic internationalization selectively, for more prosaic reasons of domestic distributional influence and political control.

Efforts to theorize illiberal adaptation usually accept another core globalization claim, that states increasingly must share economic governance authority with other actors, including private business, civil society organizations, and international corporations and financial agencies over economic policy (Mittelman 2000: 920). Beeson (2003a: 368) argues that "[t]he Southeast Asian experience dramatically highlights the way in which globalization undermines the nation-state theory of government and replaces it with a new concept of governance . . . something that is increasingly characterized by co-operation between states and between states and non-state actors." Yet he also notes that "there is nothing inherently new about the subordinate position of many Southeast Asian nations." Indeed, as described above, students of the regional political economy showed how Southeast Asia's boom-era development was embedded in global businesses' transnational networks. Rather, it is the persistence of state patrimonialism and clientelist politics, even in the midst of "deep integration," that is the more theoretically significant finding. The key point is that most Southeast Asian states are not obviously less integral to the governance of their domestic economies than in earlier eras. Their powers to shape distributional or developmental outcomes remain, as they have always been, decidedly limited, but they appear surprisingly durable.

Here, the discussion comes full circle to the second issue noted above: how Southeast Asia's patrimonial, clientelist, or developmental states might achieve relatively stable accommodations with contemporary globalization trends, permitting stable economic growth over extended periods. Although post-crisis events have belied expectations of swift convergence, the question remains whether the reign of party and family bosses, and the economic power of business oligarchies, retain long-term viability in a world economy ruled by capricious financial markets and restrictive multilateral trade rules.

This question points to a broad research agenda for which robust conclusions are only now emerging. Recent research suggests, however, that some Southeast Asian regimes are using their remaining governance power to strike mutually beneficial deals with the actors who instantiate the new forms of globalization (Weiss 2003b). The need to restore international investor confidence after the crisis has prompted Southeast Asian governments to promulgate new legal-regulatory frameworks and pledges of greater financial transparency. Yet, contrary to hard globalization arguments, it seems that global financial investors can still be satisfied with partial, discretionary reforms and meanwhile remain susceptible to the lure of profits in rapidly growing markets, even when ostensibly fundamental market principles are compromised (Rodan 2003: 520).

Despite fears of a return to clientelist populism, and the slow and unreliable performance of the new bankruptcy provisions, international investors were quick to return to Thailand as Thaksin's reflationary policies boosted growth rates after 2001. Malaysia's swift reentry into global financial markets following its imposition of capital controls, recounted above, also suggests that contradictions between financial globalization and clientelistic practices are neither acute nor systemic. Rodan's (1998, 2002, 2003) research into media and corporate governance reforms is particularly important in this debate. He shows how Singapore's government liberalized the rules under which global media corporations and content providers could enter Singapore as a base for regional operations, while preserving domestic media control for the political purpose of regime maintenance. Abbott (2001) likewise traces how Malaysia has sought to exploit the economic potential of the Internet while containing its political consequences. In these cases, incumbent regimes have widened access for international entry into info-communications and other services sectors. Yet in both countries, as well as in Thaksin's democratically elected administration in Thailand, political rulers have been able to restrict the political opposition's access to the media by relying on state-linked media companies and the selective use of coercion to foster an information culture of self-censorship (Hewison 2005). Ironically, then, these governments have been able to draw administrative, policy, and political "borders" in precisely those fields of activity where globalization's supra-territoriality is thought to challenge state sovereignty most profoundly, namely cyberspace and other "media-" and "info-scapes."

A third set of issues concerns the preconditions for illiberal adaptation. Neoliberal globalization models have coincided with rising political science interest in the economic role of social capital and in the importance of local social networks or regional governance systems in supporting flexible, internationally competitive industries (Evans 1997). A different approach emphasizes the continued importance of "embedded autonomy": coalitions of developmental states and private business that enable collaboration in pursuit of adaptive strategies and developmental goals (Evans 1995). In this vein, Doner and Ramsay (2003) argue that Thailand's adaptive failures in the face of globalization reflect the weakness of the country's coordinating institutions.

Closely related but quite distinct is the neo-Weberian argument that the internal organizational attributes and capacities of nation-states themselves remain the key variable in structuring political economies even amid global integration. As noted above, intra-regional variation within Southeast Asia is highly suggestive. In her study of the politics of Southeast Asian financial systems, Hamilton-Hart (2002: 177) argues that "states with higher levels of governing capacity are better able to maintain national policy goals under conditions of capital mobility than are states with lower levels of governing capacity." Equipped with more disciplined and capable state regulatory agencies, Singapore and Malaysia managed financial internationalization more cautiously and responded to the crisis more effectively than did Indonesia. At the same time, differential institutional endowments also limit the prospects for building regional mechanisms of financial governance as a strategy of semi-illiberal adaptation (175–180).

A fourth issue concerns the theoretical implications of illiberal adaptation for more nuanced, "soft-globalization" arguments about the relationship between globalizing structures and nation-state agency. Does illiberal adaptation signify re-empowered states, or does it signify polities being compressed into mere "competition states" (Weiss 2003c)? Jayasuriya (2002) argues that globalization is transforming Southeast Asian states into authoritarian liberal regimes that replace patrimonialism with rule by law. Glassman (1999) similarly argues that globalization, by deterritorializing markets, is also "internationalizing" Southeast Asian states, "a process in which the state apparatus becomes increasingly oriented toward facilitating capital accumulation for the most internationalized investors, regardless of their nationality." By contrast, the case studies in *Southeast Asian Responses to Globalization* (Loh and Ojendal 2005) underscore how national political struggles continue to yield widely varying institutional patterns and distributional outcomes. Although the external forces falling under the broad conceptual rubric of globalization do prompt and condition such struggles, their direct influence is often ambiguous at best. Southeast Asian research thus offers a particularly telling challenge to expectations that the nation-state's role in the political economy of developing countries has become decisively less important.

Conclusions

Both critics and exponents of globalization and the notion of "Asian capitalism[s]" saw Southeast Asia's recent crisis as epitomizing the contradictions between global market integration and distinct national political economies. Yet the economic dislocations of the crisis, along with the very real political and policy changes that followed, masked important underlying domestic continuities. From the very outset of their efforts to build state power and manage economic change, Southeast Asia's rulers have had to take their external environment as they find it or, rather, as it forcefully impinges on them. This might help explain why they have consistently proved capable of adapting to and even exploiting international economic forces in order to sustain domestic systems of power.

Southeast Asia's highly globalized political economies draw attention to an important paradox in globalization debates. Even as the nation-state's economic sovereignty withers, its importance as an agent of economic reform and governance persists. Contrary to neorealist expectations, state elites in most of Southeast Asia's polities have never primarily sought to maximize national economic sovereignty or autonomy. Rather, they have aimed to maintain their preeminent position in domestic distributional politics, frequently by brokering the internationalization of their own economies. The crisis temporarily overwhelmed elites' ability to act strategically in the face of external pressures, but intentional processes of adaptation have since resumed in many, though not all, Southeast Asian states.

Efforts to theorize national agency within globalization involve several elements. First, political economy actors' strategies and bargaining must be taken seriously, derived inductively, and be related to broader abstract logics of globalization. Another lesson from Southeast Asia is that state-society patterns display a higher degree of continuity than hard-structural globalization arguments allow. Finally, divergent trajectories of growth, crisis, and reform point to more than simple path dependence; they speak to the ways in which political influences on globalization flow up-scale as well as down, not simply through resistance that challenges existing dynamics but also through bargaining that helps to constitute them. Weak states need not delegate decisive authority to truly independent market institutions in order to make sufficiently credible commitments to protect international economic actors' interests.

The best accounts of Southeast Asia's internationalization reinforce the conceptual view of the globalizing world economy as composed of far more than disembedded markets, whether such "spaces of flows" are framed in terms of the equilibrium-tending dynamics of a global division of labor or the irrational volatility of a financialized "casino capitalism" (Strange 1997). Given the multiplicity of actors, forces, and structures operating in the transnational realm, globalization's relationship to nation-states' economic governance role is complex and contradictory. Cox (R. Cox 1987) and other critical IPE theorists long ago suggested alternative theoretical approaches to naïve neoliberal ontology. Instead of the inexorable rise of denatured markets, or the creation of integrated political-institutional orders, the global economy is being reconstructed by social and political forces pursuing specific, conflicting, and converging interests within a global capitalist system whose forms are not structurally predetermined.

The theoretical implications of Southeast Asia's experience of globalization point to an even deeper paradox relevant to many other parts of the developing world. Globalization is typically thought to challenge the civic associational bonds that have made national polities the dominant locus of loyalty and authority in modern political life. Yet in polities like those in Southeast Asia, states' *effective* sovereignty, authority, and legitimacy have always been tenuous and contested. Therefore, the ostensibly corrosive effects of globalization on *Gemeinschaft* paradoxically imply less profound transformations in the structure of state-society relations. Southeast Asian states have always sought to achieve and conserve power-cum-*Gesellschaft* and have staked legitimacy claims on their ability to act as the prime agent of development. Globalization has transposed this contested project to the pursuit of the putative dictates of national "competitiveness." Many observers assume this to be an unsustainable or at best very fragile basis for the "organized hypocrisy" of states' claims to power over populations and territories. In this regard, however, Southeast Asia's deepening embeddedness in global systems of investment, production, and trade has, if anything, afforded the rulers of at least its more advanced capitalist systems greater domestic leverage and resilience than they might otherwise have enjoyed.

Chapter Thirteen

Southeast Asia in Political Science
Terms of Enlistment

DONALD K. EMMERSON

Rational choice theory, with its claims to axiomatic reasoning, deduction as a fountainhead of truth, and universal principles of politics, is challenging political science. . . . The idea of having a political science specialist for every piece of international real estate may soon seem as arcane as having a specialist for every planet in an astronomy department.

DAVID LAITIN (1993)

Pluralism without updating is not science. . . . It would be a warping of the scientific frame if we built into the charter of any department of political science that there had to be an expert in "realism," or in "South Asia," or in "democracy," or in "qualitative methods." . . . [I]nstitutionalizing slots for particular specialties is a threat to scientific progress. . . . A pluralism that shelters defunct practitioners cannot be scientifically justified.

DAVID LAITIN (2003)

[O]n the eve of the September 11 attacks, half of the top political science departments in the United States did not have a Middle East studies program. It is certainly desirable for a social science to be rigorous, empirical and seek general rules of human behavior. But as Aristotle explained, it should not try to achieve a rigor that goes beyond what is possible given the limitations inherent in the subject matter. In fact, most of what is truly useful for policy is context-specific, culture-bound and non-generalizable. The typical article appearing today in a leading journal like the *American Political Science Review* contains a lot of complex-looking math, whose sole function is often to formalize a behavioral rule that everyone with common sense understands must be true. What is missing is any deep knowledge about the subtleties and nuances of how foreign societies work. . . .

FRANCIS FUKUYAMA (2004)

Southeast Asian studies and political science are compatible. It will always be possible to define these two fields in exclusionary ways. At the extreme, they can be made to refute one another, methodologically and epistemologically. Yet there is no reason why one cannot study an area and do political science at the same time—and satisfy criteria for quality research on both sides of this polemicized divide, *depending on what those criteria are.* The italics emphasize my theme.

On the preceding pages, my colleagues have reviewed what scholars at the interface between the area and the discipline have enabled us to know about politically relevant phenomena in Southeast Asia. In their chapters and their careers, these authors have illustrated the compatibility of area studies and political science. In this chapter I want to stand back from the literature and its findings and highlight the interface itself.

To say that Southeast Asian studies and political science are compatible, after all, leaves open the nature of that compatibility. Do the two spheres of endeavor merely coexist? Are they complementary? Do they overlap? And which (if any) of these formats—*coexistence, complementarity, overlap*—is superior to the others, and why? It is on these questions that I wish to focus here.[1]

Overlapping Spheres

As a way of describing how area and disciplinary study are related, *coexistence* is misleading. My feisty opening quotations notwithstanding, this book has not been written by area specialists gazing across a DMZ that separates them from political science, nor by political scientists on the other side of the barbed wire gazing back at the area specialists. My colleagues have amply illustrated the value of scholarship that is simultaneously and robustly Southeast Asianist *and* political scientist in character. In this context, the notion of coexistence essentializes and dichotomizes what amount to contingent differences. It overlooks the fruitful interaction between perspectives associated with these differences. And it risks implying an institutional equality between area studies and the discipline that does not exist.

Compared with mere coexistence, the case for *complementarity* between area-based and disciplinary scholarship is, on the surface, more accurate and more attractive. Beyond simple juxtaposition, a complementary relationship entails mutuality and interaction. *But on whose terms?* If the study of an area is institutionally peripheral or subordinate to the discipline, and if the discipline privileges one intellectual perspective, area scholars may face a "complementarity" with the discipline that requires them to adopt that particular approach. This is what I mean in my subtitle by "terms of enlistment." At its most invidious, such a relationship reduces the area scholar to supplying data—raw material to be sorted and processed into theory in factories downstream that are owned and operated by the discipline in accordance with its convictions.

When David Laitin, as quoted above, insists on his understanding of "science" to the exclusion of "defunct practitioners," Southeast Asianists prospectively included, he seeks to impose his own terms of enlistment. His is a methodological warning to get with the program—shape up or ship out. Fukuyama, although he may not have had Laitin specifically in mind, regards Laitin's kind of "science" as intellectually trivial and policy-useless. Fukuyama's terms of enlistment contradict Laitin's.

Compared with coexistence and complementarity, the notion of *overlap* has several advantages. Unlike coexistence, it does not reify the two sides. Unlike complementarity, it does not allocate one function or set of functions to area studies and a different set to political science. The notion of overlap implies what Peter Berger (1974: 123) called "cognitive respect." It acknowledges that scholars with political science backgrounds and Southeast Asian interests have, or ought to have, freedom of intellectual choice. It recognizes, too, that pre-defunct Southeast Asian political scientists have worked out, in their writings and careers, their own ways of meshing or balancing the area with the discipline.

Some of the scholars working inside this overlap—the zone of greatest area-discipline intimacy and transaction—may willingly conform to an assigned role in an intellectual division of labor. Others, however—emboldened, one hopes, by some of the arguments in this book—will see no necessarily fatal tension between studying an area and doing political science. They will claim for area studies a full analytic and even a theory-generating role that is at the same time consonant with what they believe political science is, or should be, about.

It is hard for a Southeast Asianist to ignore one of the two spheres. But some may enjoy spending time outside this overlap, either in the rest of the area-study sphere or in the rest of the disciplinary one—extensions where diverse conceptions of scholarship also prevail. In the nonoverlapping space on the area side, for example, some may criticize or even reject the discipline while others settle for coexistence with it, just as scholars in the extension of the disciplinary sphere will hold comparably various views of area studies.

A career is not a snapshot but a film. Intellectual preferences and priorities evolve. No scholar is likely to stay in one fixed place from the beginning of a career to its end. Some will look for cases and comparisons beyond Southeast Asia, whereas others will dig deeper into one country in that region. Some will seek greater acquaintance with other disciplines, whereas others are content to explore the perspectives and findings that political science affords. Accordingly, the zone of overlap, like the spheres themselves, will expand or contract. Necessarily, the "terms of enlistment"—the meanings and conditions that locate "the study of Southeast Asia" within "political science" (and vice versa)—will change as well.

An awareness of scholarly flux is not easily reduced to a logo suitable for emblazoning on a banner to be carried by the vanguard of a revolutionary or revisionist movement inside either Southeast Asian studies or political science. But partly for that very reason, a sense of shifting and overlapping spheres not only captures actual complexity and contingency—the dynamics of diversity—better than more schematic alternatives do; it also opens a range of possible scholarly futures for area and disciplinary study that are more appealing, at least to me, than mutual alienation at one extreme or disciplinary hegemony at the other. (Area hegemony is almost impossible to imagine, or so I shall argue.)

The zone of area-discipline overlap is the natural habitat of comparative politics, the subdiscipline of political science that is most hospitable to area studies. No subfield in the discipline is better positioned to mediate or transcend the dichotomy between area-based knowledge and political science. But it is not realistic or desirable to seek in comparative politics a neat—let alone a permanent—resolution of area-discipline tensions. Dissent and disarray in this context are encouraging signs that the terms of enlistment are still being tested, and contested.

Although arguing for dynamic overlap as the best way of illustrating the compatibility of area studies and political science, this chapter does acknowledge aspects of coexistence and complementarity in matters of professional organization and proposed practice. I begin by highlighting the institutionally hierarchical relationship of area scholarship to political science—their unequal and uneasy coexistence on some campuses. The discussion then differentiates the two spheres while noting the overlap between them and the diversity within them. Next I review in unequal detail two proposed complementarities between the area and the discipline: the "tripartite methodology" of David Laitin and the "analytic narratives" of Robert Bates.

The chapter ends by arguing against an overly monolithic or centripetal view of theory and for a more open methodology of "plural choice." My intention is not to promote an alternative to "rational choice" but to urge instead that whatever the method a scholar decides to use, the decision should be driven by the nature of the research problem at hand, rather than by professional investment or evangelical faith in a single key that supposedly fits all locks. My wish throughout is to help make the zone of overlap between Southeast Asian studies and political science more productive, intellectually and professionally, for those located there.[2]

Unequal Organization

Life is ineluctably spatial. People live their lives on location, including even the seat that temporarily locates an airline passenger between locations. Being located somewhere means interacting with the human and physical environment around you. If our shared intellectual goal is to understand these interactions—or to explain, predict, or interpret them—then it follows that we must first be able to situate them.

Indeed, there is no such thing as context-free understanding. The effort to comprehend human thinking, feeling, or behavior in a computer model or a game matrix merely substitutes an artificial environment controlled by the researcher for the more complex and diverse "natural" environments in which these phenomena occur, as the lives of billions of unique individuals elapse and intersect.

At the root of the "area idea" is the proposition that trying to get inside a relevant selection of those life worlds at relevant places and times is a necessary (if insufficient) step toward comprehending what has gone on there, or is going on there, not to mention predicting what will be going on there. Reversing Gertrude Stein's derisory view of Oakland—"there is no there there"—for area specialists there always is a there there, and a then as well. History is a core discipline in area studies.

In the organization of U.S. universities, nevertheless, Southeast Asia programs, where they even exist, are interstitial between departments that represent the disciplines and, in that capacity, form the main pillars of higher education.

Marginality has some advantages. Not being mono-disciplinary, area-studies programs can help widen intellectual horizons that may have been narrowed in departments. Not being tenure homes, such programs are less subject than departments to rancor and jealousy over hiring, firing, and promotion. In the cooperative activities of area centers—brown-bag talks, conferences, potluck dinners—political scientists may find intellectual and personal relief from the hierarchical ambience, career competition, topical constraint, and authorized methodology that may characterize their disciplinary department. There are, of course, exceptions to these judgments. But successful area programs do often serve as respites of a kind from the quotidian business of impressing one's departmental colleagues by improving one's curriculum vitae. Especially keen are the feelings of isolation among area scholars on campuses—by far the majority—that are not large or wealthy enough to sustain a Center for Southeast Asian Studies.

Note the prepositions: a Center *for* Southeast Asian Studies, but a Department *of* Political Science. To my knowledge no U.S. university—certainly no major one—houses a Department *for* Political Science or a Center *of* Southeast Asian Studies.[3] Compared with the area, the discipline needs no efforts on its behalf. A department "of" the discipline links to something already large and lasting. The notion that every university should maintain a unit devoted to studying Southeast Asia is, in contrast, fanciful. There are far fewer Southeast Asia centers than there are political science departments. When they chose to be "for" rather than "of" Southeast Asian studies, these centers may not have been self-consciously advocating their field of study. Like Marx's classes "of" and "for" themselves, this is a subtle distinction. Yet the difference in prepositional choice between area and discipline remains striking—and is at least consonant with the observation that in U.S. higher education, compared with political science, Southeast Asian studies are institutionally more precarious.

In a conversation with me years ago a U.S. political scientist, one of the best-known names in comparative politics at the time, only half-humorously dismissed proponents of area scholarship as mere "real estate" agents whose "soak and poke" methods could not withstand scrutiny. Area work, he half-implied, was too parochial and sloppy to qualify as proper political science.[4]

I have treated—this book treats—the overlap between area concerns and political science as a zone of healthy and productive collaboration, now or in prospect. As the above putdown suggests, however, that cross-hatching has also bred professional disregard, intensified sometimes by the two spheres' inequality in the organization of academe. Anyone who has moved between these fields in the course of a career has experienced, alongside mutual good will, reciprocal disdain—the area specialist dismissed as unsystematic, the disciplinist disdained as insensitive. Working in such mixtures of affinity and coolness, one may wonder where one's loyalties should lie.

Dilemmas of allegiance are especially acute among younger scholars seeking tenure. Should they publish in Asian studies journals that share their attraction to the "area idea" or in political science journals that may impress their departmental seniors more? How assiduously should beginning faculty cultivate theory, chase causality, run regressions, build models, and seek patterns in aggregate data across multiple countries? Dare they relinquish quantity for quality and scope for depth in prolonged fieldwork in a small but richly complex place? What might it mean to follow the advice of the influential anthropologist Clifford Geertz and generalize *within* a case? Or, still referencing Geertz (1973b: 26), how "thick" does description have to be to gain the respect of theoreticians? Once tenure is obtained, if it is, such choices become less acute, and personal preferences enjoy freer rein.

Methodologically, compared with area studies, political science is more presumptive. The New Shorter Oxford English Dictionary, for example, defines *political science* twice: (1) "the branch of knowledge that deals with the State and systems of government"; and (2) "the scientific analysis of political activity and behavior."

Definition (1) parallels area studies in featuring a topic, which happens to be "the State and systems of government" rather than "Southeast Asia." How the discipline deals or should deal with its preferred subject is left open. But the door of methodology is at least partly closed by definition (2), which has no counterpart in the study of an area. That second account commits the discipline to dealing with "political activity and behavior" not impressionistically or descriptively but through "scientific analysis." Political *science* implies an official tool kit; mere Southeast Asian *studies* does not. Reinforcing the epistemological gap between disciplinary and area knowledge is the difference between centripetally singular "science" and centrifugally plural "studies"—between a do-it-this-way standard and an invitation potentially to do it your own way.[5]

Crossing Borders

The multidisciplinary scope of Southeast Asian studies necessarily diversifies that set of endeavors compared with the one discipline of political science. Yet the discipline, however firmly ensconced in the academy, is not a solidly consensual monument to science. A version of the intellectual tension between area and discipline appears inside the discipline itself, as the gap between differently set barriers to entry: the low-bar eclecticism of the verb "deals with" in definition (1) and the high-bar certification of "scientific analysis" in definition (2).[6]

One might expect the transdisciplinary sweep of Southeast Asian studies to encompass topics and viewpoints so multiple and varied as to make political science appear cramped and monochrome by comparison. That might be true if practitioners of "political science" in fact dealt only with narrowly "political" topics using only narrowly construed "science" as an approach. Instead, of course, the writings and teaching of scholars housed in the discipline, including those working on Southeast Asia, span political economy, political history, political anthropology, political sociology, and so on. Nor is it difficult to see politics of some sort at work in almost any situation, entity, activity, or event.

As for the "science" in political science, there is only the loosest of agreements as to what that key qualifier means. Uncertainty and controversy over the appropriateness of this or that approach, and the difficulty faced by any one school that would impose its epistemology on other schools, help to keep a scholar's choice of method at least somewhat open. Nevertheless, that openness remains greater in Southeast Asian studies than in political science. The discipline is one of the social sciences, and they are diverse, but area studies embrace the humanities more fully and enthusiastically than political science does.

Perspectival controversies inside the discipline matter. A candidacy for tenure may be at stake. In contrast, the institutional subordination of area knowledge and its fragmentation across diverse world regions work to lower the stakes of methodological conflict.

The self-styled "perestroika" backlash in the discipline illustrates this difference. The revolt was meant in part to challenge the perceived dominance of rational-choice assumptions in political science. No such movement developed in Southeast Asian studies, and not just because skepticism toward rational-choice theorizing was already widespread among area scholars at the time. Compared with its political science equivalent, the Southeast Asianist vocation was then, and remains, too weakly organized and professionally too minor for its diverse and dispersed adherents to bother plotting reform. No hegemony, no rebellion.

For if political science combines a hierarchy with a specialty, Southeast Asian studies are a specialty with little to no hierarchy. In the United States, the American Political Science Association (APSA) is for a political scientist what the Association for Asian Studies (AAS) is for an Asianist—a professional "guild" (Emmerson 2003). Elevation to the leadership of APSA means being acknowledged as a leader of the discipline. For younger scholars, publication in APSA's peer-reviewed journal, *The American Political Science Review* (*APSR*), significantly enhances the chance of tenure.[7] Appearances on panels at the Association's annual conventions are lesser stepping-stones toward the same end. The AAS also has its leaders, its *Journal of Asian Studies*, and its yearly meetings. But the Southeast Asia Council and its members occupy a small box well inside the organizational chart of the AAS. Meeting infrequently and lacking funds and visibility, SEAC is peripheral compared with APSA.

Area studies are also weaker than the discipline in a more ironic respect. Most students of Southeast Asia are specialists on only one of its ten countries. Other things being equal, the audience at an AAS panel on one of Southeast Asia's ten states is not likely to include many specialists on the other nine. When the subject of such a panel is politics, the relative homogeneity of the audience may be not only spatial but disciplinary as well. It was partly to remedy such narrowness that the AAS some years ago began urging its members to organize "border-crossing" panels that spanned countries and disciplines alike. The irony is that this was considered an innovation in area scholarship, whose interdisciplinarity already implied broad horizons and holistic perspectives. Self-segmentation by country within Southeast Asia, let alone by region within Asia as a whole, is in its own way no less parochial than mono-disciplinarity.

Generalizing Within Area Studies

In every scholarly genre at any point in time, some ideas are emergent or ascendant while others are in relative stasis or decline. The study of an area is no exception. If today, for their field, Southeast Asianists jotted down these ideas—what's "in," what's "out"—their lists would, of course, vary. But among the more appealing and popular concepts, hybridity, constructedness, and contingency would surely recur. Conversely, among the anathemas on these lists—sins for scholars to avoid—I would expect to find frequent warnings against essentialism, reification, and givenness. Better to reach for a constructivist insight than fall back into the naturalist fallacy.

Southeast Asian studies are intellectually diverse. But they are not random. For various reasons, including globalization and the legacy of postmodernism, those who study Southeast Asia nowadays tend to feature possibility, openness, changeability—and shun imputations of permanency, closure, innateness. If explorations of indeterminacy are "in," intimations of determinism are definitely "out." Among the most relativistic Southeast Asianists, paradoxically, primordialism verges on apostasy.

Primordialism is the idea that cultural outlooks and behaviors are foundational—long-standing, slow-changing, and deeply rooted in the hearts and minds of the members of a given culture. Resistance to such an essentialist formulation, including the very notion of "a given culture," is more intense and widespread in Southeast Asian studies, where anthropology looms large, than it is in political science. Primordialism is not behavioralism, and studies of "political culture" in the discipline are passé, at least under that name. Yet the notion of a fixed or viscous culture could, in principle, satisfy a political scientist's desire to reach bedrock of some sort, and in that sense may not differ as much as one might think from the quest for universally and enduringly valid generalizations about outlooks and behaviors. Political scientist Samuel Huntington's controversial but influential study of civilizations (1996) illustrates the point (see Huntington 2004). Certainty may be chimerical, but the appetite and therefore the market for it remain.

Southeast Asia is but a small part of the larger world. Even if they could make law-like statements to account for political phenomena throughout "their" region, how would Southeast Asianists know whether or not those generalizations applied as well to the many peoples, countries, and regions elsewhere? They would not know, at least not without extending the scope of their research to include the rest of the world—that is, not without ceasing to be Southeast Asianists in the sense of specialists who confine themselves to that region. The more research undertaken entirely outside Southeast Asia, the weaker the researcher's claim to a single-area identity.

An area specialist could avoid losing that identity by staking permanent ground upstream. He or she could supply materials, all drawn from Southeast Asia, to political scientists working downstream: rough insights from "local knowledge" worth reconsidering in other settings, regionally plausible propositions worth wider testing, or mere data and descriptions to be plugged into a model or matched against a generalization that the receiving political scientist might be able to confirm or improve.

To the extent that the processing of area knowledge by disciplinists adding value downstream is aimed at the certainty and closure one associates with law-like generalizations, however, the implications may be repellent for area students who are apt to assume—even to prefer—contingency and openness in human affairs. An area specialist may be happy to generate creative ideas and insights for further consideration by others. But if raw information is all the disciplinist wants from the area-ist, the latter may not be happy at all. Why should responsibility for evidence stop there? Why should it preclude a role in making theories based on that evidence—and assessing them as well? Not all area specialists will want to be hired as hewers of wood and drawers of water on a disciplinarian plantation.

It is from such a biased complementarity that area-based resistance can arise. Instead of helping to inform the discipline, a relativistic Southeast Asianist may choose to question its susceptibility to universalist assumptions, as if any one nontrivial rule could fit all or even most cases. Rejecting a division of scholarly labor seen as invidious—area studies as a mere data bank for the discipline—such a scholar could claim and even celebrate the uniqueness of "local knowledge" (Geertz 1983; see also Emmerson 2004). He or she might use fluency in a local language to assert that local phenomena are fundamentally untranslatable, incommensurate, and thus fortunately beyond one-size-must-fit-all-if-only-we-could-find-it political science.

In this instance as well, the area specialist's professional identity could be at stake. The more that human beings everywhere think and act similarly in similar situations for similar reasons, the more arbitrarily bounded any one part of the world must be. An area specialist may warrant specializing in one region, country, or part of a country by emphasizing its uniqueness. A universal ontology jeopardizes that justification.

The most common claim for Southeast Asia's uniqueness showcases its diversity. The claim is ironic insofar as diversity implies ranges of variation, which imply variables, which invite cross-case comparisons—comparative political science. The claim is irenic in that it opens opportunities for cooperation—peace—between area and disciplinary specialists. The claim is additionally ironic, however, in a way that hampers such cooperation, epistemological disagreements aside. Although a typical university-based Southeast Asianist teaches much or most of the region, most of her or his research is likely to be limited to one or at most a few countries within it. Such a scholar is not well equipped to accomplish a fraction of the comparisons that the vaunted diversity of Southeast Asia invites, let alone to draw contrasts with other parts of the world.

Many gradations are of course possible between universalism in the service of disciplinary theory and exceptionalism in defense of local knowledge. Like my colleagues who move back and forth between area and discipline, including my co-authors here, I do not wish to essentialize the two genres. They are not necessarily opposed. But they are different—and seen to be so, as the ensuing discussion of "the state of the subdiscipline" of comparative politics will suggest.

Generalizing Within Political Science

In a paper presented at the APSA convention in 2000, the well-known, influential, and originally Africanist political scientist David Laitin reviewed "the state of the subdiscipline" of comparative politics—an essay published in 2002 in APSA's third decennial review of "the state of the discipline" (Laitin 2000, 2002). "A new consensus is on the horizon," he announced in that review, "one that emphasizes a tripartite methodology, including [1] statistics, [2] formalization, and [3] narrative" (2002: 632).

The tensions between the discipline and the area discussed here were not

Laitin's topic. In his paper he implied that such disagreements might be the fading legacy of older scholars. He was "encouraged by the orientation and training of the coming generation of comparativists, who are ready to join in on the emergent consensus that I outline here" (2000: 2, including n. 1).[8]

The three components of that would-be-emergent consensus[9] amount to a menu of methodological choices. A comparativist can (1) seek "statistical regularities across a large number of similar units," notably as reflected in "cross sectional or diachronic data"; (2) endogenize "principal variables" in "formal models"; or (3) "examine real [or virtual] cases to see if the results from the statistical analyses [method (1)] and the theoretical accounts [method (2)] apply to the world" (Laitin 2000: 1–4; see also 2002: 630–631).

Large-*n* statistics, mathematical models, reality-checking narratives . . . this division of intellectual labor compartmentalizes and sequences scholarly research. Qualitative work is reserved for "narrative." But that activity is limited to seeing whether the statistical regularities and the formal models "apply to the world."

Laitin's triptych is ecumenical in one sense at least. It reserves one panel for narration. Yet this complementarity is likely, on balance, to discourage a Southeast Asianist political scientist hoping to generate theory using qualitative methods. There is no opportunity for that activity in Laitin's summary of his scheme. The narrator is called in only after the statistician and the modeler have done their work. And it is *their work* that becomes the work of this third member of the research team.

Laitin's complementarity is also remarkable in that it reverses the invidious upstream-downstream specialization that I referred to earlier. The "narrative" function has been redesigned and relocated downstream: from generating raw input—data—at the onset of research to checking the fit between highly processed material—statistics, models—and the actual world. Does this new role empower a narrator to call a halt to the whole process if she or he determines that these statistical patterns and modeled propositions, including draft laws of causation, do not in fact "apply to the world"?

I am not sure. But I strongly suspect that the success of such a whistle-blower—the narrator's ability to persuade the statistician and the modeler to reconsider their quantitative results—would depend on how impressed the latter colleagues were with the methods behind the critique—that is, with the nature and efficacy of the whistle being blown. It may be unfair to note that the narrator-critic would be outnumbered two-to-one in Laitin's format. But it seems fair to wonder whether either the statistician or the modeler would accept correction on the basis of purely or mainly qualitative evidence, the sort that goes into the making of a constructed—interpreted—story, which is what a narrative is. Having gone to all the trouble of processing quantitative evidence and deriving mathematical parameters, why would these rigorously "scientific" colleagues have a change of heart and suddenly believe that "mere anecdotes" are "data" after all?

A different response seems more likely: Unless and until you test our products "scientifically," the way we would, using quantitative methods, we must reject your critique. A few exceptions do not overthrow a rule. The necessarily subjective character of your "narrative" makes its apparent lessons unreliable. Suggestive, perhaps. But definitive? No. Determining what is definitive can only be our own—quantitative, cross-case, model-running—task.

Laitin's three functions could be performed by one person. But the sheer range of skills and experience required is sure to daunt an individual scholar— the artificial languages of statistics and modeling, the spoken languages of field sites and secondary literatures, and the years of experience, with the computer, in the classroom, on the ground, in the stacks, before credibility across such disparate domains could be acquired.

Ideally, innumeracy should have no more place in the zone of area-discipline overlap than illiteracy does, and rational-choice comparativists should spend long periods seeking "local knowledge" in actual, complex, puzzling field settings where people speak neither math nor English. Realistically, however, collaboration among differently equipped and specialized scholars will remain necessary and desirable.

What is missing in a complementarity that either sequesters the qualitatively minded scholar farthest upstream panning for raw data *or* farthest downstream narrating reality checks is the possibility that quantitative *and* qualitative research are best brought to bear *throughout* the research process, depending on what method or combination of methods is best suited to the problem at hand.[10]

Laitin illustrated his proposal by reviewing works written from each of his three perspectives on recurring topics in comparative politics: democracy, order, and capitalism. These illustrations acknowledged the creativity of narrators in advancing and debating various answers to large questions. But it is clear from his account that the qualitative mode in which these authors worked necessarily limited their ability to generate real—that is, formal—theory.

Laitin further limited his notion of narrative by identifying it closely with history: "Questions that require sensitivity to change over time lend themselves better to historical rather than statistical analyses" (2000: 12–13). In his paper at least, Laitin admitted a role for "ethnographic, interview, or archival work" in determining whether "changes in parameter values" and "outcomes" that a theory anticipates have actually occurred (2000: 5). However, it remains clear that qualitative political anthropology, for Laitin, is a taker (if also possibly a tester) of theory, not its maker.

Laitin also implicitly dismissed, or at least demoted, other disciplines, such as sociology, anthropology, linguistics, philosophy, and literature, as makers of theory about politics—except perhaps insofar as researchers in these fields could be either explicitly statistical or historical, or could build formal models. This surely must come as a disappointment to a political-science-schooled area specialist accustomed to learning, and learning theory, from diversely insightful work by scholars in some or all of these disciplines—work that is neither exactly historical nor quantitative but does illuminate, or generalize from, aspects of the world.

Viewed against the academic organization of knowledge, such narrowness makes a certain sense. Political science would lose its identity if it became transdisciplinary—the equivalent of area studies going global. One could argue that proponents of multidisciplinary research on the area side of the divide should be pleased enough at history's incorporation into Laitin's political science scheme not to ask for more diversity than that. Yet even with history inside it, such an amputated world seems designed to induce at least mild claustrophobia in a Southeast Asianist accustomed to multidisciplinary horizons.

The difficulty is that these other disciplines come with their own preferred concepts, approaches, and methods. One can sympathize with Laitin's dilemma: (a) to organize a hierarchy that will enforce methodological tranquility within political science, and to keep the alternative universes of other disciplines outside the building, where they cannot disrupt what goes on inside it; or (b) to let them inside the building, where they can enrich political science but at the risk of importing an anarchy of assumptions and techniques.

Between these alternatives, Laitin proposed a less strict version of (a) that may still be too strict to attract many area scholars, namely: (c) a limited partnership with history and at least the possibility of openness to diachronic narratives from other parts of academe, provided that these liaisons are restricted to helping to improve, through case-specific evidence, political science theory as defined in quantified terms. In practice, the success of this middle option would depend, for example, on how many area specialists would willingly accept such a division of labor, knowing that they would have to check their own epistemologies at the door. By the light of this third option, area studies and comparative politics are compatible, but only on the latter's terms as interpreted by Laitin.

Compatibility on Whose Terms?

Two years before the APSA panel on which he reviewed the state of comparative politics, a book appeared by five other authors working from rational-choice perspectives—three political scientists and two economists. They called it *Analytic Narratives* (Bates et al. 1998), henceforth abbreviated *AN*.

In one sense, at the time, this was a breakthrough. Rational-choice theorists were admitting that "narratives" really could be analytic. In that recognition—and, by extension, the reverse admission, that analysis could be narrative—lay a possible synthesis at the end of a long dialectic in the literature. The arguments in that dialectic (Friedman 1996) could be traced back, through the antithesis to rational-choice theorizing articulated most notably by Green and Shapiro (1994), to the thesis propounded by the school itself in a literature commonly dated from the work of William Riker (1990, 1962). But the synthesis was not to be. Or if *AN* was a synthesis, it did not last long. Among other scholars, Jon Elster (2000), in a devastating review of the book in the *APSR*, kept the dialectic going.

Area scholarship was relevant but not central to these debates. One looks in vain through *AN*, or through Laitin (2002) or (2000), for a discussion of area studies as an enterprise in its own right, with its own findings and arguments, let alone its own theories or pre-theories. The omission is all the more striking for that fact that both Bates and Laitin began their careers as area specialists—in African studies.[11]

Analytic Narratives paid major attention to history. It could have been subtitled "Modeling European and American History." Of the five core chapters apparently written to illustrate what analytic narratives were, four took up, respectively, the political economy of late-medieval Genoa; absolutism in seventeenth- and eighteenth-century France and England; conscription in nineteenth-century France, Prussia, and the United States; and political stability in the United States prior to the Civil War. The fifth, by Bates, concerned the workings of the International Coffee Organization from 1962 to 1989. Here is how Bates and his collaborators summarized what they were up to:

> We call our approach analytic narrative because it combines analytic tools that are commonly employed in economics and political science [read: rational choice] with narrative form, which is more commonly employed in history. Our approach is narrative; it plays close attention to stories, accounts, and context. It is analytic in that it extracts explicit and formal lines of reasoning, which facilitate both exposition and explanation. (*AN*: 10)

What this paragraph seems to mean is that economics and political science, or more accurately the partisans of rational-choice theorizing within these disciplines, are analytic. In contrast to these fields, which have tools, history offers only a narrative form. Historians describe. They tell stories. They compose accounts of what happened. They provide context. They offer their narratives for consumption by those who add real value: namely, the authors, all of them working in genuinely analytic disciplines where supposedly genuine theory—formal theory—is made. That downstream activity "extracts explicit and formal lines of reasoning" from upstream historical narration.

At least Laitin, as I have noted, would later turn this division of labor upside down by placing "narrative" farthest downstream.[12] The narrators in his scheme were not merely adherents of a form. To run reality checks on formal theory, they would have to wield tools as well. However, the nature and provenance of those tools remained unclear. Would they be the methods of large-n, quantifying "science"? If so, in what sense would these narrators be allowed to narrate?

I began this essay by acknowledging the compatibility of area studies and political science. But that compatibility is not, and should not become, the unequal congruity of inferior and superior within a hierarchy in which the area student knows his or her place and the disciplinarian knows what counts. A less skewed and more respectful arrangement would reflect a sharing of interests and a shared sense of one's own limitations.

On both sides of the interface between area work and political science, scholars have a mutual interest in theory *broadly understood*. The problem is that for many on the disciplinary side, area students are not truly theoretical, but when viewed from the area-study side, the discipline looks too narrowly theoretical.

In this regard, the time is past due for area scholars to retire a canard about the other side. Few political scientists believe they are building a single, permanent, universal "Scientific Theory of Politics" that will put a STOP to all lesser efforts, including the qualitative fumblings of area specialists. The latter should not fear a straw man. Even Laitin, in his Darwinian vision of area studies possibly becoming "defunct" (2003: 108), did not go so far as to claim that "science" would *definitively* prevail. Here he is on the same subject, but in a still less cumulative vein:

> Comparativists will drop old questions, not because they are solved but because new questions have pushed their way onto the political agenda. . . . Choice of the dependent variable cannot be separated from the goals, interests, and generational perspectives of researchers. . . . Also, questions comparativists ask about outcomes continually get specified anew, as the way we ask our questions about political outcomes changes over time. . . . [Such] questions *never get satisfactorily solved*, as on the brink of discovery they get specified in a new way, opening up new lines of inquiry. (Laitin 2002: 632, italics added; see also 2000: 5–6)

As for Bates and his co-authors, in *AN* they quoted and rejected the accusation by Green and Shapiro (1994: x) that the failures of rational-choice theory were " 'rooted in the aspiration' " of its partisans " 'to come up with universal theories of politics.' " *AN*'s authors argued that notwithstanding their book's debt to "deductive reasoning"—each chapter, they acknowledged, "constructs, employs, or appeals to a formal model"—the essays "seek no universal laws of human behavior." They noted that the pioneer of rational-choice thinking in political science, William Riker (1962), had believed that rational choice held "the promise of a universal approach to the social sciences, capable of yielding general laws of political behavior." But the authors of *AN* were unwilling to go along. They dismissed Riker's claim as having been "based on an 'overconfident' and naïve vision of the sciences" (*AN*: 11, including n. 11).

Opponents of STOP who work wholly or partly on the area side of the interface with political science ought to relax a bit and treat Riker's imperial vision for rational choice as comparable to the withering away of the state for classical Marxists, or to the resurrection of a worldwide caliphate for committed Islamists—attractive to militants in this or that school but too fanciful to be taken seriously by others as a scenario for the future. More worthy of worry are the skewed terms on which rational-choice theorists would establish and institutionalize the compatibility of area studies with political science.

Theory and Choice

The most important question, in the end, is not whether area students feel welcome in a disciplinary club, or whether rational-choicers are imperialists. If diplomacy aims to prevent conflict, scholarship does not. Scholarship is about who is right. And scholarship is therefore necessarily also about what "being right" means. Discord is not the bane of scholarship but its lifeblood.

Is David Laitin's conception of theory right? Theory, for Laitin, is formal theory, and formal theory "(a) postulates relationships among abstract variables, (b) has rules of correspondence such that one can map values for a large number of real world cases on each of the variables, and (c) provides an internally consistent logic that accounts for the stipulated relationships" (2000: 3).

One can—I will—briefly question five aspects of this understanding of theory: *closure, scale, quantification, abstraction,* and *consistency.*

By *closure* I mean the idea that formal theory is theory period—ruling out any other kind. Is it not possible that Laitin's formula, however attractive, is only one way of specifying what theory can be and how it could be made?

By *scale* I refer to his insistence on large *ns.* Could there not also be theory on a small scale? Consider a theory of regime change that has been stretched to fit the nearly two hundred member states of the United Nations. Will that necessarily explain regime change *in Southeast Asia* better—more convincingly—than a theory that has been developed intensively in that region's ten countries and is meant to apply only to them?

Quantification is crucial to statistical analysis and formal modeling and therefore to Laitin's notion of theory. If quantifying a phenomenon entails losing some information about it, and if quantification thereby omits some phenomena, or distorts some more than others, how can the omissions and distortions be handled except by recourse to qualitative methods? Arguably, quantitative methods have made the need for qualitative ones even greater, notwithstanding Laitin's having marked only the latter for possible extinction (2003: 180).

As for postulations, relationships, variables, rules, internally consistent logic, and what they say about the "real world," these notions still must be expressed to some considerable extent in words—as part of a qualitative methodology. And if qualitative methods are essential, how can qualitative theory be overlooked? Is it not altogether possible that some phenomena are better explained by qualitative theory than by its quantitative counterpart, or at least that the balance of qualitative and quantitative methods involved should not be determined in advance? Is "informal theory" inferior to "formal theory" if, for a given empirical relationship to be explained or an analytic problem to be solved, the cost of quantification measured in omission and distortion exceeds the benefit measured in specification?

As for *abstraction*, decades ago Giovanni Sartori, writing in the *APSR*, famously distinguished three kinds of theory on the "ladder of abstraction": narrow-gauge, middle-range, and global. He went on to advocate "develop[ing] the discipline [of political science] along a medium level of abstraction" using "better intermediate categories" to improve theories of the middle range (1970: 1,044, 1,053).

Do Sartori's three types of theory differ only in degree? Does climbing the ladder imply only a larger n? Since Sartori wrote, has political science attained the highest rung, with no need to back down? Or are there intellectual issues involved that have not gone away, including what Sartori called "conceptual stretching"—a pitfall to which large-n categorizers may be especially blind? And if that is so, are there circumstances in which one would want to resist abstraction, avoiding a higher rung for the sake of greater analytic clarity and empirical certainty on a lower one? Is "local knowledge" something that a political scientist should want to leave behind?

It is conventional to assess theories by *consistency* and correspondence—the seamlessness of their internal logic on the one hand, and of their external fit with reality on the other, insofar as that reality can be independently apprehended. Between two theories about the same subject, one may appear to be modestly less consistent than the other yet seem to correspond to reality better. In such an instance, should consistency overrule correspondence? And what if the slightly less well knit but apparently more accurate theory is narrow-gauge or even micro-gauge in the sense of being limited to a single country, province, village, or even household?

Could the consistency of the analyst's mathematical logic be failing fully to capture the sometimes inconsistent thinking and behavior to be found among the people under study? If so, is the solution to climb the ladder of abstraction, enlarging the n in the hopes of ensuring actor rationality at least on average? Or to pursue the apparent anomaly more deeply in that local situation? Consistency may not be the hobgoblin of small minds, but it could be less evident in some smaller populations, whose outlooks and actions might therefore require, first and foremost, a qualitative understanding of what is going on.

None of these questions is against "science." Rather, they ask how narrowly the term should be construed.

Perhaps in the busy overlap between area studies and political science one ought to consider, alongside rational-choice methods, what might be termed a methodology of "plural choice." By "plural choice" I mean to acknowledge (a) the hypothetical multiplicity of motives and behaviors in a population under study, (b) the intellectual diversity of approaches and methods available to those who wish to study that population, and (c) the need to make the choice of a research method fit the research problem, not the other way around.

By pluralism I do not imply indecision. One must choose, and as path dependence sets in, future choices will become less plural. Nor do I imply hostility toward a "science" of rational choice. Depending on the research problem, a highly statistical, mathematically modeled, and large-n-scaled approach may indeed work best. I do, however, imply a commitment not to put theory permanently first, above all other forms of understanding, or to commit oneself first and foremost to a method, as if it fit all problems, like the proverbial man whose possession of a hammer made everything he saw resemble a nail.

A plural-choice approach need not compete with its rational-choice alternative, but could improve it by addressing objections to it: for example, that it makes insufficient allowance for nonrational choice, or that it privileges the rationality of material interest.

Within economics, there is already a literature on "bounded rationality" and a subfield, behavioral economics, that explores "quasi-rational choice."[13] Plural-choice theorists would go beyond these modifications, however, to explore awkward questions that rational-choice theorists, with their emphasis on voluntary decisions to make or break coalitions, have tended to treat as exogenous to their models or simply to ignore.

One of these questions would require the researcher to pay close and sustained attention to first-order beliefs, emotions, and intentions. By "first-order" I mean what actors actually think they are doing, and not—or not just—what a formal modeler deduces they must up be to.[14] Apparent in this context is the self-impoverishment that rational-choice theory has achieved through its lack of interest in anthropology.

Discovering and charting first-order consciousness is, of course, not all a scholar has to do. When anthropologists deploy Kenneth Pike's classic distinction between "emic" and "etic" discourse, they do not rule out the latter, second-order, analyst-driven understandings. Anthropology is far more than ethnography, and even ethnography is more than purely descriptive. The "narratives" that rational choicers consider merely atheoretical, or at best pre-theoretical, involve decisions of selection and presentation that owe at least something to the analyst's own "etic" concerns, *including theoretical ones—* matters that traditionally may have been, and may still be, external to the individuals and communities under study.

For imaginative ethnographers and sober modelers alike, however, it stands to reason that the greater the gap between what an analyst thinks is going on and what the objects of her or his analysis think is happening—and why—the greater the danger that explanations and predictions deduced from formal models will fail. For the sake of the abstraction, coverage, consistency, and specification that formal modeling requires, the modeler risks imputing to distant, diverse, and variously informed actors a motivation that plays no role, or a minor one, in the first-order mixture of motive and reason—and arguably, yes, a kind of theory—that actually leads them to do what they do.

The implications of mixed rationality as a basis for inter-specialist conciliation and synergy are unclear. But such an approach at least leaves open the chance of success. Each party to the dispute would have to be willing to give up something, but perhaps not too much. On the disciplinary side, the modelers would have to qualify their assumptions, possibly in both meanings of that verb. But a modified—diversified—conception of rationality would remain central to the interface, and thus to cooperation across it. On the area side, scholars would be nudged toward becoming more numerate, and toward a greater tolerance for comparison. Die-hard exceptionalists among them might even be persuaded to try comparing "apples and oranges" after all. At the same time, the new credibility of inductive research, and the new migration of ex-"field workers" downstream toward theories of their own making, would be welcomed by area specialists, if not also their informants, as enhancing cognitive respect and, more important, scholarly potential.

Meanwhile, pending such bargains, in the dynamic, creative zone of area-discipline overlap where this book was conceived, Southeast Asianists who are simultaneously political scientists, and vice versa, will seek their own terms of enlistment.

Chapter Fourteen

Concluding Remarks

ERIK MARTINEZ KUHONTA,
DAN SLATER, AND TUONG VU

This book has charted the process of knowledge accumulation in a range of important topics in political science. We hope the chapters have shown that Southeast Asian political studies have produced valuable scholarship regarding core theoretical questions in the discipline. Some of these works have given rise to prominent debates in political science, whereas others have had minimal impact outside Southeast Asian studies. The different chapters in this book have sought to highlight how and why some works have succeeded in defining and extending debates, whereas others have not. In this final chapter we intend to sharpen these points. We close by addressing the relevance of this book for contemporary policy debates.

Dual engagement with theory and region has long been the foundation for original and compelling work in Southeast Asian political studies. Scholars who have made effective use of these overlapping bodies of knowledge have been engaged in a dialectic conversation. Immersed in theoretical ideas or concepts from the discipline, these scholars have examined them against the real-world politics of the region and have then challenged, reformulated, or built new theoretical propositions. They have gone back and forth between the classics of the discipline, the historical narratives of the region, and the "soaking and poking" so vital to fieldwork. Theoretical lenses have been vital to the enterprise, but inductive analysis has also been indispensable for developing ideas that combine theoretical originality with solid empirical grounding.

Careful attention to history, it bears emphasizing, has been crucial to this dialectic enterprise—perhaps more than any other methodological or meta-theoretical approach. Ultimately, it is this interplay among theory, empirics, and theory again that has distinguished work in Southeast Asian political studies and influenced debate in political science.

It is worth reemphasizing in this conclusion why Southeast Asian political studies are so crucial to the study of comparative politics. First, the region itself stands out as a natural laboratory for comparative analysis. For the lay observer, Southeast Asia's religious and ethnic diversity immediately comes to mind when one thinks of objects for comparison. Although such cultural diversity is important for the comparative enterprise, the chapters in this volume have underscored other aspects that also deserve comparative treatment and that may not appear as obvious candidates for comparative work. For example, Dan Slater has emphasized the region's variation in regime type after the global "third wave" of democratization. This distinguishes Southeast Asia from other regions where democratization has either been sweeping or has made a minimal impact. Perhaps no other region at this point in time provides such a wealth of variation that can be effectively employed to build theory in the study of regimes. Other areas that have been highlighted as important foci for comparison include state structures, processes of institutional reform, types of party systems, and labor regimes. In all these substantive areas, there is significant variation within the region to merit comparative analysis. Mining these questions for theoretical insights will underline the inherent value of Southeast Asian political studies for comparative politics.

Second, the historical experience of Southeast Asia can play a critical role in addressing reigning theories. It can engage these theories by pointing out anomalies within them, elaborating on them, or building distinct theoretical frameworks. Case studies within the area studies genre are often seen as having a primary goal of confronting broader theories with empirical anomalies. But Southeast Asian political studies have the potential to move beyond simply chipping away at the margins of a theory that perhaps made no effort to incorporate cases from the region in the first place. Indeed, Southeast Asianists can aspire to use their regional knowledge to build theories that not only challenge existing ones but also provide an alternative way of visualizing politics.

Dominant theories or concepts generally reflect the political experience of the Western Hemisphere. Concepts derived from Europe and Latin America are often taken for granted in the academy and yet are incongruent—if often informatively so—with the realities of large parts of the developing world. For example, the Southeast Asia literature on political parties and elections indicates that such institutions retain political relevance in illiberal regimes as well as liberal democracies, even as they clearly fulfill different political functions. Regional scholarship on civil society makes a compelling case for disaggregating the concept to reflect the diverse character of civil *societies*, and for carefully specifying the effects of regime type on the development of social and political movements. Along the same lines, religious movements have often been superficially analyzed in the comparative politics literature, in part because of secularist assumptions that these movements are inherently destabilizing. Southeast Asian research has shown that such movements are much more complex and multifaceted because they tend to reflect and encapsulate other social tensions, such as class, ethnicity, and gender.

The prevailing neoliberal view that posits convergence as the inevitable result of globalization has been forcefully disproven in Southeast Asia's economies. Rejecting the zero-sum logic of neoliberal teleology or of a nationalist sovereignty backlash, a close analysis of Southeast Asian states' response to globalization indicates that domestic political and business elites have been able to ride the wave of globalization to their own benefit. Illiberal adaptation to the sweeping power of liberalizing forces presents a stark paradox to mainstream assumptions of globalization's trajectory. Finally, the claim that military regimes are exceptionally vulnerable to democratization pressures may generally ring true in Southeast Asia as it does in Latin America, but apparent "outliers" such as Burma and Indonesia call the presumptive causal mechanisms behind this correlation into question in interesting and provocative ways.

These challenges that emerge out of the historical experience of Southeast Asia are not simply an exercise in using deviant cases to impugn prevailing concepts and theories. Rather, they are powerful arguments for building alternative theoretical frameworks. To be sure, numerous chapters in this book have taken Southeast Asianists to task for not being attentive enough to theory. But we should not forget that our counterparts in other regions of the world are sometimes too hasty to draw theoretical conclusions that do not reflect the experience of many parts of the world, simply because these parts of the world have not been seriously incorporated into the theoretical conversation. Comparative politics would be better served by more vigorous exchange of theoretical *lessons* rather than vigorous insistence on theoretical *conclusions*.

Finally, Southeast Asian political studies have a role to play in breaking down essentialist mindsets. The chapters on ethnicity and religion have made it clear how the literature has progressed beyond primordialist views of identity. Although cultural identities clearly matter in movements that have a religious or ethnic goal, one must investigate more deeply whether these ascriptive identities are all-encompassing for their members. What studies ranging across southern Thailand, southern Philippines, and eastern Malaysia show is that class dynamics often complicate a simple clash between a dominant culture and a minority. Taking such a lesson to the level of nation-states, a nuanced analysis of Islamic doctrine, institutions, and personalities strips the globalizing "clash of civilizations" thesis of any real depth.

A number of chapters have highlighted theoretical debates in political science that are deeply indebted to Southeast Asian research: the moral economy versus rational peasant debate initiated by Scott and Popkin, the consociational versus cross-cutting cleavage debate between Lijphart and Horowitz, as well as active, ongoing disputes over whether Scott's "weapons of the weak" should be considered weapons at all. These debates are well known to most practitioners of comparative politics, yet this book has charted numerous other arguments generated by Southeast Asian research that have not resonated as forcefully in the discipline. There is clearly a gap between these noted accomplishments and the potential of Southeast Asian studies for advancing theoretical debates in comparative politics.

A critical refrain running through many chapters has been the need for Southeast Asianists to think more comparatively, engage theory more explicitly, and delineate causal findings more precisely. In highlighting this push for more comparative work and deeper engagement with theory, we again want to underscore the myriad opportunities that the region provides for addressing broader debates in political science. Too often have we read work that is compelling and richly deserves a wider readership, yet will be unlikely to gain one because of a failure to broaden out theoretical claims—whether through comparative analysis or through deeper immersion in the theoretical literature.

The chapters in this book have been heavily focused on debates in the academy, but it would be a mistake to assume that these debates are purely academic. On the contrary, the very process of knowledge accumulation is crucial—or *should* be crucial—for crafting policy. Scholars who have contributed prominently to theory and policy have recently called for a reorientation of political science toward real-world events (Diamond 2002;

Fukuyama 2004). For Southeast Asianists deeply concerned about the region they study, this call to strengthen the relationship between political science and policy making should be seen as welcome and overdue. After all, the reason that most scholars of Southeast Asian politics got drawn into the academy, we suspect, was because of a desire to devote their careers to making a contribution to the region. Yet we do not agree that the challenge is simply for scholars to make their research more *policy-relevant*; the bigger problem as we see it is that policy makers so often fail to make policies more *research-relevant*.

Here, the diversity of political outcomes in Southeast Asia makes the region especially valuable. By reaching a better understanding of the determinants of state strength *and* weakness, the malleability *and* stickiness of ethnic sentiment, the institutional determinants of economic growth *and* stagnation (as well as outright collapse), and the resilience *and* fragility of authoritarian regimes, policy analysts will clearly have more robust knowledge on which to make their assessments. Just as important for policy makers is the ability to categorize and conceptualize—in other words, to bring events, personalities, and figures into some abstract container. As sociologist Carol Weiss notes, "participants in the policy process can profit from an understanding of the forces and currents that shape events, and from the structures of meaning that [social scientists] derive from their theories and research" (quoted in Wilson 2002: 4).

Qualitative methods can play a particularly central role in policy recommendations because of their ability to closely identify causal mechanisms. For example, as Ben Kerkvliet argues in his chapter, explaining how agrarian conditions such as widespread tenancy, land inequality, or landlessness contribute to rural unrest and rebellion can be achieved only by in-depth research. It is simply inadequate to link variables to an outcome without close investigation of the causal chain (or chains).

Comparative-historical analysis is also of value for policy because of its tendency to identify broad, sweeping patterns in political life. These persistent patterns counter the common conceit of policy makers that political outcomes mostly depend on the decisions of people in charge. The macro-historical research that John Sidel has used to frame his study of local bossism in the Philippines may not appear to be immediately pertinent to policy, but its broad theoretical claim that instituting elections prior to centralizing state power can be detrimental to democratic quality has real policy value. When rebuilding war-torn states, policy makers are often forced to choose whether to institute elections quickly or wait until a stable, state apparatus has been established. Clearly, comparative-historical work has much that it can bring to this urgent problem.

Two other examples are especially noteworthy. As U.S. military forces struggle to quell stubborn insurgencies in Afghanistan and Iraq, the historical example of British success in crushing rebellion and fostering communal stability in Malaysia has served as an inspiration for some U.S. policy makers. In fact, Richard Stubbs's (1989b) classic study of the British "hearts and minds campaign" during the Malayan Emergency has recently been republished, in recognition of its obvious implications for contemporary global politics. But history teaches us that such comparisons must be drawn with great care. It should be recalled that the British strategy in Malaya was also an inspiration for the United States' disastrous experiment with "strategic hamlets" in South Vietnam in the 1960s and 1970s. Yet the knee-jerk assumption that what had worked in Malaya would work in Vietnam had been powerfully challenged as early as 1965 in a careful cross-country comparison by Milton Osborne (1965), a leading Southeast Asianist of the era. The political risks of ignoring area expertise are every bit as high in 2008 as they were in 1965.

Speaking more broadly, no Southeast Asianist with a sense of history can fail to recognize that the United States' current global war on terrorism exhibits some striking parallels with its earlier global war on communism. In both instances, policy makers have felt pressed to pay more attention to area studies in general, and to Southeast Asia in particular. But they have also felt tempted to view the complex political realities of the region through a single, simplistic conceptual frame. Witness the rush among self-described "terrorism experts" to portray Islamic militants in Southeast Asia as nothing more than an appendage of Al-Qaeda, rather than a phenomenon with important and distinct homegrown elements. If policy makers are seriously interested in understanding and addressing the complex, causal roots of Islam-tinged resistance in Southeast Asia, and not just in crushing its most militant adherents, they would be well advised to marinate themselves in the expert analyses of Surin Maisikrod and Ruth McVey (on southern Thailand), Bahtiar Effendy and Robert Hefner (on Indonesia), Clive Kessler and Hussin Mutalib (on Malaysia), and Thomas McKenna and Patricio Abinales (on the southern Philippines), among others.

In sum, such Southeast Asianists' ongoing efforts to combine theory and region should be of tremendous value for the policy community at a time when global events have reinforced the salience of area studies knowledge. Guided by theory yet grounded in empirics, the finest works in Southeast Asian political studies should just as well form the basis for sound contributions to the policy realm as they have to the accumulation of knowledge in comparative politics.

Notes

CHAPTER I

This chapter has benefited from the comments of Natasha Hamilton-Hart, Allen Hicken, Paul Hutchcroft, Jomo K. S., Suzaina Kadir, Andrew MacIntyre, Michael Montesano, and Kevin O'Brien; participants at a workshop at the Asia-Pacific Research Center, Stanford University, 18–19 June 2004; participants at a roundtable at the Asia Research Institute, National University of Singapore, 16 November 2004; and two anonymous reviewers at Stanford University Press.

1. We should note at the outset that the volume is focused on the study of comparative politics in Southeast Asia rather than scholarship on international relations.

2. The initial florescence of area studies was of course inextricably intertwined with U.S. geopolitical interests in the emerging Cold War. Fascinating as these connections are, they are not our focus here. For an excellent discussion of such themes in Southeast Asian research, see Berger (2003).

3. For those unfamiliar with these methodological debates, excellent recent resources include Shapiro and colleagues (2004) and Monroe (2005). The seminal recent texts are Brady and Collier (2004) and King and colleagues (1995), with the former serving as a polite if pointed rejoinder to the latter. A testier exchange can be found between Bates (1996) and Johnson (1997).

4. The scholar was Margaret Keck, director of Latin American studies at Johns Hopkins University. Quoted in Social Science Research Council (2001).

5. For broadly similar conclusions on dissertations as opposed to journal publications, see Maldonado and colleagues (2005). We should hasten to add that a systematic study of methods in *books* published in the field of comparative politics would almost certainly show even greater weighting in favor of qualitative approaches than Munck and Snyder's study of journal *articles*.

6. A thorough review of methodological techniques and tools in qualitative research is also beyond our limitations here. For systematic treaties on this subject, see Ragin (1987), Munck (1998), Mahoney (2000b), and Gerring (2001).

7. For instance, in the quantitative study of political conflicts, it is a routine practice for researchers to multiply their "cases" with a time unit to produce a large "n."
The basic data unit in these studies is often a "country/year," by which a single country studied over 20 years becomes 20 data points. For example, Collier and Hoeffler's
(2001) dataset has fewer than 50 wars, but they claim to have statistical samples of
more than 600 "episodes" (of "war" and "non-war"). Consider this logic as applied
to a qualitative study that scrutinizes thirty years of Russian history to search for
explanations of the Bolshevik revolution. Is it possible to say that this study actually
involves thirty "cases"? The answer would seem to be yes, because by explaining why
there was a revolution in 1917, its author also explains why a revolution did not take
place in the previous twenty-nine years.

8. The discussion of interpretivism here follows authors in the Symposium on
Interpretivism in *Qualitative Methods* (Fall 2003) in restricting interpretivism to the
kind developed in the 1950s, 1960s, and 1970s, not the later interpretivism that may
be more appropriately called post-structuralism or post-modernism. One of the
most influential works of the early interpretivist tradition is Geertz (1973b).

9. See also his first three essays in Anderson (1998b).

10. Anderson's later work is driven less by fieldwork than by comparative-
historical and literary analysis.

11. Alfred Stepan (cited in Chandra and Kammen (2002: 96–136) decried political science's "stunning neglect of the military" more than thirty years ago. Little did
he know that he was writing during what would prove to be the heyday of military
studies in the discipline.

12. McCoy's (1999: 114) hypothesized linkage from anti-Japanese struggle to
anti-authoritarian commitments gains support in the intermediate case of PMA '51,
the first *postwar* class, which gave far more active support to Marcos's dictatorial
regime than did PMA '40.

13. See also John Gerring's (2003) interview of Geertz.

CHAPTER 2

For detailed and thoughtful critiques, I thank Paul Hutchcroft, Netithorn Praditsarn, Kazue Takamura, and Tuong Vu, as well as two anonymous reviewers.

1. For an early review of the statist genre, see Skocpol (1985). For more recent reviews, see Kohli (2002) and, somewhat more broadly, Pierson and Skocpol (2002).

2. There is much that should be synthesized on socialist states in the region.
I leave this for others to pursue.

3. Unlike Esman, Chan did not assert that the administrative state could be a
major force in Singapore's impressive developmental trajectory.

4. See also Hamilton-Hart (2002: especially 79–84).

5. Note that whereas Higgott and Robison (1985: 27) are critical of Riggs's emphasis on patron-client relations and the bureaucratic polity's structural-functional

framework, they also acknowledge that Riggs and his cohorts were "aware of the role of the elites, the bureaucracy, and the 'government.'" See also Kohli's (1987: 16–19) argument that some modernization and neo-Marxist scholars did address the role of the state, even if through the lenses of sociological variables.

6. Note in particular the critique of the *theory* of the bureaucratic polity: "Unless the theoretical implications and shortcomings of the structural-functional model are confronted, it is not possible to use the theoretically-specific terminology developed by Riggs because importing the terminology brings with it the theoretical cargo" (Hewison 1989: 13).

7. Quite notably, however, Indonesianists largely ignored the functionalist and teleological elements of Riggs's model. The model of the bureaucratic polity that was transported across the region was primarily one of bureaucratic power rather than of theories of modernization. In this sense, as the concept shifted terrain, a key aspect of its edifice was left behind.

8. Although Liddle (1985) leans on balance toward the view that the New Order state is increasingly institutionalized, he submits that Suharto's personalism still suffuses much of the state. Jackson (1978: 17) makes the same argument: ". . . Indonesian bureaucratic polity is not a personalistic or sultanistic regime. The power of the president is neither unlimited nor arbitrary, and it is not based solely on charismatic authority. Suharto is as likely to be obeyed as his more magnetic predecessor."

9. Contrast, for example, Liddle (1985) and Liddle (1987).

10. Crouch (1986) makes a similar point in regard to military repression. Some areas of Indonesia were less repressed because of links between dissatisfied military officials and certain social groups. In other words, military policy, like economic policy, was not always following the dictates of the center.

11. Hutchcroft (1998: 46–58) provides a sophisticated typology of patrimonial states, contrasting what he terms the "patrimonial administrative state" (Thailand, Indonesia, Zaire) with the "patrimonial oligarchic state" (Philippines).

12. This is a central theme in Hutchcroft's work and in Anderson's (1988) brilliant essay. But note that other scholars emphasize significant elements of change rather than continuity: Kerkvliet and Mojares (1991), Kerkvliet (1996), and Doronila (1996).

13. Ironically, this is a criticism that the "Australia political economy school" has leveled at the modernization school. See Higgott and Robison (1985).

14. In the concluding chapter to MacIntyre's volume, Stephan Haggard (1994) dissents from the view that the Southeast Asian states are relatively weak and ineffective. Compared to the macroeconomic crises in Latin America, Haggard argues that states in Southeast Asia are in fact quite effective in maintaining stable macroeconomic policies.

15. That the Thai state may have possessed elements capable of propelling development was also noticed by Ruth McVey (1992a: 17): "[T]he relationships of the bureaucratic polity are not so hostile to economic growth as had been imagined. . . ."

16. In *The East Asian Miracle*, the World Bank concluded that the Southeast Asian experience was a better model for the developing world, in large part because Southeast Asia's development was not tied so closely to industrial policy.

17. See also Lev (1972: chapter 2).

18. See also Harper (1999).

19. Sidel regards the Philippine state as strong on the basis of its predatory features. However, state strength is generally conceptualized in terms of capacity and autonomy separate from social interests. If one uses predatory behavior as the benchmark, then Mobutu's Zaire would be considered a strong state under these conditions. Even if one does divide state power into "infrastructural" on one side and "despotic" on the other, it still bears emphasizing that although the Philippine state may be predatory and therefore exhibit "despotic power," this does not occur in the interests of the state-qua-state (in contrast to Suharto's New Order). If the state is conceptualized simply as an arena of power, rather than an autonomous institution, then there is ultimately no analytical distinction between state and society.

20. For a sophisticated, comparative-historical study that argues that internal conflicts did in fact strengthen states in Southeast Asia, see Slater (2005).

21. See Collier and Collier (1991: chapter 1). For some recent efforts to use "critical junctures" in the region, see Kuhonta (2003), Bertrand (2004), and Slater (2005).

22. Notable exceptions are Girling (1981) and McVey (1982). See also the comment by Benda (1982: 50).

23. An important, although apparently ignored, effort to bridge Indonesian politics and comparative politics through the concept of bureaucratic authoritarianism was undertaken by Dwight King. King (1982) argued that the New Order might be better conceptualized as a bureaucratic-authoritarian (BA) state rather than as a bureaucratic polity. An emphasis on the BA model puts the spotlight on corporatism rather than patron-client relations, which King believed deserved greater emphasis. Given Guillermo O'Donnell's emphasis on the emergence of the BA state following a conjuncture of political and economic crises that threatened the dominant classes, this might have proven a fruitful line of inquiry in Indonesian political studies. See O'Donnell (1988: 22–33).

24. See also Anderson's (1982: 83) conclusion in his review of Indonesian political studies.

CHAPTER 3

This manuscript has benefited from the comments of Jason Brownlee, Allen Hicken, Erik Kuhonta, Bill Liddle, Gabriella Montinola, Jan Teorell, Danny Unger, Tuong Vu, and two anonymous reviewers at Stanford University Press. Thanks also go to Allison Youatt for her meticulous editorial assistance. A shorter version of this chapter focused entirely on authoritarian institutions has been published in the *Taiwan Journal of Democracy* (Slater 2006). The inspiration for this chapter's title comes from an article by Thomas Risse-Kappen, "Ideas Do Not Float Freely" (1994), which argues that structural forces largely determine the fate of political ideas.

1. To my knowledge, Haggard and Kaufman (1995) and Huntington (1991) are the only major theory-building exercises in the study of democratization that give serious consideration to Southeast Asian cases. Even in these two instances, other world regions receive the lion's share of attention.

2. It is obviously troubling that all three of these countries have seen military forces acting as decisive arbiters in recent succession crises. Such problems of post-transition politics are beyond the scope of this essay, but the lingering significance of the Thai, Indonesian, and Philippine militaries surely underscores the importance of examining the institutions that make authoritarianism work and, quite often, keep democracy from working well.

3. Steven Levitsky and Lucan Way (2002) argue that regimes fail to meet this minimum democratic standard when "incumbents routinely abuse state resources, deny the opposition adequate media coverage, harass opposition candidates and their supporters, and in some cases manipulate electoral results." Although ruling parties in Malaysia, Singapore, and Cambodia may not be major manipulators of election tallies, they all harass oppositionists in ways that make elections intrinsically unfair.

4. It is symptomatic that perhaps the four most impressive recent contributions to regime theory in Latin America examine the first- or second-wave origins of regimes (when outcomes still varied) rather than third-wave transitions (when authoritarianism collapsed everywhere but Cuba). See Mahoney (2001), Lopez-Alves (2000), Yashar (1997), and Collier and Collier (1991).

5. This is a somewhat broader definition than the one Mahoney adopts in the final version of this manuscript, but one that I still find quite appropriate.

6. On Europe, see, for example, Downing (1992) and Moore (1966); on Latin America, see the citations in note 4.

7. For an explanation of region-wide democratic breakdown that parallels O'Donnell's (1973) famous structural economic explanation for authoritarian resurgence in Latin America, see Rocamora (1978).

8. Suffice it to say that Southeast Asianists have produced as much if not more useful theoretical knowledge on the role of classes, parties, states, militaries, and social movements in democratic consolidation than in democratic transition. Southeast Asian political studies pioneered the study of clientelism as a class phenomenon, showing how severe inequality undermined democratic quality. Classic studies include Scott (1972b) and Anderson (1988), with recent work by Robison and Hadiz (2004) serving as a worthy descendant of this research tradition. For recent work on the role of parties in democratic consolidation, see Ockey (2003) on Thailand, Hutchcroft and Rocamora (2003) on the Philippines, and Slater (2004) on Indonesia.

Sidel (1999) and the essays in Trocki (1998) are great contributions to our under-standing of the role of the state (including weak states) in improving or reducing democratic quality. Excellent studies of why militaries in Southeast Asia do or do not obey civilian authorities include Chandra and Kammen (2002) and McCoy (1999). Finally, Hefner (2000) and Mujani and Liddle (2004) provide theoretically insightful analyses of social movement organizations in consolidating democratic politics.

9. Examples are legion, but no single volume signaled the shift in terrain more than O'Donnell and Schmitter (1986).

10. I am grateful to Bill Liddle for reminding me of the stifling effects of theo-rists' early obsession with the social prerequisites of democracy. For the classic state-ment, see Lipset (1959).

11. Mahoney (2003) provides an excellent overview of this literature and its progress.

12. Among many others, see Moore (1966) on the bourgeoisie, Huntington (1991) on the middle class, and Rueschemeyer, Stephens, and Stephens (1992) on the working class.

13. Endogenous democratization has been most recently and rigorously cham-pioned by Boix and Stokes (2003); exogenous democratization has been most vigor-ously defended by Przeworski and Limongi (1997).

14. Theorists have been more concerned with examining how institutional weak-ness undermines democracies than dictatorships. On the role of political parties in preventing *democratic* collapse, see Bermeo (2003), Ertman (1998), and Luebbert (1991). Although Huntington (1968) ostensibly trained his sights on political in-stability regardless of regime type, his concern clearly focused on the many falling democracies of that era.

15. See the essays, including Thompson's, in Chehabi and Linz (1998).

16. I make a similar argument about Malaysia (Slater 2003), where the personaliza-tion of power under Mahathir Mohamad in the 1990s failed to undermine either state or regime. To the contrary, Mahathir ironically made use of a highly developed and loyal state apparatus to crush his opponents and personalize power in the first place.

17. See Linz and Stepan (1996).

18. For a critique and recommended amending of this typology, see Slater (2003).

19. I exclude East Timor because electoral democracy was introduced there amid a struggle for national independence, not a struggle for popular sovereignty against local authoritarian rulers. Like the former communist countries' simultaneous tran-sitions from foreign domination and authoritarian rule, East Timor's democratic transition might best be seen as a belated "second wave" transition—driven by de-colonization—rather than fitting a "third wave" logic.

20. For a fascinating analysis of revenue-mobilization strategies in Burma, see Steinberg (2001).

21. Thanks to Allen Hicken and Erik Kuhonta for alerting me to the limitations of UNTAC's influence, which were indeed considerable.

22. Beyond the existing works cited here, recent works on the role of parties and states in sustaining Southeast Asian authoritarianism include Brownlee's (2007) comparison of Malaysia and the Philippines with Iran and Egypt, Smith's (2007) comparison of Indonesia and Iran, and Slater's (2005) comparison of party, state, and regime outcomes in seven Southeast Asian cases.

CHAPTER 4

I wish to thank Bill Liddle, Gabriella Montinola, two anonymous reviewers, and the participants of the Stanford workshop on Southeast Asia in Political Science for comments on earlier drafts of this chapter.

1. Two major exceptions are the use of the Malaysian case by Lijphart (1977) and Horowitz (1985) (both general comparativists) to develop and support arguments about how to construct a stable democracy in divided societies. Landé's (1965) work on parties and factions in the Philippines has had an impact outside of Southeast Asia. These contributions are discussed in more detail below.

2. This perception holds even for the Philippines, which has the longest (albeit interrupted) history of elections in Asia. For many scholars of Philippine politics, parties and elections are seen as epiphenomenal to issues of elite, oligarchic, or clan conflict. Indeed, when I tell Filipinos I study political parties and party systems in the Philippines, a common response is "What parties? What system?"

3. Liddle's (2001) edited volume titled *Crafting Indonesia Democracy* is a good example of scholars grappling with such questions.

4. The subject of parties and elections in communist or socialist states (e.g., Vietnam, Laos, and pre-1993 Cambodia) is not covered here but is discussed in Dan Slater's chapter.

5. Anderson's highly readable, tongue-in-cheek writing style is certainly one important factor.

6. See, for example, Sartori (1976) and Horowitz (1985).

7. See G. Cox (1987), Mainwaring and Scully (1995), Kitschelt and colleagues (1999), Mainwaring (1999), Shugart and Wattenberg (2000), and Posner (2005).

8. Indeed, I would place some of my own work in the category—e.g., Hicken and Kasuya (2003).

9. See Neher (1976), Kassim (1979), Crouch and associates (1980), Surin (1992), Sombat (1993), Rahman (1994), Landé (1996), Croissant and associates (2002), Antlov and Cederroth (2004), and Liddle and Mujani (2004).

10. Sidel (1996) draws similar parallels between Thailand and the Philippines.

11. On Africa, see Zolberg (1964, 1966). On Latin America, see Martz (1964).

12. See Lev (1967) and Liddle (1970).

13. See Hicken (2002) for a more extensive review of attempts to answer these questions.

14. A fourth factor sometimes mentioned is the presence of a powerful chief executive (e.g., Grossholtz 1964; Banlaoi and Carlos 1996). Presidentialism is often associated with weak and noncohesive legislative parties (see Lijphart et al. 1993: 322). However, one must be cautious regarding the direction of causality (Shugart 1999; Hicken 2002).

15. I discuss the literature on Malaysia and Singapore later.

16. For more recent work in English, see King's study of the Palang Dharma and New Aspiration parties in Thailand (1996) and Hicken (2002). Notable research in the Thai language includes Preecha (1981), Manut (1986), Manut and colleagues (1988), and Kanok (1993).

17. For example, see Feith (1957), Geertz (1960), Liddle (1970), Imawan (1989), Chaidar (1999), and Sulistyo (2002). See also Lev's work on political parties in Indonesia (1967, 1970).

18. For the history of early party development in Malaysia (Malaya), see Maryanov (1967).

19. See also Case (1996b).

20. The article was written prior to the 2004 election, so Case does not have a chance to analyze UMNO's continued success at the polls. Obviously, disagreements among the opposition continue to hinder collective action. Perhaps also the government's ability to rein in some of its excesses, the change in UMNO leadership, and the relatively quick recovery from the 1997 crisis contributed to its electoral victory.

21. This list is by no means exhaustive of the possibilities.

22. See, for example, McRae (1974), Lijphart (1977), Horowitz (1985, 1991), and Reilly (2001).

23. See Lijphart (1995) and Reilly (2001) for a review of this debate. See Croissant (2002) for a review of consociational versus majoritarian institutions in Asia.

24. Namely, the Alternative Vote, the Supplementary Vote, and the Single Transferrable Vote.

25. Existing studies include MacDougall (1968), Kassim (1979), and Rachagan (1984). During its early history, Malaysia's system contained elements of consociationalism, but there was a move to a more majoritarian (and/or authoritarian) approach after the riots of 1969.

26. Burma considered several electoral models before adopting a largely majoritarian approach in 1948, although it also employed a Senate that attempted to mirror the ethnic divisions in the country (Silverstein 1977, 1980).

27. See Posner (2005) for an excellent analysis of how societal groups have responded to electoral incentives in Africa.

28. For a discussion of constitutional reform in Indonesia, see Liddle (2001).

29. Current debates about constitutional reform in the Philippines echo these same themes.

30. In Indonesia, parties that do not obtain a certain percentage of the votes cannot run in the subsequent election. Some small parties have maneuvered around this rule by formally dissolving and then reconstituting themselves under a new name.

31. See Hicken (2002, 2007b, 2006) and Reilly (2003a) for some examples.

32. See Alesina, Roubini, and Cohen (1997), Powell (2000), Persson and Tabellini (1999), and Chhibber and Nooruddin (2004).

33. There are other measures of the number of parties. The appropriate measure depends on the research question (see Niemi and Hsieh 2002). The formula for N is the inverse of the sum of the squared proportions of the vote or of the seats. For n parties receiving votes, and for p_i representing the proportion of popular votes received by party i, $N = 1/\sum_{i=1}^{n} p_i^2$.

34. For example, the block vote in pre-reform Thailand and the Philippines (Senate), mixed-member systems in Thailand and the Philippines, and SNTV in Thailand (Senate) and Indonesia (DPD).

35. These figures are for the 1986–1996 elections.

36. See Cox (1997, 1999), Chhibber and Kollman (1998, 2004), and Hicken (2002).

37. There is, of course, variation in the importance of and polarization along this dimension.

38. In less democratic settings, we certainly see such transfers occur. The organizational strategies of Golkar and the Indonesian military owed much to the PKI and in fact were designed to undermine and displace the PKI organization throughout Indonesia. So too did the Thai military pursue a counterinsurgency strategy that mimicked the CPT's emphasis on building support in rural villages.

39. A full research design would need to account for competing explanations and intervening variables, such as the presence of other (ethnic or regional) cleavages that may form the basis for political parties, electoral institutions, and the effect of armed communist insurgencies.

CHAPTER 5

I am indebted to helpful comments from Don Emmerson, Ben Kerkvliet, Erik Kuhonta, Bill Liddle, Kevin O'Brien, Dan Slater, and Danny Unger. Smith College and the Naval Postgraduate School provided generous funding for the research and writing of this chapter. Parts of this chapter appeared in *Theory and Society* 35(4), 393–419.

1. Among fifty-three civil wars from 1960 to 1992, twenty-three took place in Asia as opposed to nineteen in Africa and eleven in the Middle East (Henderson and Singer 2000).

2. McAdam and colleagues (2001: 5) define *contentious politics* as "episodic, public, collective interaction among makers of claims and their objects when (a) at least one government is a claimant, an object of claims, or a party to the claims and (b) the claims would, if realized, affect the interests of at least one of the claimants." Here I define *contentious mass politics* as uninstitutionalized politics that involves nonelites and a contest for power or authority in a polity but is not necessarily public or collective. For the purpose of this project, ethnic and religious conflicts are excluded.

3. "Genre" here is used with a somewhat looser meaning than a research "tradition" or "program," which is commonly based only on shared ontology or methods. Works in the same genre share an analytical focus, research methods, or both. This is only one way of breaking down the diverse and voluminous literature on the subject matter. The taxonomy tries to be comprehensive without being too cumbersome. Obviously, works belonging to different genres may overlap in many important ways.

4. Many political scientists also write political histories (hereafter *History*) of particular Southeast Asian revolutions. In this genre, these conflicts are treated as unique events that unfolded over time, not as a category of social phenomena that require causal explanations. I do not discuss this genre in this chapter, but Tables 5.1 and 5.2 include the History genre to highlight the distinct aspects of the other four "political sciency" genres.

5. According to Gurr (1970: 6), out of 2,828 articles that appeared in the *American Political Science Review* from its establishment in 1906 through 1968, only 29 had titles that concerned political disorder or violence, and more than half (15) of these appeared after 1961.

6. Adas (1979) is included in the Organization genre for its central focus on organizational factors such as leadership and mobilization processes.

7. See also Scott (1977a, 1977b, 1977c, 1979).

8. Weller and Guggenheim's (1982) edited volume applies a "mild" version of the moral economy thesis to contexts beyond Southeast Asia.

9. In fact, a prominent Southeast Asianist dismissed "people power" in the Philippines as merely bringing back *cacique* democracy (Anderson 1988). In contrast, this event was heralded in the Comparative literature as an "urban revolution" or a case of the "third wave of democratization."

10. Scott (1990) did not restrict its subjects to peasants, but they were among the principal groups examined.

11. For a description of this database, see Small and Singer (1982).

12. Extensive reviews of this genre are available in several articles and two recent edited volumes: Goldstone (1980, 2001, 2003) and Foran (1997). In this review, I will focus particularly on those Comparative studies that involve Southeast Asian cases.

13. The search used two keywords: "politics" and the name of a Southeast Asian country for the time period 1975–2003. It found 220 dissertations on Vietnam, 118 on Indonesia, 93 on the Philippines, 69 on Malaysia, 61 on Thailand, 28 on Cambodia, and 24 on Burma. The high number for Vietnam is misleading because most

dissertations focused on various dimensions of the Vietnam War, not on Vietnamese politics per se.

14. See Goodwin (1997), Lanzona (2000), and Thompson (2004).

15. For example, see the debate among Goldthorpe (1997), Ragin (1997), Rueschemeyer and Stephens (1997), and Goldstone (1997), and that between Lieberson (1991, 1994) and Savolainen (1994).

16. Examples are Berman (1974) and Paige (1975).

17. Examples are Kerkvliet (1990, 2005).

18. An example is Race (1972).

19. Scott (1976, 1985, 1990).

20. Ragin (1997: 32) explains the difference between "explanation" and "explaining variation."

21. The usage here follows P. A. Hall (2003: 374). *Ontology* refers to "premises about the deep causal structures of the world."

22. See *Qualitative Methods* 1:2 (Fall 2003) for a recent debate on the interpretivist tradition in political science.

23. In fact, social movement researchers in general overwhelmingly choose to study only movements with which they sympathize (Edelman 2001: 302). Race (1972: ix) is a rare exception: He opens his study of the Vietnamese insurgency by saying, "The reader will find few evil or incompetent characters in this book, but rather an account of how [the communist] revolutionary movement was able to gain victory despite the efforts of a considerable number of honest and conscientious [government] men, acting according to their best understanding."

24. As Collier and Hoeffler (2001: 17) conclude their study on how greed explains rebellions better than grievances do, "Our evidence does not therefore imply that rebels are necessarily criminals. But the grievances that motivate rebels may be substantially disconnected from the large social concerns of inequality, political rights, or ethnic or religious identity"—which is to say that either rebels are mistakenly motivated or they deliberately distort certain "objective" social realities.

25. For example, see Skocpol (1982: 363).

26. Ethnographic methods and interpretivism have been undervalued in the discipline, but support for them appears to be increasing. See Bayard de Volo and Schatz (2004: 67), the debate on interpretivism in *Qualitative Methods* 1:2 (Fall 2003), and the Symposium on Discourse and Content Analysis in *Qualitative Methods* 2:1 (Spring 2004).

27. For this point on descriptive concepts in the interpretivist tradition, see Bevir (2003: 20).

28. See Skocpol (1982).

29. McAdam and colleagues (2001: 23) and Amenta (2003: 115–116) view this ambiguity as a problem for the social movement literature.

30. Why? I can offer three possible reasons. First, few Southeast Asian revolutions meet the strict requirements for "great social revolutions." Second, most

revolutionary conflicts in the region involved protracted civil wars. Many of these conflicts did not end until the late 1980s, when interest in Southeast Asia had waned. Third, the Comparative genre requires reliable secondary sources, which were missing for many Southeast Asian cases, especially the Indochinese case, until the 1980s or 1990s.

31. This is in part a response to criticisms that the use of Mill's methods in Comparative works is inappropriate. See Lieberson (1991, 1994), Savolainen (1994), and Goldstone (1997).

32. Perry (1980: 533) and Skocpol and Somers (1980: 194).

33. This practice can be usefully contrasted with the common statistical practice in studying political conflicts that uses the basic data unit of "country/year," by which a national "case" studied over 20 years becomes 20 "cases" (or data points) in a regression analysis. For example, Collier and Hoeffler's (2001) data set has fewer than 50 wars, but their regression analyses claim to have statistical samples (n) of more than 600 "episodes."

34. See the discussion of "dataset observations" and "causal process observations" in the first chapter of this book.

35. For a claim to the contrary, see Wickham-Crowley (1997).

36. Walton is referring to theoretical frameworks established by James Scott, Eric Wolf, Charles Tilly, Immanuel Wallerstein, and Barrington Moore.

37. Wickham-Crowley (1992) uses only Central American cases, whereas Parsa (2000) selects cases from the Middle East, Central America, and Southeast Asia.

38. Farhi (1990) is of the former type, whereas Skocpol (1979) belongs to the latter.

39. Ragin (1997: 30–32) discusses how cases are "constituted" and not taken as given in Comparative research.

40. For discussions of definitional issues, see Goldstone (1980: 450), Walton (1984: 6–14), Goodwin (2001: 9), Goldstone (2001: 140–142), and Goldstone (2003: 52–55).

41. Lichbach and Gurr (1981) have shown that a democratic regime is associated with an increased likelihood of *protests* but a decreased likelihood of *rebellions*; see Henderson and Singer (2000: 276) for more examples. If the concept of revolution is not uniformly defined, two different researchers may reach contradictory results, yet both may be right because they are not examining the same phenomenon (even though they believe they are doing so).

42. What is presented here is only the gist of the argument and the method of inference. Of course, their models are more complex than can be summarized here.

43. The rational actor model is not new in the study of conflict. One of the earliest works is Leites and Wolf (1970), which seeks to apply the market analogy to political conflict in a formal mathematical model. Note that Popkin (1979) treats peasants as rational actors, whereas Leites and Wolf (1970) and Collier and Hoeffler (1998, 2001) focus on rebel groups and their leaders as rational actors.

44. Ross (2003, 2005) uses the case study method to examine a number of cases in Collier and Hoeffler's (2001) dataset. He shows that natural resources did not cause (although they helped sustain) civil wars, as they argue.

45. Collier and Hoeffler (1998: 7).

46. Feierabend and Feierabend (1972: 369–372), Skocpol and Somers (1980: 194), and Mahoney (2003: 131–137).

47. Hawes (1990) and Kessler (1989), which study the movement at a more macro-level, offer contrary findings.

48. For example, see Henderson and Singer (2000) and Goodwin (2001).

49. An example is Henderson and Singer (2000).

CHAPTER 6

1. I am drawing on Mahoney (2003: 132–137); discussions during the Southeast Asia in Political Science workshop, June 18–19, 2004, Stanford University, especially comments by Rick Doner, Don Emmerson, and Erik Kuhonta; and the chapter by Erik Kuhonta, Dan Slater, and Tuong Vu in this book. May I also thank Erik Kuhonta, Dan Slater, and Tuong Vu for their sound leadership and advice.

2. See the following prominent books of that period: Thompson and Adloff (1950), Hammer (1954), Trager (1959, 1966), Tanham (1961), Valeriano and Bohannan (1962), Fall (1963), and O'Ballance (1964, 1966).

3. For instance, Schwartz (1951) and North (1953). A few years later came Johnson (1962), which also received little notice among those researching rural unrest in Southeast Asia during the 1960s.

4. See Thompson and Adloff (1950: 39–41, 205–207) and much of Hammer (1954) until a section beginning on page 247 about the Viet Minh's "decisive shift into the communist camp."

5. For instance, Trager (1959: 111ff) and Thompson (1966: 21–49). An exception to this trend is McVey (1964b: 145–184).

6. The study is based primarily on two years of interviews and other research in Bandung. Another scholar at about the same time as Smail who emphasized local perspective on revolution and other phenomena and whose work influenced subsequent local studies is John A. Larkin. See Larkin (1967), which was based on a doctoral dissertation, completed in 1966 at New York University. After further extensive research in the Philippines, Larkin published a major book (1972) on Pampanga province.

7. Kahin's book also includes the perspectives of key players on the Dutch side of the struggle.

8. Some authors, such as Kheng (1983: xiii), acknowledge Smail's influence. Many researchers do not refer to Smail's work, but most probably knew it or were influenced by others before them who did. My research of the Huk rebellion in the Philippines was partly inspired by Smail's approach as well as by studies that

had been done of China's revolution, particularly Yang (1959), Johnson (1962), and Hinton (1966).

9. The book chapters that this piece is synthesizing are by eight scholars who have done extensive local-level research using documents, interviews, memoirs, and other material from and about people and organizations during the revolutionary years in Indonesia. Not all local-level studies about Indonesia have findings that substantiate this summary. See, for instance, Frederick (1989: 292–295), the research for which included living in Surabaya for long periods and using archival materials there, elsewhere in Indonesia, and in other countries.

10. To make his argument, Ileto uses archival materials, songs, memoirs, and a popular account of Jesus Christ's life and death. See also Sturtevant (1976), which draws on documents from and about various rural movements, some interviews with former participants, and newspaper accounts.

11. In addition to other research, McKenna studied for fourteen months in a Muslim Filipino community.

12. Research for this book included eighteen months in the Philippines to interview former Huk participants and supporters and to read documents and other materials from and about the rebellion.

13. See also Starobin (1954: chapters 9–11).

14. To extract the perspectives of people in the rebellion or supporting it, Stubbs examined a large number of previously inaccessible documents in Malaysia and elsewhere from and about the rebellion.

15. To do his study, the most thorough to date on the Communist Party of the Philippines (CPP) and New People's Army (NPA) of the 1970s–1980s, Collier spent two years in and around central Mindanao talking to participants, sympathizers, and opponents and analyzing hundreds of documents. The manuscript is a revision of Collier (1997).

16. Research materials for Elliott's two-volume book comprise nearly 400 interviews with people from the revolutionary movement, thousands of documents from the movement, memoirs and other writings by Vietnamese participants, and the author's longtime involvement with Vietnam, including living in My Tho, the area emphasized in the study.

17. Race's research included four stays in Vietnam (one in Long An province from late 1967 to mid-1968), interviews with "several hundred" Vietnamese, and analysis of numerous documents captured from the revolutionary movement in southern Vietnam.

18. Kiernan's studies draw heavily on numerous interviews with Cambodians and documents from the Khmer Rouge, the U.S. government, and others involved in Cambodia. Regarding the U.S. and Saigon governments' violence in the Mekong delta, Elliott says it did stifle the revolution for long periods of time by depopulating large parts of the countryside. However, the cost was the destruction of countless

villages and "a catastrophically high level of civilian casualties . . ." (Elliott: 2003: 618–619, 755, 1126–1127).

19. Countering the common explanation in the 1960s among academics and government officials in Saigon and Washington, DC, Elliott concludes that terror and intimidation "were not the main factors in mobilizing widespread popular support" for the revolutionary movement in Vietnam. Force "was a supplement to but not a substitute for incentives and moral suasion" (Elliott 2003: 5).

20. The study attracted attention in the *New York Times*, 15 October 1967: 4. It was also appreciated in some high-level U.S. policy circles, according to Robert L. Sansom, who sharply criticizes Mitchell's methodology and disputes his findings (Sansom 1970: 229–232). For his study, Sansom emphasizes selected villages in the Mekong delta that he studied off and on during 1966–1968.

21. See Sansom (1970: chapters 2–3, 11–12), Race (1972: 90, 97–98, 165–167), Trullinger (1980: 35, 41–43), White (1981: 230–232 and elsewhere), and Elliott (2003: 437–439, 1389–1390, and elsewhere). All these studies also talk about other social, economic, and political motivations and ideals of rural Vietnamese. Trullinger lived several years in Vietnam in the 1970s, including several months in a village of Thua Thien province in central Vietnam; White emphasizes the Red River delta and draws on archival material and numerous Vietnamese publications.

22. Using surviving colonial and other records as well as other materials, Adas tries to understand history from the perspective of villagers who lived in the Irrawaddy delta.

23. The most notable example is Pike (1966).

24. This is clearly elaborated in Race (1974: 169–205). See also Popkin (1979: chapter 6), Sansom (1970: 233–245), Race (1972: 165, 174, and elsewhere), Trullinger (1980: 98–113), and Elliott (2003: chapters 4, 9–11), among others. By and large compatible with this kind of analysis is Hy V. Luong's account of how the Viet Minh developed in a northern Vietnam village (Luong 1992: chapter 4), research for which draws heavily on interviews with the villagers and with former residents living abroad and on archival materials.

25. Rutten's chapter is based on research extending over several years that she has done in villages of Negros Island, central Philippines.

26. Two unusual works are McAlister (1969) and Race (1974). Although both focus on Vietnam, they reach out to wider literatures about revolution as well as such subjects as rural society, relative deprivation, and social exchanges.

27. Examples are Sjamsuddin (1985) and Stubbs (1989b).

28. Popkin's research included interviews and conversations with villagers and other Vietnamese during several extended stays in Vietnam during the second half of the 1960s.

29. For examples of that research, see *Journal of Conflict Resolution* (2005).

30. As most readers will know, patron-client is a hierarchical dyadic exchange relationship in which the person in the superior, more privileged position (the patron) grants goods and services to protect and/or benefit the subordinate person (the client), often in immediate, tangible ways. The client reciprocates by giving services, assistance, and general support that are frequently less tangible than and nearly always different from what he or she receives.

31. Rare were studies that looked at peasants' peaceful struggles for better living conditions, agrarian reform, etc. An example is Starner (1961: chapters 5–6), which considers villagers' views on political matters and examines peasant unions.

32. Cederroth began doing research in one of the villages in 1972 and in the other in 1986. See also Pelras (2000), an analysis of persisting patron-client relations in Indonesia's South Sulawesi based on years of fieldwork there.

33. Kimura did research in the Philippines for several years in the 1980s, including closely observing election campaigns in Batangas province.

34. Methodologies for each of these studies included lengthy and repeated stays in villages; each book has an appendix that elaborates how the author did the research.

35. Stoler's research included fieldwork among plantation workers in North Sumatra as well as extensive use of archival material. Hefner's methodology, which included numerous stays in the Tengger highlands, is explained in an appendix in his book. See also Mortimer (1974: 278–279), whose research stretched over several years during which he interviewed Indonesians inside and outside the country, collected documents, and used other sources.

36. Sidel's book is based on more than two years of research in the Philippines, primarily in two provinces. Among other in-depth research into violent and fraudulent aspects of electoral politics in the Philippines are some chapters in McCoy (1993a). National governments also use intimidation and violence to win elections and remain in power. See Liddle (1972: especially 14–17), a suggestive, though brief, study of elections in the early years of the Suharto regime, and Turton (1984: 50–62), a discussion of political violence in rural Thailand.

37. The research for this study involved talking to people and observing political and other activities during several stays, totaling more than two years, in a rural subdistrict. Others have also written about vote buying in Thailand, but few have tried as Arghiros has to look deeply into why rural people sell their votes.

38. Research for the study included seventeen months of fieldwork in a regency and municipality in North Sumatra. Issues were also important in the Javanese village that Liddle studied (1972: 12).

39. This comes through in several scholars' studies, based on long-term research in various parts of the country, published in Kerkvliet and Mojares (1991).

40. The author did research in the village three times for a total of eighteen months; see also Strauch (1981).

41. This book is based largely on research during the author's two lengthy stays in a Kelantanese community.

42. Research for this book included two years of fieldwork in a Malaysian village.

43. Oorthuizen's research included nearly two years of fieldwork with irrigation users and managers in Central Luzon. The Kerkvliet (2005) study draws on more than two years of research in Vietnam that included interviews with villagers in and archival materials about Red River delta provinces.

44. Research for this study included several years living in and studying northern Thailand.

CHAPTER 7

1. This problem seems endemic to area studies rather than unique to Southeast Asia.

2. For instance, Ben Kerkvliet (1995b) outlines the difficulties of conducting research on state-society relations in Vietnam and posits an ongoing, if inconsistent, interaction between the party and the masses. Even there, though, scholars (including Kerkvliet) have begun to speak of a nascent civil society and to debate on how to understand and classify organizations and individuals active in the public sphere (Kerkvliet 2003). There are undoubtedly also other works out there of which I am unaware because of the language in which they are written.

3. I recognize that I veer in this chapter toward the same false aggregation, implying a lack of internal differentiation in any given "civil society."

4. As a contributor to the volume, I include myself in this critique!

5. He backs these claims up with a strong theoretical discussion of democratization, Asian values (promoted as a counterweight to demands for liberalism in places such as Singapore), pervasive elitism, and more about the region.

6. Unfortunately (but not uncommonly), these theoretical insights are largely crammed into a concluding chapter after an extended historical exegesis on Clarke's primary and secondary cases; the volume would arguably be more useful to nonarea specialists were that pattern redressed.

7. Putnam's formulation thus differs in an important way from Alexis de Tocqueville's pioneering analysis of American society. The latter saw Christianity as practiced in the United States as central to the country's democratic culture (2000 [1835]: especially 530–539).

8. Brunei seems lacking much of a civil society, but arguably more as an artifact of absolute monarchy than of Islam per se—and certainly not from too strong an affiliation with a transnational *ummah*. In fact, Brunei's most significant prodemocratic reform movements (in 1962 and 1985) were Islamist to at least some extent.

9. On the other hand, William Liddle points out that Islamic organizations may be part of a state corporatist framework. He presents the case of the Association of Indonesian Muslim Intellectuals (ICMI), a mass organization forged by the New Order regime "for the purpose of controlling important social groups" (1996: 615) rather than an oppositional political movement, even if endorsed by students and Islamist activists. Other mass organizations of the period—for instance, the (non-Islamist) youth movement Pemuda Pancasila (see Ryter 1998)—would generally fall into the same state corporatist category.

10. Aspinall writes on later student activism as well (for instance, 1999).

11. Hong Liu (1998) offers a bridge between these two streams via his explicit focus on cross-national and cross-regional links among overseas Chinese voluntary organizations as transnational movements, with implications for the political forms and impacts of the Chinese diaspora.

12. Uhlin offers a handy snapshot version in a table of ten "foreign influences," from Marxism to feminism to variants of Islamism (1997: 240–241).

13. This preference is reinforced by the dearth of the sort of datasets that add a quantitative dimension to examinations of civil society elsewhere, as through event coding and statistical assessment.

14. Southeast Asia was at one time a font of pivotal studies on peasant movements, by James Scott, Eric Wolf, Sartono Kartodirdjo, Harry Benda, and others.

15. Betraying a shared immersion in the "contentious politics" school, fellow Cornellian Eva-Lotta Hedman (1998) likewise uses a well-grounded social movements approach to investigate knotty questions of mobilization.

16. Bell and Jayasuriya likewise propose: "Whereas the Western experience of 'democratization' emerged as a response to a growing demand for autonomy on the part of groups and classes in civil society, the dominant and intrusive role of state power in most aspects of East and Southeast Asian social life channels political change to serve the managerial and technocratic ends of the state" (1995: 15).

CHAPTER 8

1. For the general trend of the increasingly prominent role of religion in the public sphere, see, for example, Casanova (1994).

2. For a more comprehensive debate about the constructivist view and its critique of the primordialist view, see Laitin (1986).

3. Alfred Stepan, a prominent political scientist, is one of the most enthusiastic scholars committed to rectifying this analytical parochialism in studies of religion and politics. See his seminal study *Arguing Comparative Politics* (Stepan 2001).

4. See also Inglehart (2000).

5. Keyes (1999) later acknowledges sectarian trends and other divisive issues in Thai Buddhism.

6. The later sections discuss impacts and controversies related to Geertz's primordial approach and this conceptualization in particular.

7. Peletz (2002) explores intersections between local culture and *Syariah*, and how Islamic legal officials interpret, balance, and adopt the two in local Islamic courts in Malaysia.

8. See also Bowen's "The Forms Culture Takes" (1995) and *Religions in Practice* (2002) for a methodological debate about studying religion in Southeast Asia.

9. For a more comprehensive study on the *Sangha* and its relations to state and society, see Ishii (1986).

10. The somewhat reverse trend of the Thai state's laissez-faire policy toward religion since the mid-1980s is discussed in White (2005).

11. For a discussion of the institutional development of the Islamic court system, see Lev (1972) and Noer (1978: 42–52). For the development of the religious education system, see Noer (1973, 1978).

12. Che Man's (1990) comparative study on Muslim separatist movements in Southern Thailand and Southern Philippines adopts a similar approach.

13. Kessler (1979) explicitly challenges the classically oriented studies of Islam and religion, which influenced social scientists' earlier efforts to solve contemporary social and political problems.

14. Muslim intellectuals and scholars use the term "cultural Islam" or "civil Islam" to refer to Islamic activity that serves as a source of ethical and cultural guidance. "Political Islam" refers to Islamic activism that emphasizes involvement in party politics and other political activities.

15. See also Ong (1995, 1999) for anthropological analysis of gender-based Islamic movements in Malaysia.

16. Jackson's study sheds light on the sectarian character of the religion—both ideologically and organizationally—challenging earlier studies that presented Buddhist institutions as an ideologically homogeneous unitary actor (Keyes 1987). Jackson raises the possibility that sectarian trends within the *Sangha* can challenge the legitimacy of religious and political authorities in religious terms, and channel dissent against ruling elites. The best example of the symbolic association between religion and an oppositional force is provided by the student uprising against the Thai authoritarian regime in October 1973 (Reynolds 1978).

17. The current popular proclivity for magic and cults can also be understood from this sociological perspective. Jackson, for example, explores the popularity of magical monks in Thailand (Jackson 1999).

18. Literatures on this subject have grown in the context of the post-9/11 U.S.-led global war on terror. For a critical review of the terrorism literature, see Hamilton-Hart (2005).

19. See also Fealy (2004). International Crisis Group (ICG) reports offer an excellent analysis of the topic. Sidney Jones is the regional director of the group.

20. Van Bruinessen (2002) also emphasizes the local roots of radical Islam. He argues that the roots of most of the radical Islamic groups in Indonesia can be traced back to indigenous Muslim political movements dating back to the 1940s.

21. Middle East specialists, in particular, have made a significant theoretical contribution by bridging area studies and comparative politics (e.g., Brynen, Korany, and Noble 1995; Tessler, Nachtwey, and Banda 1999).

22. Interviews conducted in those countries contain questions about governance and democracy, and about conceptions and practices relating to Islam.

23. Other examples are Barton (1994) and Barton and Fealy (1996).

24. Hefner and Horvatich's edited volume, *Islam in an Era of Nation-States* (1997), is one such study. See also Nakamura, Siddique, and Bajunid (2001).

25. Hefner draws inspiration from Putnam (1993).

26. Nevertheless, this study acknowledges the immediate political interests of individuals closely linked to the regime who have been involved in the ICMI's foundation. It also notes an increasing tension in the organization between those who wished to use the organization to seek the government's patronage and those who wished to make it an independent body to represent the interests of the urban, middle-class Muslim community.

27. Levine (1981) has produced a number of comparative studies on the topic and other relevant issues covering not only Brazil and Colombia but also other nations in the region.

28. The relationship between organized religion and the state and its effect on oppositional mobilization are discussed in Hedman (1997).

29. Recent studies highlight the declining influence and coherence of established ecclesiastical establishments in Thailand. See, for example, Jackson (1997).

30. For relevant contributions, see, for instance, Esposito (1987) and Esposito and Voll (1996).

CHAPTER 9

Participants from the workshop out of which this volume was born offered insightful comments on an earlier draft. In particular, I would like to acknowledge the help of Pek Koon Heng, Tuong Vu, Dan Slater, and also two anonymous reviewers and Portia Reyes. The chapter's shortcomings remain the author's responsibility alone.

1. On globalization in Southeast Asia, see Felker's essay in this volume.

2. Given Hamayotsu's essay on religion in this volume, this chapter where possible will also seek to distinguish religious from ethnic ascriptions. This is done despite the trend in the literature to subsume all such differences—also including language, caste, and tribe—under an ethnic umbrella. See Horowitz (1985), Brown and Ganguly (1997a), and Varshney (2002).

3. This paragraph I draw from Bentley (1987).

4. These "universal" attributes are from Parsons (1982).

5. See Pye's chapter on political development in Southeast Asia in Almond and Coleman (1960).

6. For a convincing critique, see Sidel (1999).

7. Of the time, see also Milne (1967: 3) and Esman (1972: 17).

8. This also signaled a move in anthropology from "rural tribalism" to "urban ethnicity."

9. Hence, it is sometimes referred to as the circumstantialist school.

10. According to Bentley (1987), Leach put ethnicity in the anthropologist's purview.

11. For a critique of these reforms, see Anderson (1978). On the specific use of the map in this state-building project, see Thongchai (1994).

12. A modified (and reified) version of the plural society went on to influence a generation of African and Caribbean scholarship (M. G. Smith 1965; Kuper and Smith 1969).

13. The essay does, nevertheless, mark Geertz as a modernizationist.

14. Geertz's influence on Anderson is particularly pronounced in the latter's famous piece on Javanese conceptions of power (1990a [1972]).

15. Perhaps a short explanation is needed as to why I bypass Anderson's *Imagined Communities*. Only recently has the intricate link between ethnicity and nationalism been assumed. Gellner (1983) mentions ethnicity in passing, and in the first edition (1983) of his magnum opus, Anderson also downplays the role of ethnicity. In the second edition (1991), he adds a short discussion on ethnicity with respect to the colonial census, but he cites the work of Hirschman, which we will examine independently below. On Anderson's inattention to ethnicity, see Verdery (1994: 43) and Banks (1996: 126–128).

16. See also Stockwell (1982).

17. For a more recent, nuanced historical constructivist approach to ethnicity that draws on changing census categorizations over time in Laos, see Pholsena (2002).

18. Subsequent edited volumes have furthered this state-oriented, ethnic policy approach. Duncan (2004) focuses on modernizing state policies toward peripheral indigenous peoples; Mackerras (2003) is more general in nature.

19. On this dynamic, see also Dournes (1980), Evans (1992), and De Koninck (1996).

20. In this way, although focusing on Indonesia, Bertrand's study can be conceived as comparative in scope.

21. Beyond Malaysia, Horowitz sees consociationalism as a defective mechanism for conflict reduction for several reasons. Here we deal with just two. First is the model's overly universalistic assumptions, which deny variegated local contexts.

Second, leaders in many Asian and African states typically lack the political freedom to negotiate and compromise in the ways that consociationalism dictates. To be touched on below, Horowitz champions electoral engineering and in particular electoral systems that reward politicians for making appeals across ethnic groups. Other mechanisms such as federalism and regional autonomy are considered equally efficacious (1985: part V).

22. For other comparative works where Malaysia figures prominently, see also Nordlinger (1972) and Harff and Gurr (2004).

23. Exemplary is Skinner (1996).

24. On the studies of and explanations for state-Chinese business relations, see Abrami and Doner's essay in this volume.

CHAPTER 10

The authors thank two anonymous reviewers for their comments and thank Angela Tsang for editorial assistance.

1. "Post-socialist" indicates countries that no longer operate as planned economies. Vietnam and Laos remain communist regimes.

2. See Bates (1995), Meier and Stiglitz (2001), and Rodrik (2003).

3. On the distinction between upgrading and diversification (or structural change), see Gereffi (1999), Waldner (1999), and Weiss (1998).

4. For empirical studies of economic performance differences between the NICs and the ASEAN-4, see Amsden (2001), Wong and Ng (2001), Booth (1999), and Rasiah (2003).

5. In some cases, as in Chalmers Johnson's work on the Japanese developmental state, the anomaly was enough to stimulate a whole range of concept and theory development. Linda Lim's hard-hitting (1983) correction to Milton Friedman's naive paean to Singapore's free-market economy highlighted an equally significant anomaly, but with less impact.

6. See Chapter 1 of this text for a review of this literature.

7. See Bowie (1991) and Crouch (1996) on Malaysia, Winters (1996) on Indonesia, Muscat (1994) and Unger (1998) on Thailand, Hutchcroft (1998) on the Philippines, and Rodan (1989) and Hamilton-Hart (2000a) on Singapore.

8. On the benefits of distributional policies, see the useful piece by Donald Crone (1988).

9. We are grateful to David Kang for discussions on this issue. On the concept of "pockets of efficiency," see Evans (1995).

10. This argument seems consistent with Hamilton-Hart's (2000a) emphasis on institutional capacity as the basis for variation in responses to the 1997 crisis.

11. An earlier example of task-specific analysis is Noble's superb analysis of industrial policy in Taiwan and Japan (1998).

12. Cross-national, single-sector studies include Hamilton-Hart (2002), McKendrick, Doner, and Haggard (2000), and Doner (1991b). For single-country, cross-task, or cross-industry/sector studies, see Unger (1998), MacIntyre (1990), and Doner and Ramsay (2003).

13. See Amsden (1989), Haggard (1990), Wade (1990), and World Bank (1993).

14. See the various chapters in Khan and Jomo (2000).

15. On administrative reform, see Unger (2003). On the Philippines, see Hutchcroft (2000b). On patronage in Malaysia, see Gomez and Jomo (1997). On rent seizing, see Ross (2001).

16. On "getting prices wrong" in Northeast Asia, see Amsden (1989). On Southeast Asia, see, for example, Lim (1983), Rodan (1989), Wong (2001), Hamilton-Hart (2002), Unger (1998), and Rock (2000).

17. See, for example, Muscat (1994).

18. This discussion draws on Doner, Ritchie, and Slater (2005), especially Section II.

19. In addition to work cited earlier, cross-national comparisons include Maxfield (1997) and Kang (2003). Within-country, cross-sectoral studies include Thitinan (2001), Lauridsen (2000), and especially Christensen (1993). One of the rare studies of inter-regional differences within one country is Rasiah's (2000) study of Penang.

20. Studies include Hewison (1986, 1989), Robison (1986), and MacIntyre (1990).

21. Pioneering works include Skinner (1958), Suehiro (1989), Mackie (1992), and Robison (1986).

22. See Lim and Gosling (1983) and more generally Greif (1994).

23. See Unger (1998).

24. See Borrus, Ernst, and Haggard (2000).

25. See Anek (1992), MacIntyre (1990), Felker (1998), and Doner and Schneider (2000). On "industrial agglomerations," the pioneering work is Rasiah (1994).

26. See, for example, the World Bank workshop on "Business-Government Consultative Mechanisms in Market-Oriented Reforms," Washington, DC, January 31, 2000. See also Campos and Root (1996).

27. For references, see Section II in Doner, Ritchie, and Slater (2005).

28. On the concept of "competitive clientelism," see Doner and Ramsay (1997).

29. Deyo's analysis (1989) is drawn from the four East Asian NICs but essentially applies to the ASEAN countries.

30. See Rasiah (2003) and Abrami (2003).

31. See Kuruvilla and Erickson (2002) and Deyo (1989).

32. See useful reviews by Thelen (1999: 373, 2003).

33. For more nuanced discussions of path dependency, see, for example, Thelen (2003: 216–222).

34. See the useful review by Ross (1999).

35. See the chapters in Rodrik (2003).

36. For an overview of Chinese family firms in Southeast Asia, see Lim and Gosling (1983). For a critique of cultural explanations of the Chinese family firm, see Greenhalgh (1994).

37. See Mackie (1992) and Hutchcroft (1998).

38. See Schneider (2004) and Doner and Schneider (2000).

39. This view is found in both cultural and organizational accounts of state socialism. See, for example, Porter (1993), Jowitt (1992), Oi (1989), and Walder (1986).

40. See Szelenyi and Kostello (1998) and Nee (1989).

41. See Kerkvliet (2005), Fforde (1989), and Beresford (1988).

42. See Kerkvliet, Heng, and Koh (2003) and Chan, Kerkvliet, and Unger (1999).

43. Outside the Vietnamese context, see McDermott (2002), Woodruff (2000a, 2000b), Oi and Walder (1999), Wank (1999), Eyal, Szelenyi, and Townsley (1998), Grabher and Stark (1997), Walder (1996), and Stark (1992, 1996).

44. The classic demonstration of the disjunctures among motive, institutions, and outcome is Weber's Protestant ethic. For an application to the developmental state model, see Underhill and Zhang (2005).

45. See Collier and Mahoney (1996: 84).

CHAPTER 11

I would like to thank Ben Kerkvliet, Natasha Hamilton-Hart, Tuong Vu, Gerald Houseman, and two anonymous reviewers for their insightful comments and suggestions.

1. This focus has been regarded by James Caporaso and David Levine (1992: 220) as a "power-centered" approach. The limitation involved in this approach is "not where to find it [power] but what to ignore" because "power is nearly everywhere."

2. I will use the terms "farmers," "peasants," and "rural producers" interchangeably. Peasants are rural producers who produce for their own consumption and for sale, using their own and family labor, and occasionally hiring and selling labor. They may have a certain degree of control over the resources and production equipment, unlike workers who work in a factory owned by someone else.

3. E-mail communication with Tom Brass, June 8, 2004.

4. A "locally specific" explanation or a "process-oriented" approach is inspired by Migdal's "state-in-society" approach. It disaggregates the state into different levels of analysis, takes into account local variations, and identifies a combination of the types of agricultural policies and the nature of personal interactions between local authorities and rural populations as central to understanding peasants' varying perceptions of local and state authorities. See Thawnghmung (2004).

5. The ideas in this chapter are inspired by Oi (1993).

6. See a special volume on "Urban Bias," *Journal of Development Studies* 29 (July 1993).

7. Some argue that share tenancy is inefficient because it fails to provide incentives, as the tenant stands to receive only a share of output. Others argue that sharecropping has certain advantages, including risk sharing between landlords and tenants. Tenants under fixed-rent contract, on the other hand, have to face all the risks, whereas wage laborers have no incentives to work. See Rashid and Quibria (1995: 133–134).

8. Richter quotes the following works as examples: Kesselman (1973), Huntington (1968), and Hoadley (1975).

9. Riedinger reviews the following works that assess the relationships between democratic political institutions and socioeconomic inequality: Marshall (1964), Lipset (1981 [1960]), and Jackman (1986).

10. Bernstein highlights timing and duration as keys to understanding variations in transitional trajectories. "Duration" analyzes the relatively more leisurely or compressed processes and stages of transition from its inception to completion. For instance, the defeat of the seigneurial reaction in England provided an initial condition for a transition of exceptionally leisurely duration, from the fifteenth to the eighteenth century. On the other hand, agrarian transitions appear to have been of relatively short duration, from the 1790s to the 1830s, in the northeastern United States and from the 1870s to the 1920s in Japan, and intensely compressed in Taiwan and South Korea, in the 1950s and 1960s.

11. The first type of rent seizing is generally known as "rent seeking," under which firms seek rents created by the state by bribing politicians and bureaucrats. The second type of rent is referred to as "rent extraction," in which politicians and bureaucrats seek rents held by firms, or threaten firms with costly regulation.

CHAPTER 12

The author thanks Danny Unger, Natasha Hamilton-Hart, Richard Doner, Regina Abrami, and other participants in the Stanford Workshop on Southeast Asia in Political Science: Theory, Region, and Qualitative Analysis, June 18–19, 2004. Special thanks are due to Dan Slater for many helpful suggestions on several drafts. The author is solely responsible for any errors or misinterpretations contained in this chapter.

1. Globalization is the object of a variety of literatures spanning the social sciences and humanities disciplines. In order to keep the discussion reasonably limited, this chapter restricts its focus to prominent debates in political economy—in particular, changing state-market relationships. It does not attempt to survey related political science literatures analyzing the relationships between globalization and democratization, cultural change, or other issues.

2. In this essay, the terms "region-specific" and "regional specialization" are used to denote research that takes conventional regional geopolitical demarcations as analytic frames of reference (even if it problematizes or modifies them) and that emphasizes historical and contextual knowledge as integral to the construction of valid hypotheses and inferences.

3. Quoted in Agence France-Presse, September 14, 1998.

4. Quoted in *Business Times* (Kuala Lumpur), January 26, 1999.

5. Quoted in *The Star* (Kuala Lumpur), February 9, 1999.

6. The paraphrase is from Weiss (1998).

7. In a similar critique, Bernard (1996: 656–657) argues that regional and global structures "need to be thought of as integral components of the political economy of individual countries rather than as constituting a set of 'exogenous factors' at the 'international level.'"

8. His acknowledged reference is Ruggie (1983), and his model adapts Pempel's (1998) concept of political economy regimes—stable amalgams of state institutions, socioeconomic orders, and foreign economic strategies or modes of international integration.

CHAPTER 13

I received helpful comments on a draft of this chapter from Rick Doner, Andrew MacIntyre, and Nikki Velasco, among other participants in "Southeast Asia in Political Science: Theory, Region, and Qualitative Analysis," Southeast Asia Forum, Stanford University, June 18–19, 2004, the workshop out of which this book grew. I owe particular thanks to Erik Kuhonta for his suggestions. Any remaining inadequacies are mine alone.

1. Every choice of focus forgoes others. In keeping with this volume's main concern, this chapter is about the sometimes troubled intersection of Southeast Asian studies and political science. It is not a history of Southeast Asian studies. It does not explore how such studies have been affected by government and foundations, for example, or by World War II and the Vietnam War. Nor does it discuss in any depth disciplines other than political science, or trans-disciplinary "international studies." These are important omissions, as an anonymous reviewer has helpfully reminded me. I acknowledge, too, that my present scope is rather parochially American. To read beyond these limitations, see, for example, Sears (2007), Chou and Houben (2006), Reid (2003, including Emmerson 2003), SSRC Staff (2000), Hirschman et al. (1992), Morse (1984), and Emmerson (1984).

2. In 2005 a sharply worded essay by South Asianist–cum–political scientist Susanne Hoeber Rudolph illustrated both the tension and the tolerance that mark area-discipline relations. She defended the "situated knowledge" sought by area students against the "conversionary project" of discipline-first rationalists in po-

litical science who touted Lockean ideology as "universal knowledge." Yet she had originally delivered this critique to the annual convention of the American Political Science Association in her capacity as president of that explicitly disciplinary body (Rudolph 2005: 12; see also Laitin 1993).

3. Centers *for* Southeast Asian Studies and Departments *of* Political Science, on the other hand, exist at Northern Illinois University, Ohio University, and the Universities of California–Berkeley, California–Los Angeles, Hawaii–Manoa, Michigan–Ann Arbor, Washington–Seattle, and Wisconsin–Madison.

4. In the still more sweeping opinion of another political scientist, Robert Bates (1996: 1), scholars of all disciplines agree that "area studies has failed to generate scientific knowledge." See also Laitin's reference to "real estate" in my first epigraph. Compare, however, the defense of "soaking and poking" by political scientist Richard Fenno (1978: xiv, 249–250).

5. In Southeast Asian studies the uniqueness, holism, and nuanced complexity of particular individuals and groups, especially in villages frequented by cultural anthropologists, have been cited as reasons not to aggregate human behavior using quantitative techniques. But the difference should not be overdrawn. Southeast Asian area studies of political economy routinely display and discuss statistical data on, for example, the member states of the Association of Southeast Asian Nations (ASEAN).

6. The institutional security of political science is one thing; unanimity about ontology among political scientists is quite another. Among the social sciences, only political science embeds its scientific status in its very name—as if to allay self-doubt as to whether there can really ever be a cumulative and causal science of politics. Extending this speculation, one might even imagine alongside each Department of Political Science an invisible Department of Government ready to seize power in the event of a paradigm failure. Most economists, in contrast, have not felt a need to rechristen their enterprise "economic science," which sounds almost redundant, notwithstanding the dissensus within that field when it comes to explaining the past, never mind predicting the future. Political science is not exactly oxymoronic. Certainly one can try to study politics "scientifically," whatever exactly that means. But neither has the discipline been especially successful in doing so, if success means the discovery and accumulation of reliable, nontrivial, and durable laws that explain political attitudes, organization, and behavior.

7. In 2003, responding to "perestroika"-style criticism of the *APSR*, the Association began publishing a second professional journal, *Perspectives on Politics*. It will be interesting to compare the relative career boost associated with an appearance in the former versus the latter venue.

8. It would be helpful to know the average ages of "perestroikans" and their opponents in political science—and if older political scientists are more skeptical of, say, rational-choice theory than younger ones are, how much of that difference to

attribute to epistemological progress and how much to intellectual fashion. In the meantime, the growing prominence of Laitin's methodology in graduate student socializations and tenure-track job descriptions will be explained by different observers in different ways.

9. I write "would-be-emergent" because of Laitin's candor in acknowledging that "this essay has, I admit, a Leninist goal of creating a vanguard to facilitate what is historically emergent" (2000: 3, n. 3)—a cohort capable of "pushing history along" (2002: 631). Should his desire to create such a vanguard fail, what "is historically emergent" may not be. There is also some shrinkage between the essay's grand opening vision of "a new consensus" that is already "on the horizon" and the modesty of its closing claim to have shown only "specks of evidence" that one really is emerging (2002: 630, 659).

10. Consonant with this advice is the idea that the most productive way to reconcile quantitative and qualitative approaches "is not through the unilateral imposition of norms, but rather through mutual learning" (Brady et al. 2004: 5).

11. Had Bates and Laitin been Sinologists, would they have evolved in the same intellectual direction? Or would the temptation of exceptionalism have been too great to resist?

12. Laitin (2002: 659; 2000: 38) recommended for political science a division of labor comparable to the one in physics, where empirical realities were reported by "experimentalists" (the equivalent of "field workers" in political science) for "theorists" to explain. Missing from this parallelism, however, were two ideas: that the experimenters and field workers themselves might already be in the explaining business, and that they might already be doing theory.

13. Illustrations include Nelson and Winter (1982) on "bounded rationality" and Thaler (1991) on "quasi-rational choice."

14. For more on this topic, see Emmerson (1982).

Bibliography

Abbott, J. 2001. "Democracy@internet.asia? The Challenges to the Emancipatory Potential of the Net: Lessons from China and Malaysia." *Third World Quarterly* 22(1): 99–114.

Abinales, P. 1997. "State Building, Communist Insurgency, and *Cacique* Politics in the Philippines." In P. B. Rich and R. Stubbs, eds., *The Counter-Insurgent State.* New York: St. Martin's.

———. 2000. *Making Mindanao: Cotabato and Davao in the Formation of the Philippine Nation-State.* Manila: Ateneo de Manila University.

Abrami, R. 2002. "Self-Making, Class Struggle, and Labor Autarky: The Political Origins of Private Entrepreneurship in Vietnam and China." Ph.D. diss., University of California, Berkeley.

———. 2003. "Worker Rights and Global Trade: The U.S.-Cambodia Bilateral Textile Trade Agreement." Harvard Business School Case 703-034.

———. 2005a. "The Delta Blues: U.S.-Vietnam Catfish Trade Dispute (A)." Harvard Business School Case 706-003.

———. 2005b. "The Delta Blues: U.S.-Vietnam Catfish Trade Dispute (B)." Harvard Business School Case 706-006.

———, and N. Henaff. 2004. "The City and the Countryside: Economy, State and Socialist Legacies in the Vietnamese Labor Market." In M. Beresford and A. Tran, eds., *Reaching for the Dream: Challenges of Sustainability in Vietnamese Economic Development.* Copenhagen: Nordic Institute of Asian Studies.

Abuza, Z. 2003. *Militant Islam in Southeast Asia.* Boulder: Lynne Rienner.

Acharya, A. 1999. "Realism, Institutionalism, and the Asian Economic Crisis." *Contemporary Southeast Asia* 21(1): 1–29.

———. 2003. "Democratisation and the Prospects for Participatory Regionalism in Southeast Asia." *Third World Quarterly* 24(2): 375–390.

Adas, M. 1974. *The Burma Delta: Economic Development and Social Change on an Asian Rice Frontier, 1852–1941.* Madison: University of Wisconsin Press.

————. 1979. *Prophets of Rebellion: Millenarian Protest Movements Against the European Colonial Order*. Chapel Hill: University of North Carolina Press.

————. 1980. "'Moral Economy' or 'Contest State'? Elite Demands and the Origins of Peasant Protest in Southeast Asia." *Journal of Social History* 13(4): 521–540.

————. 1981. "From Avoidance to Confrontation: Peasant Protest in Precolonial and Colonial Southeast Asia." *Comparative Studies in Society and History* 23(2): 217–247.

————. 1982. "Bandits, Monks, and Pretender Kings: Patterns of Peasant Resistance and Protest in Colonial Burma, 1826–1941." In R. Weller and S. Guggenheim, eds., *Power and Protest in the Countryside*.

————. 1986. "From Footdragging to Flight: The Evasive History of Peasant Avoidance Protest in South and Southeast Asia." In J. Scott and B. Kerkvliet, eds., *Everyday Forms of Peasant Resistance in South-East Asia*.

————. 1998. *State, Market, and Peasant in Colonial South and Southeast Asia*. Aldershot: Ashgate.

Alagappa, M., ed. 1995. *Political Legitimacy in Southeast Asia: The Quest for Moral Authority*. Stanford: Stanford University Press.

————. 2004a. "Civil Society and Democratic Change: Indeterminate Connection, Transforming Relations." In M. Alagappa, ed., *Civil Society and Political Change in Asia*.

————. 2004b. "Civil Society and Political Change: An Analytical Framework." In M. Alagappa, ed., *Civil Society and Political Change in Asia*.

————. 2004c. "Introduction." In M. Alagappa, ed., *Civil Society and Political Change in Asia*.

————. 2004d. "The Nonstate Public Sphere in Asia: Dynamic Growth, Institutionalization Lag." In M. Alagappa, ed., *Civil Society and Political Change in Asia*.

————, ed. 2004e. *Civil Society and Political Change in Asia: Expanding and Contracting Democratic Space*. Stanford: Stanford University Press.

Alesina, A., and N. Roubini, with G. D. Cohen. 1997. *Political Cycles and the Macroeconomy*. Cambridge, MA: MIT Press.

Alexander, P., P. Boomgaard, and B. Whites. 1994. *In the Shadow of Agriculture: Non-Farm Activities in the Javanese Economy, Past and Present*. Amsterdam: Royal Tropical Institute.

Almond, G. A. 1960. "Introduction: A Functional Approach to Comparative Politics." In G. A. Almond and J. S. Coleman, eds., *The Politics of Developing Areas*. Princeton: Princeton University Press.

Alvarez, S. 1990. *Engendering Democracy in Brazil: Women's Movements in Transition Politics*. Princeton: Princeton University Press.

Amenta, E. 2003. "What We Know About the Development of Social Policy." In J. Mahoney and D. Rueschemeyer, eds., *Comparative Historical Analysis in the Social Sciences*.

Ammar Siamwalla. 2000. "Anatomy of the Thai Crisis." Unpublished manuscript, Thailand Development Research Institute.

Amorim-Neto, O., and G. C. Cox. 1997. "Electoral Institutions, Cleavage Structures, and the Number of Parties." *American Journal of Political Science* 41(1): 149–174.

Amsden, A. 1989. *Asia's Next Giant: South Korea and Late Industrialization.* New York: Oxford University Press.

———. 2001. *The Rise of "the Rest": Challenges to the West from Late-Industrializing Economies.* New York: Oxford University Press.

Ananta, A., E. N. Arifin, and L. Suryadinata. 2004. *Indonesian Electoral Behaviour: A Statistical Perspective.* Singapore: Institute of Southeast Asian Studies.

Anderson, B. 1972. *Java in a Time of Revolution.* Ithaca: Cornell University Press.

———. 1978. "Studies of the Thai State: State of Thai Studies." In E. B. Ayal, ed., *The Study of Thailand.* Athens: Ohio University Center for International Studies, Southeast Asia Program.

———. 1982. "Perspective and Method in American Research on Indonesia." In B. Anderson and A. Kahin, eds., *Interpreting Indonesian Politics.*

———. 1983. "Old State, New Society: Indonesia's New Order in Comparative Historical Perspective." *Journal of Asian Studies* 42(3): 477–496.

———. 1987. "Introduction." In B. Anderson, ed., *Southeast Asian Tribal Groups and Ethnic Minorities.* Cambridge, MA: Cultural Survival, Report 22.

———. 1988. "Cacique Democracy in the Philippines: Origins and Dreams." *New Left Review* 169: 3–33.

———. 1990a [1972]. "The Idea of Power in Javanese Culture." In B. Anderson, ed., *Language and Power: Exploring Political Cultures in Indonesia.* Ithaca: Cornell University Press.

———. 1990b. "Murder and Progress in Modern Siam." *New Left Review* 81: 33–48.

———. 1991 [1983]. *Imagined Communities.* London: Verso.

———. 1996. "Elections and Participation in Three Southeast Asian Countries." In R. Taylor, ed., *The Politics of Elections in Southeast Asia.*

———, ed. 1997. *Democratization in Southeast and East Asia.* New York: St. Martin's.

———. 1998a. "From Miracle to Crash." *London Review of Books* 20(8): 3–7.

———. 1998b. *The Spectre of Comparisons: Nationalism, Southeast Asia and the World.* London: Verso.

———, and A. Kahin, eds. 1982. *Interpreting Indonesian Politics.* Ithaca: Cornell Modern Indonesia Project, Cornell University.

Anderson, L. 2003. "Islam and Comparative Politics." *Newsletter: APSA-CP* 14(1): 25–27.

Anek Laothamatas. 1992. *Business Associations and the New Political Economy of Thailand.* Boulder: Westview.

————. 1996. "A Tale of Two Democracies: Conflicting Perceptions of Elections and Democracy in Thailand." In R. Taylor, ed., *The Politics of Elections in Southeast Asia*.

————. 1997. "Development and Democratization: A Theoretical Introduction with Reference to the Southeast Asian and East Asian Cases." In L. Anek, ed., *Democratization in Southeast and East Asia*. Singapore: Institute of Southeast Asian Studies.

Antlov, H. 1995. *Exemplary Center, Administrative Periphery: Rural Leadership and the New Order in Java*. London: Curzon.

————, and S. Cederroth, eds. 2004. *Elections in Indonesia: The New Order and Beyond*. London: Routledge.

Anusorn Limmanee. 1995. *Political Business Cycles in Thailand, 1979–1992*. Research report. Institute of Thai Studies, Chulalongkorn University.

Arghiros, D. 1995. *Political Structures and Strategies: A Study of Electoral Politics in Contemporary Rural Thailand*. Occasional Paper No. 31. Hull: University of Hull, Centre for South-East Asian Studies.

————. 2000. "The Local Dynamics of the 'New Political Economy': A District Business Association and Its Role in Electoral Politics." In R. McVey, ed., *Money and Power in Provincial Thailand*.

————. 2001. *Democracy, Development and Decentralization in Provincial Thailand*. Richmond: Curzon.

Aspinall, E. 1993. "Student Dissent in Indonesia in the 1980s." Working paper 79. Clayton: Centre of Southeast Asian Studies, Monash University.

————. 1999. "The Indonesian Student Uprising of 1998." In A. Budiman, B. Hatley, and D. Kingsbury, eds., *Reformasi: Crisis and Change in Indonesia*. Clayton: Monash Asia Institute.

————. 2005. *Opposing Suharto: Compromise, Resistance, and Regime Change in Indonesia*. Stanford: Stanford University Press.

Aung-Thwin, M. 1989. "1948 and Burma's Myth of Independence." In J. Silverstein, ed., *Independent Burma at Forty Years*. Ithaca: Southeast Asia Program, Cornell University.

Banks, M. 1996. *Ethnicity: Anthropological Constructions*. London: Routledge.

Banlaoi, R. C., and C. R. Carlos. 1996. *Political Parties in the Philippines: From 1900 to the Present*. Makati: Konrad Adenauer Foundation.

Barraclough, S. 1985. "The Dynamics of Coercion in the Malaysian Political Process." *Modern Asian Studies* 19(4): 797–822.

Barth, F. 1969. "Introduction." In F. Barth, ed., *Ethnic Groups and Boundaries*. Bergen: Universitets Forlaget.

Barton, G. 1994. "The Impact of Neo-Modernism on Indonesian Islamic Thought: The Emergence of a New Pluralism." In D. Bourchier and J. Legge, eds., *Democracy in Indonesia 1950s and 1990s*. Clayton: Centre of Southeast Asian Studies, Monash University.

———, and G. Fealy, eds. 1996. *Nahdlatul Ulama, Traditional Islam and Modernity in Indonesia*. Clayton: Monash Asia Institute.

Bates, R. 1981. *Markets and States in Tropical Africa*. Berkeley: University of California Press.

———. 1995. "Social Dilemmas and Rational Individuals: An Assessment of the New Institutionalism." In J. Harriss, J. Hunter, and C. M. Lewis, eds., *The New Institutional Economics and Third World Development*. London: Routledge.

———. 1996. "Letter from the President: Area Studies and the Discipline." *APSA-CP* 7(1): 1–2.

———, A. Greif, M. Levi, J. Rosenthal, and B. Weingast. 1998. *Analytic Narratives*. Princeton: Princeton University Press.

Bayard de Volo, L., and E. Schatz. 2004. "From the Inside Out: Ethnographic Methods in Political Research." *PS* 27(2): 267–272.

Beckert, J. 2002. *Beyond the Market: The Social Foundations of Economic Efficiency*. Princeton: Princeton University Press.

Beeson, M. 1999. "Reshaping Regional Institutions: APEC and the IMF in East Asia." *Pacific Review* 12(1): 1–24.

———. 2001. "Japan and Southeast Asia: The Lineaments of Quasi-Hegemony." In G. Rodan, K. Hewison, and R. Robison, eds., *The Political Economy of Southeast Asia*.

———. 2003a. "Sovereignty Under Siege: Globalisation and the State in Southeast Asia." *Third World Quarterly* 24(2): 357–374.

———. 2003b. "East Asia, the International Financial Institutions and Regional Regulatory Reform." *Journal of the Asia Pacific Economy* 8(3): 305–326.

———. 2003c. "ASEAN Plus Three: The Rise of Reactionary Regionalism." *Contemporary Southeast Asia* 25(2): 251–268.

———, and R. Robison. 2000. "Introduction: Interpreting the Crisis." In R. Robison et al., eds., *Politics and Markets in the Wake of the Asian Crisis*. London: Routledge.

Bell, D., D. Brown, K. Jayasuriya, and D. M. Jones, eds. 1995. *Towards Illiberal Democracy in Pacific Asia*. New York: St. Martin's.

———, and K. Jayasuriya. 1995. "Understanding Illiberal Democracy: A Framework." In D. Bell, D. Brown, K. Jayasuriya, and D. M. Jones, eds., *Towards Illiberal Democracy in Pacific Asia*.

Bellin, E. 2002. *Stalled Democracy: Capital, Labor, and the Paradox of State-Sponsored Development*. Ithaca: Cornell University Press.

Benda, H. 1958. *The Crescent and the Rising Sun*. The Hague: W. van Hoeve.

———. 1982. "Democracy in Indonesia." In B. Anderson and A. Kahin, eds., *Interpreting Indonesian Politics*.

Bentley, C. G. 1987. "Ethnicity and Practice." *Comparative Studies in Society and History* 29(1): 24–55.

Beresford, M. 1988. *Vietnam: Politics, Economics, and Society*. London: Pinter.

Berger, M. 2003. "Decolonisation, Modernisation and Nation-Building: Political Development Theory and the Appeal of Communism in Southeast Asia, 1945–1975." *Journal of Southeast Asian Studies* 34(3): 421–448.

Berger, P. L. 1974. *Pyramids of Sacrifice: Political Ethics and Social Change.* New York: Basic Books.

Berlin, I. 1953. *The Hedgehog and the Fox.* New York: Simon and Schuster.

Berman, P. 1974. *Revolutionary Organization.* Lexington: Lexington Books.

Berman, S. 1997. "Civil Society and the Collapse of the Weimar Republic." *World Politics* 49(3): 401–429.

Bermeo, N. 2003. *Ordinary People in Extraordinary Times: The Citizenry and the Breakdown of Democracy.* Princeton: Princeton University Press.

Bernard, M. 1996. "States, Social Forces, and Regions in Historical Time: Toward a Critical Political Economy of Eastern Asia." *Third World Quarterly* 17(4): 649–665.

———. 1999. "East Asia's Tumbling Dominoes: Financial Crises and the Myth of the Regional Model." In L. Panitch, ed., *The Socialist Register 1999: Global Capitalism Versus Democracy.* London: Merlin.

———, and J. Ravenhill. 1995. "Beyond Product Cycles and Flying Geese: Regionalization, Hierarchy, and the Industrialization of East Asia." *World Politics* 47(2): 171–209.

Bernstein, H. 1996. "Agrarian Questions Then and Now." *Journal of Peasant Studies* 24(1): 22–59.

———, and T. Brass. 1996. "Questioning the Agrarian: The Work of T. J. Byres." In Henry Bernstein and Tom Brass, eds., *Agrarian Questions: Essays in Appreciation of T. J. Byres.* London: Taylor and Francis.

Bertrand, J. 1998. "Growth and Democracy in Southeast Asia." *Comparative Politics* 30(3): 355–375.

———. 2004. *Nationalism and Ethnic Conflict in Indonesia.* Cambridge: Cambridge University Press.

Bevir, M. 2003. "Interpretivism: Family Resemblances and Quarrels." *Qualitative Methods* 1(2): 9–13.

Bhavnani, R., and M. Ross. 2003. "Announcement, Credibility and Turnout in Popular Rebellions." *Journal of Conflict Resolution* 47(3): 340–366.

Blais, A., and A. Dobrzynska. 1998. "Turnout in Electoral Democracies." *European Journal of Political Research* 33(2): 239–261.

Blondel, J. 1968. "Party Systems and Patterns of Government in Western Democracies." *Canadian Journal of Political Science* 1(2): 180–203.

Boix, C., and S. C. Stokes. 2003. "Endogenous Democratization." *World Politics* 55(4): 517–549.

Booth, A. 1988. *Agricultural Development in Indonesia.* Wellington: Allen and Unwin.

———. 1999. "Initial Conditions and Miraculous Growth: Why Is Southeast Asia Different from Taiwan and South Korea?" *World Development* 27(2): 301–321.

———. 2003. "The Burma Development Disaster in Comparative Historical Perspective." *SOAS Bulletin of Burma Research* 1(1): 1–23.

Borrus, M. 1993. "The Regional Architecture of Global Electronics: Trajectories, Linkages, and Access to Technology." In P. Gourevitch and P. Guerrieri, eds., *New Challenges to International Cooperation: Adjustments of Firms, Policies, and Organizations to Global Competition.* San Diego: University of California at San Diego Press.

———. 1999. "Exploiting Asia to Beat Japan: Production Networks and the Comeback of U.S. Electronics." In D. Encarnation, ed., *Japanese Multinationals in Asia.* New York: Oxford University Press.

———, D. Ernst, and S. Haggard. 2000. *International Production Networks in Asia.* New York: Routledge.

Boswell, T., and W. Dixon. 1990. "Dependency and Rebellion: A Cross-National Analysis." *American Sociological Review* 55(4): 540–559.

———, and W. Dixon. 1993. "Marx's Theory of Rebellion: A Cross-National Analysis of Class Exploitation, Economic Development, and Violent Revolt." *American Sociological Review* 58(5): 681–702.

Boudreau, V. 1996a. "Of Motorcades and Masses: Mobilization and Innovation in Philippine Protest." In P. Abinales, ed., *The Revolution Falters.* Ithaca: Southeast Asia Program, Cornell University.

———. 1996b. "Northern Theory, Southern Protest: Opportunity Structure Analysis in Cross-National Perspective." *Mobilization* 1(2): 175–189.

———. 1999. "Diffusing Democracy? People Power in Indonesia and the Philippines." *Bulletin of Concerned Asian Scholars* 31(4): 3–18.

———. 2001. *Grass Roots and Cadre in the Protest Movement.* Manila: Ateneo de Manila University Press.

———. 2004. *Resisting Dictatorship: Repression and Protest in Southeast Asia.* New York: Cambridge University Press.

Bowen, John R. 1995. "The Forms Culture Takes: A State-of-the-Field Essay on the Anthropology of Southeast Asia." *Journal of Asian Studies* 54(4): 1047–1078.

———. 2002. *Religions in Practice: An Approach to the Anthropology of Religion.* Boston: Allyn and Bacon.

———. 2003. *Islam, Law, and Equality in Indonesia: An Anthropology of Public Reasoning.* Cambridge: Cambridge University Press.

Bowie, A. 1991. *Crossing the Industrial Divide.* New York: Columbia University Press.

———, and D. Unger. 1997. *The Politics of Open Economies.* New York: Cambridge University Press.

Bowie, K. 1992. "Unraveling the Myth of the Subsistence Economy: Textile Production in Nineteenth Century Northern Thailand." *Journal of Asian Studies* 51(4): 797–823.

———. 1997. *Rituals of National Loyalty: An Anthropology of the State and the Village Scout Movement in Thailand.* New York: Columbia University Press.

Bowles, P. 2002. "Asia's Post-Crisis Regionalism: Bringing the State Back In, Keeping the United States Out." *Review of International Political Economy* 92: 244–270.

Brady, H., and D. Collier, eds. 2004. *Rethinking Social Inquiry*. Lanham: Rowman and Littlefield.

Brady, H., D. Collier, and J. Seawright. 2004. "Refocusing the Discussion of Methodology." In H. Brady and D. Collier, eds., *Rethinking Social Inquiry*.

Brass, P. R. 1991. *Ethnicity and Nationalism*. New Delhi: Sage.

Bratton, M., and N. van de Walle. 1997. *Democratic Experiments in Africa*. New York: Cambridge University Press.

Bray, F. 1983. "Patterns of Evolution in Rice-Growing Societies." *Journal of Peasant Studies* 11(1): 3–33.

Brenner, S. 2005. "Islam and Gender Politics in Late New Order Indonesia." In A. C. Willford and K. George, eds., *Spirited Politics*.

Brinton, C. 1938. *The Anatomy of Revolution*. New York: Norton.

Broad, R. 1988. *Unequal Alliance: The World Bank, the International Monetary Fund, and the Philippines*. Berkeley: University of California Press.

Brocheux, P. 1983. "Moral Economy or Political Economy? The Peasants Are Always Rational." *Journal of Asian Studies* 42(4): 791–803.

Brown, D. 1994. *The State and Ethnic Politics in Southeast Asia*. London: Routledge.

———, and D. M. Jones. 1995. "Democratization and the Myth of the Liberalizing Middle Classes." In D. Bell, D. Brown, K. Jayasuriya, and D. M. Jones, eds., *Towards Illiberal Democracy in Pacific Asia*.

Brown, I. 1988. *The Elite and the Economy in Siam, c. 1890–1920*. Singapore: Oxford University Press.

Brown, M. E. 1997. "The Impact of Government Policies on Ethnic Relations." In M. E. Brown and S. Ganguly, eds., *Government Policies and Ethnic Relations in Asia and the Pacific*.

———, and S. Ganguly, eds. 1997a. *Government Policies and Ethnic Relations in Asia and the Pacific*. Cambridge, MA: MIT Press.

———, and S. Ganguly. 1997b. "Introduction." In M. E. Brown and S. Ganguly, eds., *Government Policies and Ethnic Relations in Asia and the Pacific*.

———, and S. Ganguly, eds. 2003. *Fighting Words: Language Policy and Ethnic Relations in Asia*. Cambridge, MA: MIT Press.

Brown, N. 1989. "The Conspiracy of Silence and the Atomistic Political Activity of the Egyptian Peasantry." In F. Colburn, ed., *Everyday Forms of Peasant Resistance*.

Brownlee, J. 2007. *Authoritarianism in an Age of Democratization*. New York: Cambridge University Press.

Brusco, V., M. Nazareno, and S. C. Stokes. 2002. "Clientelism and Democracy: Evidence from Argentina." Paper presented at the Conference on Political Parties and Organization in Parliamentary and Presidential Regimes, Yale University.

Brynen, R., B. Korany, and P. Noble, eds. 1995. *Political Liberalization and Democratization in the Arab World: Theoretical Perspective*, Vol. 1. Boulder: Lynne Rienner.

Budiman, A., ed. 1990. *State and Civil Society in Indonesia*. Clayton: Center of Southeast Asian Studies, Monash University.

Bunce, V. 2003. "Rethinking Recent Democratization: Lessons from the Post-Communist Experience." *World Politics* 55(2): 167–192.

Burchett, W. 1956. *North of the Seventeenth Parallel*. Delhi: People's Publishing House.

Callaghy, T. 1984. *The State-Society Struggle: Zaire in Comparative Perspective*. New York: Columbia University Press.

Callahan, M. 2003. *Making Enemies: War and State Building in Burma*. Ithaca: Cornell University Press.

Callahan, W. A. 1998. *Imagining Democracy: Reading "The Events of May" in Thailand*. Singapore: Institute of Southeast Asian Studies.

———. 2000. *Pollwatching, Elections and Civil Society in Southeast Asia*. Burlington: Ashgate.

Campos, E., and H. L. Root. 1996. *The Key to the East Asian Miracle: Making Shared Growth Credible*. Washington, DC: Brookings Institution.

Camroux, D. 1996. "State Responses to Islamic Resurgence in Malaysia: Accommodation, Co-Option, and Confrontation." *Asian Survey* 36(9): 852–868.

Caporaso, J., and D. Levine. 1992. *Theories of Political Economy*. Cambridge: Cambridge University Press.

Carey, J. M., and M. S. Shugart. 1995. "Incentives to Cultivate a Personal Vote: A Rank Ordering of Electoral Formulas." *Electoral Studies* 14(4): 417–439.

Carlos, C. R. 1997. *Handbook of Political Parties and Elections in the Philippines*. Makati: Konrad Adenauer Foundation.

———. 1998. *Selected Elections Cases in the Philippines: From the Supreme Court and Electoral Tribunals*. Makati: Konrad Adenauer Foundation.

———, and R. C. Banlaoi. 1996. *Elections in the Philippines: From Pre-Colonial Period to the Present*. Makati: Konrad Adenauer Foundation.

Carothers, T. 2002. "The End of the Transition Paradigm." *Journal of Democracy* 13(1): 5–21.

Carter, M., B. Barham, and D. Mesbah. 1996. "Agroexport Booms and the Rural Poor in Chile, Guatemala and Paraguay." *Latin America Research Review* 31(1): 33–60

Casanova, J. 1994. *Public Religions in the Modern World*. Chicago: University of Chicago Press.

Case, W. 1996a. "UMNO Paramountcy: A Report on Single Party Dominance in Malaysia." *Party Politics* 2(1): 115–127.

———. 1996b. "Can the 'Halfway House' Stand? Semidemocracy and Elite Theory in Three Southeast Asian Countries." *Comparative Politics* 28(4): 437–464.

———. 2001. "Malaysia's Resilient Pseudodemocracy." *Journal of Democracy* 12(1): 43–57.

———. 2002. *Politics in Southeast Asia: Democracy or Less*. Richmond: Curzon.

———. 2004. "New Uncertainties for an Old Pseudo-Democracy: The Case of Malaysia." *Comparative Politics* 37(1): 83–104.

———. 2005. "Malaysia: New Reforms, Old Continuities, Tense Ambiguities." *Journal of Development Studies* 41(2): 284–309.

Casson, A., and K. Obidzinski. 2002. "From New Order to Regional Autonomy: Shifting Dynamics of 'Illegal' Logging in Kalimantan, Indonesia." *World Development* 30(12): 2133–2151.

Cederroth, S. 1991. "From PNI to Golkar: Indonesian Village Politics, 1955–87." In M. Morner and T. Svenson, eds., *The Transformation of Rural Society in the Third World*. London: Routledge.

Centeno, M. A. 1997. "Blood and Debt: War and Taxation in Nineteenth-Century Latin America." *American Journal of Sociology* 102(6): 1565–1605.

———. 2002. *Blood and Debt: War and the Nation-State in Latin America*. University Park: Pennsylvania State University Press.

Cerny, P. G. 1999. "Reconstructing the Political in a Globalising World: States, Institutions, Actors and Governance." In F. Buelens, ed., *Globalisation and the Nation-State*. Cheltenham: Edward Elgar.

Chai-Anan Samudavanija. 1989. "Democracy in Thailand: A Case Study of a Stable Semi-Democratic Regime." In L. Diamond, J. Linz, and S. M. Lipset, eds., *Democracy in Developing Countries: Asia*. Boulder: Lynne Rienner.

———. 1995. "Thailand: A Stable Semidemocracy." In L. Diamond, J. Linz, and S. M. Lipset, eds., *Politics in Developing Countries*. Boulder: Lynne Rienner.

———. 1998. "Beyond Transition in Thailand." In L. Diamond and M. F. Plattner, eds., *Democracy in East Asia*. Baltimore: Johns Hopkins University Press.

Chaidar, A. 1999. *Pemilu 1999: Pertarungan Ideologis Partai-partai Islam Versus Partai-partai Sekuler*. Jakarta: Darul Falah.

Chamberlain, H. B. 1993. "On the Search for Civil Society in China." *Modern China* 19(2): 199–215.

Chan, A., B. J. T. Kerkvliet, and J. Unger, eds. 1999. *Transforming Asian Socialism: China and Vietnam Compared*. Canberra: Allen and Unwin.

Chan, H. C. 1975. "Politics in an Administrative State: Where Has the Politics Gone?" In S. C. Meow, ed., *Trends in Singapore*. Singapore: Singapore University Press.

———. 1976. *The Dynamics of One Party Dominance: The PAP at the Grassroots*. Singapore: Singapore University Press.

Chandra, S., and D. Kammen. 2002. "Generating Reforms and Reforming Generations: Military Politics in Indonesia's Democratic Transition and Consolidation." *World Politics* 55(1): 96–136.

Chazan, N. 1992. "Africa's Democratic Challenge." *World Policy Journal* 9(2): 279–307.

Che Man, W. K. 1990. *Muslim Separatism: The Moros of Southern Philippines and the Malays of Southern Thailand.* Singapore: Oxford University Press.

Chehabi, H., and J. Linz, eds. 1998. *Sultanistic Regimes.* Baltimore: Johns Hopkins University Press.

Chhibber, P. K., and K. Kollman. 1998. "Party Aggregation and the Number of Parties in India and the United States." *American Political Science Review* 92(2): 329–342.

———, and K. Kollman. 2004. *The Formation of National Party Systems: Federalism and Party Competition in Canada, Great Britain, India, and the United States.* Princeton: Princeton University Press.

———, and I. Nooruddin. 2004. "Do Party Systems Count? The Number of Parties and Government Performance in the Indian States." *Comparative Political Studies* 37(2): 152–187.

Choi, J. 2001. "Philippine Democracies Old and New: Elections, Term Limits, and Party Systems." *Asian Survey* 41(3): 488–501.

Chou, C., and V. Houben, eds. 2006. *Southeast Asian Studies: Debates and New Directions.* Singapore: Institute of Southeast Asian Studies.

Christensen, S. 1993. "Coalitions and Collective Choice: The Politics of Institutional Change in Thai Agriculture." Ph.D. diss., University of Wisconsin, Madison.

Chua, B. H. 1995. *Communitarian Ideology and Democracy in Singapore.* New York: Routledge.

———. 2000. "Consuming Asians: Ideas and Issues." In Chua Beng Huat, ed., *Consumption in Asia: Lifestyles and Identities.* London: RoutledgeCurzon.

———, and J. E. Tan. 1999. "Singapore: Where the Middle Class Sets the Standard." In M. Pinches, ed., *Culture and Privilege in Capitalist Asia.* London: Routledge.

Clarke, G. 1998. *The Politics of NGOs in South-East Asia: Participation and Protest in the Philippines.* New York: Routledge.

Clear, A. 2000. "The International Dimension of Democratization: Foreign Aid for the 1999 Indonesian Elections." Paper presented at the Annual Meeting of the American Political Science Association, Washington, DC.

Cohen, A. 1969. *Custom and Politics in Urban Africa.* Berkeley: University of California Press.

Colburn, F., ed. 1989. *Everyday Forms of Peasant Resistance.* Armonk: M. E. Sharpe.

Collier, C. J. 1997. "The Politics of Insurrection in Davao, Philippines." Ph.D. diss., University of Hawaii.

———. 2002. "The Politics of Insurrection in Davao, Philippines." Book manuscript.

Collier, D., and J. Mahoney. 1993. "Conceptual 'Stretching' Revisited: Adapting Categories in Comparative Analysis." *American Political Science Review* 87(4): 845–855.

———, and J. Mahoney. 1996. "Insights and Pitfalls: Selection Bias in Qualitative Research." *World Politics* 49(1): 56–91.

———, and S. Levitsky. 1997. "Democracy with Adjectives: Conceptual Innovation in Comparative Research." *World Politics* 49(3): 430–451.

Collier, P. 2000. "Doing Well Out of War: An Economic Perspective." In M. Berdal and D. Malone, eds., *Greed and Grievance: Economic Agendas in Civil Wars.* Boulder: Lynne Rienner.

———, and A. Hoeffler. 1998. "On Economic Causes of Civil War." *Oxford Economic Papers* 50: 563–573.

———, and A. Hoeffler. 2001. *Greed and Grievance in Civil War.* Washington, DC: World Bank.

———, and N. Sambanis, eds. 2005. *Understanding Civil War* (2 volumes). Washington, DC: World Bank.

Collier, R., and D. Collier. 1991. *Shaping the Political Arena.* Princeton: Princeton University Press.

Connors, M. 1999. "Political Reform and the State in Thailand." *Journal of Contemporary Asia* 29(2): 201–226.

Coppedge, M. 1998. "The Dynamics of Latin American Party Systems." *Party Politics* 4(4): 547–568.

Cox, G. 1987. *The Efficient Secret: The Cabinet and the Development of Political Parties in Victorian England.* Cambridge: Cambridge University Press.

———. 1997. *Making Votes Count.* Cambridge: Cambridge University Press.

———. 1999. "Electoral Rules and Electoral Coordination." *Annual Review of Political Science* 2: 145–161.

———, and M. D. McCubbins. 2001. "The Institutional Determinants of Policy Outcomes." In S. Haggard and M. D. McCubbins, eds., *Presidents, Parliaments, and Policy.* Cambridge: Cambridge University Press.

Cox, R. 1987. *Production, Power, and World Order.* New York: Columbia University Press.

Croissant, A. 2002. "Majoritarian and Consensual Democracy, Electoral Systems and Democratic Consolidation in Asia." *Asian Perspective* 26(2): 5–39.

———, and J. Dosch. 2001. "Parliamentary Elections in Thailand, March 2000 and January 2001." *Electoral Studies* 22(1): 153–193.

———, G. Bruns, and M. John, eds. 2002. *Electoral Politics in Southeast and East Asia.* Friedrich-Ebert-Stiftung, Office for Regional Co-operation in Southeast Asia.

Crone, D. 1982. *The ASEAN States.* New York: Praeger.

———. 1988. "State, Social Elites, and Government Capacity in Southeast Asia." *World Politics* 40(2): 252–268.

Crouch, H. 1978. *The Army and Politics in Indonesia.* Ithaca: Cornell University Press.

———. 1984. *Domestic Political Structures and Regional Economic Co-operation.* Singapore: Institute of Southeast Asian Studies.

———. 1986. "Patrimonialism and Military Rule in Indonesia." In A. Kohli, ed., *The State and Development in the Third World*. Princeton: Princeton University Press.

———. 1996. *Government and Society in Malaysia*. Ithaca: Cornell University Press.

———. 1998. "Indonesia's 'Strong State.'" In P. Dauvergne, ed., *Weak and Strong States in Asia-Pacific Societies*. St. Leonards: Allen and Unwin.

———, K. H. Lee, and M. Ong, eds. 1980. *Malaysian Politics and the 1978 Election*. Kuala Lumpur: Oxford University Press.

———, and J. Morley. 1999. "The Dynamics of Political Change." In J. Morley, ed., *Driven by Growth: Political Change in the Asia-Pacific Region*.

Crozier, B. 1965. *South-East Asia in Turmoil*. Harmondsworth: Penguin.

Davis, W. 1987. "Religion and Development: Weber and the East Asian Experience." In M. Weiner and S. P. Huntington, eds., *Understanding Political Development*. Boston: Little, Brown.

de Castro, I., Jr. 1992. "Money and Moguls: Oiling the Campaign Machinery." In L. Kalaw-Tirol and S. S. Colonel, eds., *1992 and Beyond: Forces and Issues in Philippine Elections*. Quezon City: Philippine Center for Investigative Journalism and Ateneo Center for Social Policy and Public Affairs.

De Koninck, R. 1996. "The Peasantry as the Territorial Spearhead of the State in Southeast Asia: The Case of Vietnam." *Sojourn* 11(2): 231–258.

de Leon, J. 1986. "Election Manipulation: The Case of the February 1986 Presidential Election." *Philippine Journal of Public Administration* 30(2): 154–183.

de Tocqueville, A. 2000 [1835]. *Democracy in America*. Translated by H. Reeve. 2 vols. New York: Bantam.

Dearden, P. 1996. "Development, the Environment, and Social Differentiation in Northern Thailand." In J. Rigg, ed., *Counting the Costs: Economic Growth and Environmental Change in Thailand*. Singapore: Institute of Southeast Asian Studies.

Denzau, A. T., and D. C. North. 1994. "Shared Mental Models: Ideologies and Institutions." *Kyklos* 47(1): 3–31.

Deyo, F. 1989. *Beneath the Miracle: Labor Subordination in the New Asian Industrialism*. Berkeley: University of California Press.

———. 1997. "Labour and Industrial Restructuring in South-East Asia." In G. Rodan, K. Hewison, and R. Robison, eds., *The Political Economy of Southeast Asia*.

———, and K. Agartan. 2003. "Markets, Workers and Economic Reforms: Reconstructing East Asian Labor Systems." *Journal of International Affairs* 57(1): 55–79.

Diamond, L. 1996. "Toward Democratic Consolidation." In L. Diamond and M. F. Plattner, eds., *The Global Resurgence of Democracy*. Baltimore: Johns Hopkins University Press.

———. 2002. "What Political Science Owes to the World." *PS: Political Science and Politics* Online Special (March).

————, and M. F. Plattner, eds. 1998. *Democracy in East Asia*. Baltimore: Johns Hopkins University Press.

DiGregorio, M. 2001. "Iron Works: Excavating Alternative Futures in a Northern Vietnamese Craft Village." Ph.D. diss., University of California, Los Angeles.

Doner, R. F. 1991a. "Approaches to the Politics of Economic Growth in Southeast Asia." *Journal of Asian Studies* 50(4): 818–849.

————. 1991b. *Driving a Bargain: Automobile Industrialization and Japanese Firms in Southeast Asia*. Berkeley: University of California Press.

————. 1992. "Limits of State Strength: Toward an Institutionalist View of Economic Development." *World Politics* 44(3): 398–431.

————. 1993. "Japanese Foreign Investment and the Creation of a Pacific Asian Region." In M. Kahler and J. Frankel, eds., *Regionalism and Rivalry: Japan and the United States in Pacific Asia*. Chicago: University of Chicago Press.

————. 1997. "Japan in East Asia: Institutions and Regional Leadership." In P. Katzenstein and T. Shiraishi, eds., *Network Power: Japan and Asia*. Ithaca: Cornell University Press.

————. 2000. "Rent-Seeking and Economic Development in Thailand." In M. Khan and K. S. Jomo, eds., *Rents, Rent-Seeking and Economic Development*.

————. 2004. "Growing into Trouble: Institutions and Politics in the Thai Sugar Industry." *Journal of East Asian Studies* 4(1): 97–138.

————, and A. Ramsay. 1997. "Competitive Clientelism and Economic Governance: The Case of Thailand." In B. Schneider and S. Maxfield, eds., *Business and the State in Developing Countries*. Ithaca: Cornell University Press.

————, and B. Schneider. 2000. "Business Associations and Economic Development." *Business and Politics* 2(3): 261–288.

————, and A. Ramsay. 2003. "Economic Upgrading in Liberalizing Thailand: Institutional and Political Challenges." In Linda Weiss, ed., *States in the Global Economy: Bringing Domestic Institutions Back In*. Cambridge: Cambridge University Press.

————, B. Ritchie, and D. Slater. 2005. "Systemic Vulnerability and the Origins of Developmental States: Northeast and Southeast Asia in Comparative Perspective." *International Organization* 59(2): 327–361.

Doronila, A. 1996. *A New Paradigm for Understanding Philippine Politics*. Manila: Asian Center for the Study of Democratic Institutions.

Dournes, J. 1980. *Minorities of Central Vietnam: Autochthonous Indochinese People*, trans. Mark Goetzke, Stephen Headley, and Stephen Varro. London: Minority Rights Group.

Downing, B. M. 1992. *The Military Revolution and Political Change*. Princeton: Princeton University Press.

Duncan, C. 2001. "The Social Construction of Developmental Labour Systems: South-East Asian Industrial Restructuring." In G. Rodan, K. Hewison, and R. Robison, eds., *The Political Economy of South-East Asia*.

———, ed. 2004. *Civilizing the Margins: Southeast Asian Government Policies for the Development of Minorities*. Ithaca: Cornell University Press.

Duverger, M. 1954. *Political Parties: Their Organization and Activity in the Modern State*. New York: Wiley.

Edelman, M. 2001. "Social Movements: Changing Paradigms and Forms of Politics." *Annual Review of Anthropology* 30: 285–317.

Eder, J. 1993. "Family Farming and Household Enterprise in a Philippine Community, 1971–1988: Persistence or Proletarianization?" *Journal of Asian Studies* 52(3): 647–671.

Effendy, B. 2003. *Islam and the State in Indonesia*. Singapore: Institute of Southeast Asian Studies.

Ekiert, G., and J. Kubik. 1998. "Contentious Politics in New Democracies: East Germany, Hungary, Poland, and Slovakia, 1989–93." *World Politics* 50: 547–581.

Eldridge, P. 1990. "NGOs and the State in Indonesia." In A. Budiman, ed., *State and Civil Society in Indonesia*.

———. 1995. *Non-government Organizations and Democratic Participation in Indonesia*. Kuala Lumpur: Oxford University Press.

———. 1996. "Development, Democracy and Non-government Organisations in Indonesia." *Asian Journal of Political Science* 4(1): 17–35.

Elliott, D. 2003. *The Vietnamese War: Revolution and Social Change in the Mekong Delta 1930–1975*. Armonk: Sharpe.

Elster, J. 2000. "Rational Choice History: A Case of Excessive Ambition." *American Political Science Review* 94(3): 685–695.

Emmerson, D. 1978. "The Bureaucracy in Political Context: Weakness in Strength." In K. Jackson and L. Pye, eds., *Political Power and Communications in Indonesia*.

———. 1982. "Orders of Meaning: Understanding Political Change in a Fishing Community in Indonesia." In B. Anderson and A. Kahin, eds., *Interpreting Indonesian Politics*.

———. 1983. "Understanding the New Order: Bureaucratic Pluralism in Indonesia." *Asian Survey* 23(11): 1220–1241.

———. 1984. "'Southeast Asia': What's in a Name?" *Journal of Southeast Asian Studies* 15(1): 1–21.

———. 1995. "Region and Recalcitrance: Rethinking Democracy Through Southeast Asia." *Pacific Review* 8(2): 223–248.

———. 1998. "Americanizing Asia?" *Foreign Affairs* 77(3): 46–56.

———. 1999. "A Tale of Three Countries." *Journal of Democracy* 10(4): 35–53.

———. 2000. "Will Indonesia Survive?" *Foreign Affairs* 79(3): 95–106.

———. 2003. "Situating Southeast Asian Studies: Realm, Guild, and Home." In A. Reid, ed., *Southeast Asian Studies*.

———. 2004. "Clashing Inspirations: Presumptive Universals and the Cult of Local Knowledge." Keynote speech, Graduate Student Research Conference, Institute of Asian Research and Centre for Japanese Research, University of British

Columbia, Canada, February 5–7. Available online at <http: //aparc.stanford .edu/docs/people/emmerson/>.

Encarnation, D. 1992. *Rivals Beyond Trade: America Versus Japan in Global Competition*. Ithaca: Cornell University Press.

Ertman, T. 1998. "Democracy and Dictatorship in Interwar Europe Revisited." *World Politics* 50(3): 475–505.

Esman, M. J. 1972. *Administration and Development in Malaysia*. Ithaca: Cornell University Press.

Esposito, J. L., ed. 1987. *Islam in Asia: Religion, Politics, and Society*. New York: Oxford University Press.

———, and J. Piscatori. 1991. "Democratization and Islam." *Middle East Journal* 45(3): 424–440.

———, and J. O. Voll. 1996. *Islam and Democracy*. New York: Oxford University Press.

Eulau, H. 1962. "Comparative Political Analysis: A Methodological Note." *Midwest Journal of Political Science* 6(4): 397–407.

Evans, G. 1992. "Internal Colonialism in the Central Highlands of Vietnam." *Sojourn* 7(2): 274–304.

Evans, P. 1995. *Embedded Autonomy*. Princeton: Princeton University Press.

———. 1997. "The Eclipse of the State? Reflections on Stateness in an Era of Globalization." *World Politics* 50(1): 62–87.

———, D. Rueschemeyer, and T. Skocpol, eds. 1985. *Bringing the State Back In*. Cambridge: Cambridge University Press.

Eyal, G., I. Szelenyi, and E. Townsley. 1998. *Making Capitalism Without Capitalists*. London: Verso.

Fall, B. 1963. *The Two Viet-Nams*. New York: Praeger.

Farhi, F. 1990. *States and Urban-Based Revolution: Iran and Nicaragua*. Urbana: University of Illinois Press.

Fealy, G. 2001. "Review of Robert W. Hefner, *Civil Islam: Muslims and Democratization in Indonesia*." *Contemporary Southeast Asia* 23(2): 363–368.

———. 2004. "Islamic Radicalism in Indonesia: The Faltering Revival?" In *Southeast Asian Affairs 2004*. Singapore: Institute of Southeast Asian Studies.

Fearon, J. D., and D. D. Laitin. 2000. "Violence and the Social Construction of Ethnic Identity." *International Organization* 54(4): 845–877.

Federspiel, H. M. 1998. *Indonesia in Transition: Muslim Intellectuals and National Development*. Commack: Nova Science.

Fei, J., and G. Ranis. 1964. *Development of the Labor Surplus Economy*. Homewood: Irwin.

Feierabend, I., and R. Feierabend. 1972 [1966]. "Systemic Conditions of Political Aggression: An Application of Frustration-Aggression Theory." In I. Feierabend, R. Feierabend, and T. Gurr, eds., *Anger, Violence, and Politics*.

————, R. Feierabend, and B. Nesvold. 1972 [1969]. "Social Change and Political Violence: Cross-National Patterns." In I. Feierabend, R. Feierabend, and T. Gurr, eds. *Anger, Violence, and Politics.*

————, R. Feierabend, and T. Gurr, eds. 1972. *Anger, Violence, and Politics.* Englewood Cliffs: Prentice Hall.

Feillard, A. 1997. "Traditionalist Islam and the State in Indonesia: The Road to Legitimacy and Renewal." In R. Hefner and P. Horvatich, eds., *Islam in an Era of Nation-States.*

Fein, H. 1993. "Revolutionary and Antirevolutionary Genocides: A Comparison of State Murders in Democratic Kampuchea, 1975 to 1979, and in Indonesia, 1965 to 1966." *Comparative Studies in Society and History* 35(4): 796–823.

Feith, H. 1957. *The Indonesian Elections of 1955.* Ithaca: Cornell Modern Indonesia Project.

————. 1962. *The Decline of Constitutional Democracy in Indonesia.* Ithaca: Cornell University Press.

————. 1982. "History, Theory and Indonesia: A Reply to Harry J. Benda." In B. Anderson and A. Kahin, eds., *Interpreting Indonesian Politics.*

Felker, G. 1998. "Upwardly Global? The State, Business, and MNCs in Malaysia and Thailand's Technological Transformation." Ph.D. diss., Woodrow Wilson School, Princeton University.

————. 2004. "Mahathir and the Politics of Economic Policy in Malaysia." In B. Welsh, ed., *Reflections: The Mahathir Years.* Washington, DC: Johns Hopkins University School of Advanced International Studies.

————, and K. S. Jomo. 2003. "New Approaches to Investment Policy in the ASEAN 4." In K. S. Jomo, ed., *Southeast Asian Paper Tigers?* London: Routledge.

Fenno, R. F. 1978. *Home Style: House Members in Their Districts.* Boston: Little, Brown.

Ferejohn, J. 1991. "Rationality and Interpretation: Parliamentary Elections in Early Stuart England." In K. R. Monroe, ed., *The Economic Approach to Politics: A Critical Reassessment of the Theory of Rational Action.* New York: HarperCollins.

Fforde, A. 1989. *The Agrarian Question in North Vietnam, 1974–1979.* Armonk: Sharpe.

————. 2004. "Vietnamese State Owned Enterprises (SOEs): 'Real Property,' Commercial Performance and Political Economy." Working Paper Series 69, Southeast Asia Research Center, City University of Hong Kong.

Filippov, M., P. Ordeshook, and O. Shvetsova. 2004. *Designing Federalism: A Theory of Self-Sustainable Federal Institutions.* Cambridge: Cambridge University Press.

Foran, J. 1992. "A Theory of Third World Social Revolutions: Iran, Nicaragua and El Salvador Compared." *Critical Sociology* 19(2): 3–27.

————, ed. 1997. *Theorizing Revolutions.* New York: Routledge.

Ford, M. 2000. "Challenge to NGOs' Domination of the Indonesian Labour
Movement During the Habibie Interregnum." Paper presented at the Asian
Studies Association of Australia Annual Meeting, Melbourne.

Franzese, R., Jr. 2002. *Macroeconomic Policies of Developed Democracies*. Cambridge:
Cambridge University Press.

Frederick, W. 1989. *Visions and Heat: The Making of the Indonesian Revolution*. Athens: Ohio University Press.

Friedman, J., ed. 1996. *The Rational Choice Controversy*. New Haven: Yale University
Press.

Frieson, K. G. 1996. "The Cambodian Elections of 1993: A Case of Power to the
People?" In R. Taylor, ed., *The Politics of Elections in Southeast Asia*.

Fukuyama, F. 2004. "How Academia Failed the Nation: The Decline of Regional
Studies." *SAISPHERE* (Winter). Available online at <http://www.sais-jhu
.edu/pubaffairs/publications/saisphere/winter04/index.html>.

Funston, J. 2000. "Malaysia's Tenth Elections: Status Quo, Reformasi or Islamization?" *Contemporary Southeast Asia* 22(1): 23–59.

Furnivall, J. S. 1944 [1939]. *Netherlands India: A Study of Plural Economy*. Cambridge:
Cambridge University Press.

———. 1956 [1948]. *Colonial Policy and Practice: A Comparative Study of Burma and
Netherlands India*. New York: New York University Press.

———. 1991 [1939]. *The Fashioning of Leviathan: The Beginnings of British Rule in
Burma* (ed. Gehan Wijeyewardane). Canberra: Department of Anthropology,
Australian National University.

Gainsborough, M. 2003a. "Corruption and the Politics of Decentralization in Vietnam." *Journal of Contemporary Asia* 33: 69–84.

———. 2003b. *Changing Political Economy of Vietnam: The Case of Ho Chi Minh City*.
London: RoutledgeCurzon.

Geddes, B. 1999a. "Authoritarian Breakdown: Empirical Test of a Game Theoretic
Argument." Paper presented at the Annual Meeting of the American Political
Science Association, Atlanta.

———. 1999b. "What Do We Know About Democratization After Twenty Years?"
Annual Review of Political Science 2: 115–144.

Geertz, C. 1960. *The Religion of Java*. Chicago: University of Chicago Press.

———. 1963. *Agricultural Involution: The Processes of Ecological Change in Indonesia*.
Berkeley: University of California Press.

———. 1968. *Islam Observed: Religious Development in Morocco and Indonesia*. Chicago and London: University of Chicago Press.

———. 1973a [1963]. "The Integrative Revolution: Primordial Sentiments and
Civil Politics in the New States." In *The Interpretation of Cultures: Selected Essays*.
New York: Basic Books.

———. 1973b. *The Interpretation of Cultures: Selected Essays*. New York: Basic Books.

———. 1983. *Local Knowledge: Further Essays in Interpretive Anthropology.* New York: Basic Books.

Gellner, E. 1983. *Nations and Nationalism.* Oxford: Blackwell.

———. 1994. *Conditions of Liberty: Civil Society and Its Rivals.* London: Penguin.

George, A., and A. Bennett. 2005. *Case Studies and Theory Development in the Social Sciences.* Cambridge, MA: MIT Press.

George, T. J. S. 1980. *Revolt in Mindanao: The Rise of Islam in Philippine Politics.* Kuala Lumpur: Oxford University Press.

Gereffi, G. 1999. "International Trade and Industrial Upgrading in the Apparel Commodity Chain." *Journal of International Economics* 48: 37–70.

Gerring, J. 2001. *Social Science Methodology: A Criterial Framework.* New York: Cambridge University Press.

———. 2003. "Interview with Clifford Geertz." *Qualitative Methods* 1(2): 24–28.

Girling, J. 1981. *The Bureaucratic Polity in Modernizing Societies: Similarities, Differences, and Prospects in the ASEAN Region.* Singapore: Institute of Southeast Asian Studies.

Glassman, J. 1999. "State Power Beyond the 'Territorial Trap': The Internationalization of the State." *Political Geography* 18(6): 669–696.

———. 2004. "Economic 'Nationalism' in a Post-Nationalist Era: The Political Economy of Economic Policy in Post-Crisis Thailand." *Critical Asian Studies* 36(1): 37–64.

Golden, M. 2002. "Electoral Connections: The Effect of the Personal Vote on Political Patronage, Bureaucracy and Legislation in Postwar Italy." *British Journal of Political Science* 33(2): 189–202.

Goldstone, J. 1980. "Theories of Revolution: The Third Generation." *World Politics* 32(3): 425–453.

———. 1997. "Methodological Issues in Comparative Macrosociology." *Comparative Social Research* 16: 107–120.

———. 2001. "Toward a Fourth Generation of Revolutionary Theory." *Annual Review of Political Science* 4: 139–187.

———. 2003. "Comparative Historical Analysis and Knowledge Accumulation in the Study of Revolutions." In J. Mahoney and D. Rueschemeyer, eds., *Comparative Historical Analysis in the Social Sciences.*

Goldthorpe, J. 1997. "Current Issues in Comparative Macrosociology: A Debate on Methodological Issues." *Comparative Social Research* 16: 1–26.

Gomez, E. T. 1998. "Authoritarianism, Elections and Political Change in Malaysia." *Public Policy* 2(3): 113–144.

———, ed. 2002. *Political Business in East Asia.* London: Routledge.

———, and K. S. Jomo. 1997. *Malaysia's Political Economy.* Cambridge: Cambridge University Press.

Goodwin, J. 1997. "The Libidinal Constitution of a High-Risk Social Movement: Affectual Ties and Solidarity in the Huk Rebellion, 1946 to 1954." *American Sociological Review* 62(1): 53–69.

———. 2001. *No Other Way Out: States and Revolutionary Movements, 1945–1991.* New York: Cambridge University Press.

Goss, J., D. Burch, and R. Rickson. 2000. "Agro-Food Restructuring and Third World Transnationals: Thailand, the CP Group and the Global Shrimp Industry." *World Development* 28(3): 513–530.

Gourevitch, P. 2003. "The Politics of Corporate Governance Regulation." *Yale Law Journal* 112: 101–152.

Gowing, P. 1979. *Muslim Filipinos: Heritage and Horizon.* Quezon City: New Day.

———, and R. D. McAmis. 1974. "Irresistible Forces, Immovable Objects." In P. Gowing and R. D. McAmis, eds., *The Muslim Filipinos.* Manila: Solidaridad.

Grabher, G., and D. Stark. 1997. *Restructuring Networks in Post-Socialism.* Oxford: Oxford University Press.

Green, D., and I. Shapiro. 1994. *Pathologies of Rational Choice Theory.* New Haven: Yale University Press.

Greenhalgh, S. 1994. "De-Orientalizing the Chinese Family Firm." *American Ethnologist* 21(4): 746–770.

Greif, A. 1994. "Cultural Beliefs and the Organization of Society: A Historical and Theoretical Reflection on Collectivist and Individualist Societies." *Journal of Political Economy* 102: 912–950.

Grossholtz, J. 1964. *Politics in the Philippines.* Boston: Little, Brown.

Gunaratna, R. 2002. *Inside Al Qaeda.* New York: Columbia University Press.

Gunn, G. 1988. *Political Struggles in Laos (1939–1954).* Bangkok: Duang Kamol.

———. 1990. *Rebellions in Laos.* Boulder: Westview.

Gurr, T. 1970. *Why Men Rebel.* Princeton: Princeton University Press.

Habermas, J. 1974 [1964]. "The Public Sphere: An Encyclopedia Article." *New German Critique* 1(3): 49–55.

Hadiz, V. 1997. *Workers and the State in New Order Indonesia.* New York: Routledge.

———. 2002. "Globalization, Labour, and Economic Crisis: Insights from Southeast Asia." *Asian Business and Management* 1: 249–266.

Haggard, S. 1990. *Pathways from the Periphery.* Princeton: Princeton University Press.

———. 1994. "Business, Politics, and Policy in Northeast and Southeast Asia." In A. MacIntyre, ed., *Business and Government in Industrializing Asia.*

———. 1999. "Governance and Growth: Lessons from the Asian Economic Crisis." *Asian-Pacific Economic Literature* 13(2): 30–42.

———. 2000. *The Political Economy of the Asian Financial Crisis.* Washington, DC: Institute for International Economics.

———, and R. Kaufman. 1995. *The Political Economy of Democratic Transitions.* Princeton: Princeton University Press.

Hall, D. 2003. "The International Political Ecology of Industrial Shrimp Aquaculture and Industrial Plantation Forestry in Southeast Asia." *Journal of Southeast Asian Studies* 34(2): 251–265.

Hall, J. A. 1995. "In Search of Civil Society." In J. A. Hall, ed., *Civil Society: Theory, History, Comparison.* Cambridge: Polity.

Hall, P. A. 2003. "Aligning Ontology and Methodology in Comparative Research." In J. Mahoney and D. Rueschemeyer, eds., *Comparative Historical Analysis in the Social Sciences.*

———, and D. Soskice. 2001. *Varieties of Capitalism: The Institutional Foundations of Comparative Advantage.* New York: Oxford University Press.

Hamayotsu, K. 2002. "Islam and Nation Building in Southeast Asia: Malaysia and Indonesia in Comparative Perspective." *Pacific Affairs* 75(3): 353–375.

Hamilton, G., ed. 1991. *Business Networks and Economic Development in East and Southeast Asia.* Hong Kong: Center of Asian Studies, University of Hong Kong.

Hamilton-Hart, N. 2000a. "The Singapore State Revisited." *Pacific Review* 13(2): 195–216.

———. 2000b. "Thailand and Globalization." In S. Kim, ed., *East Asia and Globalization.* Lanham: Rowman and Littlefield.

———. 2002. *Asian States, Asian Bankers: Central Banking in Southeast Asia.* Ithaca: Cornell University Press.

———. 2005. "The Regionalization of Southeast Asian Business: Transnational Networks in National Contexts." In T. J. Pempel, ed., *Remapping East Asia.*

Hammer, E. 1954. *The Struggle for Indochina.* Stanford: Stanford University Press.

Harff, B., and T. Gurr. 1988. "Toward Empirical Theory of Genocides and Politicides: Identification and Measurement of Cases Since 1945." *International Studies Quarterly* 32(3): 359–371.

———, and T. Gurr. 2004. *Ethnic Conflict in World Politics.* 2nd ed. Boulder: Westview.

Harper, T. N. 1999. *The End of Empire and the Making of Malaya.* Cambridge: Cambridge University Press.

Harrison, L. E. 1992. *Who Prospers? How Cultural Values Shape Economic and Political Success.* New York: Basic Books.

Harriss, J. 1982. *Rural Development, Theories of Peasant Economy and Agrarian Change.* London: Hutchinson University Library.

———, J. Hunter, and C. M. Lewis, eds. 1995. *The New Institutional Economics and Third World Development.* New York: Routledge.

Hart, G. 1986. *Power, Labor, and Livelihood: Processes of Change in Rural Java.* Berkeley: University of California Press.

———. 1991. "Engendering Everyday Resistance: Gender, Patronage and Production Politics in Rural Malaysia." *Journal of Peasant Studies* 19(1): 93–121.

———, A. Turton, and B. White. 1989. *Agrarian Transformations: Local Processes and the State in Southeast Asia.* Berkeley: University of California Press.

Hasan, N. 2002. "Faith and Politics: The Rise of the Laskar Jihad in the Era of Transition in Indonesia." *Indonesia* 73: 145–169.

Hassall, G., and C. Saunders, eds. 1997. *The People's Representatives: Electoral Systems in the Asia Region.* Sydney: Allen and Unwin.

Hassan, S. 2002. "Political Non-governmental Organizations: Ideals and Realities." In K. W. F. Loh and K. B. Teik, eds., *Democracy in Malaysia: Discourses and Practices.* Richmond: Curzon.

Hatch, W., and K. Yamamura. 1996. *Asia in Japan's Embrace: Building a Regional Production Alliance.* New York: Cambridge University Press.

Hawes, G. 1987. *The Philippine State and the Marcos Regime: The Politics of Export.* Ithaca: Cornell University Press.

———. 1990. "Theories of Peasant Revolution: A Critique and Contribution from the Philippines." *World Politics* 42(2): 261–298.

———, and H. Liu. 1993. "Explaining the Dynamics of the Southeast Asian Political Economy: State, Society, and the Search for Economic Growth." *World Politics* 45(4): 629–660.

Hayami, Y., and M. Kikuchi. 1981. *Asian Village Economy at the Crossroads: An Economic Approach to Institutional Change.* Tokyo: University of Tokyo Press.

———, A. R. Quisumbing, and L. Adriano. 1990. *Toward an Alternative Land Reform Paradigm: A Philippine Perspective.* Manila: Ateneo de Manila University Press.

Hedman, E. E. 1997. "In Search of Oppositions: South East Asia in Focus." *Government and Opposition* 32(4): 578–597.

———. 1998. "In the Name of Civil Society: Contesting Free Elections in the Post-colonial Philippines." Ph.D. diss., Cornell University.

———. 2001. "Contesting State and Civil Society: Southeast Asian Trajectories." *Modern Asian Studies* 35(4): 921–951.

Hefner, R. W. 1990. *The Political Economy of Mountain Java.* Berkeley: University of California Press.

———. 1993. "Islam, State, and Civil Society: ICMI and the Struggle for the Indonesian Middle Class." *Indonesia* 56 (October): 1–35.

———. 1997. "Islamization and Democratization in Indonesia." In R. W. Hefner and P. Horvatich, eds., *Islam in an Era of Nation-States.*

———. 2000. *Civil Islam: Muslims and Democratization in Indonesia.* Princeton: Princeton University Press.

———, and P. Horvatich, eds. 1997. *Islam in an Era of Nation-States.* Honolulu: University of Hawaii Press.

Henderson, E., and J. D. Singer. 2000. "Civil War in the Post-Colonial World, 1946–92." *Journal of Peace Research* 37(3): 275–299.

Heng, P. K. 1996. "Chinese Responses to Malay Hegemony in Peninsular Malaysia 1957–96." *Tonan Ajia Kenkyu* 34(3): 32–55.

Henin, B. 2002. "Agrarian Change in Vietnam's Northern Upland Region." *Journal of Contemporary Asia* 32(1): 3–29.

Herbst, J. 1989. "How the Weak Succeed: Tactics, Political Goods, and Institutions in the Struggle over Land in Zimbabwe." In F. Colburn, ed., *Everyday Forms of Peasant Resistance*.

———. 2000. *States and Power in Africa*. Princeton: Princeton University Press.

Herrera, Y. M. 2004. *Imagined Economies: The Sources of Russian Regionalism*. New York: Cambridge University Press.

Heryanto, A. 1998. "Ethnic Identities and Erasure: Chinese Indonesians in Public Culture." In J. Kahn, ed., *Southeast Asian Identities: Culture and the Politics of Representation in Indonesia, Malaysia, Singapore, and Thailand*. Singapore: Institute of Southeast Asian Studies.

———. 1999. "The Years of Living Luxuriously: Identity Politics of Indonesia's New Rich." In M. Pinches, ed., *Culture and Privilege in Capitalist Asia*. London: Routledge.

———, and S. K. Mandal. 2003a. "Challenges to Authoritarianism in Indonesia and Malaysia." In A. Heryanto and S. K. Mandal, eds., *Challenging Authoritarianism in Southeast Asia*.

———, and S. K. Mandal, eds. 2003b. *Challenging Authoritarianism in Southeast Asia*. New York: RoutledgeCurzon.

Hewison, K. 1986. "Capital in the Thai Countryside: The Sugar Industry." *Journal of Contemporary Asia* 16(1): 3–17.

———. 1989. *Bankers and Bureaucrats: Capital and the Role of the State in Thailand*. New Haven: Yale University Southeast Asia Studies.

———. 1999. "Political Space in Southeast Asia: 'Asian-Style' and Other Democracies." *Democratization* 6(1): 224–245.

———. 2000. "Thailand's Capitalism Before and After the Economic Crisis." In R. Robison et al., eds. *Politics and Markets in the Wake of the Asian Crisis*.

———. 2001. "Nationalism, Populism, Dependency: Old Ideas for a New Southeast Asia?" Hong Kong: City University of Hong Kong Southeast Asia Research Centre Working Papers No. 4.

———. 2005. "Neo-Liberalism and Domestic Capital: The Political Outcomes of the Economic Crisis in Thailand." *Journal of Development Studies* 41(2): 310–330.

———, R. Robison, and G. Rodan, eds. 1993. *Southeast Asia in the 1990s: Authoritarianism, Democracy, and Capitalism*. Sydney: Allen and Unwin.

———, and G. Rodan. 1996. "The Ebb and Flow of Civil Society and the Decline of the Left in Southeast Asia." In G. Rodan, ed., *Political Oppositions in Industrialising Asia*.

———, and R. Robison, eds. 2006. *East Asia and the Trials of Neo-Liberalism*. London: Routledge.

Hicken, A. D. 2002. "Parties, Pork and Policy: Policymaking in Developing Democracies." Ph.D. diss., University of California, San Diego.

———. 2004. "Asia: General Overview." In J. Colomer, ed., *Handbook of Electoral System Choice*. New York: Palgrave.

———. 2006. "Party Fabrication: Constitutional Reform and the Rise of Thai Rak Thai." *Journal of East Asian Studies* 6(3): 381–408.

———. 2007a. "How Do Rules and Institutions Encourage Vote Buying?" In F. C. Schaffer, ed., *Elections for Sale*.

———. 2007b. "How Effective Are Institutional Reforms?" In F. C. Schaffer, ed., *Elections for Sale*.

———, and B. Ritchie. 2002. "The Origin of Credibility Enhancing Institutions in Southeast Asia." Paper presented at the Annual Meeting of the American Political Science Association, Boston.

———, and Y. Kasuya. 2003. "A Guide to the Constitutional Structures and Electoral Systems of East, South, and Southeast Asia." *Electoral Studies* 22(1): 121–151.

Higgott, R. 1998. "The Asian Economic Crisis: A Study in the Politics of Resentment." *New Political Economy* 33: 333–356.

———. 2000. "The Political Economy of Globalisation in East Asia: The Salience of 'Region Building.'" In K. Olds et al., eds., *Globalisation and the Asia-Pacific*. London: Routledge.

———, and R. Robison. 1985. "Theories of Development and Underdevelopment: Implications for the Study of Southeast Asia." In R. Higgott and R. Robison, eds., *Southeast Asia: Essays in the Political Economy of Structural Change*. London: Routledge.

Hikam, M. A. S. 1996. *Demokrasi dan Civil Society*. Jakarta: LP3ES.

———. 2000. "'Civil Society' Sebagai Proyek Pencerahan." *Tashwirul Afkar* 7: 83–87.

Hinton, W. 1966. *Fanshen: A Documentary of Revolution in a Chinese Village*. New York: Monthly Review Press.

Hirsch, P. 1990. *Development Dilemmas in Rural Thailand*. New York: Oxford University Press.

Hirschman, C. 1986. "The Making of Race in Colonial Malaya: Political Economy and Racial Ideology." *Sociological Forum* 1(2): 330–361.

———. 1987. "The Meaning and Measurement of Ethnicity in Malaysia: An Analysis of Census Classifications." *Journal of Asian Studies* 46(3): 555–582.

———. 2003. "The Development of the Social Sciences Prior to Globalization and Some Thoughts on the Future." In A. Reid, ed., *Southeast Asian Studies*.

———, C. F. Keyes, and K. Hutterer, eds. 1992. *Southeast Asian Studies in the Balance*. Ann Arbor: Association for Asian Studies.

Hoadley, J. S. 1975. *The Military in the Politics of Southeast Asia*. Cambridge, MA: Schenkman.

Hobsbawm, E., and T. Ranger, eds. 1983. *Invention of Tradition*. New York: Cambridge University Press.

Hobson, J. 2000. *The State and International Relations*. New York: Cambridge University Press.

———, and M. Ramesh. 2002. "Globalisation Makes of States What States Make of It: Between Agency and Structure in the State/Globalisation Debate." *New Political Economy* 71: 5–22.

Hollnsteiner, M. R. 1963. *The Dynamics of Power in a Philippine Municipality*. Quezon City: Community Development Research Council, University of the Philippines.

———. 1968. "Reciprocity in the Lowland Philippines." In F. Lynch, ed., *Four Readings on Philippine Values*. Quezon City: Ateneo de Manila University Press.

Honna, J. 2003. *Military Politics and Democratization in Indonesia*. New York: RoutledgeCurzon.

Horowitz, D. L. 1985. *Ethnic Groups in Conflict*. Berkeley: University of California Press.

———. 1990a. "Ethnic Conflict Management for Policymakers." In J. Montville, ed., *Conflict and Peacemaking in Multiethnic Societies*.

———. 1990b. "Making Moderation Pay." In J. Montville, ed., *Conflict and Peacemaking in Multiethnic Societies*.

———. 1991. *A Democratic South Africa? Constitutional Engineering in a Divided Society*. Berkeley: University of California Press.

———. 2001. *The Deadly Ethnic Riot*. Berkeley: University of California Press.

Hudson, W. 2003. "Problematizing European Theories of Civil Society." In D. Schak and W. Hudson, eds., *Civil Society in Asia*.

Huntington, S. P. 1968. *Political Order in Changing Societies*. New Haven: Yale University Press.

———. 1984. "Will More Countries Become Democratic?" *Political Science Quarterly* 99(2): 193–218.

———. 1991. *The Third Wave: Democratization in the Late Twentieth Century*. Norman: University of Oklahoma Press.

———. 1996. *The Clash of Civilizations and the Remaking of World Order*. New York: Simon and Schuster.

———. 2004. *Who Are We? The Challenges to America's National Identity*. New York: Simon and Schuster.

Husken, F., and B. White. 1989. "Java: Social Differentiation, Food Production, and Agrarian Control." In G. Hart, A.Turton, B. White, eds., *Agrarian Transformations*.

Hutchcroft, P. D. 1991. "Oligarchs and Cronies in the Philippine State: The Politics of Patrimonial Plunder." *World Politics* 43(3): 414–459.

———. 1998. *Booty Capitalism: The Politics of Banking in the Philippines*. Ithaca: Cornell University Press.

———. 2000a. "Colonial Masters, National Politicos, and Provincial Lords: Central Authority and Local Autonomy in the American Philippines, 1900–1913." *Journal of Asian Studies* 59(2): 277–306.

———. 2000b. "Obstructive Corruption: The Politics of Privilege in the Philippines." In M. H. Khan and K. S. Jomo, eds., *Rents, Rent-Seeking and Economic Development*.

———, and J. Rocamora. 2003. "Strong Demands and Weak Institutions: The Origins and Evolution of the Democratic Deficit in the Philippines." *Journal of East Asian Studies* 3(2): 259–292.

Huynh, K. K. 1982. *Vietnamese Communism 1925–1945.* Ithaca: Cornell University Press.

Ileto, R. C. 1979. *Pasyon and Revolution.* Quezon City: Ateneo de Manila University Press.

———. 1999. "Religion and Anti-Colonial Movements." In N. Tarling, ed., *The Cambridge History of Southeast Asia.* Cambridge: Cambridge University Press.

Imawan, R., 1989. "The Evolution of Political Party Systems in Indonesia: 1900 to 1987." Ph.D. diss., Northern Illinois University.

Inglehart, R. 2000. "Culture and Democracy." In L. E. Harrison and S. P. Huntington, eds., *Culture Matters: How Values Shape Human Progress.* New York: Basic Books.

IRI (International Republican Institute). 2003. "Cambodia 2003: National Assembly Elections" <http://www.iri.org/asia/cambodia/pdfs/Cambodia's%202003%20National%20Assembly%20Elections.pdf>.

Ishii, Y. 1986. *Sangha, State, and Society: Thai Buddhism in History.* Kyoto: Center for Southeast Asian Studies, Kyoto University.

Jackman, R. 1986. "Elections and the Democratic Class Struggle." *World Politics* 39(1): 123–146.

Jackson, K. D. 1978. "Bureaucratic Polity: A Theoretical Framework for the Analysis of Power and Communications in Indonesia." In K. Jackson and L. Pye, eds., *Political Power and Communications in Indonesia.*

———. 1980. *Tradition, Authority, Islam and Rebellion.* Berkeley: University of California Press.

———, and L. Pye, eds. 1978. *Political Power and Communications in Indonesia.* Berkeley: University of California Press.

Jackson, P. A. 1989. *Buddhism, Legitimation, and Conflict: The Political Functions of Urban Thai Buddhism.* Singapore: Institute of Southeast Asian Studies.

———. 1997. "Withering Centre, Flourishing Margins: Buddhism's Changing Political Roles." In K. Hewison, ed., *The Political Change in Thailand: Democracy and Participation.* London: Routledge.

———. 1999. "The Enchanting Spirit of Thai Capitalism: The Cult of Luan Phor Khoon and the Post-Modernization of Thai Buddhism." *South East Asia Research* 7(1): 5–60.

Jacobs, N. 1971. *Modernization Without Development: Thailand as an Asian Case Study*. New York: Praeger.

Jayasuriya, K. 1999. "See Through a Glass, Darkly: Models of the Asian Currency Crisis of 1997–98." In H. Henke and I. Boxhill, eds., *The End of the "Asian Model"?* Amsterdam: John Benjamins.

———. 2002. "The Rule of Law and Governance in East Asia." In M. Beeson, ed., *Reconfiguring East Asia: Regional Institutions and Organizations After the Crisis*. London: RoutledgeCurzon.

———. 2003. "Embedded Mercantilism and Open Regionalism: The Crisis of a Regional Political Project." *Third World Quarterly* 24(2): 339–355.

Jesudason, J. 1996. "The Syncretic State and the Structuring of Oppositional Politics in Malaysia." In G. Rodan, ed., *Political Oppositions in Industrialising Asia*.

———. 1999. "The Resilience of the Dominant Parties of Malaysia and Singapore." In H. Giliomee and C. Simkins, eds., *The Awkward Embrace: The Dominant Party and Democracy in Mexico, South Africa, Malaysia and Taiwan*. Amsterdam: Harwood Academic Publishers.

Johan, K. 1984. *The Emergence of the Malay Administrative Elite*. Singapore: Oxford University Press.

Johnson, C. 1962. *Peasant Nationalism and Communist Power*. Stanford: Stanford University Press.

———. 1975. "Political Science and East Asian Area Studies." In L. Pye, ed., *Political Science and Area Studies: Rivals or Partners*. Bloomington: Indiana University Press.

———. 1982. *MITI and the Japanese Miracle: The Growth of Industrial Policy, 1925–1975*. Stanford: Stanford University Press.

———. 1997. "Preconception vs. Observation, or the Contributions of Rational Choice Theory and Area Studies to Contemporary Political Science." *PS: Political Science and Politics* 30(2): 170–174.

———, and T. Forsyth. 2002. "In the Eyes of the State: Negotiating a 'Right-Based Approach' to Forest Conservation in Thailand." *World Development* 30(9): 1591–1605.

Jomo, K. S. 1986. *A Question of Class: Capital, the State, and Uneven Development in Malaya*. Singapore: Oxford University Press.

———. 2001. "Rethinking the Role of Government Policy in Southeast Asia." In J. Stiglitz and S. Yusuf, eds., *Rethinking the East Asian Miracle*. Washington, DC: Oxford University Press for the World Bank.

———, et al. 1997. *Southeast Asia's Misunderstood Miracle*. Boulder: Westview.

Jones, D. M. 1998. "Democratization, Civil Society, and Illiberal Middle Class Culture in Pacific Asia." *Comparative Politics* 30(2): 147–169.

———, and D. Brown. 1994. "Singapore and the Myth of the Liberalizing Middle Class." *Pacific Review* 7(1): 79–87.

Jones, S. 2005. "The Changing Nature of Jemaah Islamiyah." *Australian Journal of International Affairs* 59(2): 169–178.

Journal of Conflict Resolution. 2005. 49(3–4): 319–633.

Jowitt, K. 1992. *New World Disorder: The Leninist Extinction.* Berkeley: University of California Press.

Kadir, S. 2002. "When the 'Other' Isn't Clear: Islamic Society and the State in Indonesia's Democratic Transition." Paper presented at the Annual Meeting of the American Political Science Association, Boston.

Kahin, A. 1985. "Overview." In A. Kahin, ed., *Regional Dynamics of the Indonesian Revolution.* Honolulu: University of Hawaii Press.

Kahin, G. 1952. *Nationalism and Revolution in Indonesia.* Ithaca: Cornell University Press.

Kalaw-Tirol, L., and S. S. Coronel, eds. 1992. *1992 and Beyond: Forces and Issues in Philippine Elections.* Quezon City: Philippine Center for Investigative Journalism and Ateneo Center for Social Policy and Public Affairs.

Kalyvas, S. N. 1996. *The Rise of Christian Democracy in Europe.* Ithaca: Cornell University Press.

Kang, D. 2003. *Crony Capitalism.* New York: Cambridge University Press.

Kanok Wongtrangan. 1993. *Phakkanmuang Thai* (Thai Political Parties). Bangkok: Chulalongkorn.

Karim, H., and S. N. Hamid, eds. 1984. *With the People! The Malaysian Student Movement 1967–74.* Petaling Jaya: Institute for Social Analysis (INSAN).

Kassim, I. 1979. *Race, Politics and Moderation: A Study of the Malaysian Electoral Process.* Singapore: Times Books International.

Kasuya, Y. 2001. "Party System Linkage: Explaining Its Variation in the Philippine Case." Paper presented at the Annual Meeting of the American Political Science Association, San Francisco.

Katzenstein, P. 1997. "Introduction: Asian Regionalism in Comparative Perspective." In P. Katzenstein and T. Shiraishi, eds., *Network Power: Japan and Asia.* Ithaca: Cornell University Press.

———. 2000. "Varieties of Asian Regionalism." In P. Katzenstein et al., eds., *Asian Regionalism.* Ithaca: East Asia Program, Cornell University.

Katznelson, I., and H. Milner, eds. *Political Science: The State of the Discipline.* New York: Norton.

Kaviraj, S., and S. Khilnani. 2001. "Introduction: Ideas of Civil Society." In S. Kaviraj and S. Khilnani, eds., *Civil Society: History and Possibilities.* New York: Cambridge University Press.

Kell, T. 1995. *The Roots of Acehnese Rebellion, 1989–1992.* Ithaca: Cornell Modern Indonesian Project.

Kelliher, D. 1992. *Peasant Power in China.* New Haven: Yale University Press.

Kerkvliet, B. 1977. *The Huk Rebellion.* Berkeley: University of California Press.

————. 1978. Review of "Popular Uprisings in the Philippines, 1840–1940." *American Political Science Review* 72(2): 771–772.

————. 1979. "Land Reform: Emancipation or Counterinsurgency." In D. Rosenberg, ed., *Marcos and Martial Law in the Philippines.*

————. 1982. "Martial Law in Nueva Ecija Village, the Philippines." *Bulletin of Concerned Asian Scholars* 14 (October/December): 2–19.

————. 1990. *Everyday Politics in the Philippines: Class and Status Relations in a Central Luzon Village.* Berkeley: University of California Press.

————. 1995a. "Rural Society and State Relations." In B. Kerkvliet and D. Porter, eds., *Vietnam's Rural Transformation.* Boulder: Westview.

————. 1995b. "Village-State Relations in Vietnam: The Effect of Everyday Politics of Decollectivization." *Journal of Asian Studies* 54(2): 396–418.

————. 1996. "Contested Meanings of Elections in the Philippines." In R. Taylor, ed., *The Politics of Elections in Southeast Asia.*

————. 1998. "Land Regimes and State Strengths and Weaknesses in the Philippines and Vietnam." In P. Dauvergne, ed., *Weak and Strong States in Asia-Pacific Societies.* Sydney: Allen and Unwin.

————. 2003. "Introduction: Grappling with Organizations and the State." In B. Kerkvliet, R. Heng, and D. Koh, eds., *Getting Organized in Vietnam.*

————. 2005. *The Power of Everyday Politics: How Vietnamese Peasants Transformed National Policy.* Ithaca: Cornell University Press.

————, and R. B. Mojares, eds. 1991. *From Marcos to Aquino: Local Perspectives on Political Transition in the Philippines.* Honolulu: University of Hawaii Press, and Quezon City: Ateneo de Manila University Press.

————, and D. Porter. 1995. *Vietnam's Rural Transformation.* Boulder: Westview.

————, R. Heng, and D. Koh, eds. 2003. *Getting Organized in Vietnam.* Singapore: Institute of Southeast Asian Studies.

Kesselman, M. 1973. "Order of Movement? The Literature of Political Development as Ideology." *World Politics* 26(1): 139–154.

Kessler, C. S. 1978. *Islam and Politics in a Malay State: Kelantan 1838–1969.* Ithaca: Cornell University Press.

————. 1979. "Islam, Society and Political Behaviour: Some Comparative Implications of the Malay Case." *British Journal of Sociology* 23: 33–50.

Kessler, R. 1989. *Rebellion and Repression in the Philippines.* New Haven: Yale University Press.

Keyes, C. F. 1967. *Isan: Regionalism in Northeastern Thailand.* Ithaca: Cornell Thailand Project, Interim Reports Series no. 10.

————. 1971. "Buddhism and National Integration in Thailand." *Journal of Asian Studies* 30(3): 551–568.

————. 1979. "Introduction." In C. F. Keyes, ed., *Ethnic Adaptation and Identity: The Karen on the Thia Frontier with Burma.* Philadelphia: ISHI.

———. 1981. "Dialectics of Ethnic Change." In C. F. Keyes, ed., *Ethnic Change*. Seattle: University of Washington Press.

———. 1987. *Thailand: Buddhist Kingdom as Modern Nation-State*. Boulder: Westview.

———. 1999. "Moral Authority of the Sangha and Modernity in Thailand: Sexual Scandals, Sectarian Dissent, and Political Resistance." In *Socially Engaged Buddhism for the New Millennium*. Bangkok: Sathirakoses-Nagapradipa Foundation and Foundation for Children.

Khan, M. H., and K. S. Jomo, eds. 2000. *Rents, Rent-Seeking and Economic Development*. Singapore: Cambridge University Press.

Kheng, C. B. 1983. *Red Star Over Malaya*. Singapore: Singapore University Press.

Kiefer, T. 1972. *The Tausug: Law and Violence in a Philippine Moslem Society*. New York: Holt, Rinehart and Winston.

Kiernan, B. 1985. *How Pol Pot Came to Power*. London: Verso.

———. 1996. *The Pol Pot Regime*. New Haven: Yale University Press.

Kimura, M. 1992. "Philippine Political Parties and the Party System in Transition: Leaders, Factions and Blocs." *Pilipinas* 18 (Spring): 43–65.

———. 1997. *Elections and Politics Philippines Style: A Case in Lipa*. Manila: De La Salle University Press.

King, D. E. 1996. "New Political Parties in Thailand: A Case Study of the Palang Dharma Party and the New Aspiration Party." Ph.D. diss., University of Wisconsin–Madison.

King, D. Y. 1982. "Indonesia's New Order as a Bureaucratic Polity, a Neo-Patrimonial Regime or a Bureaucratic-Authoritarian Regime: What Difference Does It Make?" In B. Anderson and A. Kahin, eds., *Interpreting Indonesian Politics*.

———. 2003. *Half-Hearted Reform: Electoral Institutions and the Struggle for Democracy in Indonesia*. Westport: Praeger.

King, G., R. Keohane, and S. Verba. 1995. *Designing Social Inquiry*. Princeton: Princeton University Press.

Kitschelt, H., Z. Mansfeldova, R. Markowskis, and G. Toka. 1999. *Post-Communist Party Systems: Competition, Representation, and Inter-Party Cooperation*. Cambridge: Cambridge University Press.

Knight, J. 1992. *Institutions and Social Conflict*. New York: Cambridge University Press.

Knutsen, O. 1998. "The Strength of the Partisan Component of Left-Right Identity: A Comparative Longitudinal Study of Left-Right Party Polarization in Eight West European Countries." *Party Politics* 4: 5–31.

Koh, G., and G. L. Ooi. 2000. "The Relative Authorities of the State and Civil Society." In G. Koh and G. L. Ooi, eds., *State-Society Relations in Singapore*. Singapore: Oxford University Press.

Kohli, A. 1986. "Introduction." In A. Kohli, ed., *The State and Development in the Third World*. Princeton: Princeton University Press.

———. 1987. *The State and Poverty in India*. Cambridge: Cambridge University Press.

———. 1999. "Where Do High-Growth Political Economies Come From? The Japanese Lineage of South Korea's Developmental State." In M. Woo-Cumings, ed., *The Developmental State*. Ithaca: Cornell University Press.

———. 2002. "State, Society and Development." In I. Katznelson and H. Milner, eds., *Political Science*.

———. 2004. *State-Directed Development*. Cambridge: Cambridge University Press.

———, et al. 1996. "The Role of Theory in Comparative Politics: A Symposium." *World Politics* 48(1): 1–49.

Koppel, B., and D. Zurick. 1988. "Rural Transformation and the Future of Agricultural Development Policy in Asia." *Agricultural Administration and Extension* 28: 283–301.

———, J. Hawkins, and W. James. 1994. *Development or Deterioration: Work in Rural Asia*. Boulder: Lynne Rienner.

Kornai, J. 1990. *Vision and Reality, Market and State*. London: Routledge.

Kramol Tongdhamachart. 1982. *Towards a Political Party Theory in Thai Perspective*. Singapore: Maruzen Asia.

Krasner, S. D. 1999. *Sovereignty: Organized Hypocrisy*. Princeton: Princeton University Press.

Kuhonta, E. M. 2003. "The Political Foundations of Equitable Development: State and Party Formation in Malaysia and Thailand." Ph.D. diss., Princeton University.

Kuo, C. 1995. *Global Competitiveness and Industrial Growth in Taiwan and the Philippines*. Pittsburgh: University of Pittsburgh Press.

Kuper, L., and M. G. Smith, eds. 1969. *Pluralism in Africa*. Berkeley: University of California Press.

Kuruvilla, S., and C. Erickson. 2002. "Change and Transformation in Asian Industrial Relations." *Industrial Relations* 41(2): 171–228.

Laakso, M., and R. Taagepera. 1979. "Effective Number of Parties: A Measure with Application to West Europe." *Comparative Political Studies* 12: 3–27.

Laitin, D. D. 1986. *Hegemony and Culture: Politics and Religious Change Among the Yoruba*. Chicago: University of Chicago Press.

———. 1993. "Letter from the Incoming President." *APSA-CP* 4(2): 3, 18.

———. 2000. "Comparative Politics: The State of the Subdiscipline." Paper presented at the Annual Meeting of the American Political Science Association, Washington, DC.

———. 2002. "Comparative Politics: The State of the Subdiscipline." In I. Katznelson and H. Milner, eds., *Political Science*.

———. 2003. "The Perestroikan Challenge to Social Science." *Politics & Society* 31(1): 163–184.

Lake, D., and M. Baum. 2001. "The Invisible Hand of Democracy: Political Control and the Provision of Public Services." *Comparative Political Studies* 34(6): 587–621.

Landa, J. T. 1991. "A Theory of the Ethnically Homogeneous Middleman Group: An Institutional Alternative to Contract Law." *Journal of Legal Studies* 10(2): 349–362.

Landé, C. 1965. *Leaders, Factions and Parties*. New Haven: Southeast Asian Studies, Yale University.

———. 1971. "Party Politics in the Philippines." In G. Guthrie, ed., *Six Perspectives on the Philippines*. Manila: Bookmark.

———. 1996. *Post-Marcos Politics: A Geographic and Statistical Analysis of the 1992 Philippine Elections*. Singapore: Institute of Southeast Asian Studies.

Lange, M., and D. Rueschemeyer, eds. 2005. *States and Development*. New York: Palgrave MacMillan.

Lanzona, V. 2000. "Gender, Sex, Family and Revolution: Women in the Huk Rebellion on the Philippines 1942–1956." Ph.D. diss., University of Wisconsin, Madison.

Laquian, A. A. 1966. *The City in Nation-Building: Politics and Administration in Metropolitan Manila*. Manila: School of Public Administration, University of the Philippines.

Larkin, J. A. 1967. "Place of Local History in Philippine Historiography." *Journal of Southeast Asian History* 8 (September): 306–317.

———. 1972. *The Pampangans: Colonial Society in a Philippine Province*. Berkeley: University of California Press

———. 1993. *Sugar and the Origins of Modern Philippine Society*. Berkeley: University of California Press.

Larson, O. 1968. "Rural Society." In D. Sills, ed., *Encyclopedia of the Social Sciences*, Vol. 13. New York: MacMillan.

Lauridsen, L. 2000. "Industrial Policies, Political Institutions and Industrial Development in Thailand 1959–1991." Working Paper No. 21, International Development Studies, Roskilde University.

Leach, E. 1954. *Political Systems of Highland Burma: A Study of Kachin Social Structure*. Cambridge, MA: Harvard University Press.

Ledgerwood, J. 1998. "Rural Development in Cambodia: The View from the Village." In F. Brown and D. Timberman, eds., *Cambodia and International Community*. Singapore: Asian Society Publications.

———, and J. Vijghen. 2002. "Decision-Making in Rural Khmer Villages." In J. Ledgerwood, ed., *Cambodia Emerges from the Past*. DeKalb: Center for Southeast Asian Studies, Northern Illinois University.

Leheny, D. 2005. "The War on Terrorism in Asia and the Possibility of Secret Regionalism." In T. J. Pempel, ed., *Remapping East Asia*.

Leites, N., and C. Wolf, Jr. 1970. *Rebellion and Authority*. Chicago: Markham.

Leonard, P., and D. Kaneff. 2002. *Post-Socialist Peasant? Rural and Urban Constructions of Identity in Eastern Europe, East Asia and the Former Soviet Union*. Basingstoke: Palgrave.

Leshkowich, A. M. 2000. "Tightly Woven Threads: Gender, Kinship and 'Secret Agency' Among Cloth and Clothing Traders in Ho Chi Minh City's Ben Thanh Market (Vietnam)." Ph.D. diss., Harvard University.

Lev, D. 1967. "Political Parties in Indonesia." *Journal of Southeast Asian History* (March).

———. 1970. "Parties, Functional Groups, and Elections in Indonesia." *Asia* 19 (Autumn).

———. 1972. *Islamic Courts in Indonesia*. Berkeley: University of California Press.

Levine, D. H. 1981. *Religion and Politics in Latin America*. Princeton: Princeton University Press.

———, and S. Mainwaring. 1989. "Religion and Popular Protest in Latin America: Contrasting Experiences." In S. Eckstein, ed., *Power and Popular Protest: Latin American Social Movements*. Berkeley: University of California Press.

Levitsky, S., and L. A. Way. 2002. "The Rise of Competitive Authoritarianism." *Journal of Democracy* 13(2): 51–64.

Lewis, J., ed. 1974. *Peasant Rebellion and Communist Revolution in Asia*. Stanford: Stanford University Press.

———. 1986. "Overview: Development Promotion: A Time for Regrouping." In J. Lewis et al., eds., *Development Strategies Reconsidered: US Third World Policy Perspectives No. 5*. Washington, DC: Overseas Development Council.

Liang, D. 1970. *Philippine Parties and Politics*. San Francisco: Gladstone.

Lichbach, M. 1989. "An Evaluation of 'Does Economic Inequality Breed Political Conflict?' Studies." *World Politics* 41(4): 431–470.

———. 1995. *The Rebel's Dilemma*. Ann Arbor: University of Michigan Press.

———, and T. Gurr. 1981. "The Conflict Process: A Formal Model." *Journal of Conflict Resolution* 25(1): 3–29.

Liddle, R. W. 1970. *Ethnicity, Party and National Integration: An Indonesian Case Study*. New Haven: Yale University Press.

———. 1972. "The 1971 Indonesian Elections: A View from the Village." *Asia* 27 (Autumn): 4–18.

———. 1978. "Indonesia 1977: The New Order's Second General Election." *Asian Survey* 18(2): 175–185.

———. 1985. "Soeharto's Indonesia: Personal Rule and Political Institutions." *Pacific Affairs* 58(1): 68–90.

———. 1987. "The Politics of Shared Growth: Some Indonesian Cases." *Comparative Politics* 19(2): 127–146.

————. 1992. "Indonesia's Democratic Past and Future." *Comparative Politics* 24(4): 443–462.

————. 1996. "The Islamic Turn in Indonesia: A Political Explanation." *Journal of Asian Studies* 55(3): 613–634.

————, ed. 2001. *Crafting Indonesian Democracy*. Indonesian Institute of Science and the Ford Foundation.

————. 2002. "Indonesia's Democratic Transition: Playing by the Rules." In A. Reynolds, ed., *The Architecture of Democracy*. Oxford: Oxford University Press.

————, and S. Mujani. 2004. "Indonesia's Approaching Elections: Politics, Islam, and Public Opinion." *Journal of Democracy* 15(1): 109–123.

Lieberman, E. 2001. "Causal Inference in Historical Institutional Analysis: A Specification of Periodization Strategies." *Comparative Political Studies* 34(9): 1011–1035.

Lieberson, S. 1991. "Small N's and Big Conclusions: An Examination of the Reasoning in Comparative Studies Based on a Small Number of Cases." *Social Forces* 70(2): 307–320.

————. 1994. "More on the Uneasy Case for Using Mill-Type Methods in Small N Comparative Studies." *Social Forces* 72(4): 1225–1237.

Lijphart, A. 1975. "The Comparable-Cases Strategy in Comparative Research." *Comparative Political Studies* 8(2): 158–177.

————. 1977. *Democracy in Plural Societies*. New Haven: Yale University Press.

————. 1990. "The Power-Sharing Approach." In J. Montville, ed., *Conflict and Peacemaking in Multiethnic Societies*.

————. 1994. *Electoral Systems and Party Systems*. New York: Oxford University Press.

————. 1995. "Multiethnic Democracy." In S. M. Lipset et al., eds., *The Encyclopedia of Democracy*. Washington, DC: Congressional Quarterly.

————, R. Rogowski, and K. Weaver. 1993. "Separation of Powers and Cleavage Management." In K. Weaver and B. A. Rockman, eds., *Do Institutions Matter? Government in the United States and Abroad*. Washington, DC: Brookings Institution.

Lim, L. 1983. "Singapore's Success: The Myth of the Free Market Economy." *Asian Survey* 23: 752–764.

————. 1995. "Southeast Asia: Success Through International Openness." In B. Stallings, ed., *Global Change, Regional Response*. New York: Cambridge University Press.

————. 1996. "The Evolution of Southeast Asian Business Systems." *Journal of Asian Business* 12(11): 51–74.

————, and P. Gosling, eds. 1983. *The Chinese in Southeast Asia*. Vol. I, *Ethnicity and Economic Activity*. Singapore: Maruzen Asia.

Linz, J. 1994. *The Failure of Presidential Democracy*. Baltimore: Johns Hopkins University Press.

———, and A. Stepan. 1996. *Problems of Democratic Transition and Consolidation.* Baltimore: Johns Hopkins University Press.

Lipset, S. M. 1959. "Some Social Requisites of Democracy: Economic Development and Political Legitimacy." *American Political Science Review* 53(1): 69–105.

———. 1981 [1960]. *Political Man: The Social Bases of Politics.* Baltimore: Johns Hopkins University Press.

———, and Stein Rokkan, eds. 1967. *Party Systems and Voter Alignments.* New York: Free Press.

Lipton, M. 1977. *Why Poor People Stay Poor.* Cambridge, MA: Harvard University Press.

Liu, H. 1998. "Old Linkages, New Networks: The Globalization of Overseas Chinese Voluntary Associations and Its Implications." *China Quarterly* 155: 582–609.

Loh, F. 2003. "NGOs and Non-Electoral Politics." *Aliran Monthly* 22(11): 2–9.

———. 2005. "Globalization, Development and Democratization in Southeast Asia." In F. Loh and J. Ojendal, eds., *Southeast Asian Responses to Globalization.*

———, and J. Ojendal, eds. 2005. *Southeast Asian Responses to Globalization.* Copenhagen: Nordic Institute of Asian Studies.

Long, N. 1996. "Rural Sociology." In A. Kuper and J. Kuper, eds., *The Social Science Encyclopedia.* London: Routledge.

Lopez-Alves, F. 2000. *State Formation and Democracy in Latin America, 1810–1900.* Durham: Duke University Press.

Luebbert, G. M. 1991. *Liberalism, Fascism, or Social Democracy: Social Classes and the Political Origins of Regimes in Interwar Europe.* New York: Oxford University Press.

Luong, H. V. 1985. "Agrarian Unrest from an Anthropological Perspective: The Case of Vietnam." *Comparative Politics* 17(2): 153–174.

———. 1992. *Revolution in the Village.* Honolulu: University of Hawaii Press.

Lynch, F. 1968. "Social Acceptance." In F. Lynch, ed., *Four Readings on Philippine Values.* Quezon City: Ateneo de Manila University Press.

———. 1984 [1975]. "Big and Little People: Social Class in the Rural Philippines." In A. A. Yengoyan and P. Q. Makil, eds., *Philippine Society and the Individual: Selected Essays of Frank Lynch, 1949–1976.* Ann Arbor: Center for South and Southeast Asian Studies, University of Michigan.

MacDougall, J. 1968. "Shared Burdens: A Study of Communal Discrimination by the Political Parties of Malaysia and Singapore." Ph.D. diss., Harvard University.

Machado, K. 1995. "Japanese Foreign Direct Investment in East Asia: The Expanding Division of Labor and the Future of Regionalism." In S. Chan, ed., *Foreign Direct Investment in a Changing Global Political Economy.* Basingstoke: MacMillan.

———. 1999. "Complexity and Hierarchy in the East Asian Division of Labour: Japanese Technological Superiority and ASEAN Industrial Development." In

K. S. Jomo and G. Felker, eds., *Technology, Competitiveness and the State: Malaysia's Industrial Technology Policies*. London: Routledge.

MacIntyre, A. 1990. *Business and Politics in Indonesia*. St. Leonards: Allen and Unwin.

———, ed. 1994a. *Business and Government in Industrializing Asia*. Ithaca: Cornell University Press.

———. 1994b. "Business, Government and Development: Northeast and Southeast Asian Comparisons." In A. MacIntyre, ed., *Business and Government in Industrializing Asia*.

———. 1994c. "Introduction: Northeast Asian and Southeast Asian Comparisons." In A. MacIntyre, ed., *Business and Government in Industrializing Asia*.

———. 2003. *The Power of Institutions: Political Architecture and Governance*. Ithaca: Cornell University Press.

———, and K. Jayasuriya. 1992. "The Politics and Economics of Economic Policy Reform in South-East Asia and the South-West Pacific." In A. J. MacIntyre and K. Jayasuriya, eds., *The Dynamics of Economic Policy Reform in South-East Asia and the South-West Pacific*. Singapore: Oxford University Press.

Mackerras, C., ed. 2003. *Ethnicity in Asia*. London: RoutledgeCurzon.

Mackie, J. 1992. "The Changing Patterns of Chinese Big Business in Southeast Asia." In R. McVey, ed., *Southeast Asian Capitalists*.

Magadia, J. C. J. 1999. "Interest Representation in Public Policy Deliberations in Post-Authoritarian Philippines." Ph.D. diss., Columbia University.

Mahoney, J. 2000a. "Knowledge Accumulation in Comparative-Historical Analysis: The Case of Democracy and Authoritarianism." Paper presented at workshop on "Comparative-Historical Analysis," Harvard University.

———. 2000b. "Strategies of Causal Inference in Small-N Research." *Sociological Methods and Research* 28(4): 387–424.

———. 2001. *The Legacies of Liberalism: Path Dependence and Political Regimes in Central America*. Baltimore: Johns Hopkins University Press.

———. 2003. "Knowledge Accumulation in Comparative Historical Research: The Case of Democracy and Authoritarianism." In J. Mahoney and D. Rueschemeyer, eds., *Comparative Historical Analysis in the Social Sciences*.

———, and D. Rueschemeyer, eds. 2003. *Comparative Historical Analysis in the Social Sciences*. New York: Cambridge University Press.

Mai, U. 1990. *Peasant Peddlers and Professional Traders: Subsistence Trade in Rural Markets of Minahasa, Indonesia*. Singapore: Institute of Southeast Asian Studies.

Mainwaring, S. P. 1999. *Rethinking Party Systems in the Third Wave of Democratization: The Case of Brazil*. Stanford: Stanford University Press.

———, and T. Scully. 1995. "Introduction." In S. Mainwaring and T. Scully, eds., *Building Democratic Institutions: Party Systems in Latin America*. Stanford: Stanford University Press.

Maldonado, C., et al. 2005. "Dissertations in Comparative Politics 1985–2004." *APSA-CP* 16(2).

Malesky, E. 2004. "Push, Pull, and Reinforcing: The Channels of FDI Influence on Provincial Governance in Vietnam." In B. Kerkvliet and D. G. Marr, eds., *Beyond Hanoi: Local Government in Vietnam*. Singapore: Institute of Southeast Asian Studies.

———. 2005. "Gerrymandering—Vietnamese Style: The Political Geography of Economic Transition." Working Paper, University of California–San Diego, School of International Relations/Pacific Studies.

———. 2007. "Foreign Direct Investors: Agents of Economic Transition." Paper in revision.

———. Forthcoming. "Straight Ahead on Red: How Foreign Direct Investment Empowers Sub-National Leaders." *Journal of Politics*.

Malley, M. 2003. "Indonesia: The Erosion of State Capacity." In R. I. Rotberg, ed., *State Failure and State Weakness in a Time of Terror*. Washington, DC: Brookings Institution.

Manut Wathanakomen. 1986. *Khomunphunthan phakkanmuang patchuban lae phakkanmuang kap kanluaktang pi 2522–2529* (Basic Data on Contemporary Political Parties and on Political Parties in the Elections of 1979–1986). Bangkok: Social Science Association of Thailand.

———, et al. 1988. *Khomunphunthan phakkanmuang patchuban lae phakkanmuang kap kanluaktang pi 2531* (Basic Data on Contemporary Political Parties and on Political Parties in the Elections of 1988). Bangkok: Social Science Association of Thailand.

Marks, T. 1994. *Making Revolution: The Insurgency of the Communist Party of Thailand in Structural Perspective*. Bangkok: White Lotus.

———. 1995. *Maoist Insurgency Since Vietnam*. London: Frank Cass.

Marr, D., and C. White, eds. 1988. *Postwar Vietnam: Dilemmas in Socialist Development*. Ithaca: Cornell Southeast Asia Program Series No. 3.

Marshall, T. H. 1964. *Class, Citizenship, and Social Development*. Garden City: Doubleday.

Martz, J. D. 1964. "Dilemmas in the Study of Latin American Political Parties." *Journal of Politics* 26(3): 509–531.

Maryanov, G. S. 1967. "Political Parties in Mainland Malaya." *Journal of Southeast Asian History* 8(1).

Masuyama, S., and D. Vandenbrink. 2001. "Industrial Restructuring in East Asian Economies for the Twenty-First Century." In S. Masuyama and D. Vandenbrink, eds., *Industrial Restructuring in East Asia: Towards the 21st Century*. Tokyo: Nomura Research Institute.

Matthews, B. 1993. "Buddhism Under a Military Regime: The Iron Heel in Burma." *Asian Survey* 33(4): 408–423.

Mauzy, D. K. 2002. "Electoral Innovation and One-Party-Dominance in Singapore." In J. Hsieh and D. Newman, eds., *How Asia Votes*. New York: Chatham.

Maxfield, S. 1997. *Gatekeepers of Growth: The International Political Economy of Central Banking in Developing Countries*. Princeton: Princeton University Press.

McAdam, D., S. Tarrow, and C. Tilly. 2001. *Dynamics of Contention*. New York: Cambridge University Press.

McAlister, J. 1969. *Vietnam: The Origins of Revolution*. New York: Knopf.

———, and P. Mus. 1970. *The Vietnamese and Their Revolution*. New York: Harper and Row.

McCargo, D., ed. 2002. *Reforming Thai Politics*. Copenhagen: Nordic Institute of Asian Studies.

McCarthy, J. 2004. "Changing to Gray: Decentralization and the Emergence of Volatile Socio-Legal Configurations in Central Kalimantan, Indonesia." *World Development* 32(7): 1199–1223.

McCoy, A., ed. 1993a. *An Anarchy of Families: State and Family in the Philippines*. Madison: Center for Southeast Asian Studies, University of Wisconsin.

———. 1993b. "An Anarchy of Families: The Historiography of State and Family in the Philippines." In A. McCoy, ed., *An Anarchy of Families*.

———. 1999. *Closer Than Brothers: Manhood at the Philippine Military Academy*. New Haven: Yale University Press.

McDermott, G. 2002. *Embedded Politics: Industrial Networks and Institutional Change in Post-Communism*. Ann Arbor: University of Michigan Press.

McKay, J. 1982. "An Exploratory Synthesis of Primordial and Mobilizationist Approaches to Ethnic Phenomena." *Ethnic and Racial Studies* 5(4): 395–420.

McKendrick, D. G., R. Doner, and S. Haggard. 2000. *From Silicon Valley to Singapore: Location and Competitive Advantages in the Disk Drive Industry*. Stanford: Stanford University Press.

McKenna, T. M. 1998. *Muslim Rulers and Rebels: Everyday Politics and Armed Separatism in the Southern Philippines*. Berkeley: University of California Press.

McKeown, T. 1999. "Case Studies and the Statistical Worldview." *International Organization* 53(1).

McRae, K., ed. 1974. *Consociational Democracy: Political Accommodation in Segmented Societies*. Toronto: McClelland and Stewart.

McVey, R. 1964a. *The Rise of Indonesian Communism*. Ithaca: Cornell University Press.

———. 1964b. "The Southeast Asian Insurrectionary Movements." In C. E. Black and T. P. Thornton, eds., *Communism and Revolution*. Princeton: Princeton University Press.

———. 1982. "The Beamtenstaat in Indonesia." In B. Anderson and A. Kahin, eds., *Interpreting Indonesian Politics*.

———. 1989. "Identity and Rebellion Among Southern Thai Muslims." In A. D. W. Forbes, ed., *The Muslims of Thailand*. Gaya: Center for South East Asian Studies.

Bibliography 399

———. 1992a. "The Materialization of the Southeast Asian Entrepreneur." In R. McVey, ed., *Southeast Asian Capitalists*.

———, ed. 1992b. *Southeast Asian Capitalists*. Ithaca: Southeast Asia Program, Cornell University.

———. 1998. "Globalization, Marginalization, and the Study of Southeast Asia." In *Southeast Asian Studies: Reorientations*. Ithaca: Southeast Asia Program, Cornell University.

———. 2000a. "Of Greed and Violence, and Other Signs of Progress." In R. McVey, ed., *Money and Power in Provincial Thailand*.

———. ed, 2000b. *Money and Power in Provincial Thailand*. Honolulu: University of Hawaii Press.

Means, G. P. 1970. *Malaysian Politics*. London: University of London Press.

Medina, L. F., and S. Stokes. 2002. "Clientelism as a Political Monopoly." Working paper.

Meier, G., and J. Stiglitz, eds. 2001. *Frontiers of Development Economics*. New York: Oxford University Press.

Mellor, J. W. 1986. "Agriculture on the Road to Industrialization." In J. P. Lewis and V. Kallab, eds., *Development Strategies Reconsidered*. New Brunswick: Transaction.

Midgal, J. 1974. *Peasants, Politics, and Revolution*. Princeton: Princeton University Press.

———. 1988. *Strong Societies and Weak States*. Princeton: Princeton University Press.

———. 2001. *State in Society*. Cambridge: Cambridge University Press.

———, A. Kohli, and V. Shue, eds. 1994. *State Power and Social Forces*. Cambridge: Cambridge University Press.

Milne, R. S. 1967. *Government and Politics in Malaysia*. Boston: Houghton Mifflin.

Milner, A. C. 2002 [1995]. *The Invention of Politics in Colonial Malaya*. New York: Cambridge University Press.

MINDS, ed. 1997. *Masyarakat Madani: Satu Tinjauan Awal*. Ampang, Selangor: Malaysian Institute of Development Strategies.

Missingham, B. 2003. *The Assembly of the Poor in Thailand*. Bangkok: Silkworm.

Mitchell, E. J. 1968. "Inequality and Insurgency: A Statistical Study of South Vietnam." *World Politics* 20(3): 421–438.

———. 1969. "Some Econometrics of the Huk Rebellion." *American Political Science Review* 63(4): 1159–1171.

Mittleman, J. H. 2000. *The Globalization Syndrome: Transformation and Resistance*. Princeton: Princeton University Press.

———, and N. Othman, eds. 2001. *Capturing Globalization*. London: Routledge.

Moise, E. 1983. *Land Reform in China and North Vietnam*. Chapel Hill: University of North Carolina Press.

Molloy, I. 1988. "The Decline of the Moro National Liberation Front in the Southern Philippines." *Journal of Contemporary Asia* 18(1): 59–76.

Monroe, K., ed. 2005. *Perestroika! The Raucous Rebellion in Political Science*. New Haven: Yale University Press.

Montinola, G. 1999. "Parties and Accountability in the Philippines." *Journal of Democracy* 10(1): 126–140.

Montville, J., ed. 1990. *Conflict and Peacemaking in Multiethnic Societies*. Lexington: Lexington Books.

Moon, C., and S. Rhyu. 2000. "The State, Structural Rigidity, and the End of Asian Capitalism." In R. Robison et al., eds., *Politics and Markets in the Wake of the Asian Crisis*.

Moore, B. 1966. *Social Origins of Dictatorship and Democracy*. Boston: Beacon.

Morley, J. W., ed. 1999. *Driven by Growth: Political Change in the Asia-Pacific Region*. Armonk: Sharpe.

Morse, R. A., ed. 1984. *Southeast Asian Studies: Options for the Future*. Washington, DC: Wilson Center.

Mortimer, R. 1974. *Indonesian Communism Under Sukarno*. Ithaca: Cornell University Press.

Mujani, S., and R. W. Liddle. 2004. "Politics, Islam, and Public Opinion." *Journal of Democracy* 15(1): 109–123.

Muller, E. 1985. "Income Inequality, Regime Repressiveness, and Political Violence." *American Sociological Review* 50(1): 47–61.

———, and M. Seligson. 1985. "Inequality and Insurgency." *American Sociological Review* 81(2): 425–452.

Munck, G. 1998. "Canons of Research Design in Qualitative Analysis." *Studies in Comparative International Development* 33(3): 18–45.

———, and R. Snyder. 2004. "What Has Comparative Politics Accomplished?" *APSA-CP* 15(2): 26–31.

———, and R. Snyder. 2005. "Debating the Direction of Comparative Politics: An Analysis of Leading Journals." Paper presented at the Annual Meeting of the American Political Science Association, Washington, DC.

Murashima, E., et al., eds. 1991. *The Making of Modern Thai Political Parties*. Tokyo: Institute of Developing Economies, Joint Research Program Series No. 86.

Murphy, A. 2000. "Indonesia and Globalization." In S. Kim, ed., *East Asia and Globalization*. Lanham: Rowman and Littlefield.

Muscat, R. 1994. *The Fifth Tiger: A Study of Thai Development Policy*. Armonk: Sharpe.

Mutalib, H. 2000. "The Socio-Economic Dimension in Singapore's Quest for Security and Stability." *Pacific Affairs* 75(1): 39–56.

———. 2003. *Political Parties in Singapore*. Singapore: Eastern Universities Press.

Nagata, J. 1974. "What Is a Malay? Situational Selection of Ethnic Identity in a Plural Society." *American Ethnologist* 1(2): 331–350.

Nair, S. 1995. "States, Societies and Societal Movements: Power and Resistance in Malaysia and Singapore." Ph.D. diss., University of Minnesota.

Nakamura, M., S. Siddique, and O. F. Bajunid, eds. 2001. *Islam and Civil Society in Southeast Asia.* Singapore: Institute of Southeast Asian Studies.

Narine, S. 1997. "ASEAN and the ARF: The Limits of the 'ASEAN Way.'" *Asian Survey* 37(10): 961–978.

Nash, M. 1963. "Party Building in Upper Burma." *Asian Survey* 3(4): 197–121.

———. 1965. *The Golden Road to Modernity: Village Life in Contemporary Burma.* New York: Wiley.

Naya, S. F., and J. Tan. 1995. *Asian Transitional Economies.* Singapore: Institute of Southeast Asian Studies.

NDI (National Democratic Institute for International Affairs). 2001. "The Political Process and the 2001 Parliamentary Elections in Singapore." <http://www .accessdemocracy.org/library/1326_sgp_2001parlelect.pdf>.

Nee, V. 1989. "A Theory of Market Transition: From Redistribution to Markets in State Socialism." *American Sociological Review* 54: 663–681.

Neher, C. D. 1976. "Constitutionalism and Elections in Thailand." In C. D. Neher, ed., *Modern Thai Politics.* Cambridge, MA: Schenkman.

———, and R. Marlay. 1995. *Democracy and Development in Southeast Asia.* Boulder: Westview.

Nelson, M. H. 1998. *Central Authority and Local Democratization in Thailand.* Bangkok: White Lotus.

———. 2000. "The Senate Elections of March 4, 2000 (etc., etc.)." *KPI Newsletter* 1(3): 3–7.

Nelson, R., and S. G. Winter. 1982. *An Evolutionary Theory of Economic Change.* Cambridge, MA: Harvard University Press.

Nesadurai, H. E. S. 2003. *Globalisation, Domestic Politics and Regionalism: The ASEAN Free Trade Area.* London: Routledge.

Ness, G. 1967. *Bureaucracy and Rural Development in Malaysia.* Berkeley: University of California Press.

The New Shorter Oxford English Dictionary [NSOED]. 1993. Oxford: Clarendon.

Nicholas, C. 2000. *The Orang Asli and the Contest for Resources: Indigenous Politics, Development and Identity in Peninsular Malaysia.* Copenhagen: International Work Group for Indigenous Affairs.

Niemi, R. G., and J. F. Hsieh. 2002. "Counting Candidates: An Alternative to the Effective N." *Party Politics* 8(1): 75–99.

Noble, G. 1998. *Collective Action in East Asia: How Ruling Parties Shape Industrial Policy.* Ithaca: Cornell University Press.

Noer, D. 1973. *The Modernist Muslim Movement in Indonesia: 1900–1942.* Singapore: Oxford University Press.

———. 1978. *Administration of Islam in Indonesia.* Ithaca: Cornell Modern Indonesia Project.

Nohlen, D., F. Grotz, and C. Hartmann, eds. 2001. *Elections in Asia and the Pacific: A Data Handbook*. Vol. 2. Oxford: Oxford University Press.

Nordlinger, E. A. 1972. *Conflict Regulation in Divided Societies*. Cambridge, MA: Harvard University, Center for International Affairs.

North, R. C. 1953. *Moscow and the Chinese Communists*. Stanford: Stanford University Press.

Norton, A. R. 1995. *Civil Society in the Middle East*. Vol. 1. Leiden: Brill.

———. 1996. *Civil Society in the Middle East*. Vol. 2. Leiden: Brill.

———. 1999. "Associational Life: Civil Society in Authoritarian Political Systems." In M. Tessler, J. Nachtwey, and A. Banda, eds., *Area Studies and Social Science*.

Nowak, T. C., and K. A. Snyder. 1974. "Economic Concentration and Political Change in the Philippines." In B. Kerkvliet, ed., *Political Change in the Philippines*. Hawaii: University of Hawaii Press.

Numazaki, I. 2000. "Chinese Business Enterprise as Inter-Family Partnership: A Comparison with the Japanese Case." In Chan Kwok Bun, ed., *Chinese Business Networks: State, Economy and Culture*. Singapore: Prentice Hall, Pearson Education Asia.

O'Ballance, E. 1964. *Indo-China War 1945–1954: A Study in Guerilla Warfare*. London: Faber and Faber.

———. 1966. *Malaya: The Communist Insurgent War, 1948–60*. London: Faber and Faber.

O'Donnell, G. A. 1973. *Modernization and Bureaucratic-Authoritarianism*. Berkeley: University of California Institute of International Studies.

———. 1988. *Bureaucratic Authoritarianism: Argentina, 1966–1973, in Comparative Perspective*. Berkeley: University of California Press.

———, and P. C. Schmitter. 1986. *Transitions from Authoritarian Rule: Tentative Conclusions About Uncertain Democracies*. Baltimore: Johns Hopkins University Press.

Ockey, J. 1991. "Business Leaders, Gangsters and the Middle Class." Ph.D. diss., Cornell University.

———. 2000. "The Rise of Local Power in Thailand: Provincial Crime, Elections and the Bureaucracy." In R. McVey, ed., *Money and Power in Provincial Thailand*.

———. 2002. "Civil Society and Street Politics in Historical Perspective." In D. McCargo, ed., *Reforming Thai Politics*.

———. 2003. "Change and Continuity in the Thai Political Party System." *Asian Survey* 43(4): 663–680.

Oi, J. 1989. *State and Peasant in Contemporary China*. Berkeley: University of California Press.

———. 1993. "Reform and Urban Bias in China." *Journal of Development Studies* 29: 129–147.

———, and A. Walder. 1999. *Property Rights and Economic Reform in China*. Stanford: Stanford University Press.

Ong, A. 1995. "State Versus Islam: Malay Families, Women's Bodies, and the Body Politics in Malaysia." In A. Ong and M. Peletz, eds., *Bewitching Women, Pious Men: Gender and Body Politics in Southeast Asia*. Berkeley: University of California Press.

———. 1999. "Muslim Feminism: Citizenship in the Shelter of Corporatist Islam." *Citizenship Studies* 3(3): 355–371.

Oorthuizen, J. 2003. *Water, Works, and Wages: The Everyday Politics of Irrigation Management Reform in the Philippines*. Hyderabad: Orient Longman.

Ordeshook, P. C., and O. Shvetsova. 1994. "Ethnic Heterogeneity, District Magnitude and the Number of Parties." *American Journal of Political Science* 38(1): 100–123.

Osborne, M. E. 1965. *Strategic Hamlets in South Viet-Nam*. Ithaca: Southeast Asia Program, Cornell University.

Othman, N., and C. Kessler. 2000. "Capturing Globalization: Prospects and Projects." *Third World Quarterly* 21(6): 1013–1026.

Oxhorn, P. 1994. "Where Did All the Protesters Go? Popular Mobilization and the Transition to Democracy in Chile." *Latin American Perspectives* 82(21): 49–68.

Ozawa, T. 1999. "Pacific Economic Integration and the 'Flying Geese' Paradigm." In A. M. Rugman and G. Boyd, eds., *Deepening Integration in the Pacific Economies*. Cheltenham: Elgar.

———, et al. 2001. "The Internet Revolution, the 'McCluhan' Stage of Catch-Up, and Institutional Reforms in Asia." *Journal of Economic Issues* 35(2): 289–298.

Paige, J. 1970. "Inequality and Insurgency in Vietnam: A Re-Analysis." *World Politics* 23(1): 24–37.

———. 1975. *Agrarian Revolution*. New York: Free Press.

Panggabean, S. 2000. "'Civil Society' Sebagai Kawasan Kebebasan." *Tashwirul Afkar* 7: 88–95.

Parreñas, R. S. 2001. "Transgressing the Nation-State: The Partial Citizenship and 'Imagined (Global) Community' of Migrant Filipina Domestic Workers." *Signs: Journal of Women in Culture and Society* 26(4): 29–54.

Parsa, M. 2000. *States, Ideologies, and Social Revolutions: A Comparative Analysis of Iran, Nicaragua and the Philippines*. New York: Cambridge University Press.

Parsonage, J. 1997. "Trans-State Developments in South-East Asia: Subregional Growth Zones." In G. Rodan, K. Hewison, and R. Robison, eds., *The Political Economy of Southeast Asia*.

Parsons, T. 1982. "Evolutionary Universals in Society." In L. H. Matthews, ed., *Talcott Parsons on Institutions and Social Evolution*. Chicago: University of Chicago Press.

Pasuk Phongpaichit. 1999. "Civilising the State: State, Civil Society, and Politics in Thailand." Amsterdam: The Wim Wertheim Lecture, Center for Asian Studies.

———. 2000. "*Chao Sua, Chao Pho, Chao Thi*: Lords of Thailand's Transition." In R. McVey, ed., *Money and Power in Provincial Thailand*.

———, and C. Baker. 1995. *Thailand: Economy and Politics.* Kuala Lumpur: Oxford University Press.

———, and C. Baker. 2004. *Thaksin: The Business of Politics in Thailand.* Bangkok: Silkworm.

Peletz, M. 2002. *Islamic Modern: Religious Courts and Cultural Politics in Malaysia.* Princeton: Princeton University Press.

Pelras, C. 2000. "Patron-Client Ties Among the Bugis and Makassarese of South Sulawesi." *Bijdragen tot de Taal-, Land- en Volkenkunde* 156(3): 15–54.

Peluso, N. 1992. *Rich Forests, Poor People: Resource Control and Resistance in Java.* Berkeley: University of California Press.

———, P. Vandergeest, and L. Potter. 1995. "Social Aspects of Forestry in Southeast Asia: A Review of Postwar Trends in the Scholarly Literature." *Journal of Southeast Asian Studies* 26(1): 196–218.

Pelzer, K. 1978. "Swidden Cultivation in Southeast Asia: Historical, Ecological, and Economic Perspectives." In P. Kunstadter, E. C. Chapman, and S. Babhasri, eds., *Farmers in the Forest.* Honolulu: University of Hawaii Press.

Pempel, T. J. 1998. *Regime Shift: Comparative Dynamics of the Japanese Political Economy.* Ithaca: Cornell University Press.

———, ed. 2005. *Remapping East Asia: The Construction of a Region.* Ithaca: Cornell University Press.

Peralta, L. V. 1977. *Philippine Elections from the Pre-Spanish Period to 1907.* Quezon City: University of the Philippines.

Perry, E. 1980. "States and Social Revolution." *Journal of Asian Studies* 39(3): 533–535.

Persson, T., and G. Tabellini. 1999. "The Size and Scope of Government: Comparative Politics with Rational Politicians." *European Economic Review* 43(4–6): 699–735.

Pettee, G. S. 1938. *The Process of Revolution.* New York: Harper and Row.

Phillips, H. 1965. *Thai Peasant Personality.* Berkeley: University of California Press.

Pholsena, V. 2002. "Nation/Representation: Ethnic Classification and Mapping Nationhood in Contemporary Laos." *Asian Ethnicity* 3(2): 175–197.

Pierson, P., and T. Skocpol. 2002. "Historical Institutionalism in Contemporary Political Science." In I. Katznelson and H. Milner, eds., *Political Science.*

Pike, D. 1966. *Viet Cong: The Organization and Techniques of the National Liberation Front of South Vietnam.* Cambridge, MA: MIT Press.

Pingali, P. 1997. "From Subsistence to Commercial Production Systems: The Transformation of Asian Agriculture." *American Journal of Agricultural Economics* 79(2): 638–646.

Piper, N., and A. Uhlin. 2002. "Transnational Advocacy Networks, Female Labor Migration and Trafficking in East and Southeast Asia: A Gendered Analysis of Opportunities and Obstacles." *Asian and Pacific Migration Journal* 11(2): 171–195.

———, and A. Uhlin, eds. 2004. *Transnational Activism in Asia: Problems of Power and Democracy*. London: Routledge.

Pisan Suriyamongkol, and J. Guyot. n.d. *The Bureaucratic Polity at Bay*. Bangkok: Graduate School of Public Administration, National Institute of Development Administration.

Pitsuwan, S. 1982. "Islam and Malay Nationalism: A Case Study of the Malay Muslims of Southern Thailand." Ph.D. diss., Harvard University.

Polanyi, K. 1944. *The Great Transformation*. Boston: Beacon.

Popkin, S. 1979. *The Rational Peasant*. Berkeley: University of California Press.

Porter, G. 1993. *Vietnam: The Politics of Bureaucratic Socialism*. Ithaca: Cornell University Press.

Posner, D. N. 2003. "The Colonial Origins of Ethnic Cleavages: The Case of Linguistic Divisions in Zambia." *Comparative Politics* 35(2): 127–146.

———. 2005. *Institutions and Ethnic Politics in Africa*. Cambridge: Cambridge University Press.

Powell, G. B. 2000. *Elections as Instruments of Democracy*. New Haven: Yale University Press.

Preecha Hongkrailvet. 1981. *Phakkanmuang lae banha phakkanmuang thai* (Political Parties and the Problems of Thai Political Parties). Bangkok: Thai Watthanaphanit.

Pretty, J. 1995. *Regenerating Agriculture: Policies and Practice for Sustainability and Self-Reliance*. Washington, DC: Henry.

Pritchett, L. 2003. "A Toy Collection, a Socialist Star, and a Democratic Dud?" In D. Rodrik, ed., *In Search of Prosperity*.

Pryor, F. 1991. "Third World Decollectivization: Guyana, Nicaragua, and Vietnam." *Problems of Communism* 40(3): 97–109.

———. 1992. *The Red and the Green: The Rise and Fall of Collectivized Agriculture in Marxist Regimes*. Princeton: Princeton University Press.

Przeworski, A., and F. Limongi. 1997. "Modernization: Theories and Facts." *World Politics* 49(2): 155–183.

———, M. Alvarez, and J. Cheibub. 2000. *Democracy and Development: Political Institutions and Well-Being in the World, 1950–1990*. New York: Cambridge University Press.

Puthucheary, M. 1978. *The Politics of Administration: The Malaysian Experience*. Singapore: Oxford University Press.

Putnam, R. D. 1993. *Making Democracy Work: Civic Tradition in Modern Italy*. Princeton: Princeton University Press.

Pye, L. W. 1956. *Guerrilla Communism in Malaya*. Princeton: Princeton University Press.

———. 1960. "The Politics of Southeast Asia." In G. A. Almond and J. S. Coleman, eds., *The Politics of Developing Areas*. Princeton: Princeton University Press.

————. 1962. *Politics, Personality and Nation Building: Burma's Search for Identity.* New Haven: Elliott's.

————, with M. W. Pye. 1985. *Asian Power and Politics.* Cambridge, MA: Harvard University Press.

Race, J. 1972. *War Comes to Long An.* Berkeley: University of California Press.

————. 1974. "Toward an Exchange of Theory of Revolution." In J. Lewis, ed., *Peasant Rebellion and Communist Revolution in Asia.*

Rachagan, S. S. 1980. "The Development of the Electoral System." In H. Crouch et al., eds., *Malaysian Politics and the 1978 Election.*

————. 1984. "Ethnic Representation and the Electoral System." In S. H. Ali, ed., *Ethnicity, Class and Development: Malaysia.* Kuala Lumpur: Persatuan Sains Sosial Malaysia.

————. 1993. *Law and the Electoral Process in Malaysia.* Kuala Lumpur: University of Malaya Press.

Ragin, C. 1987. *The Comparative Method.* Berkeley: University of California Press.

————. 1997. "Turning the Tables: How Case-Oriented Research Challenges Variable-Oriented Research." *Comparative Social Research* 16: 27–42.

————. 2000. *Fuzzy-Set Social Science.* Chicago: University of Chicago Press.

Rahman, A. R. 1994. *The Conduct of Elections in Malaysia.* Kuala Lumpur: Berita.

Ramage, D. 1995. *Politics in Indonesia: Democracy, Islam and the Ideology of Tolerance.* London: Routledge.

Ramsay, A. 1986. "Thai Domestic Politics and Foreign Policy." In K. Jackson, S. Paribatra, and J. S. Djiwandono, eds., *ASEAN in Regional and Global Context.* Berkeley: Institute of East Asian Studies, University of California.

Rashid, S., and M. G. Quibria. 1995. "Is Land Reform Passé? With Special Reference to Asian Agriculture." In M. G. Quibria, ed., *Critical Issues in Asian Development.* New York: Oxford University Press.

Rasiah, R. 1994. "Flexible Production Systems and Local Machine Tool Subcontracting: Electronics Components Transnationals in Malaysia." *Cambridge Journal of Economics* 18(3): 278–298.

————. 2000. "Politics, Institutions and Flexibility: Microelectronics Transnationals and Machine Tool Linkages in Malaysia." In F. Deyo, R. Doner, and E. Hershberg, eds., *Economic Governance and the Challenge of Flexibility in East Asia.* Boulder: Rowman and Littlefield.

————. 2003. "Manufacturing Export Growth in Indonesia, Malaysia and Thailand." In K. S. Jomo, ed., *Southeast Asian Paper Tigers? From Miracle to Debacle and Beyond.* London: Routledge.

Ravenhill, J. 2003. "The New Bilateralism in the Asia Pacific." *Third World Quarterly* 24(2): 255–282.

Reid, A. 2003a. "Southeast Asian Studies: Decline or Rebirth?" In A. Reid, ed., *Southeast Asian Studies.*

———, ed. 2003b. *Southeast Asian Studies: Pacific Perspectives*. Tempe: Program for Southeast Asian Studies, Arizona State University.

Reilly, B. 2001. *Democracy in Divided Societies: Electoral Engineering for Conflict Management*. Cambridge: Cambridge University Press.

———. 2003a. "Political Engineering of Parties and Party Systems." Paper presented at the Annual Meeting of the American Political Science Association.

———. 2003b. "Political Parties and Political Engineering in the Asia Pacific Region." *Asia Pacific Issues* 71: 1–8.

Rex, J. 1980 [1959]. "The Plural Society in Sociological Theory." In H. Evers, ed., *Sociology of South-East Asia*. Kuala Lumpur: Oxford University Press.

Reynolds, A. 1999. "Women in the Legislatures and Executives of the World: Knocking at the Highest Glass Ceiling." *World Politics* 51(4): 547–572.

Reynolds, F. E. 1978. "Legitimization and Rebellion: Thailand's Civic Religion and the Student Uprising of October, 1973." In B. L. Smith, ed., *Religion and Legitimization of Power in Thailand, Laos, and Burma*. Chambersburg: ANIMA.

Rice, E. E. 1988. *Wars of the Third Kind: Conflict in Underdeveloped Countries*. Berkeley: University of California Press.

Richter, L. 1982. *Land Reform and Tourism Development: Policy-Making in the Philippines*. Cambridge, MA: Schenkman.

Riedel, J., and W. S. Turley. 1999. "The Politics and Economics of Transition to an Open Market Economy in Vietnam." OECD Technical Papers No. 152.

Riedinger, J. 1995. *Agrarian Reform in the Philippines*. Stanford: Stanford University Press.

Rigg, J. 1994. "Redefining the Village and Rural life: Lessons from Southeast Asia." *Geographical Journal* 160(2): 123–135.

———. 2001. *More Than the Soil: Rural Change in Southeast Asia*. Harlow: Prentice Hall.

———. 2003. *Southeast Asia: The Human Landscape of Modernization and Development*. London: Routledge.

Riggs, F. 1966. *Thailand: The Modernization of a Bureaucratic Polity*. Honolulu: East-West Center.

Riker, W. 1962. *The Theory of Political Coalitions*. Westport: Greenwood.

———. 1990. "Political Choice and Rational Choice." In J. Alt and K. Shepsle, eds., *Perspectives on Positive Political Economy*. New York: Cambridge University Press.

Risse-Kappen, T. 1994. "Ideas Do Not Float Freely: Transnational Coalitions, Domestic Structures, and the End of the Cold War." *International Organization* 48(2): 185–214.

Ritchie, B. 2001. "Innovation Systems, Collective Dilemmas, and the Formation of Technical and Intellectual Capital in Malaysia, Singapore, and Thailand." *International Journal of Business and Society* 2(2): 21–48.

Rix, A. 1993. "Japan and the Region: Leading from Behind." In R. Higgott, R. Leaver, and J. Ravenhill, eds., *Pacific Economic Relations in the 1990s: Cooperation or Conflict?* Boulder: Lynne Rienner.

Robertson, P. S., Jr. 1996. "The Rise of the Rural Network Politician: Will Thailand's New Elite Endure?" *Asian Survey* 36(9): 924–941.

Robison, R. 1986. *Indonesia: The Rise of Capital*. London: Allen and Unwin.

———, and D. Goodman, eds. 1996. *The New Rich in Asia*. London: Routledge.

———, et al., eds. 2000. *Politics and Markets in the Wake of the Asian Crisis*. New York: Routledge.

———, G. Rodan, et al. 2002. "Transplanting the Regulatory State in Southeast Asia: A Pathology of Rejection." *Southeast Asia Research Centre Working Papers Series* 33.

———, and V. Hadiz. 2004. *Reorganising Power in Indonesia: The Politics of Oligarchy in an Age of Markets*. London: RoutledgeCurzon.

———, and V. Hadiz. 2005. "Neo-Liberal Reforms and Illiberal Consolidations: The Indonesian Paradox." *Journal of Development Studies* 41(2): 220–241.

———, and K. Hewison. 2005. "Introduction: East Asia and the Trials of Neo-Liberalism." *Journal of Development Studies* 41(2): 183–196.

Rocamora, J. 1978. "The Structural Imperative of Authoritarian Rule." *Southeast Asia Chronicle* 65: 7–19.

———. 1998. "Philippine Political Parties, Electoral System and Political Reform." *Philippines International Review* 1(1).

Rock, M. 2000. "Thailand's Old Bureaucratic Polity and Its New Semi-Democracy." In M. H. Khan and K. S. Jomo, eds., *Rents, Rent-Seeking and Economic Development*.

Rodan, G. 1989. *The Political Economy of Singapore's Industrialization: National State and International Capital*. London: Macmillan.

———. 1993. "Reconstructing Divisions of Labour: Singapore's New Regional Emphasis." In R. Higgott, R. Leaver, and J. Ravenhill, eds., *Pacific Economic Relations in the 1990s: Cooperation or Conflict?* Boulder: Lynne Reinner.

———, ed. 1996. *Political Oppositions in Industrialising Asia*. New York: Routledge.

———. 1997a. "Civil Society and Other Political Possibilities in Southeast Asia." *Journal of Contemporary Asia* 27(2): 156–178.

———. 1997b. "Singapore: Economic Diversification and Social Divisions." In G. Rodan, K. Hewison, and R. Robison, eds., *The Political Economy of Southeast Asia: An Introduction*.

———. 1998. "The Internet and Political Control in Singapore." *Political Science Quarterly* 113(1): 63–89.

———. 2001. "Singapore: Globalisation and the Politics of Economic Restructuring." In G. Rodan, K. Hewison, and R. Robison, eds., *The Political Economy of Southeast Asia: Conflicts, Crises, and Change*.

———. 2002. "Do Markets Need Transparency? The Pivotal Cases of Singapore and Malaysia." *New Political Economy* 71: 23–46.

————. 2003. "Embracing Electronic Media but Suppressing Civil Society: Authoritarian Consolidation in Singapore." *Pacific Review* 16(4): 503–534.

————, K. Hewison, and R. Robison, eds. 1997. *The Political Economy of Southeast Asia: An Introduction.* Oxford: Oxford University Press.

————, K. Hewison, and R. Robison, eds. 2001. *The Political Economy of Southeast Asia: Conflicts, Crises, and Change.* Oxford: Oxford University Press.

Rodrik, D., ed. 2003. *In Search of Prosperity: Analytic Narratives on Economic Growth.* Princeton: Princeton University Press.

Roff, W. R. 1994. *The Origins of Malay Nationalism.* 2nd ed. Kuala Lumpur: Oxford University Press.

Rohde, D. 2001. "Indonesia Unraveling." *Foreign Affairs* 80(1): 110–124.

Rosenberg, D., ed. 1979. *Marcos and Martial Law in the Philippines.* Ithaca: Cornell University Press.

Ross, M. 1999. "The Political Economy of the Resource Curse." *World Politics* 51(2): 297–322.

————. 2001. *Timber Booms and Institutional Breakdown in Southeast Asia.* Cambridge: Cambridge University Press.

————. 2003. "Oil, Drugs, and Diamonds: The Varying Roles of Natural Resources in Civil War." In K. Ballentine and J. Sherman, eds., *The Political Economy of Armed Conflict.* Boulder: Lynne Rienner.

————. 2004. "How Do Natural Resources Influence Civil War? Evidence from 13 Cases." *International Organization* 58(1): 35–67.

————. 2005. "Resources and Rebellion in Aceh, Indonesia." In P. Collier and N. Sambanis, eds., *Understanding Civil War.* Washington, DC: World Bank.

Rosser, A. 2002. *The Politics of Economic Liberalisation in Indonesia: State, Market and Power.* Richmond: Curzon.

————. 2003. "Coalitions, Convergence and Governance Reform in Indonesia." *Third World Quarterly* 24(2): 319–337.

Rudolph, S. 1997. "Introduction: Religion, States, and Transnational Civil Society." In S. Rudolph and J. Piscatori, eds., *Transnational Religion and Fading States.* Boulder: Westview.

————. 2005. "The Imperialism of Categories: Situating Knowledge in a Globalizing World." *Perspectives on Politics* 3(1): 5–14.

Rueschemeyer, D., E. Stephens, and J. Stephens. 1992. *Capitalist Development and Democracy.* Chicago: University of Chicago Press.

————, and J. Stephens. 1997. "Comparing Historical Sequences—A Powerful Tool for Causal Analysis." *Comparative Social Research* 16: 55–72.

Ruggie, J. 1983. "International Regimes, Transactions, and Change: Embedded Liberalism in the Postwar Economic Order." In S. Krasner, ed., *International Regimes.* Ithaca: Cornell University Press.

Russo, A. 1972. "Economic and Social Correlates of Government Control in South

Vietnam." In I. Feierabend, R. Feierabend, and T. Gurr, eds., *Anger, Violence, and Politics.*

Rustow, D. 1970. "Transitions to Democracy: Toward a Dynamic Model." *Comparative Politics* 2(2): 337–363.

Rutten, M. 1999. "Rural Capitalists in India, Indonesia, and Malaysia: Three Cases, Two Debates, One Analysis?" *Sojourn* 14(1): 57–58.

Rutten, R. 1996. "Popular Support for the Revolutionary Movement CPP-NPA: Experiences in a Hacienda in Negros Occidental, 1978–1995." In P. Abinales, ed., *The Revolution Falters.* Ithaca: Southeast Asia Program, Cornell University.

Ryter, L. 1998. "Pemuda Pancasila: The Last Loyalist Free Men of Suharto's Order?" *Indonesia and the Malay World* 66: 45–73.

Sachsenroder, W., and U. E. Frings, eds. 1998. *Political Party Systems and Democratic Development in East and Southeast Asia. Volume I: Southeast Asia.* Aldershot: Ashgate.

Samson, A. 1971–1972. "Army and Islam in Indonesia." *Pacific Affairs* 44(4): 545–565.

Sansom, R. 1970. *The Economics of Insurgency in the Mekong Delta of Vietnam.* Cambridge, MA: MIT Press.

Saravanamuttu, J. 1997. "Transforming Civil Societies in ASEAN Countries (with special focus on Malaysia and Singapore)." CIS Working Paper 1997-8, Center for International Studies, University of Toronto.

Sartori, G. 1970. "Concept Misformation in Comparative Politics." *American Political Science Review* 64(4): 1033–1053.

———. 1976. *Parties and Party Systems.* Cambridge: Cambridge University Press.

Savolainen, J. 1994. "The Rationality of Drawing Big Conclusions Based on Small Samples: In Defense of Mill's Methods." *Social Forces* 72(4): 1217–1224.

Scaff, A. H. 1955. *The Philippine Answer to Communism.* Stanford: Stanford University Press.

Schaffer, F. C., ed. 2007. *Elections for Sale: The Causes, Consequences, and Reform of Vote Buying.* Boulder: Lynne Rienner.

Schak, D., and W. Hudson., eds. 2003a. *Civil Society in Asia.* Burlington: Ashgate.

———, and W. Hudson. 2003b. "Civil Society in Asia." In D. Schak and W. Hudson, eds., *Civil Society in Asia.*

Schmitter, P. 1992. "The Consolidation of Democracy and the Representation of Social Groups." *American Behavioral Scientist* 35(4/5): 422–449.

———. 1997. "Civil Society East and West." In L. Diamond et al., eds., *Consolidating the Third Wave Democracies.* Baltimore: Johns Hopkins University Press.

Schneider, B. 2004. *Business Politics and the State in Twentieth-Century Latin America.* New York: Cambridge University Press.

Schock, K. 2005. *Unarmed Insurrections: People Power Movements in Nondemocracies.* Minneapolis: University of Minnesota Press.

Schwartz, B. 1951. *Chinese Communism and the Rise of Mao*. Cambridge, MA: Harvard University Press.

Scott, G., Jr. 1990. "A Resynthesis of Primordial and Circumstantialist Approaches to Ethnic Group Solidarity." *Ethnic and Racial Studies* 13(2): 147–171.

Scott, J. 1972a. *Comparative Political Corruption*. Englewood Cliffs: Prentice Hall.

———. 1972b. "Patron-Client Politics and Political Change in Southeast Asia." *American Political Science Review* 66(1): 91–113.

———. 1976. *The Moral Economy of the Peasant: Rebellion and Subsistence in Southeast Asia*. New Haven: Yale University Press.

———. 1977a. "Peasant Revolution: A Dismal Science." *Comparative Politics* 9(2): 231–248.

———. 1977b. "Hegemony and the Peasantry." *Politics and Society* 7(3): 267–296.

———. 1977c. "Protest and Profanity: Agrarian Revolt and the Little Tradition." *Theory and Society* 4(1): 1–39 and 4(2): 210–242.

———. 1979. "Revolution in the Revolution: Peasants and Commissars." *Theory and Society* 7(1–2): 97–134.

———. 1985. *Weapons of the Weak: Everyday Forms of Peasant Resistance*. New Haven: Yale University Press.

———. 1990. *Domination and the Arts of Resistance: Hidden Transcripts*. New Haven: Yale University Press.

———. 1998. *Seeing Like a State*. New Haven: Yale University Press.

———, and B. Kerkvliet, eds. 1986. *Everyday Forms of Peasant Resistance in South-East Asia*. London: Frank Cass.

Sears, L., ed. 2007. *Knowing Southeast Asian Subjects*. Seattle: University of Washington Press.

Seidman, I. 1998. *Interviewing as Qualitative Research*. New York: Teachers College Press.

Selden, M. 1993. "Agrarian Development Strategies in China and Vietnam." In W. Turley and M. Selden, eds., *Reinventing Vietnamese Socialism*. Boulder: Westview.

Shapiro, I., et al., eds. 2004. *Problems and Methods in the Study of Politics*. New York: Cambridge University Press.

Shefter, M. 1994. *Political Parties and the State*. Princeton: Princeton University Press.

Sherlock, S. 2004. "The 2004 Indonesian Elections: How the System Works and What the Parties Stand For. A Report on Political Parties." Center for Democratic Institutions.

Shue, V. 1977. *The Reach of the State*. Stanford: Stanford University Press.

———. 1988. *The Reach of the State*. Stanford: Stanford University Press.

Shugart, M. S. 1999. "Efficiency and Reform: A New Index of Government Responsiveness and the Conjunction of Electoral and Economic Reform." Working Paper.

————, and S. Mainwaring. 1997. *Presidentialism and Democracy in Latin America.* Cambridge: Cambridge University Press.

————, and M. P. Wattenberg, eds. 2000. *Mixed-Member Electoral Systems: The Best of Both Worlds?* Oxford: Oxford University Press.

Sidel, J. T. 1996. "Siam and Its Twin? Democratization and Bossism in Contemporary Thailand and the Philippines." *IDS Bulletin* 27(2).

————. 1998. "*Macet Total:* Logics of Circulation and Accumulation in the Demise of Indonesia's New Order." *Indonesia* 66: 159–194.

————. 1999. *Capital, Coercion, and Crime: Bossism in the Philippines.* Stanford: Stanford University Press.

————. 2001. "It Takes a *Madrasah?* Habermas Meets Bourdieu in Indonesia." Review of Robert Hefner's *Civil Islam: Muslims and Democratization in Indonesia. South East Asia Research* 9(1): 109–122.

————. 2003. "Other Schools, Other Pilgrimages, Other Dreams: The Making and Unmaking of *Jihad* in Southeast Asia." In J. Siegel and A. Kahin, eds., *Southeast Asia over Three Generations.* Ithaca: Southeast Asia Program, Cornell University.

Silverstein, J. 1977. *Burma: Military Rule and the Politics of Stagnation.* Ithaca: Cornell University Press.

————. 1980. *Burmese Politics: The Dilemma of National Unity.* New Brunswick: Rutgers University Press.

Silvey, R., and R. Elmhirst. "Engendering Social Capital: Women Workers and Rural-Urban Networks in Indonesia's Crisis." *World Development* 31(5): 865–879.

Sisk, T. D. 1996. *Power Sharing and International Mediation in Ethnic Conflicts.* Washington, DC: United States Institute of Peace Press.

Sjamsuddin, N. 1985. *The Republican Revolt: A Study of the Acehnese Rebellion.* Singapore: Institute of Southeast Asian Studies.

Skinner, W. 1958. *Leadership and Power in the Chinese Community of Thailand.* Ithaca: Cornell University Press.

————. 1996. "Creolized Chinese Societies in Southeast Asia." In A. Reid, K. Alilunas-Rodgers, and J. Cushman, eds., *Sojourners and Settlers.* Sydney: Paul.

Skocpol, T. 1979. *States and Social Revolutions.* New York: Cambridge University Press.

————. 1982. "What Makes Peasants Revolutionary?" *Comparative Politics* 14: 351–375.

————. 1985. "Bringing the State Back In: Strategies of Analysis in Current Research." In P. Evans, D. Rueschemeyer, and T. Skocpol, eds., *Bringing the State Back In.*

————, and M. Somers. 1980. "The Uses of Comparative History in Macrosocial Inquiry." *Comparative Studies in Society and History* 22(2): 174–197.

Slater, D. 2003. "Iron Cage in an Iron Fist: Authoritarian Institutions and the Personalization of Power in Malaysia." *Comparative Politics* 36(1): 81–101.

———. 2004. "Indonesia's Accountability Trap: Party Cartels and Presidential Power After Democratic Transition." *Indonesia* 78: 61–92.

———. 2005. "Ordering Power: Contentious Politics, State-Building, and Authoritarian Durability in Southeast Asia." Ph.D. diss., Emory University.

———. 2006. "The Architecture of Authoritarianism: Southeast Asia and the Regeneration of Democratization Theory." *Taiwan Journal of Democracy* 2(2): 1–22.

Smail, J. 1964. *Bandung in the Early Revolution, 1945–1945.* Ithaca: Cornell Modern Indonesia Project.

Small, M., and D. Singer. 1982. *The Resort to Arms: International and Civil Wars 1916–1980.* Beverly Hills: Sage.

Smith, B. 2007. *Hard Times in the Land of Plenty: Oil Booms and Opposition in Late Developing States.* Ithaca: Cornell University Press.

Smith, D. E. 1965. *Religion and Politics in Burma.* Princeton: Princeton University Press.

Smith, M. G. 1965. *The Plural Society in the British West Indies.* Berkeley: University of California Press.

Snyder, J. 2000. *From Voting to Violence: Democratization and Nationalist Conflict.* New York: Norton.

So, A. 2001. "The 'Globalization Project' and East Asia: An Opportunity or a Trap?" In J. C. Hsiung, ed., *Twenty-First Century World Order and the Asia-Pacific.* New York: Palgrave.

Social Science Research Council (SSRC). 2001. "Rethinking Social Science Research on the Developing World in the 21st Century." Conference report (June): 35.

Solingen, E. 1999. "ASEAN, *Quo Vadis?* Domestic Coalitions and Regional Cooperation." *Contemporary Southeast Asia* 21(1): 30–53.

Sombat Chantornvong. 1993. *Luaktang wikrit: Panha lae thang ok* (Thai Elections in Crisis: Problems and Solutions). Bangkok: Kobfai.

———. 2000. "Local Godfathers in Thai Politics." In R. McVey, ed., *Money and Power in Provincial Thailand.*

SSRC Staff, Roundtable Participants. 2000. *Weighing the Balance: Southeast Asian Studies Ten Years After.* New York: Social Science Research Council Southeast Asia Program.

Stark, D. 1992. "Path Dependency and Privatization Strategies in East-Central Europe." *East European Politics and Societies* 6(1): 17–54.

———. 1996. "Recombinant Property in East European Capitalism." *American Journal of Sociology* 101: 993–1027.

Starner, F. 1961. *Magsaysay and the Philippine Peasantry.* Berkeley: University of California Press.

Starobin, J. R. 1954. *Eyewitness in Indo-China.* New York: Cameron and Kahn.

Stauffer, R. B. 1975. *The Philippine Congress: Causes of Structural Change.* London: Sage.

Steinberg, D. I. 2001. "The Burmese Conundrum: Approaching Reformation of the Political Economy." In R. Taylor, ed., *Burma: Political Economy Under Military Rule*. London: Hurst.

Stenson, M. 1970. *Industrial Conflict in Malaya: Prelude to the Communist Revolt of 1948*. London: Oxford University Press.

Stepan, A. 1978. *The State and Society: Peru in Comparative Perspective*. Princeton: Princeton University Press.

———. 1987. *Rethinking Military Politics: Brazil and the Southern Cone*. Princeton: Princeton University Press.

———. 2001. *Arguing Comparative Politics*. Oxford: Oxford University Press.

Stoler, A. 1995. *Capitalism and Confrontation in Sumatra's Plantation Belt, 1870–1979*. Ann Arbor: University of Michigan Press.

Strange, S. 1996. *The Retreat of the State: The Diffusion of Power in the World Economy*. New York: Cambridge University Press.

———. 1997. *Casino Capitalism*. Manchester: Manchester University Press.

Strauch, J. 1980. "The General Election at the Grassroots: Perspectives from a Chinese New Village." In H. Crouch et al., eds., *Malaysian Politics and the 1978 Election*.

———. 1981. *Chinese Village Politics in the Malaysian State*. Cambridge, MA: Harvard University Press.

Stromseth, J. 2003. "Business Associations and Policy-Making in Vietnam." In B. Kerkvliet, R. Heng, and D. Koh, eds., *Getting Organized in Vietnam*.

Stubbs, R. 1989a. "Geopolitics and the Political Economy of Southeast Asia." *International Journal* 44: 517–540.

———. 1989b. *Hearts and Minds in Guerrilla Warfare: The Malayan Emergency 1948–1960*. Singapore: Oxford University Press.

———. 1999. "War and Economic Development: Export-Oriented Industrialization in East and Southeast Asia." *Comparative Politics* 31(3): 337–355.

———. 2002. "ASEAN Plus Three: Emerging East Asian Regionalism?" *Asian Survey* 42(3): 440–455.

———. 2005. *Rethinking Asia's Economic Miracle: The Political Economy of War, Prosperity, and Crisis*. New York: Palgrave Macmillan.

Sturtevant, D. 1976. *Popular Uprisings in the Philippines, 1840–1940*. Ithaca: Cornell University Press.

Suehiro, A. 1989. *Capital Accumulation in Thailand: 1885–1985*. Tokyo: Center for East Asian Cultural Studies.

Sulistyo, H. 2002. "Electoral Politics in Indonesia: A Hard Way to Democracy." In A. Croissant, G. Bruns, and M. John, eds., *Electoral Politics in Southeast and East Asia*.

Surin Maisikrod. 1992. *Thailand's Two General Elections in 1992: Democracy Sustained*. Research Notes and Discussion Paper No. 75. Singapore: Institute of Southeast Asian Studies.

Suryadinata, L. 2002. *Elections and Politics in Indonesia.* Singapore: Institute of Southeast Asian Studies.

Swift, M. G. 1965. *Malay Peasant Society in Jelebu.* London: Athlone.

Szelenyi, I., and E. Kostello. 1998. "Outline of an Institutionalist Theory of Inequality: The Case of Socialist and Postcommunist Eastern Europe." In V. Nee and M. Brinton, eds., *The New Institutionalism in Sociology.* New York: Russell Sage Foundation.

Taagepera, R., and M. S. Shugart. 1989. *Seats and Votes: The Effects and Determinants of Electoral Systems.* New Haven: Yale University Press.

Tamada, Y. 1991. "Itthiphon and Amnat: An Informal Aspect of Thai Politics." *Southeast Asian Studies* 28(4): 445–465.

Tan, B. K., and B. Singh. 1994. *Uneasy Relations: The State and NGOs in Malaysia.* Kuala Lumpur: Gender and Development Programme, Asian and Pacific Development Centre.

Tan, L. E. 1997. *The Politics of Chinese Education in Malaya 1945–1961.* Kuala Lumpur: Oxford University Press.

Tan, P. J. 2001. "Political Parties and the Consolidation of Democracy in Indonesia." *Panduan Parlemen Indonesia (Indonesian Parliament Guide).* Jakarta: API.

———. 2002. "Anti-Party Reaction in Indonesia: Causes and Implications." *Contemporary Southeast Asia* 24(3): 484–508.

Tan, S. K. 1977. *The Filipino Muslim Armed Struggle, 1900–1972.* Makati: Filipinas Foundation.

———. 1990. "The Rise of State Authoritarianism in Malaysia." *Bulletin of Concerned Asian Scholars* 22(3): 32–42.

Tancangco, L. 1992. *The Anatomy of Electoral Fraud.* Manila: MLAGM.

Tanham, G. K. 1961. *Communist Revolutionary Warfare: From the Vietminh to the Viet Cong.* New York: Praeger.

Tanter, R. 1990. "Oil, IGGI, and US Hegemony: The Global Pre-conditions for Indonesian Rentier-Militarization." In A. Budiman, ed., *State and Civil Society in Indonesia.*

Taylor, M. 1988. *Rationality and Revolution.* New York: Cambridge University Press.

Taylor, P. 2004. *Goddess on the Rise: Pilgrimage and Popular Religion in Vietnam.* Honolulu: University of Hawaii Press.

Taylor, R. 1982. "Perceptions of Ethnicity in the Politics of Burma." *Southeast Asian Journal of Social Science* 10(1): 7–20.

———. 1987. *The State in Burma.* London: Hurst.

———, ed. 1996. *The Politics of Elections in Southeast Asia.* New York: Cambridge University Press.

Teehankee, J. 2002. "Electoral Politics in the Philippines." In A. Croissant, G. Bruns, and M. John, eds., *Electoral Politics in Southeast and East Asia.*

Temple, J. 2003. "Growing into Trouble: Indonesia After 1966." In D. Rodrik, ed., *In Search of Prosperity*.

Tessler, M. 2002. "Islam and Democracy in the Middle East: The Impact of Religious Orientation on Attitudes Toward Democracy in Four Arab Countries." *Comparative Politics* 34(3): 337–354.

———, J. Nachtwey, and A. Banda, eds. 1999. *Area Studies and Social Science: Strategies for Understanding Middle East Politics*. Bloomington: Indiana University Press.

Thaler, R. H. 1991. *Quasi-Rational Economics*. New York: Russell Sage Foundation.

Than, M., and J. Tan. 1990. *Myanmar Dilemmas and Option*. Singapore: Institute of Southeast Asian Studies.

Thaveeporn Vasavakul. 1997. "Sectoral Politics and Party Building." In A. Fforde, ed., *Doi Moi: Ten Years After the 1986 Party Congress*. Canberra: Australia National University.

———. 2003. "Language Policy and Ethnic Relations in Vietnam." In M. E. Brown and S. Ganguly, eds., *Fighting Words*.

Thawnghmung, A. 1998. "The State-Centric Analysis of Urban Bias in the Transitions To and From Socialism." Paper presented at the Annual Meeting of the Association for Asian Studies, Washington DC.

———. 2003. "Rural Perceptions of State Legitimacy in Burma/Myanmar." *Journal of Peasant Studies* 30(2): 1–40.

———. 2004. *Behind the Teak Curtain: Authoritarianism, Agricultural Policies and Political Legitimacy in Rural Burma/Myanmar*. London: Kegan Paul.

Thelen, K. 1999. "Historical Institutionalism in Comparative Politics." *Annual Review of Political Science* 2(1): 369–404.

———. 2003. "How Institutions Evolve: Insights from Comparative Historical Analysis." In J. Mahoney and D. Rueschemeyer, eds., *Comparative Historical Analysis in the Social Sciences*.

Thitinan Pongsudirak. 2001. "Crisis from Within: The Politics of Macroeconomic Management in Thailand, 1947–1997." Ph.D. diss., London School of Economics.

Thomas, N. 2002. "Building an East Asian Community: Origins, Structure, and Limits." *Asian Perspective* 26(4): 83–112.

Thompson, M. R. 1995. *The Anti-Marcos Struggle*. New Haven: Yale University Press.

———. 2004. *Democratic Revolutions: Asia and Eastern Europe*. New York: Routledge.

Thompson, R. 1966. *Defeating Communist Insurgency: Experiences from Malaya and Vietnam*. London: Chatto and Windus.

Thompson, V., and R. Adloff. 1950. *The Left Wing in Southeast Asia*. New York: William Sloane.

Thongchai Winichakul. 1994. *Siam Mapped: A History of the Geo-Body of a Nation*. Honolulu: University of Hawaii Press.

Thorner, D., B. Kerblay, and R. Smith, eds. 1986. *A. V. Chayanov on the Theory of Peasant Economy*. Madison: University of Wisconsin Press.

Tilly, C. 1975. "Reflections on the History of European State-Making." In C. Tilly, ed., *The Formation of National States in Western Europe*. Princeton: Princeton University Press.

———. 1985. "War Making and State Making as Organized Crime." In P. Evans, D. Rueschemeyer, and T. Skocpol, eds., *Bringing the State Back In*.

———. 1992. *Coercion, Capital, and European States, AD 990–1992*. Cambridge: Blackwell.

Tilman, R. O. 1964. *Bureaucratic Transition in Malaya*. Durham: Duke University Press.

Tønnesson, S. 2000. "The Layered State in Vietnam." In K. E. Brødsgaard and S. Young, eds., *State Capacity in East Asia: Japan, Taiwan, China, and Vietnam*. New York: Oxford University Press.

Trager, F., ed. 1959. *Marxism in Southeast Asia: A Study of Four Countries*. Stanford: Stanford University Press.

———. 1966. *Why Viet Nam?* London: Pall Mall.

Tremewan, C. 1994. *The Political Economy of Social Control in Singapore*. New York: St. Martin's.

Trocki, C. 1998. "Democracy and the State in Southeast Asia." In C. Trocki, ed., *Gangsters, Democracy, and the State in Southeast Asia*. Ithaca: Southeast Asia Program, Cornell University.

Trullinger, J. W., Jr. 1980. *Village at War: An Account of Revolution in Vietnam*. New York: Longman.

Truong, Q. 1987. "Agricultural Collectivization and Rural Development in Vietnam: A North/South Study (1955–1985)." Ph.D. diss., Vrije Universiteit te Amsterdam.

Tsebelis, G. 1995. "Veto Players in Presidentialism, Parliamentarism, Multicameralism and Multipartyism." *British Journal of Political Science* 25(3): 289–325.

Turton, A. 1984. "Limits of Ideological Domination and the Formation of Social Consciousness." In A. Turton and S. Tanabe, eds., *History and Peasant Consciousness in South East Asia*. Osaka: National Museum of Ethnology.

Uhlin, A. 1997. *Indonesia and the "Third Wave of Democratization."* Richmond: Curzon.

Underhill, G., and X. Zhang. 2005. "The Changing State-Market Condominium in East Asia: Rethinking the Political Underpinnings of Development." *New Political Economy* 10(1): 1–24.

Unger, D. 1993. "Japan's Capital Exports: Molding East Asia." In D. Unger and P. Blackburn, eds., *Japan's Emerging Global Role*. Boulder: Lynne Rienner.

———. 1998. *Building Social Capital in Thailand*. Cambridge: Cambridge University Press.

———. 2001. "A Regional Economic Order in East and Southeast Asia?" *Journal of Strategic Studies* 24(2): 179–202.

———. 2003. "Principals of the Thai State." In B. Heredia and B. Schneider, eds., *Administrative Reform in the Developing World*. Coral Gables: North-South Center Press.

Vail, L., ed. 1989. *The Creation of Tribalism in Southern Africa*. Berkeley: University of California Press.

Valeriano, N. N., and C. L. R. Bohannan. 1962. *Counter-Guerrilla Operations: The Philippine Experience*. New York: Praeger.

van Bruinessen, M. 2002. "Genealogies of Islamic Radicalism in Post-Suharto Indonesia." *South East Asia Research* 10(2): 117–154.

———. 2003. "Post-Suharto Muslim Engagement with Civil Society and Democracy." Paper presented at the Third International Conference and Workshop "Indonesia in Transition," organized by the KNAW and Labsosio, University of Indonesia, August 24–28, 2003. Depok, Indonesia.

van Klinken, G. 2001. "The Maluku Wars: Bringing Society Back In." *Indonesia* 71: 1–26.

Varshney, A. 2002. *Ethnic Conflict and Civic Life: Hindus and Muslims in India*. New Haven: Yale University Press.

Velasco, R. 1999. "Philippines." In I. Marsh, J. Blondel, and T. Inoguchi, eds., *Democracy, Governance, and Economic Performance: East and Southeast Asia*. New York: U.N. Press.

Verdery, K. 1994. "Ethnicity, Nationalism, and State-Making." In H. Vermeulen and C. Govers, eds., *The Anthropology of Ethnicity: Beyond "Ethnic Groups and Boundaries."* Amsterdam: Spinhuis.

Verma, V. 2002. *Malaysia: State and Civil Society in Transition*. Boulder: Lynne Rienner.

Vickerman, A. 1986. *The Fate of the Peasantry*. New Haven: Yale Southeast Asia Studies.

Viola, L. 1996. *Peasant Rebels Under Stalin*. New York: Oxford University Press.

Vo, N. T. 1990. *Vietnam's Economic Policy Since 1975*. Singapore: Institute of Southeast Asian Studies.

von der Mehden, F. R. 1963. *Religion and Nationalism in Southeast Asia: Burma, Indonesia, the Philippines*. Madison: University of Wisconsin Press.

Wade, R. 1990. *Governing the Market*. Princeton: Princeton University Press.

———. 2001. "The US Role in the Long Asian Crisis of 1990–2000." In A. J. Lukausas and F. L. Rivera-Batiz, eds., *The Political Economy of the East Asian Financial Crisis and Its Aftermath*. Cheltenham: Elgar.

———. 2003. "What Strategies Are Viable for Developing Countries Today? The World Trade Organization and the Shrinking of 'Development Space.'" *Review of International Political Economy* 10(4): 621–644.

———, and F. Veneroso. 1998. "The Asian Crisis: The High Debt Model Versus the Wall Street–Treasury–IMF Complex." *New Left Review* 22(8): 1–24.

Wakeman, F., Jr. 1993. "The Civil Society and Public Sphere Debate: Western Reflections on Chinese Political Culture." *Modern China* 19(2): 108–138.

Walder, A. 1986. *Communist Neo-Traditionalism*. Berkeley: University of California Press.

———. 1996. "Markets and Inequality in Transitional Economies: Toward Testable Theories." *American Journal of Sociology* 101(4): 1060–1073.

Waldner, D. 1999. *State Building and Late Development*. Ithaca: Cornell University Press.

Walker, M. 1996. *NGO Participation in a Corporatist State: The Example of Indonesia*. Berkeley: Institute of Urban and Regional Development, University of California–Berkeley.

Walton, J. 1984. *Reluctant Rebels*. New York: Columbia University Press.

Wanandi, J. 2002. "Indonesia: A Failed State?" *Washington Quarterly* 25(3): 135–146.

Wank, D. 1999. *Commodifying Communism: Business, Trust and Politics in a Chinese City*. Cambridge: Cambridge University Press.

Weigle, M. A., and J. Butterfield. 1992. "Civil Society in Reforming Communist Regimes: The Logic of Emergence." *Comparative Politics* 25(1): 1–23.

Weiss, L. 1998. *The Myth of the Powerless State*. Ithaca: Cornell University Press.

———. 2003a. "Introduction: Bringing Domestic Institutions Back in." In L. Weiss, ed., *States in the Global Economy: Bringing Domestic Institutions Back In*. Cambridge: Cambridge University Press.

———. 2003b. "Guiding Globalisation in East Asia: New Roles for Old Developmental States." In L. Weiss, ed., *States in the Global Economy: Bringing Domestic Institutions Back In*. Cambridge: Cambridge University Press.

———. 2003c. "Is the State Being 'Transformed' by Globalisation?" In L. Weiss, ed., *States in the Global Economy: Bringing Domestic Institutions Back In*. Cambridge: Cambridge University Press.

———, and J. M. Hobson. 2000. "State Power and Economic Strength Revisited: What's So Special About the East Asian Crisis?" In R. Robison, M. Beeson, K. Jayasuriya, and H.-R. Kim, eds., *Politics and Markets in the Wake of the Asian Crisis*. London: Routledge.

Weiss, M. 2000. "The 1999 Malaysian General Elections: Issues, Insults, and Irregularities." *Asian Survey* 40(3): 413–435.

———. 2006. *Protest and Possibilities: Civil Society and Coalitions for Political Change in Malaysia*. Stanford: Stanford University Press.

———, and S. Hassan, eds. 2003. *Social Movements in Malaysia: From Moral Communities to NGOs*. London: RoutledgeCurzon.

Weiss, T., D. Forsythe, and R. Coate. 2004. *The United Nations and Changing World Politics*. Boulder: Westview.

Weller, R., and S. Guggenheim, eds. 1982. *Power and Protest in the Countryside: Studies of Rural Unrest in Asia, Europe, and Latin America*. Durham: Duke University Press.

Welsh, B. 2000. "Malaysia and Globalization." In S. Kim, ed., *East Asia and Globalization*. Lanham: Rowman and Littlefield.

Wertheim, W. F. 1965. *East-West Parallels*. Chicago: Quadrangle Books.

West, L. 1997. *Militant Labor in the Philippines*. Philadelphia: Temple University Press.

White, B. 1997. "Agroindustry and Contract Farmers in Upland West Java." *Journal of Peasant Studies* 24(3): 100–136.

White, C. 1981. "Agrarian Reform and National Liberation in the Vietnamese Revolution, 1920–1957." Ph.D. diss., Cornell University.

———. 1983. "Recent Debates in Vietnamese Development Policy." In G. White, R. Murray, and C. White, eds., *Revolutionary Socialist Development in the Third World*. Lexington: University Press of Kentucky.

———. 1986. "Everyday Resistance, Socialist Revolution and Rural Development: The Vietnamese Case." In J. Scott and B. Kerkvliet, eds., *Everyday Forms of Peasant Resistance in South-East Asia*.

———. 1988. "Alternative Approaches to the Socialist Transformation of Agriculture in Postwar Vietnam." In D. Marr and C. White, eds., *Postwar Vietnam*.

White, E. 2005. "Fraudulent and Dangerous Popular Religiosity in the Public Sphere: Moral Campaigns to Prohibit, Reform, and Demystify Thai Spirit Mediums." In A. C. Willford and K. George, eds., *Spirited Politics*.

Wiant, J., and D. Steinberg. 1988. "Burma: The Military and National Development." In Soedjati Djiwandono and Yong Mun Cheong, eds., *Soldiers and Stability in Southeast Asia*. Singapore: Institute of Southeast Asian Studies.

Wickham, C. R. 2002. *Mobilizing Islam: Religion, Activism, and Political Change in Egypt*. New York: Columbia University Press.

———. 2004. "Interests, Ideas, and Islamist Outreach in Egypt." In Q. Wiktorowicz, ed., *Islamic Activism*.

Wickham-Crowley, P. 1992. *Guerrillas and Revolution: A Comparative Study of Insurgents and Regimes Since 1956*. Princeton: Princeton University Press.

Wickham-Crowley, T. 1997. "Structural Theories of Revolution." In J. Foran, ed., *Theorizing Revolutions*.

Wiktorowicz, Q., ed. 2004. *Islamic Activism: A Social Movement Theory Approach*. Bloomington: Indiana University Press.

Willford, A. C., and K. George, eds. 2005. *Spirited Politics: Religion and Public Life in Contemporary Southeast Asia*. Ithaca: Southeast Asia Program, Cornell University.

Wilson, D. A. 1962. *Politics in Thailand*. Ithaca: Cornell University Press.

Wilson, W. J. 2002. "Expanding the Domain of Policy-Relevant Scholarship in the Social Sciences." *PS: Political Science and Politics* Online Special (March).

Winters, J. 1996. *Power in Motion: Capital Mobility and the Indonesian State.* Ithaca: Cornell University Press.

———. 2000. "The Financial Crisis in Southeast Asia." In R. Robison et al., eds., *Politics and Markets in the Wake of the Asian Crisis.*

Wolf, C., Jr. 1966. "Insurgency and Counterinsurgency: New Myths and Old Realities." *Yale Review* 56 (October): 225–241.

Wolf, E. 1969. *Peasant Wars in the Twentieth Century.* New York: Harper Torchbooks.

Wolpe, H. 1974. *Urban Politics in Nigeria.* Berkeley: University of California Press.

Wolters, E. P., ed. 1976. *Australia's Northern Neighbors: Independent or Dependent?* Melbourne: Nelson.

Wolters, W. 1983. *Politics, Patronage, and Class Conflict in Central Luzon.* The Hague: Institute of Social Studies.

Wong, P. 2001. "The Role of the State in Singapore's Industrial Development." In P. Wong and C. Ng, eds., *Industrial Policy, Innovation and Economic Growth.* Singapore: Singapore University Press.

———, and C. Ng. 2001. "Rethinking the Development Paradigm: Lessons from Japan and the Four Asian NIEs." In P. Wong and C. Ng, eds., *Industrial Policy, Innovation and Economic Growth.* Singapore: Singapore University Press.

Woo-Cumings, M. 1998. "National Security and the Rise of the Developmental State in South Korea and Taiwan." In H. Rowen, ed., *Behind East Asian Growth.* New York: Routledge.

Woodruff, D. M. 2000a. "Rules for Followers: Institutional Theory and the New Politics of Economic Backwardness in Russia." *Politics & Society* 28(4): 437–482.

———. 2000b. *Money Unmade: Barter and the Fate of Russian Capitalism.* Ithaca: Cornell University Press.

———. 2006. "Understanding Rules and Institutions: Possibilities and Limits of Game Theory." *Qualitative Methods* 4(1): 13–17.

———, and R. Abrami. 2004. "Towards a Manifesto: Interpretive Materialist Political Economy." Paper presented at the Annual Meeting of the American Political Science Association, Chicago.

World Bank. 1968. *Political Order in Changing Societies.* New Haven: Yale University Press.

———. 1986. *World Development Report 1986.* New York: Oxford University Press.

———. 1993. *The East Asian Miracle.* New York: Oxford University Press.

———. 2000. Workshop on Business-Government Consultative Mechanisms in Market-Oriented Reforms. Washington, DC, January 31.

———. 2005. "Thailand: Investment Climate, Firm Competitiveness, and Growth." Bangkok: World Bank Draft Report, August 30.

Wurfel, D. 1988. *Filipino Politics: Development and Decay*. Ithaca: Cornell University Press.

Yamamoto, T., ed. 1995. *Emerging Civil Society in the Asia Pacific Community*. Singapore: Institute of Southeast Asian Studies.

Yamazawa, I. 1995. "On Pacific Economic Integration." In R. Garnaut and P. Drysdale, eds., *Asia Pacific Regionalism: Readings in International Economic Relations*. Pymble, New South Wales: Harper Educational.

Yang, C. K. 1959. *A Chinese Village in Early Communist Transition*. Cambridge, MA: MIT Press.

Yanow, D. 2003. "Interpretive Empirical Political Science: What Makes This Not a Subfield of Qualitative Methods." *Qualitative Methods* 1(2): 9–13.

Yashar, D. J. 1997. *Demanding Democracy: Reform and Reaction in Costa Rica and Guatemala, 1870s–1950s*. Stanford: Stanford University Press.

Yegar, M. 1979. *Islam and Islamic Institutions in British Malaya*. Jerusalem: Magnes Press, Hebrew University.

Yin, R. 2003. *Case Study Research*. Thousand Oaks: Sage.

Yoshihara, K. 1988. *The Rise of Ersatz Capitalism in South-East Asia*. Singapore: Oxford University Press.

Young, C. 1976. *The Politics of Cultural Pluralism*. Madison: University of Wisconsin Press.

Young, K. 1999. "Consumption, Social Differentiation and Self-Definition of the New Rich in Industralising Southeast-Asia." In M. Pinches, ed., *Culture and Privilege in Capitalist Asia*. London: Routledge.

Youngblood, R. L. 1990. *Marcos Against the Church*. Ithaca: Cornell University Press.

Zakaria, A. 1989. "Malaysia: Quasi-Democracy in a Divided Society." In L. Diamond, J. Linz, and S. M. Lipset, eds., *Politics in Developing Countries*. Boulder: Lynne Rienner.

Zakaria, F. 1997. "The Rise of Illiberal Democracy." *Foreign Affairs* 76: 22–43.

Zasloff, J. 1973. *The Pathet Lao*. Lexington: Lexington Books.

Zifirdaus, A. 1990. "Islamic Religion: Yes, Islamic Ideology: No! Islam and the State in Indonesia." In A. Budiman, ed., *State and Civil Society in Indonesia*.

Zolberg, A. 1964. *One Party Government in the Ivory Coast*. Princeton: Princeton University Press.

———. 1966. *Creating Political Order: The Party States of West Africa*. New York: Rand McNally.

Zweig, D. 1989. "Struggling Over Land in China: Peasant Resistance After Collectivization, 1966–1986." In F. Colburn, ed., *Everyday Forms of Peasant Resistance*.

Index

Beyond Bilateralism: U.S.-Japan Relations in the New Asia Pacific
Edited by Ellis S. Krauss and T. J. Pempel
2004

Population Change and Economic Development in East Asia:
Challenges Met, Opportunities Seized
Edited by Andrew Mason
2001

Capital, Coercion, and Crime: Bossism in the Philippines
By John T. Sidel
1999

Making Majorities: Constituting the Nation in Japan, Korea, China, Malaysia,
Fiji, Turkey, and the United States
Edited by Dru C. Gladney
1998

Chiefs Today: Traditional Pacific Leadership and the Postcolonial State
Edited by Geoffrey M. White and Lamont Lindstrom
1997

Political Legitimacy in Southeast Asia: The Quest for Moral Authority
Edited by Muthiah Alagappa
1995